A2-Level Contents

Section One — Functional Objectives and Strategies

Section Two — Financial Strategies and Accounts

Section Three — Marketing Strategies

Section Four — Operational Strategies

Section Five — Human Resource Strategies

Section Six — Corporate Aims and Objectives

Section Seven — Assessing Change

Section Eight — Managing Change

Do Well in Your Exam

Published by CGP

Editors:
Heather Gregson, Rachael Powers, Jennifer Underwood, Emma Warhurst

Contributors:
Angela Anthonisz, Jane Barnes, P. M. Brockbank, Charley Darbishire, John Grant, Peter Gray, Gemma Hallam, Jeff Harris, Luke von Kotze, Jonathan Mace, David Morris, Adrian Murray, Andy Park, Nagu Rao, Kate Redmond, Katherine Reed, Julie Watkins, Keith Williamson

Proofreaders:
Andy Park, Glenn Rogers and Victoria Skelton

ISBN: 978 1 84762 427 7

Groovy website: www.cgpbooks.co.uk
Jolly bits of clipart from CorelDRAW®
Printed by Elanders Ltd, Newcastle Upon Tyne.

Based on the classic CGP style created by Richard Parsons.

AS-Level
Business Studies

Exam Board: AQA

How Businesses Work

Here's a bit of background for you. You'd be hard-pushed to get as far as your A-levels and not have some idea about what a business is, but there's a bit more to it than that. Here's the basics on how to start up your own business.

*There are **Advantages** to owning a **Business***

1) People set up businesses mainly to make a **profit**. This means a firm **makes** more money than it **spends**. Starting a business is risky, but many people take the risk because of the possibility of big **financial rewards**.
2) People usually only set up their own business if they expect to make **more** than they could earn working as an **employee** of another company.
3) People may set up their own business so that they can be **their own boss** and make their own decisions — they don't have to answer to anyone else.
4) Setting up your own business also gives you the opportunity to do a job you're really **interested** in.

What Ian didn't realise was that if he had his own business, he wouldn't have to answer to anyone.

*Most **Businesses** exist to make a **Profit***

1) Businesses aim to make a profit by selling **products** or **services** to customers who are willing to **pay** for them — e.g. a paperclip manufacturer sells a product, and a hair salon sells a service.
2) Some businesses sell **necessities** — products or services that you **need** (like gas and electricity). Other firms provide **luxury** products or services — things you **want** but don't need (like holidays and jewellery).
3) Businesses have to **make a profit** or **break even** (see p.28) to survive.
4) This is especially true in the **private sector** — if a business doesn't make enough money to survive it could go **bankrupt** and have to **close down**.
5) In the **public sector**, it's not as clear-cut. Organisations like the army, the police, hospitals and state schools aren't there to **make money** — they provide a service to the community. **Charities** are another exception. For more on not-for-profit businesses, see p.17.

Public sector = government-owned
Private sector = privately owned

***Businesses** can have **Other Objectives** too*

As well as making a profit, businesses may have **other objectives**, such as:

- Offering the **highest quality** goods and services possible.
- Attempting to grow by increasing their **market share**, opening **more outlets** or **taking over** another business.
- Giving good **customer service**.
- Having a good **image** and **reputation**.
- Trying to limit their **impact** on the **environment**.
- **Diversifying** by offering a wider range of products or services.
- **Surviving**. This is essential for **new businesses**, especially in competitive markets (see p.72). It's also important when there's a weak economy (see p.59).

The size of a company has a big impact on its objectives. An independent shop owner will tend to focus on trying to survive, while a big international company will pay more attention to its corporate image and is likely to try to diversify its product range.

Businesses might **give up some profit** to help them meet **other objectives**. However, most business owners are **ultimately** only interested in **profit**. Everything else comes **after**.

How Businesses Work

Businesses have several different Functions

Production of products or services isn't enough on its own — businesses have **other tasks** to do before they can **make a profit**. These different tasks are usually looked after by different departments.

	Business departments and their roles
Production	A business turns **raw materials** into a finished **good** or **service** that they can sell. They must also monitor the **quality** of what they are producing. For more on turning raw materials into goods and services, see p.4. For more on quality, see p. 48-49.
Finance	Businesses have to keep a careful eye on their finances. They must keep detailed and accurate **financial records**. A business must try to get the best **value for money** for every pound it spends. For more on finance, see Section 2.
HRM	**(Human Resources Management)** Businesses must make sure they have the right number of employees of the right quality in the right place at the right time. HRM is on p.40.
Marketing	Businesses have to identify what customers **want** or **need** and figure out how best to **sell** it to them. For more on marketing, see Section 5.
Admin	Businesses have to **run their own affairs** as efficiently as possible.
R&D	**(Research and Development)** Businesses may need to discover **new ideas** for products that might be wanted in the future, and get them ready to be launched onto the market. For more on new product development, see p.60-61.

1) Businesses need to **plan** what activities to do in the future.
2) They need to **control** what workers in the business are doing, and control the amount of money that's spent.
3) Businesses need to **coordinate** all their different functions and departments and make sure that all the departments are working towards common objectives.

Businesses all need certain Key Things

Before businesses can sell things and make a profit, they need certain things:

1)	**Labour**	Businesses need people to do the work.
2)	**Finance**	It costs money to provide goods and services.
3)	**Customers**	Every business needs people to buy the goods and services, and pay for them.
4)	**Suppliers**	Suppliers provide raw materials, equipment and human resources.
5)	**Premises**	Businesses need buildings to work in.
6)	**Enterprise**	Entrepreneurs come up with original ideas and take risks to make a profit.

There's more on different sources of finance on p 18-19.

Practice Questions

Q1 Give three benefits of owning your own business.

Q2 What objectives might a private sector business have? Which objective is the most important and why?

Q3 Give five examples of departments that you might find in a typical business.

Q4 Name at least four essential things that a business needs to produce goods and services.

Exam Questions

Q1 Suggest why Anna White, a fashion designer, might want to leave her job designing clothes for a high street store and set up her own business. (6 marks)

Q2 Discuss the idea that businesses exist to make a profit. (10 marks)

Some businesses only have one function — the office Christmas party...

This first section covers fairly basic business ideas. If you've done GCSE Business Studies, some of it might seem a bit dull. Don't assume you already know it all though — it's worth reading through to make sure you really know what's what. Some of these things will crop up again later in the book — so stick with this section. And then go on to the good stuff...

What Businesses Do

If you're wondering what businesses actually do then you've come to the right page. Businesses are involved in transforming raw materials into finished products, or providing services, and they try to make a profit along the way.

Businesses *Add Value* to raw materials

1) Businesses **pay** for raw materials, then **transform** them into finished products and **sell** them. Customers pay more for the finished product than the business originally paid for the raw materials used to make it.

2) The difference between the **cost** of the raw materials bought by the business to make each product and the **price** the customer pays for the finished product is known as the **value added**. E.g. if a bakery buys the ingredients for a cake for **80p** and sells the finished cake for **£3**, the value added is £3 – £0.80 = **£2.20**.

3) The value added leaves a **surplus** — the business uses that to pay its other costs (like wages, rent and electricity — see p. 26 for more on costs), and any money left over after this is **profit**.

4) Some products have **high** value added — usually **luxury** items like designer clothes or meals in expensive restaurants. Other products, like basic grocery items, have much **lower** value added.

5) The greater the **value added**, the higher the **profits** are likely to be — businesses want the value added to be as high as possible in order to increase their profits.

Betty had plenty of raw materials — now all she needed to do was work out how to add value.

The *Supply Chain* is the product's journey from *Raw Materials* to *Consumer*

1) **Raw materials** (also called resources or input) go through various stages on their way to reaching the consumer as **finished products** (output). These stages are sometimes called **transformation** and they all form part of the **supply chain**.

2) The supply chain always starts with **raw materials** and finishes with the **consumer**, and the intermediate stages usually include suppliers (businesses that sell products to other businesses), manufacturing, distribution getting products into shops so customers can buy them) and retailers. The supply chain can be short or long depending on the product.

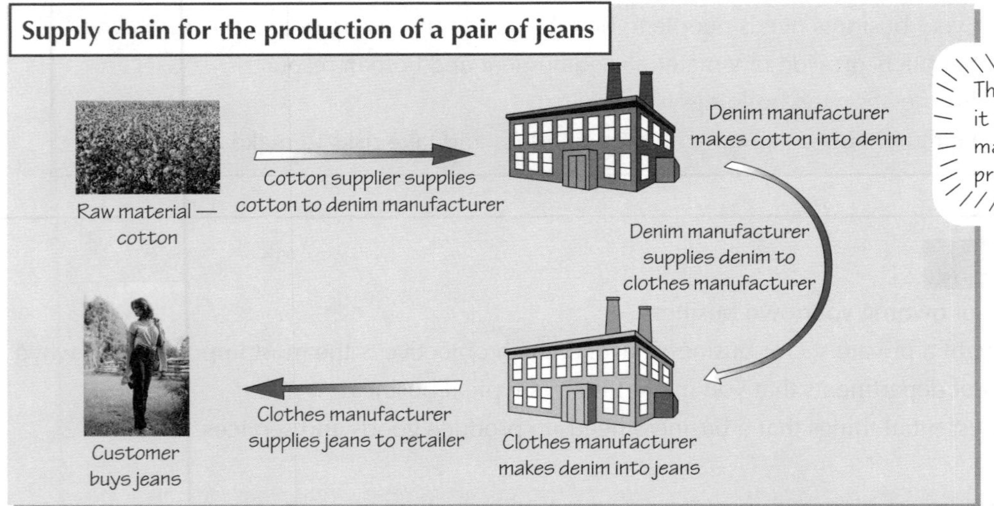

Supply chain for the production of a pair of jeans
Raw material — cotton
Cotton supplier supplies cotton to denim manufacturer
Denim manufacturer makes cotton into denim
Denim manufacturer supplies denim to clothes manufacturer
Clothes manufacturer makes denim into jeans
Clothes manufacturer supplies jeans to retailer
Customer buys jeans

This diagram is simplified — it takes lots of different raw materials to produce the end product in most cases.

3) The various steps in the supply chain often happen in different businesses and different places.

4) All businesses — wherever they are in the supply chain — are dependent on their **suppliers** and **customers** — e.g. a problem with cocoa bean crops in Africa might cause a problem for a shop selling chocolate bars in England.

5) **Value** is normally added at **each stage** in the supply chain — e.g. a bead-making factory turns plastic into beads, which can then be sold for more than the plastic was worth. If a handbag manufacturer uses the beads to decorate handbags, the handbags will be sold for more than it cost the manufacturer to buy the fabric and beads.

What Businesses Do

Businesses can be classified by Production Stage

You can classify businesses according to what **stage** of the **production process** (from raw material to finished product) the business is involved in. There are three divisions — **primary**, **secondary** and **tertiary**.

Primary Sector

1) These are industries that **extract raw materials** from natural resources.
2) This sector covers the **farming**, **fishing** and **mining** industries.
3) Primary sector industries are in **decline** in the UK, mainly because it is often **cheaper** to **import** raw materials from other countries, and trade barriers have made it more **difficult** for UK companies to **export** raw materials. E.g. in 1984 there were **170** coal mines open around the UK — more than **150** of these have now been **closed**.
4) There has also been a decline in the number of people employed in **farming** — the number of people working in farming in the UK is now **less than half** what it was at the start of the 1970s.

Secondary Sector

1) The secondary sector **processes** the raw materials that come from the primary sector.
2) Secondary industry includes **manufacturing** (e.g. cars, tinned food, steel) and **construction** (e.g. building houses, factories, roads).
3) Secondary sector industries have also been **declining** in the UK for the past 25 years, mainly due to companies **moving** production to other parts of the world where manufacturing costs are **lower**. This increases their profits because they can still sell their products to UK consumers at the same price, despite producing them more cheaply. E.g. in 2006, **645** jobs were lost at Nestlé®'s chocolate factory in York when Nestlé® moved production of several products to Europe.

Tertiary Sector

1) This is the **service sector** which provides services (like banking) to **businesses** in the primary and secondary sectors and so helps them to sell their goods, e.g. shops, banks, insurance companies, restaurants, hotels, and healthcare services. It also includes some **direct personal services** to individuals.
2) In most developed countries the tertiary sector has **expanded** over the last few decades — the UK economy is now mainly made up of tertiary sector companies.
3) The main tertiary sector growth in the UK has been in **financial** and **business** services like banking and accounting — the proportion of people working in these jobs in the UK has **doubled** in the last 25 years.

Jon was glad to hear that the tertiary sector was on the increase — he'd always wanted to be an accountant.

Practice Questions

Q1 Give two examples of products with high value added.

Q2 What is the supply chain?

Q3 Give an example of: a) a primary sector business, b) a secondary sector business, c) a tertiary sector business.

Q4 Which is the main production sector in the UK?

Exam Question

Q1 Prawnfree Ltd sell salmon fishcakes. Analyse the effect that a drop in salmon supplies might have on their supply chain. (10 marks)

I'm in the middle of a (supply) chain reaction...

The whole point of businesses is to add value to whatever they buy so that they can sell it for more than they paid for it — simple really. Learn the definitions of primary, secondary and tertiary sector businesses and a couple of examples of each in case you're asked for them in the exam. And don't forget about the supply chain — it affects all businesses.

Enterprise and Entrepreneurs

Starting a small business is easy, but making a living out of it is blimmin' hard. The examiners want you to show that you understand that starting a successful small firm is not just about having an idea.

People who start businesses are called **Entrepreneurs**

1) An entrepreneur is a person (or one of a group of people) who **raises the resources** and **organises the activities** needed to **start a business**.
2) Entrepreneurs have an **idea** for new businesses, then they organise everything they need to set up their business, including financial investment, staff, buildings, research and development, and marketing.
3) If the entrepreneur **organises** things well, and consumers **want** the good or service, the business will succeed. If they get it **wrong** the business will have to give up and stop trading.

EXAMPLE: **Richard Branson** was only 20 when he set up **Virgin** as a mail-order music retailer. He then **expanded** the company to include a record shop and recording studio, and he has since continued the expansion successfully — it now includes air travel, mobile, internet, rail and music services. Richard Branson is now one of the **wealthiest** men in Britain, and he was **knighted** for services to business in 1999.

Entrepreneurs are **Innovative Risk-takers**, **Planners** and **Organisers**

1) Successful entrepreneurs tend to be **creative** — they're **innovators** who have spotted a **gap in the market**. A gap in the market is either an **original idea**, or a way of making an **existing** idea **different** from the competition, e.g. selling goods to a new segment of the market.
2) They have **perseverance**. James Dyson took years to get his new design of vacuum cleaner to the market because he couldn't get an existing manufacturer to adopt his ideas. Eventually, he raised the **finance** himself and started his **own small business** to make what's now one of the best-selling cleaners in the world.
3) They're **risk-takers**. When starting a business, many entrepreneurs have to use their **own financial resources** to provide start-up capital. If the business fails, they lose their investment. They're **prepared** to take the risk because they believe that they will gain financial **rewards** — they're motivated by **profit**. As a general rule, low risk = low rewards, and high risk = high rewards.
4) They're good **organisers** and **planners**. Successful entrepreneurs plan what financial, technical and human resources they'll need and organise resources so that they're used cost-effectively.

Entrepreneurs research **Profitable Business Opportunities**

1) Entrepreneurs get ideas for new businesses from **brainstorming** or from personal or professional **experience**.
2) They need to consider the strengths and weaknesses of each idea. E.g. there might be lots of demand for a new Italian restaurant, but no suitable premises to locate the business in.
3) Successful entrepreneurs won't **commit** large resources to an idea until they're confident it will **work**. They need to be sure that there's enough **demand** for their product or service and that they have the **skills** to produce it.
4) Entrepreneurs need to figure out how much money they'll make — it's only worth going ahead with a business idea if it's **profitable**. If they're not likely to make big profits then it's not worth the **risk**.
5) A new business won't usually attract customers unless it can offer something different — a **unique selling point**. This could be quality, low price, good customer service etc.
6) It's really important to get the **price** right. If the price is too high, sales will be too low to make enough money. If the price is too low, the total revenue won't be enough to cover the costs.

The **Government** encourages **Enterprise**

1) The UK government encourages entrepreneurs to set up businesses because enterprise benefits the **economy** — new businesses **increase productivity** and create **new jobs**. The government is especially keen to promote enterprise in areas that need economic **regeneration**.
2) The government has set up organisations like **Business Link** to provide **advice** and **support** to owners of small businesses and to people thinking of starting their own business. They can offer advice on many aspects of setting up and running a small business, including creating a business plan and financing a new business.
3) The government also provides **grants** and **incentives** for entrepreneurs to set up businesses. Entrepreneurs can get grants from various sources, including local authorities and **Regional Development Agencies** like Yorkshire Forward and Advantage West Midlands (see p. 21 for more on this). The **Enterprise Investment Scheme** is another government scheme that offers tax incentives to people who invest in small businesses.

Enterprise and Entrepreneurs

Entrepreneurs have to do **Market Research** on a **Small Budget**

1) Before start-up, it's important to get to know the **market**. Entrepreneurs need to know about the social, environmental, legal and economic factors that limit how they market their product.
2) New businesses can easily do **secondary research** (looking at data that's already available) on a **small budget**, and they can also do low-budget **primary market research** (gathering new data) — this may be a **survey** asking potential customers their opinions of the idea, or **observation** of activities in a similar business.
3) It's really important to be **objective** and **scientific** when doing your own primary research. It's easy and tempting to ask **loaded questions** that lead people into giving the answer you want. It's easy to ask **friends** and **family** who give "nice" answers out of politeness. Watch out for this in exam questions — the new business owner in the case study may have done **unreliable** market research. You'd be spot-on to **question** their methods and their findings. For more on market research, see p. 12-13.

Entrepreneurs have to do **Marketing** on a budget too

1) At the start, a new business doesn't have loads of money to spend on **advertising** campaigns. An advert in the **local paper** and a few cheaply printed **leaflets** are going to be the limit.
2) **Sales promotions** can be **cheap** to organise. Special offers like "buy one, get one free" tend to get people buying.
3) It's important to not stimulate demand **too much** — when demand is greater than the **capacity** of the business, the business has to turn customers away, which isn't good for customer relations, to say the least...
For more on marketing, see p. 11.

New businesses often **Fail**

New start-ups are **risky** — lots of small businesses **fail** within a couple of years of starting up. The reasons for this vary from business to business, but it's often because:

> Nearly all new businesses have limited resources so they have to be very careful about what they spend when setting up.

1) The entrepreneur lacks **experience**. Small business owners, especially **sole traders** (see p.14), have to be a "Jack of all trades" — they're responsible for running all aspects of the business, including finance, managing employees, marketing, etc. Many entrepreneurs don't have enough experience to do all these things properly.
2) Entrepreneurs may have false **expectations** of what running their own business will be like — they expect huge profits or lots of free time, and give up when their expectations aren't met.
3) Many businesses fail because they simply run out of **money** — entrepreneurs sometimes underestimate costs, or overestimate demand or sales, and the business fails because of a **cash flow** crisis (see p.30-31).
4) If a business has an **inaccurate** or **unrealistic** business plan to start with, it's likely to fail.
5) Unexpected delays or a lack of available supplies can cause a business to fail — this is **poor stock control**.
6) Not doing enough **market research**, or not making sure that the research is reliable can also be a cause of failure.
7) The wrong **location** can cause a business to fail, as can changing **market conditions**, such as a recession.

Practice Questions

Q1 Why does the government encourage entrepreneurs to start their own businesses?

Q2 Give three personal characteristics of a successful entrepreneur.

Q3 Why is it important to get the price of a product right?

Q4 Give three reasons why a new business might fail.

Exam Question

Q1 Johan Möller has invented a new tin-opener, and he is setting up his own business to make and sell it.
(a) Discuss where Johan might get help with setting up his business. (4 marks)
(b) Outline two possible strengths and two possible weaknesses of Johan's idea (4 marks)

All you need is an idea... and lots of research... and the right attitude...

Starting a new business sounds like a great idea — you get to be your own boss, and hopefully make loads of money to spend on fast cars and bling. But it can be scary — there are an awful lot of things to be responsible for. It seems that entrepreneurs have to do a heck of a lot of legwork to find out what the market's like and what they need to do to succeed.

New Business Ideas

Before setting up a small business, entrepreneurs need to be sure that they can make money out of their ideas. If they don't have any business ideas of their own, starting a franchise business instead can be a good option.

Entrepreneurs can target **Niche** or **Mass Markets**

Jeffrey and Phil were convinced there would be a mass market for their origami tableware.

1) Some business ideas are aimed at a **mass market** — they are goods or services that are designed to appeal to **lots of consumers** e.g. Coca-Cola®. Mass markets generally have a **high volume** of sales, but fairly **low profit margins**.
2) Other products may be aimed at a **niche market** — a **smaller** and **more specific** group of consumers. E.g. a new type of fishing bait is unlikely to appeal to people who don't go fishing, but could still generate a good profit if it sold well to fishermen.
3) **Small businesses** can be more successful if they focus on **niche markets** — this often means they don't have to compete **directly** with larger businesses, (who don't normally target niche markets because they can find bigger rewards elsewhere). E.g. if an entrepreneur wants to set up a small business selling microwave meals, they could **establish a niche** by **specialising** in, say, meals for people with nut allergies — this allows the business to make a profit even though there are lots of large ready-meal businesses. Niche markets often have high profit margins, because there's a big **difference** between what it **costs** to make something, and what it can be **sold** for.
4) Small niche **markets** suit small niche **manufacturers**. A small manufacturer can **meet the demand** of a **small segment** of the market. It might not be able to meet the demand of a **mass market**.

Entrepreneurs need to **Know the Market**

1) Entrepreneurs need a good **background knowledge** of the market they want to sell to — it's much easier to know what will sell well in a particular market if you have **personal experience** of that market. E.g. if you don't know anything about dancing it's probably a bad idea to design a new type of dancing shoe — you won't know what dancers want or need.
2) When they're designing a new product, entrepreneurs need to check if any **similar products** are already on the market — otherwise they could waste time inventing something that's **already** been invented, or coming up with a product that's **less suitable** than what's already available. If there are plenty of competitors in the market already, there might not be any demand for a new product unless it's offering something different.
3) Just because a product hasn't been invented before **doesn't** mean that it'll be commercially successful — some things simply aren't profitable, or won't catch on even if they're original.

Original **Ideas** are business **Assets** that can be **Protected** by law

Businesses and individuals who produce **original work** and earn an income through it need to **protect their ideas** from being copied by others. You can get protection in several ways, depending on what is being protected:

1) A patent is a way of registering and protecting a new invention

If you have a new invention, you can apply for a **patent** from the **Patent Office** (a government agency that checks that an invention is an original design). If you have a patent for your **product**, or your **method** for producing it, no one else can copy it unless you give them a **licence** — and you can **charge** for the licence.

2) Trademarks (™) protect logos and slogans etc.

If you want to protect your business' name, logo or slogan, you can register it as a **trademark** (™) so that nobody else can use it. E.g. the McDonald's golden arches logo is the **intellectual property** of the McDonald's Corporation and it can't be used by any other company. McDonald's promote a certain **brand image** — if the logo was used by other companies, McDonald's **reputation** might be damaged. McDonald's might also lose **profits** if consumers went to another restaurant by mistake because it had the same logo.

3) Copyright gives protection to written work and music

It's **illegal** to reproduce other people's work without their permission. Authors and musicians or their publishers receive **royalties** (payment) every time their work is published or played on the radio.

Franchises

Franchises are *Special Agreements* between *One Business and Another*

1) Franchises aren't really a type of business ownership as such. They're **agreements** (contracts) which allow one business to use the **business idea**, **name** and **reputation** of another business.
2) The **franchisor** is the business which is willing to sell, or license, the use of its idea, name and reputation. The **franchisee** is the business which wants to use the name.
3) Several well-known retail chains in the UK operate as franchises, e.g. KFC®, BURGER KING®, McDonald's, Pizza Hut® and The Body Shop®.

The franchisee gets these benefits from running a franchise business:

1) A **well-known name**.
2) A **successful** and **proven** business idea — there is **less risk** of a franchise failing than a totally new business
3) **Training** and **financial support** to set up a new franchise outlet.
4) **Marketing**, **advertising** and **promotion** are done **nationally** by the franchisor.
5) **Buying** is done **centrally** by the franchisor — this helps franchise **outlets** keep **costs** down.
6) Expensive equipment can be **leased** from the franchisor.
7) It can be **easier to finance** a business if it's a franchise — banks can be **more willing** to lend money to people who want to buy a franchise from an established franchisor rather than set up a business from scratch.

A franchise business has these drawbacks for the franchisee:

1) They have to **pay** the franchisor for the right to use the name.
2) They have to pay the franchisor part of the **profits** or an **agreed sum**.
3) They have to run the business according to the franchisor's **rules** — they can't choose their own decor, etc.
4) It might be difficult to **sell** the franchise — they can only sell it to someone the franchisor approves of.
5) The franchise could get a **bad reputation** if other franchisees give bad customer service or sell sub-standard products.

The franchisor gets these benefits from franchising their business:

1) Someone else **runs** bits of their business for them and saves them **wage** costs.
2) They **get paid** for the use of their name, and they get a share of the **profits**.
3) The more franchises there are, the faster the **name** of the business can be **spread**.
4) The **risk** involved in opening an outlet in a new location is **reduced** because the franchisee takes on some of the risk.

A franchise business has these drawbacks for the franchisor:

1) They have to **help** the franchisee set up a new franchise.
2) They provide a good business **concept**, but they have to **share** the rewards with the franchisee.
3) If their franchisees don't have good standards, the franchisor's brand could get a **bad reputation**.

Practice Questions

Q1 What's the difference between a mass market and a niche market?

Q2 How can entrepreneurs legally protect new inventions?

Q3 What's the purpose of copyright?

Q4 What's meant by the terms "franchisee" and "franchisor"?

Exam Question

Q1 Evaluate the advantages and disadvantages of franchising, for both the franchisor and the franchisee. (10 marks)

I always thought patents were just really shiny leather shoes...

There's lots to learn on these pages, but don't let that get you down — just keep going over all the information until you're sure you've learnt it all. You need to know how entrepreneurs identify and protect a gap in the market, and understand how franchises work — don't forget to learn the advantages and disadvantages for the franchisee and franchisor too.

Understanding Markets

Businesses make a profit if they provide products that customers want or need. In order to do that, they need to understand the market they're trying to sell to, and find out what customers actually want and need.

Markets are where Sales Happen — they aren't Limited to a Physical Place

The market is where the buyer and seller meet. Traditionally the term "**market**" meant the physical **place** where people traded their goods — now it can mean **websites**. "Market" also describes the **type** of **product or service** being bought and sold — e.g. the leisure market, the computer hardware market, the global oil market.

1) **Industrial markets** are where businesses sell to other businesses, such as wholesalers supplying retailers.
2) **Consumer markets** are where firms sell to individual customers — e.g. high street shops like Currys and Next.
3) **Local markets** are where firms sell to customers who live nearby. Selling to a **national market** means selling to people who live all over the country.
4) **Electronic markets** are **virtual markets** where customers don't physically interact with sellers — instead, buying and selling is done over the internet through websites like eBay™ and Amazon.co.uk®. Firms in electronic markets that sell to other companies are called "**business-to-business**" (**B2B**) companies, and the ones that sell to individual customers are called "**business-to-consumer**" (**B2C**) companies.

Market Analysis tells a Business about the Market it's in

Market analysis lets businesses spot **opportunities** in a market by looking at **market conditions**. The most important conditions are **market size**, **growth** in the market and **market share**.

The more a firm understands about their market, the more likely they are to make good marketing decisions.

MARKET SIZE — by volume and by value

Businesses estimate the **size** of their market by the **total number of sales** (volume of sales) in the **whole market** or by the **value** in pounds of **all the sales** in the market. Market size is calculated by adding together all the sales made by different firms operating in a particular market. E.g. if there are three firms in the confectionery market, and Firm A sells £526 000 of products, Firm B sells £497 000 of products and Firm C sells £977 000 of products, the market size is £2 million.

Market size and share have to be considered together. E.g. 10% of a £1m market is worth £100k, while 25% of a £200k market is only worth £50k.

MARKET SHARE — sales as a percentage of total market size

Businesses like to know what **share** of the market they have. If **1 out of every 4** PCs bought was a Dell™, this would mean that Dell™ had a **25% market share** (in terms of units sold). If **£1 out of every £10** spent on perfume was spent on Chanel, this would mean Chanel had a **10% market share** (in terms of sales value).

Market share (%) = sales ÷ total market size × 100

MARKET GROWTH

Businesses need to know if the market is **growing** or **shrinking**. Competition is fierce in a shrinking market — there are fewer customers to go around. In a **growing** market, **several** firms can **grow easily**. Businesses may want to get out of a market that's getting smaller.

Market growth (%) = difference between size of old and new market ÷ size of old market x 100

E.g. if the confectionery market is worth £2 million in 2007, and £4 million in 2008, market growth = £2 000 000 ÷ £2 000 000 x 100 = 100%

As well as size, share and growth, market analysis takes into account things like **profitability** and the **costs** of buying equipment and training staff so you can get into the market (entry costs).

Demand affects Market Size, Share and Growth

Businesses try to increase their market share by increasing **demand** for their products among consumers. If demand for their products increases, they'll sell more products and make bigger profits. Several factors affect demand — some of these can be controlled by the business, but others can't. The main factors affecting demand are:

1) The **price of the product**. As the price rises, demand tends to go down — as the price falls, demand goes up.
2) The **actions of competitors**. When one manufacturer increases its prices, demand for **cheaper competitor products** tends to **rise**.
3) **Customer income**. When people have **more money to spend**, there's more demand.
4) **Seasonality** — e.g. the demand for ice cream is greater in the **summer**.
5) **Marketing** — successful marketing stimulates demand.

The market was small. But if you will insist on trying to sell belly button fluff...

Understanding Markets

Markets are *Segmented* into groups of *Similar Customers* for analysis

Businesses use marketing to find out what customers **need and want**, and to try to convince them to buy their products. Different groups of customers have different needs and wants. **Analysing** different parts (**segments**) of a market allows a business to **focus** on the needs of **specific groups** within a target market. Segmentation can be done by:

1) **Income**, e.g. Chanel make-up is aimed at customers with **high incomes**, and Tesco's own-brand make-up is aimed at lower-income customers. **Luxury products** are usually aimed at high income groups.
2) **Socio-economic class**, e.g. businesses can segment their market based on the kind of **jobs** people have — e.g. **electronic organisers** are aimed at **senior professionals** with busy schedules.
3) **Age**, e.g. firms often target products at specific **age groups** — e.g. 'Sugar' magazine is aimed at teenagers.
4) **Gender**, e.g. chocolate companies aim some products at **women** (e.g. Flake) and some at **men** (e.g. Yorkie®).
5) **Geographical region**, e.g. the core market for **Irn-Bru** is **Scotland**.
6) **Amount of use**, e.g. mobile phone suppliers market **differently** to heavy users and light users.
7) **Ethnic grouping**, e.g. new **ethnic minority** TV channels make it easier for businesses to target **advertising** at particular ethnic groups.
8) **Family size**, e.g. large "**family packs**" of breakfast cereal, loo roll, etc. are aimed at large families. New houses are built with a number of bedrooms to suit the **target customer**.
9) **Lifestyle**, e.g. busy **young workers** might tend to buy lots of microwaveable ready-meals, so a company making **ready-meals** might target this market segment.

All these methods focus on a **characteristic of the customer**. Businesses can also segment markets according to the **reason** for buying a product — as an essential, to cheer yourself up, as a gift, etc. Segmentation is useful for **identifying** potential new **customers**, new **markets**, and the best way of **marketing** a product, but it also has **disadvantages**, e.g.:

1) It can cause a firm to **ignore** the **needs** of other **potential customers**, e.g. if they target a chocolate bar at one particular gender.
2) It can be **difficult** to break the market into **obvious segments**. For example, it is hard to place consumers of washing up liquid into clear categories.
3) Even if a business knows which segments of the market are likely to be interested in its product, it might not know how to **target** its **marketing** to reach them — e.g. how could it target single dads over the age of 40?

Marketing is a Continual Process

1) Businesses start by deciding on **marketing objectives** — figuring out what they want to **achieve** in terms of **sales**.
2) Firms plan **marketing strategies** to achieve their objectives. They **decide** which marketing **activities** to do, based on their **research** and **analysis**.
3) They put their **strategies** into **action** and carry out **marketing activities**, e.g. advertising campaigns.
4) They **monitor sales** to make sure their marketing strategies are having the **right effect**.
5) They **change and improve** their marketing **strategies** and **activities** — if they **need** to.

Practice Questions

Answer on p. 82.

Q1 Name the three most important market conditions that a business can choose to analyse.

Q2 If a business sells 30 000 televisions and the total number of televisions sold is 150 000, what is its market share?

Q3 What is "market segmentation"?

Q4 How can a business make sure its marketing strategies are having the right effect?

Exam Questions

Q1 Outline how a business might estimate its market size and its market share. (4 marks)

Q2 Discuss how a retailer of women's clothing, such as Next, might segment their market. (6 marks)

Did you know — agoraphobia is literally "fear of the marketplace"...

...and although there are lots of different kinds of market out there, you don't need to be frightened of any of them, cos' your mum probably does the shopping anyway. Marketing's about knowing your market, knowing what people want, and knowing how to sell it to them. And to know all this stuff, you've got to do a bit of analysis to find out what's going on.

Market Research

Market research is the collection and analysis of market information such as customer likes and dislikes. It's especially important before starting a new business or launching a new product — it helps prevent disastrous errors.

Market Research is done for **Three Main Reasons**

1) It helps businesses **spot opportunities**. Businesses research **customer buying patterns** to help them predict what people will be buying in the future. A business might use **research** to help them spot growing markets to get into — and declining markets to get out of. Research on customer likes and dislikes might show a gap in the market.
2) It helps them **work out what to do next**. Businesses research before launching a product or advertising campaign.
3) It helps them see if their **plans are working**. A business that keeps a keen eye on sales figures will notice if their marketing strategy is having the right effect.

Market research can be **expensive**. **Bad market research** can lead to **disastrous business decisions**. Businesses need to **plan carefully** to make sure they get the **maximum benefit** from market research.

There's **Quantitative** *and* **Qualitative** *market research*

1) Quantitative research produces **numerical statistics** — facts and figures. It often uses multiple-choice **questionnaires** that ask questions like: "When did you last buy this product? A: within the last day, B: within the last week, C: within the last month, D: within the last year, E: longer ago, F: have never bought this product." These are called **closed questions** because they have **fixed**, **predetermined** answers.
2) Qualitative research looks into the **feelings** and **motivations** of consumers. It uses **focus groups** that have in-depth discussions on a product, and asks questions like: "How does this product make you feel?" These are called **open questions**. The answer isn't restricted to multiple-choice options.

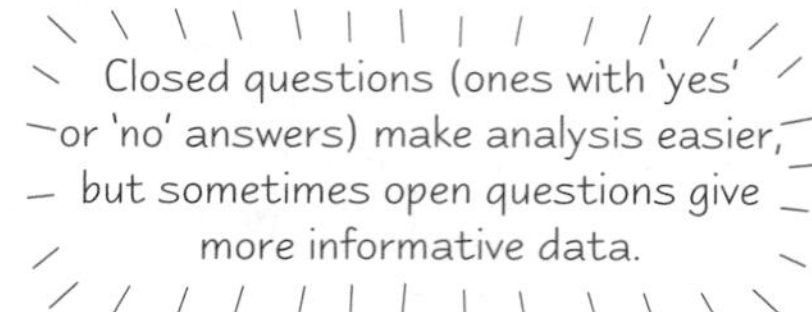

Closed questions (ones with 'yes' or 'no' answers) make analysis easier, but sometimes open questions give more informative data.

There's **Primary** *and* **Secondary** *market research*

Primary market research is where a business **gathers new data** (or employs someone to do it on their behalf).
Secondary market research is done by **analysing data** that's already available.

Primary Research

1) Primary data is gathered with **questionnaires**, **interviews**, post / phone / internet **surveys**, **focus groups** (e.g. a group of well-informed people) and by observation (e.g. looking at CCTV to see how people shop in stores). Businesses do **test marketing** — e.g. they launch a product in one **region** and measure **sales** and **customer response** before launching it across the country.
2) Primary research uses **sampling** to make predictions about the **whole market** based on a sample (see p.13).
3) Primary data is needed to find out what consumers think of a **new product** or **advert**. You can't use secondary data because, erm, there won't be any secondary data on a brand new product.
4) Primary data is **specific** to the purpose it's needed for. This is great for **niche markets** — secondary data might be too broad or too mainstream to tell you anything useful.
5) Primary data is **exclusive** to the business who commissioned the research, so **competitors can't benefit** from it.
6) Primary research is always **up to date**.
7) **But**, primary research is **labour-intensive**, **expensive** and **slow**.

Secondary Research

1) **Internal sources** of data include loyalty cards, feedback from company salesmen and analysis of company sales reports, financial accounts, and stock records.
2) **External sources** include government publications like the Social Trends report, marketing agency reports, pressure groups and trade magazines.
3) **Secondary data** is much **easier**, **faster** and **cheaper** to get hold of than primary data.
4) **But**, secondary data that was gathered for a different purpose might be **unsuitable**. It may contain **errors** and it may be **out of date**.
5) Secondary data is often used to get an **initial understanding** of a market. A business may then do more specific primary research to investigate any **issues** or problems that are shown up by the secondary data.

Market Research

Market researchers need a **Representative Sample**

1) Market researchers can't ask the **whole** of a **market** to fill in a survey. They select a sample.
2) The sample should try to **represent** the market. It must have **similar proportions** of people in terms of things like age, income, class, ethnicity and gender. If the sample isn't representative, you've got **problems**. However, it isn't always easy to get a representative sample.
3) A **big sample** has a better **chance** of being representative than a **small sample** — but even a big sample won't necessarily be 100% representative. There's always a **margin of error**.
4) The **size** of the **sample** may depend on how many people a **company** can **afford** to ask. If the **cash** available for research is **limited**, the **risk** of the information being **inaccurate** increases.
5) The **size** of the **sample** and the **sampling method** is also affected by the **type** of product or business, the **risk** involved and the **target market**. E.g. a company producing wedding dresses won't use random sampling (see below) as men don't form part of their target market. They're more likely to use quota sampling instead.

There are **three** main types of sample:

1) **Simple Random Sample** — Names are picked **randomly** from a list (usually from the electoral register).
2) **Stratified Sample** — The population is divided into groups and people are selected randomly from each group. The number of people picked from each group is **proportional** to the size of the group.
3) **Quota Sample** — People are picked who fit into a **category** (e.g. mums between 30 and 40). Businesses use quota sampling to get opinions from the people the product is directly targeted at.

Market research needs to **Avoid Bias**

The quality of decisions made using market research is only as good as the **accuracy** of the research.

1) Researchers have to be careful to avoid any possible **bias**.
2) Questionnaires and interviews should avoid **leading questions** — questions that are phrased in a way that **leads** the respondent to give a particular answer, e.g "You do like chocolate, don't you?"
3) Interviews suffer from "**interviewer effects**". This is when the **response** isn't what the interviewee **really thinks**. This can be caused by the **personality** of the interviewer — their **opinions** can **influence** the interviewee.
4) Interviewers should only ask for personal data at the **end** of an interview so that they aren't influenced by knowing the **age** or **social background** of the interviewee.
5) The more **representative** a sample is, the more **confidence** a business can have in the results of the research.

Not Spending enough on market research increases the **Risk**

1) **Market research** can be very expensive. Small businesses don't usually have a lot of money to spend — they may think that research is a waste of money, and spend their cash on fine-tuning the product instead.
2) Not doing enough market research before starting a business **increases the risk** that it will **fail** — businesses don't stand much chance of getting the product right if they **don't know** whether it's really what the market **wants**.
3) It's much less risky to do market research **before** finalising the details of a product or service. Research may tell a firm that they have to seriously **adapt** and **develop** their original idea to make it **fit in** with what the market **needs**.

Practice Questions

Q1 A toy company is researching the market for a new board game.
Write three open and three closed questions that they could use in a consumer survey.

Q2 List two internal and two external sources of secondary data.

Q3 Give three reasons why firms carry out market research.

Q4 What are the three main types of sample, and what are the differences between them?

Exam Question

Q1 Discuss why a new business might pay a market research company to gather primary research for them. (8 marks)

Surveys show that most people lie in surveys...

Research takes time and costs money — businesses must make sure the data's accurate or it'll be as much use as a chocolate fireguard. They also have to actually use the findings to provide what their customers want. If a business can use market research to increase their sales and profits, the market research will pay for itself. Everyone's a winner.

Legal Structure of Businesses

If you're setting up your own business you need to choose a legal structure for it — each type of structure has benefits and drawbacks. It's quite complicated but the next few pages will help you work out what's what.

Sole Trader Businesses are run by an Individual

1) A sole trader is an **individual** trading in his or her own name, or under a suitable trading name. Sole traders are **self-employed**, for example as shopkeepers, plumbers, electricians, hairdressers or consultants.
2) The essential feature of this type of business is that the sole trader has **full responsibility** for the **financial control** of his or her own business and for meeting **running costs** and **capital requirements**. Having full responsibility for all the **debts** of the business is called **unlimited liability**.
3) There are **minimal legal formalities** — the trader simply has to start trading. However, if the business isn't run under the **proprietor's** (owner's) name, the trader has to **register** the company name under the Business Names Act (1985).
4) There are several **advantages** of being a sole trader:

'Capital' just means 'money'. 'Capital requirement' is money invested to set up a business or fund growth.

- **Freedom** — the sole trader is his or her **own boss** and has complete **control** over decisions.
- **Profit** — the sole trader is entitled to **all the profit** made by the business.
- **Simplicity** — there's **less form-filling** than for a limited company. Bookkeeping is less complex.
- **Savings on fees** — there aren't any legal costs like you'd get with drawing up a partnership agreement or limited company documentation.

5) There are **disadvantages** too:

- **Risk** — there's **no one** to **share the responsibilities** of running the business with.
- **Time** — sole traders often need to **work long hours** to meet tight deadlines.
- **Expertise** — the sole trader may have **limited skills** in areas such as finance.
- **Vulnerability** — there's **no cover** if the trader **gets ill** and can't work.
- **Unlimited liability** — the sole trader is **responsible** for all the debts of the business.

A Partnership is a Group of Individuals working together

1) Examples of partnerships include groups of doctors, dentists, accountants and solicitors.
2) The law allows a partnership to have between **two** and **twenty partners**, although some **professions**, e.g. accountants and solicitors, are allowed **more** than twenty.
3) A partnership can either trade in the **names** of the partners, or under a suitable **trading name**.
4) Partnerships need rules. Most partnerships operate according to the terms of a **partnership agreement** (also called a **deed of partnership**). This is a document drawn up by a **solicitor** which sets out:

- The amount of **capital** contributed by each partner.
- The procedure in case of **partnership disputes**.
- How the **profit** will be shared between partners.
- Partners' **voting rights**.
- The procedures for **bringing in new partners** and old partners retiring.

There are **advantages** to a partnership:

1) More owners bring **more capital** to invest at start-up.
2) Partners can bring **more ideas** and **expertise** to a partnership.
3) Partners can **cover** for each other's **holidays** and **illness**.

There are **disadvantages** to a partnership:

1) Partners still have **unlimited liability**.
2) Each partner is liable for **decisions** made by **other partners** — even if they had **no say** in the decision.
3) There's a **risk of conflict** between partners.

Legal Structure of Businesses

Liability to pay off *Business Debts* can be *Limited* or *Unlimited*

Sole traders and partnerships have unlimited liability

1) The **business** and the **owner** are **seen as one** under the **law**.
2) This means **business debts** become the **personal debts** of the owner. Sole traders and partners can be forced to **sell personal assets** like their **house** to pay off business debts.
3) Unlimited liability is a **huge financial risk** — it's an important factor to consider when deciding on the type of ownership for a new business.

When Louise's clothes-designing business failed, unlimited liability became a real pain.

Limited liability is a much smaller risk

1) Limited liability means that the owners **aren't personally responsible** for the debts of the business.
2) The **shareholders** of both **private** and **public limited companies** (see p.16) have limited liability, because a limited company has a **separate legal identity** from its owners.
3) The **most** the shareholders in a limited company can lose is the money they have **invested** in the company.

In a limited company, the shareholders own the business.

The difference between limited liability and unlimited liability is **really important**. E.g. a builder puts **£1500** into their own business. The business hits bad times, and eventually goes bankrupt, owing **£20 000**. If the owner is a **sole trader**, he or she is liable to pay the **full amount**. If they're a **shareholder** of a limited company, they only lose the **£1500** they put in.

Some Partners in a partnership can have *Limited Liability*

1) The Limited Partnership Act (1907) allows a **partnership** to claim **limited liability** for **some** of its partners.
2) The partners with limited liability are called **sleeping partners**.
3) Sleeping partners can put **money** into the partnership but they **aren't allowed** to do anything to **run** the business.
4) There must be at least one **general partner** who **is fully liable** for all **debts** and obligations of the partnership.

Practice Questions

Q1 What legal requirements does a sole trader have to fulfil before he or she can start trading?
Q2 What's the maximum number of partners allowed in a dental practice?
Q3 What's the difference between limited liability and unlimited liability?
Q4 Which represents the biggest risk to the owners of a business — limited liability or unlimited liability?
Q5 Under what circumstances can partners in a partnership have limited liability?

Exam Question

Q1 Eric, a plumber trading as a sole trader, wants to go into partnership with his friend Sandra (also a plumber). Explain why he might want to change the type of ownership of his business? Evaluate the implications of doing so. (6 marks)

Sole traders — they're not just shoemakers...

...They can also be plumbers, window cleaners, greengrocers... You get the idea. The important thing to remember here is that sole traders and partnerships both have unlimited liability, so if you're going to set up one of these types of businesses you need to be pretty sure that it's not going to fail. Otherwise you're in big trouble...cos debts don't mind getting personal.

Legal Structure of Businesses

Companies are different from sole traders and partnerships. They have limited liability for a start.

There are two kinds of **Limited Liability Companies — Ltds and PLCs**

More on shares on p.19.

1) There are **private limited companies** and **public limited companies**.
2) Public and private limited companies have **limited liability** (see p.15).
3) They're owned by **shareholders** and run by **directors**.
4) The **capital value** (see p.14 for the meaning of capital) of the company is divided into **shares** — these can be **bought** and **sold** by shareholders.
5) Both require a **minimum** of **two shareholders**, and there's **no upper limit** on the number of shareholders.

Private Limited Companies	Public Limited Companies
Can't sell shares to the public. People in the company own all the shares.	Can sell shares to the **public**. They must issue a **prospectus** to inform people about the company before they buy.
Don't have share prices quoted on **stock exchanges**.	Their share prices can be quoted on the **Stock Exchange**.
Shareholders may not be able to sell their shares without the **agreement** of the **other shareholders**.	Shares are **freely transferable** and can be bought and sold through stockbrokers, banks and share shops.
They're often **small** family businesses.	They usually start as private companies and then **go public** later to raise more capital.
There's **no minimum share capital** requirement.	They need **over £50 000** of share capital, and if they're listed on a stock exchange, **at least 25%** of this must be publicly available. People in the company can own the rest of the shares.
They end their name with the word "limited" or **Ltd**.	They always end their name with the initials **PLC**.

Companies are governed by the **Companies Act** (1985)

The Companies Act (1985) says that two important documents must be drawn up **before** a company can start trading. These are the **memorandum of association** and the **articles of association**.

Memorandum of Association

1) The **memorandum of association** gives the company name followed by **Ltd**, if it's a private limited company, or **PLC**, if it's a public limited company, and it gives the company's business address.
2) The Memorandum of Association says what the **objectives** of the company are.
3) It gives **details** of the company's capital, e.g. £250 000 divided into 250 000 Ordinary Shares of £1 each.
4) It states clearly that the **shareholders' liability is limited.**

Articles of Association

1) The **articles of association** are the **internal rules** of the company.
2) They give the **names** of the **directors**.
3) They say **how directors are appointed** and what kind of **power** they have.
4) The articles of association say what the **shareholders' voting rights** are.
5) They set out when and how the company will hold **shareholders' meetings.**
6) The articles of association set out how the company will **share** its **profits**.

Companies House is where records of all UK companies are kept.

The **memorandum of association** and **articles of association** must both be sent to **Companies House**.
The Registrar of Companies issues a **certificate of incorporation** so that the company can start trading.
Once it's up and running, the company is legally obliged to produce **annual reports** of its financial activities.

Companies are controlled by **Shareholders** and **Directors**

1) All the shareholders in a **small** private limited company are usually the **directors**. The shareholders who hold the **most shares** have the **most power**.
2) In larger private limited companies, directors are **elected** to the board by **shareholders**. The board makes the important decisions. **Shareholders vote** on the performance of the board at the Annual General Meeting (**AGM**).
3) Shares in a PLC can be owned by **anyone**. The people who **own** the company (the shareholders) don't necessarily **control** the company — it's **controlled** by the **directors**. This is called the "**divorce of ownership and control**".

Legal Structure of Businesses

Not-for-Profit businesses are another type of business structure

1) As their name suggests, not-for-profit businesses are **not** set up to make a **profit**. Instead, they have other aims, often to **help** people in need or benefit the community.
2) **Not-for-profit** businesses are run in a similar way to other businesses. They usually have money coming into and going out of the business — the main difference is that the money generated by the business **doesn't** go to the owners or shareholders as **profit**.
3) **Public-sector** organisations providing free services to the public are not-for-profit businesses. NHS hospitals are one example — their aim is to provide healthcare rather than to make a profit. The NHS and other organisations like UK police forces and the fire service are run in a similar way to other businesses, but they don't charge for their services so they don't make a profit — they are funded by the UK **tax system**.
4) **Charities** like the Red Cross, Oxfam and Amnesty International are also not-for-profit businesses — they make money from **donations** and business activities (like charity shops), but this money is used to fund charitable activities, e.g. setting up hospitals in developing countries. Charities get **tax reductions** because of their not-for-profit structure.
5) Many **local organisations** and societies are also run as not-for-profit businesses — e.g. amateur theatre groups might charge for tickets to see their performances, but the money generated from ticket sales is put back into the business, e.g. to cover the costs of renting a building for the performance, buying costumes, etc.

Entrepreneurs have to Choose a Legal Structure for their business

1) When someone sets up a business, they have to **decide** whether to set up as a sole trader, a partnership, a private limited company (Ltd.) or a public limited company (PLC). Each of the business structures has **advantages** and **disadvantages** — the entrepreneur has to decide which is most **suitable** for their needs.
2) Setting up a **sole trader** business gives the owner **control** over the business, but **unlimited liability** is a drawback. It's a **simple** way to set up a small business, but there's a lot of **risk** involved for the owner.
3) A **partnership** means more people with more **money** and more **ideas**, but there's a risk of **disagreements** between partners and there's still **unlimited liability**.
4) A **private limited company** (Ltd.) has **limited liability** and the shareholders keep **control** over who other shares are sold to, but it's much more **complicated** to set up than a sole trader business.
5) **Public limited companies** aren't usually a suitable option for new businesses because they need at least **£50 000** of share capital to start with, and most new businesses can't raise that much money.
6) Businesses can **change** their structure — sole traders can join together to form a partnership, or they can become a private limited company if the business is successful and they want to expand. Lots of private limited companies become PLCs when they want to raise more money to **expand** the business. It's much less common, but PLCs can also become private limited companies if they are taken over by a private limited company or if the managers **buy out** the **shareholders**. For example, in 2002, Arcadia Group PLC was taken over by Philip Green's private limited company Taveta Investments Ltd. and is now Arcadia Group Ltd.

Practice Questions

Q1 State two differences between private and public limited companies.
Q2 What are the names of the two documents a company needs to draw up before it can start trading?
Q3 Why are new businesses not usually set up as PLCs?
Q4 Give three examples of not-for-profit businesses.

Exam Question

Q1 Made-Up Organics, a company selling organic make-up and toiletries, is owned by Isabelle Greenberg, a sole trader. The business has been growing over the past few years and she is thinking of becoming a private limited company instead. Discuss the advantages and disadvantages of doing this. (6 marks)

All this legal stuff seemed much more entertaining on Ally McBeal...

It's a bit of a pain having to learn all the legal ins and outs of different business structures, but make sure you do because this is quite likely to crop up in the exam. You might be asked to decide whether a particular business would be better off as a sole trader, partnership, private limited company or PLC, so you need to be able to choose between them.

Financing a New Business

Entrepreneurs need to find finance for their business if they want to turn it from an idea into reality. There are loads of different sources of finance out there, so it's just a case of choosing the right one.

Lots of **Costs** are involved in starting a new business

1) New businesses **can't** usually **put off** paying costs like employee's wages, rent on business premises and payment for equipment and raw materials. This is a **problem** because money won't start coming into the business until much **later**, when the business starts being **paid** for its products.
2) If the business **can't** pay what it owes in time, it will have to **close down**.
3) To make sure that the business will **survive** until revenue starts coming in, and to pay all the **bills** once the business starts trading, the entrepreneur needs to find a way of **financing** the business.
4) There are several possible ways of financing a new business — they all have **benefits** and **drawbacks**, and are suitable in different **circumstances**. Most businesses use a combination of different sources of finance.

Entrepreneurs can use their **Savings** to finance their business

1) Most entrepreneurs use some of their **own** money to finance their business.
2) Investing some of your own money shows that you have **faith** that the business will be **successful** — this can **encourage** banks to give you a loan or other people to invest in the business.
3) Not many entrepreneurs will have enough savings to cover **all** the money they need to start up their business — most need to find **additional** sources of finance too.

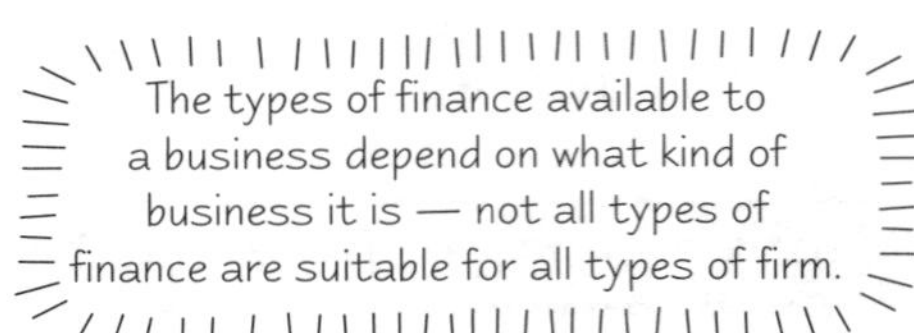

The types of finance available to a business depend on what kind of business it is — not all types of finance are suitable for all types of firm.

Entrepreneurs can take out **Loans** to finance their business

1) Entrepreneurs can get **loans** from **banks** to finance their business. They borrow a fixed amount of **money** and pay it back over a fixed period of **time** with **interest** — the amount they have to pay back depends on the interest rate and the length of time the loan is for.
2) Banks need **security** for a loan, usually in the form of property.
3) Loans are a good way of financing the **start-up** of a business and paying for **assets** like machinery and computers. They are **not** a good way to cover the **day-to-day** running costs of the business.

Advantages of bank loans

1) You're **guaranteed** the money for the duration of the loan (the bank can't suddenly demand it back).
2) You only have to pay back the **loan** and **interest** — the bank won't **own** any of your business and you don't have to give them a share of the **profits**.
3) The interest charges for a loan are usually **lower** than for an overdraft.

Disadvantages of bank loans

1) They can be **difficult** to arrange because the bank will only lend the entrepreneur money if they think they are going to get it back. If the entrepreneur doesn't own any property or other assets that can be used for security, they might not be able to get a loan.
2) Keeping up with the **repayments** can be difficult if cash isn't coming into the business quickly enough. The entrepreneur might **lose** whatever the loan is secured on (e.g. their home) — the bank can sell it to get their money back.
3) The entrepreneur might have to pay a **charge** if they decide to pay the loan back **early**.

Entrepreneurs may also be able to borrow money from **friends** or **family** — they will probably charge **less interest** than banks, or even none at all. They're also unlikely to ask for security for the loan, and might be more **flexible** about when repayments are made. However, if the business fails then the lender will **lose** the money that they lent to the entrepreneur — this could have a very negative effect on the **relationship** between the entrepreneur and the lender.

Financing a New Business

Entrepreneurs can use **Overdrafts** to finance their business

1) **Overdrafts** are where a bank lets a business spend **more** money **than** it **has** in its account, up to a **limit**. The overspend is recorded as a **negative** figure.
2) Many businesses use overdrafts to cover some of their day-to-day costs, especially if they have **short-term** cash flow problems (see p.30-31). They're **not** suitable for **long-term** finance though.

Advantages of overdrafts

1) They're **quick** and **easy** to set up — banks will usually offer them to anyone, unlike loans.
2) They're **flexible** — the business can borrow any amount up to the overdraft limit, and only has to pay interest on the amount that it borrows.

Disadvantages of overdrafts

1) The interest rate is usually very **high** so they are **expensive** if they're used over long periods of time.
2) The bank can **remove** the overdraft facility at any time and demand all the money back.

Limited companies can sell **Shares** to raise finance

1) If the business is set up as a **private limited company**, the entrepreneur can finance it using **ordinary share capital** — money raised by selling **shares** in the business.
2) Entrepreneurs can sell shares to their **friends** and **family**, or to **venture capitalists** — professional investors who buy shares in new businesses that they think have the potential to be successful.
3) The drawback of selling shares rather than taking out a loan is that the entrepreneur no longer **owns** all of the business — they have to give the shareholders a share of the **profits**, and they also have to give them a **say** in how the business is run.

Sally tried using her feminine wiles, but nothing could persuade Steve to buy shares in her suede raincoat business.

Practice Questions

Q1 Explain why a new business needs finance.

Q2 What is the main drawback of borrowing money from friends and family?

Q3 What is the difference between an overdraft and a loan?

Q4 What is meant by the term "venture capitalist"?

Exam Questions

Q1 Suggest what type of finance might be suitable for financing the launch of a cybercafé business. (6 marks)

Q2 Discuss the advantages and disadvantages of financing a new business using a bank loan. (8 marks)

Unfortunately you can't sell shares in being slightly bored with BS...

I was planning on financing my business with £1 coins from the back of the sofa. Guess not, then. All kidding aside, it's worth knowing about the different kinds of finance that entrepreneurs can use to start up their business. Learn what types of finance are suitable for the short- and long-term running of a firm too and you'll be laughing if it comes up in the exam.

Location

When you're deciding where to set up a business, it's all about location, location, location.

Businesses use **Cost-Benefit Analysis** to choose a **Location**

1) **Cost-benefit analysis** means **weighing** up the **costs** of an opportunity against its potential **benefits**.
2) Renting or buying somewhere is a big **investment** for a business. When deciding where to locate, businesses consider how each location will affect **costs** and **revenues** (e.g. rents and labour costs in Newcastle are likely to be lower than rents and labour costs in London). Businesses use **quantitative analysis** techniques such as **break-even analysis** to measure this (see p. 28-29).
3) Businesses calculate how many sales they'll need to break even at each potential location. Where the **costs of operating** from a location are **high**, the **break-even output** will be higher. It's better to put your business where break-even output is low.

Businesses make **Location** decisions based on **Practical** factors

The best location for a business depends on several factors, and is different for different types of business.

Transport costs affect where businesses are located

1) **Manufacturing** businesses which provide **bulky finished products** should be located near to their **customers** to cut down on distribution costs. Bulky products made from **lightweight** components are called "**bulk increasing**" goods.
2) Other products need **bulky raw materials** to make a **lightweight end product** — these are "**bulk decreasing**" goods. They need to be located near the source of **raw materials** to keep transport costs down.
3) A good **transport infrastructure** (see below) cuts distribution costs.
4) **Services** don't have large distribution costs. Decisions on where to locate services are based mainly on other criteria.

E.g. beer — made of water (available anywhere), plus hops and barley (low in bulk compared to the finished product). Breweries tend to be located near consumers and transport infrastructure, not near hop or barley fields.

E.g. a small business producing bottled mineral water is likely to be based near the source of the water — otherwise it would be very expensive to transport the water to the bottling factory.

A good location needs a good infrastructure

1) Business organisations benefit from access to **motorways**, fast **rail** links, **sea ports** and **airports**.
2) Transport infrastructure is needed for the **import** of **raw materials**, the **distribution** of **finished products**, and for **staff** to get to work.
3) Businesses also need **support services**. Most business organisations need some form of **commercial** support such as **banking**, **insurance** and **marketing** agencies.
4) Often there's a need for **technical** support such as engineering services and **IT** assistance.

Businesses need a location with good land and labour resources

1) There must be a **good supply** of labour resources in the area where a business will be located.
2) The labour force must also be **suitable** — e.g. they might need to be literate, they might need special skills such as IT, technical knowledge of machinery, etc.
3) The area might need **local training facilities** for staff, e.g. a college or university.
4) The area needs **facilities** such as affordable housing, suitable schooling, medical facilities and retail and leisure outlets to provide a good **quality of life** for staff.
5) Businesses can afford to pay workers less in areas where the **cost of living** is lower. To take full advantage of this, businesses need to locate **overseas** where labour costs are far lower than in the UK.
6) Businesses also need the right land resources. They might need to **expand** in the future.
7) The **cost** of **land** and **property** for factories and business premises varies significantly from area to area — land in the London area is far more expensive than land in mid-Wales, for example.
8) **International** location decisions must take account of variations in the cost of water and **electricity**.

Location decisions depend on the market

1) Some businesses such as **retailers** need to locate **near customers**, in order to catch the passing trade.

Location

The Government provides Incentives to locate in certain areas

Governments usually want to attract businesses to areas with high **unemployment**.

1) In 1998, the UK government set up 8 **Regional Development Agencies** (RDAs) to coordinate and encourage development. They can provide **financial assistance** to businesses through grants, loans and equity (share) investment. They provide **financial** and **management advice**, and can help businesses find the right location.
2) They can provide **financial assistance** to business through grants, loans and equity (share) investment. They also provide **financial guidance** and **management support**.
3) They can also help businesses find the right **location**.
4) As another part of its regional policy, the UK government has named certain economically less-developed parts of the country as **assisted areas**. In these areas government **grants** are available to persuade manufacturing and service businesses to locate there. Cornwall and the Scottish Highlands are two examples of assisted areas.

The government often use "**carrots**" and "**sticks**" to encourage businesses to locate in deprived areas.
E.g. a "**carrot**" would be a **grant** given to a business locating in an area of high unemployment.
A **"stick"** would be **refusing planning permission** to build a factory in an area where there are already lots of jobs.

There are also Qualitative Factors involved in Choosing a Location

1) Decisions about where to base a business are not always just based on things that can be **measured**.
2) Entrepreneurs might choose to start a business near where they **live** — e.g. Dyson™ is based in Wiltshire, near the owner and inventor's home.
3) Some places have a **good image** which suits the image of the product. High fashion works better in London or Paris than in Scunthorpe or Workington — London and Paris already have a fashionable image.

Businesses don't usually find an Ideal Location

1) All these factors rarely, if ever, combine in one place to create an **ideal** location. It's more likely that the decision of where to locate a business is based on a **compromise** between different factors.
2) The **importance** of each factor depends on the **type** of business. A coffee shop needs to prioritise being near its customers, but a top restaurant might cut costs by locating in a rural area, because people will travel to eat there.
3) Small businesses don't usually have much **choice** about which area of the country to locate in — entrepreneurs don't usually have spare cash to move location, so they tend to set up the business in the area where they already live. They still have to decide whereabouts in the town/city to locate — e.g. someone thinking of opening a coffee shop might choose to set up close to a university to attract students.
4) Small businesses can be at a **disadvantage** because they might not be able to afford the best location — e.g. an entrepreneur setting up a clothes shop might not be able to afford the rent in the city centre, so their shop might be in a side street where fewer people pass by.
5) **Modern technology** means that many businesses can be more **flexible** about their location. Businesses that trade over the internet rather than face-to-face can be based anywhere in the country. Doing business over the internet can be a useful way for entrepreneurs who don't live in big cities to reach customers.

Practice Questions

Q1 Identify and briefly explain three factors which affect location cost.

Q2 What are assisted areas?

Q3 Why is it difficult for small businesses to find an ideal location?

Exam Question

Q1 Discuss the factors that an entrepreneur should consider when deciding where to locate a restaurant business. (10 marks)

Phil and Kirstie can't help you now...

You're going to have to learn the factors which affect business location, no maybes about it. If this comes up in the exam (more than likely) you'll probably get a case study with some facts and figures about a business, and you'll be asked to say why the business chose to locate where it did. Or you might have to write a report recommending a location for a business.

Employing People

Even the most brilliant entrepreneurs can't do all the work themselves — they're going to need to take on more staff at some point. But there are more options than just taking on full-time employees, so sorting out staffing can be tricky.

Small businesses need to **Consider** their **Staffing Needs**

Small businesses might need to increase or decrease their staffing levels in the following situations:

1) The business is **expanding** — businesses may need **extra staff** to cope with the increased workload.
2) **Demand** increases — **extra staff** might be needed so that the business can keep up with demand.
3) A change in **direction** — if a business decides to move into a new area (e.g. if a hair salon decides to start providing beauty treatments), new staff with new **expertise** might be required.
4) **Quiet periods** — having too high staff levels at these times can cause problems for a small business because they have to **pay** all their staff even if they don't really need them.

Staff can be **Full-Time** or **Part-Time**

Most small businesses employ mainly **full-time** staff (staff working 35 hours or more per week). However, full-time staff are not always the best option for small businesses. Employing **part-time** staff can be better in some circumstances:

Advantages of part-time staff

1) Employing part-time staff can **save** the business **money**. There's no point paying full-time staff to be at work all week if there's not enough work for them to do.
2) Businesses have more **flexibility** to manage **workloads** — the business can use part-time workers to cover times when the workload is greater due to higher demand.
3) Part-time staff may have a better **work/life balance** (a good split between working for money and leisure time), so they are less likely to take time off with stress, or take sick days. Employing part-time staff to deal with increased workloads also eases the **pressure** on full-time staff, so stress and absenteeism among full-time staff are also likely to be reduced.
4) A better work/life balance is likely to mean **happier** staff — this could lead to an increase in **productivity**.
5) There is a wider range of **skills** among the workforce — by increasing the number of employees the business increases its pool of skills and experience.

Disadvantages of part-time staff

1) It can be difficult to **find** good part-time workers because most jobseekers are likely to be looking for **full-time** work.
2) Part-time employees can sometimes be less **dedicated** and **loyal** than full-time workers — they spend a lower proportion of their time working for the business so it's not such an important part of their life.
3) Part-time employees spend less time working for the business so they might not have as much **experience** of how the business works as full-time staff do.
4) The recruitment and training processes are **time-consuming** and **expensive** — it's only worth spending money on hiring part-time employees if you're sure they're going to save you money.

1) It's important for small businesses to get the **balance** between part-time and full-time staff **right** — e.g. an entrepreneur who sets up a small clothes shop might employ one full-time member of staff, and a part-time member of staff to work on Fridays and Saturdays, when the shop is busiest.
2) When entrepreneurs start up new businesses, they might be **unsure** of how **busy** they are likely to be, or how many employees they'll need to cope with **demand** — it's usually best to take on **part-time** staff until they are sure that demand will be high enough to need full-time workers.
3) **Job-sharing** is when two (or more) employees work **part-time** sharing the **same** job. They usually work on different days of the week or alternate weeks, and they share the responsibility and pay of the job. This can be a good way of allowing higher-level staff like **managers** to work part-time without disrupting the business' activities, although it needs careful planning.

Laura found balancing crockery on her feet much easier than balancing her staffing levels.

Employing People

Staff can be Temporary or Permanent

1) **Permanent** staff have an **ongoing contract** to work for a business and a **guaranteed salary**.
2) A business can only stop employing its **permanent staff** by **dismissing** them (if they behave badly or are incapable of doing their job) or making them **redundant** (if the business no longer needs anyone to do their job). It's **expensive** to make permanent employees redundant — the firm has to give them redundancy pay.
3) **Temporary** staff work for the business for a **fixed period** of time (e.g. 6 months) or on a **weekly basis** — the business can renew the employee's contract if extra staff are needed for longer than this.
4) A small business can employ **temporary** workers in **high-risk** periods when the business' future is uncertain — then they can easily **reduce** their number of employees without having to pay redundancy money.
5) Recruitment is an **expensive** process, so businesses often use **employment agencies** to find temporary staff — the agency advertises the job and finds a suitable candidate, and the business has to pay a fee to the agency. In this case, workers are employed by the **agency** rather than the business.
6) **Contractors** can be used if a business needs staff with **specialist** skills on a **short-term** basis. Contractors charge a set fee for doing a **specific job** for a limited period of time, and staff are employed by the **contractor** rather than the business. Businesses tend to use contractors for services such as gardening, cleaning, building work, IT support and security.

Attracting new employees is Difficult

1) Businesses invest a lot of time and money in recruiting staff, so it's important to find the **right** employees.
2) It's hard for small businesses to find good employees because they have **limited resources** to spend on recruitment — e.g. advertising jobs in national newspapers and magazines may be the best way to reach the best potential employees, but it may be too expensive for a small business.
3) Small businesses also find it difficult to attract good candidates because they cannot offer the same **salaries** and **benefits** as larger companies with more resources.
4) Businesses also have to consider **legal issues** when recruiting new staff. It's **illegal** for businesses to **discriminate** against potential employees because of their age, gender, race, religion, sexual orientation or because they have a disability. If a business refused to employ someone on these grounds, candidates could take them to an **employment tribunal**, and the business might have to pay **compensation**.

Businesses can get Advice on Employment Matters

1) Getting staffing **wrong** causes big **problems** for small businesses — if they don't have **enough** staff they won't be able to meet **demand**, and **too many** staff will create unnecessary **costs** for the business.
2) It's useful for small businesses to get expert **advice** on employment — small businesses can get **free** advice from Business Link or the Small Business Advisor at their bank.
3) Business owners who are members of the British Chambers of Commerce, the Federation of Small Businesses or the Institute of Directors can get expert employment advice — there's a membership **fee** for joining though.
4) Businesses can also **pay** specialist **consultants** to advise them, but this is an **expensive** option for small businesses.

Practice Questions

Q1 Give three examples of situations that might require businesses to consider their staffing needs.

Q2 State two advantages and two disadvantages of part-time staff.

Q3 Name three potential sources of advice on employment matters.

Exam Question

Q1 Discuss the practical and legal difficulties for small businesses of finding and attracting good employees. (10 marks)

You could always employ a lookalike to sit the exam for you...

Finding the right employees might be stressful for entrepreneurs, but it shouldn't be too much of a headache for you — as long as you make sure that you know the difference between part-time, full-time, permanent and temporary staff, and learn the advantages and disadvantages of each, you'll be able to sail through any employment questions that pop up in the exam.

Business Plans

Making a plan is one of the keys to business success. If you want your business to work, you've got to be prepared — any boy scout'll tell you that.

A **Business Plan** sets out the **Objectives** of the business

A business plan is a document that states **what** the owner(s) want to do and **how** they intend to do it. There are several reasons for writing a business plan before starting a business:

1) The main purpose of a business plan is usually to get financial backing for the business. A business plan shows the **financial risk** involved in setting up the business — this is important for potential **lenders** or **investors** who may want to help finance the start-up. Banks and venture capitalists will want to see a business plan before they'll think about investing.
2) Setting down all the plans for the business in a report helps the entrepreneur to assess the business' **strengths** and **weaknesses**, and allows them to see whether their idea is actually **realistic**. It also allows them to identify areas that they need to think about and plan more thoroughly.
3) The business plan is an important **management** tool — it gives details of business **objectives**, which the entrepreneur can compare with the **actual** performance of the business once it starts trading in order to track its progress. It also reminds the owner of the **ideas** they had before the business started.

Business plans are divided into **Sections**

Most business plans contain the following sections:

1) **Executive summary** — a general **overview** of the business which contains the **key points** from all the other sections. It's really important because if potential investors aren't impressed by the executive summary then they might not bother to read the rest of the business plan.
2) **Business summary** — describes what **type** of business the entrepreneur wants to set up, what **product(s)** or **service(s)** the business intends to provide, **why** it wants to provide them, and what makes it different from/better than the competition (its **competitive advantage**). It also includes the **legal structure** of the business, and the entrepreneur's vision for the **future** of the business.

> E.g. if the type of business is a **cookery school**, the service it offers would be **cookery lessons**, and it might also offer products like **recipe books** and **cooking equipment**.
>
> The entrepreneur might want to provide these things because there isn't a cookery school in the area and there is **demand** for cooking lessons due to the popularity of TV chefs like Jamie Oliver and Nigella Lawson.
>
> Its **competitive advantage** might be that it can **source** all its fresh **ingredients locally**.
>
> The entrepreneur might be a **sole trader**, or the business could be a **partnership** or **limited company**
>
> The entrepreneur's vision for the **future** might be:
> (a) to have a **revenue** of **£30 000** in the third year of trading,
> (b) to attract customers from all over the **UK** for cooking holidays as well as holding classes for **local** people,
> (c) to eventually open a **bed-and-breakfast** where students on the holiday courses can stay.

3) **Production plan** — sets out **how many** products the business intends to produce, and how it will go about **producing** them (e.g. how many workers will be required, what the costs of production will be, etc.).
4) **Marketing plan**, the entrepreneur defines the **market** for the business and explains who its main **competitors** are, who the **target customers** are and what the product's **unique selling point** is (see p.60). It includes details of any **market research** that the entrepreneur has done, and any **promotions** that they intend to run.
5) **Human resources plan** — outlines the relevant **qualifications** and **experience** of the entrepreneur and other people involved in setting up the business. It also sets out how many **employees** the business intends to take on, and how much it intends to pay them.
6) **Operations plan** — gives details of where the business will be **located**, whether the business will **own** or **rent** property and machinery, etc.
7) **Financial plan** — covers all of the financial **forecasts** for the business, e.g. how much **capital** they need to start the business, how they are going to **finance** the business (see p. 18-19), their **break-even** calculations (see p. 28-29), and a **cash flow forecast** (see p. 30-31). The financial information explains how the business will **survive** in the start-up period.

Business Plans

It's **Difficult** to produce an **Accurate** business plan

1) Business plans are **never** 100% accurate because it's **impossible** for a business to get accurate information about costs, revenue, etc. **before** it has started trading.
2) Just because the business plan says that the business should be making a profit of £2000 a month doesn't mean that that's what will actually happen — there's no way of knowing for definite, so there's always **risk** involved in setting up a business.
3) However, producing a thorough business plan **reduces** the risk of the business failing.

Entrepreneurs can get **Advice** on creating a business plan

If only Bryan had taken some professional advice before setting up his cruise business, it might have worked out a lot better.

1) The business plan is **really important**, so entrepreneurs need to get it right.
2) Entrepreneurs can get **free** help and advice on writing a business plan from a government organisation like Business Link, or from the manager or Small Business Advisor at their bank — they can give entrepreneurs sample business plans or CDs that guide you through the process of writing a business plan. Some **websites** also provide sample business plans free of charge, which entrepreneurs can adapt to their own business.
3) Entrepreneurs can also get expert guidance and advice from business consultants or accountants, but this is a more **expensive** option.

Established Businesses produce business plans too

1) Business plans are not just for new start-up businesses — it can also be very useful for **established** businesses to write a new business plan in certain situations.
2) If a business is planning to launch a **new product**, creating a new business plan can allow managers to see whether it is likely to be **profitable**. If not, they might decide not to go ahead with the launch.
3) A new business plan can also be useful if the business is planning to **expand** (e.g. if the owner of a successful restaurant decides to open another branch in a different town), especially since they might need to find external **finance** to do it.

Eilidh's clothes shop was a big success in Dundee, but she'd have saved a lot of money if she'd done a new business plan before she opened the branch in Chelmsford.

Practice Questions

Q1 What is usually the main reason for producing a business plan?
Q2 Why is the executive summary important?
Q3 Give five examples of information that's covered in a business plan.
Q4 Name three sources of expert advice on creating a business plan.

Exam Question

Q1 Explain why every new business should have a business plan. (10 marks)

"Slaps bunnies" and "painless buns" — anagrams of "business plan"...

Business plans are quite simple really — if you're going to open a business it makes sense to plan what you're going to do. Learn the key things a business plan includes, why entrepreneurs need them, and remember that writing an accurate plan for a new firm is always a bit of a problem. An anagram of problem is "lob perm" — which isn't a plan for a new hairdresser...

Costs, Revenues and Profits

Businesses need to know how much their revenue and costs are — otherwise they wouldn't have a clue how much profit they were making. Costs, revenues and profits are all related.

Revenue is the Money a business makes from Sales

1) Revenue is the **value of sales** — it's sometimes just called **sales**, and can also be called **turnover**. It's the amount of money generated by sales of a product, **before** any deductions are made.
2) You can work out the revenue by multiplying the **price** that the customer pays for each item by the **number of items** that the business sells:

   Revenue = selling price per item × quantity of items sold

   E.g. if a business sells **2000** teapots for **£8** each, the revenue is £8 × 2000 = **£16 000**.

Costs can be Fixed or Variable

1) **Fixed costs** don't change with output. **Rent** on a factory, business **rates**, **senior managers' salaries** and the cost of **new machinery** are fixed costs. When output increases, a business makes more use of the facilities it's already got. The **cost** of those facilities **doesn't change**.
2) **Variable costs** rise and fall as output changes. Hourly **wages**, **raw material costs** and the **packaging costs** for each product are all variable costs.
3) **Semi-variable costs** have fixed and variable parts. **Telephone bills** are a good example of **semi-variable** costs. Businesses have to pay a **fixed** amount for their phone line plus a **variable** amount depending on the phone calls they've made.

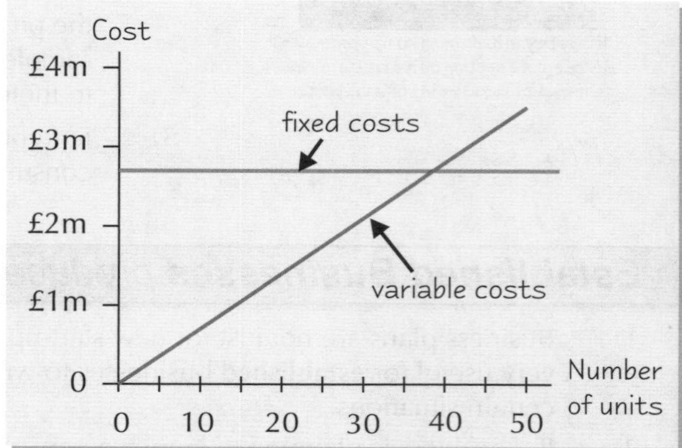

Profit = Revenue – Costs

1) When you deduct the costs from the revenue, what is left is the **profit**.
2) **Net profit** is what you get when you subtract **fixed and variable** costs from revenue — see above for explanations of fixed and variable costs.

   E.g. a teapot business has fixed costs of £4000 pcm and variable costs of £4 per teapot. It sells 2000 teapots in one month for £8 each, so its revenue is £16 000. Its variable costs that month are 2000 × £4 = £8000. The **net profit** would be: £16 000 – (£8000 + £4000) = **£4000**.
3) As well as being affected by costs, **revenue** and **profit** are affected by both **sales volume** and **price**. The amount of sales you lose by putting the price up varies — see **price elasticity of demand** on p. 68-69.
4) Businesses can do two things with profits. They can **give them to the shareholders** as dividend payments (sole traders and partnerships usually vary their salary according to how much profit they've made) or they can **re-invest** their profits in new activities.
5) **Shareholders** often want a **short-term** reward for supporting the business. In the long term, it's often better for the business to hold on to the profit and **re-invest** it in future projects.

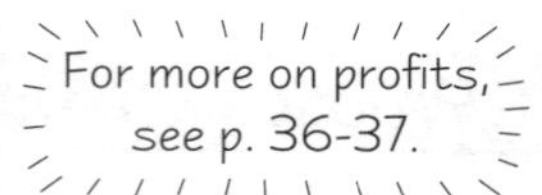
For more on profits, see p. 36-37.

Cost, revenue and profit were all related.

Costs, Revenues and Profits

Large-Scale Production *helps keep costs* ***Low***

The more a business produces, the **lower** the **cost per unit** produced. This is because the **fixed costs** are **shared out** between **more items**. The best way to show this is with an example:

1) MicroDave make microwave ovens. The **fixed costs** of running MicroDave are £200 000 per year. The **variable costs** of materials and labour are £15 per microwave.
2) If MicroDave make **5000 microwaves a year**, the total production costs are... £200 000 + (£15 × 5000) = **£275 000**. The **cost per microwave** is £275 000 ÷ 5000 = **£55**.
3) If MicroDave make **20 000 microwaves a year**, the total production costs are... £200 000 + (£15 × 20 000) = **£500 000**. The **cost per microwave** is £500 000 ÷ 20 000 = **£25**.

Businesses use information on ***Product Costs*** *to* ***Make Decisions***

1) Businesses use **cost** information to set the **selling price** of their products and services (see p.28). They set the price to make sure they'll make a **profit**. (Number of sales × price) – costs = profit.
2) If a business is a "**price taker**" in a very competitive market, it **doesn't have control** of the **selling price** of its products — it takes whatever price the market will pay. Businesses in this situation need accurate **costing** information to work out if it's **profitable** to make and sell a product at all. E.g. farmers have to sell milk, carrots, potatoes, etc to supermarkets for whatever price the supermarkets are willing to pay — if they try to put their prices up, supermarkets will just buy from other farmers instead.
3) Businesses set **budgets** (see p.32-33) which forecast how much costs are going to be over a year. Managers need to know what costs they're incurring **now**, so that they can know whether they're **meeting** the budget.

Costs also relate to ***Missed Opportunities***

Two cars... or 30 holidays... or 8000 McDonald's Value Meals...

1) **Opportunity cost** puts a value on a product or business decision in terms of what the business had to give up to have it.
2) Businesses must **choose** where to spend their limited finance. Managers **compare opportunity costs** when making their decisions. The opportunity cost of an advert half way through an episode of X Factor might be five screenings of the same advert in the middle of Emmerdale.

Practice Questions

Q1 What is the formula for calculating revenue?

Q2 Give three examples of a fixed cost.

Q3 How is net profit calculated?

Q4 What is an opportunity cost?

Exam Questions

Q1 Explain what is meant by the term 'variable costs', (2 marks)

Q2 Beth Brook Hats employs two hat-makers, each at £280/week. Beth, as Managing Director, pays herself £400/week. The other fixed costs are £300/week. The variable costs of raw materials are £14 per hat. Hats sell for £50.
(a) Draw a graph to show fixed, variable and total costs for outputs from 0 hats/week to 100 hats/week. (6 marks)
(b) Calculate the profit that Beth is making at her current output level of 60 hats per week, assuming weekly sales match output. (4 marks)

Answer on p.82.

If you don't learn this, it'll cost you...

Costs, revenue and profit are kind of at the heart of this section. They're pretty simple concepts, but they're used to work out everything else, so make sure you get them straight in your head. You need to be able to calculate revenue and profit, so learn the formulas well, and make sure you're clear on the difference between fixed and variable costs too. Oh joy...

Break-Even Analysis

Break-even analysis is a great way of working out how much you need to sell to make a profit.

Breaking Even means **Covering** your **Costs**

1) The **break-even point** is the level of sales a business needs to **cover their costs**. At this point, costs = revenue.
2) When sales are **below** the break-even point, costs are more than revenue — the business makes a **loss**. When sales are **above** the break-even point, revenue exceeds costs — the business makes a **profit**.
3) **New businesses** should always do a **break-even analysis** to **find** the break-even point. It tells them how much they will need to sell to break even. Banks and venture capitalists thinking of **loaning** money to the business will need to **see** a break-even analysis as part of the **business plan**. This helps them to decide whether to lend money to the firm — if they think that the business is unlikely to sell enough to break even, they won't lend their money.
4) **Established businesses** preparing to launch **new products** use break even analysis to work out how much **profit** they are likely to make, and also to predict the impact of the new activity on **cash flow** (see p.30-31).

Contribution is used to work out **the Break-Even Output**

1) **Contribution** is the difference between the **selling price** of a product and the **variable costs** it takes to produce it.

Contribution per unit = selling price per unit – variable costs per unit

Learn this formula for calculating break-even output

2) Contribution is used to **pay fixed costs**. The amount left over is profit.
3) **The break-even point** is where **contribution = fixed costs**. **Break-even output** is fixed costs over contribution per unit.

$$\text{Break-even output} = \frac{\text{fixed costs}}{\text{contribution per unit}}$$

Example: Harry sets up a business to print T-shirts. The **fixed costs** of premises and the T-shirt printers are **£3000**. The **variable costs** per T-shirt (the T-shirt, ink, wages) are **£5**. Each printed T-shirt sells for **£25**.

Contribution per unit = £25 – £5 = **£20**

Break-even output = £3000 ÷ £20 = **150** So, Harry has to sell **150** T-shirts to **break even**.

Draw a **Break-Even Chart** to show the **Break-Even Point**

1) Break-even charts show **costs** and **revenues** plotted against **output**. Businesses use break-even charts to see how costs and revenues **vary** with different levels of output.
2) **Output** goes on the **horizontal axis**. The scale needs to let you plot output from 0 to the maximum possible.
3) **Costs and revenue** both go on the vertical axis. Use a scale that lets you plot from 0 to the maximum revenue.
4) Plot **fixed** costs. (On the diagram on the right, fixed costs are the blue horizontal line.)
5) **Add** variable costs to fixed costs to get the **total cost**, and plot it on the graph. (The total costs are shown by the purple line, starting at the same point as the fixed costs line.)
6) Next, plot **revenue** (see p.26 for how to calculate it) on the graph . (It's the green line on the diagram.)
7) The **break-even point** is where the **revenue** line crosses the **total costs** line.

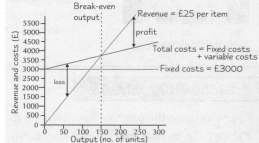

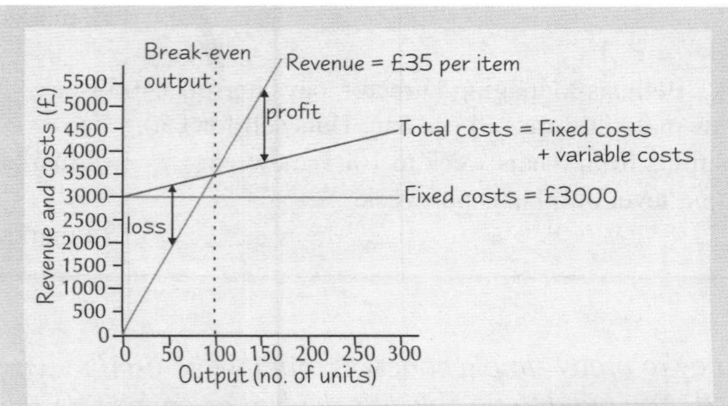

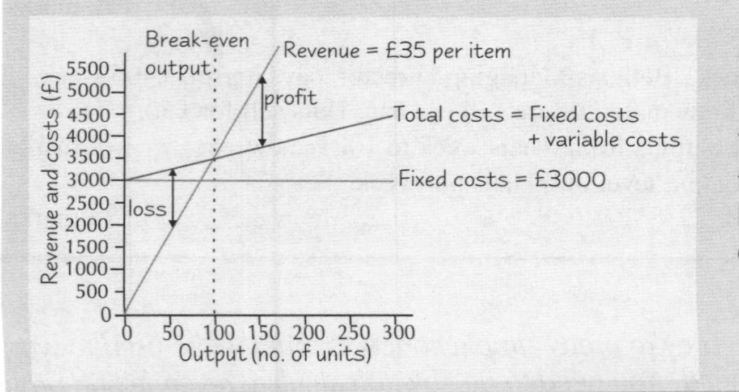

Changing either the **variable costs** or the **price** of the products will affect the break-even point.

This graph shows that if Harry **increased the price** of the T-shirts to £35 each, his break-even output would be **lowered** to 100 units. You could also work this out using the formula for break-even output:

Contribution per unit = £35 – £5 = **£30**
Break-even output = £3000 ÷ £30 = **100**

Break-Even Analysis

The Margin of Safety is the amount between Current Output and Break Even

Margin of safety = current output – break-even output

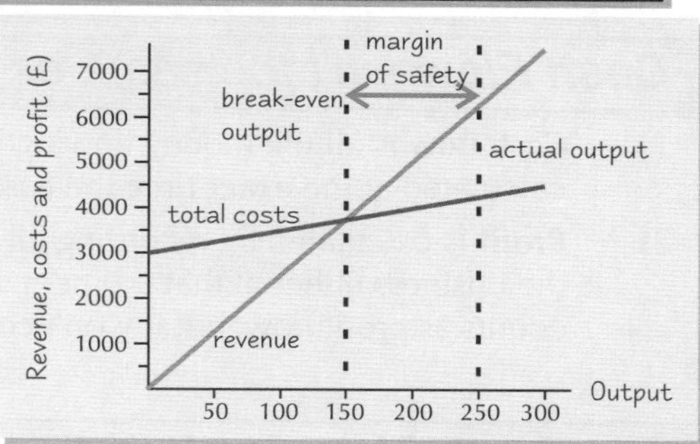

1) OK, back to Harry's T-shirt business again. The diagram on the right shows the margin of safety for Harry's business when his output is 250 T-shirts. If Harry sells **250** T-shirts, the margin of safety is 250 – 150 = **100** — he could sell up to 100 fewer T-shirts before he started losing money.
2) If his output changed to **300** T-shirts, the margin of safety would go up to 300 – 150 = **150**.
3) Knowing the break-even point and margin of safety allows businesses to make **important decisions** — if Harry's calculations show that his T-shirt business has a low margin of safety, he can take action to increase it by either **lowering his costs** or **increasing his revenue**.
4) This would **lower** his break-even point, so he'd have a **greater** margin of safety. A big margin of safety is useful for a business because it means less risk.

Break-Even Analysis has Advantages and Disadvantages

Advantages of break-even analysis	Disadvantages of break-even analysis
It's **easy** to do. If you can plot figures on a graph accurately, you can do break-even analysis.	Break-even analysis assumes that **variable costs** always rise steadily. This isn't always the case — a business can get **discounts** for buying in bulk so costs don't go up in **direct proportion** to output.
It's **quick** — managers can see the **break-even point** and **margin of safety** immediately so they can take **quick action** to cut costs or increase sales if they need to **increase** their margin of safety.	Break-even analysis is simple for a **single product** — but most businesses sell lots of different products, so looking at the business as a whole can get a lot more complicated.
Break-even charts let businesses **forecast** how variations in sales will affect **costs**, **revenue** and **profits** and, most importantly, how variations in **price** and **costs** will affect how **much** they **need** to **sell**.	If the **data** is wrong, then the **results** will be wrong.
Businesses can use break-even analysis to help **persuade** the bank to give them a **loan**.	Break-even analysis assumes the business sells **all the products**, without any wastage. But, for example, a restaurant business will end up throwing away food if fewer customers turn up than they're expecting.
Break-even analysis influences decisions on whether **new products** are launched or not — if the business would need to sell an unrealistic volume of products to break even, they would probably decide **not** to launch the product.	Break-even analysis only tells you how many units you **need** to sell to break even. It doesn't tell you how many you're **actually going to sell**.

Practice Questions

Q1 Write down the formula for contribution, and the formula for break-even output.

Q2 Write down two advantages and two disadvantages of break-even analysis.

Exam Questions

Answer on p.82.

Q1 Bob is deciding whether to set up in business selling fishing equipment. Evaluate the value of break-even analysis in helping Bob decide whether or not to go ahead with the business. (10 marks)

Q2 Muneer Khan has a small restaurant. The average price per customer per meal is £13. The variable costs of materials and labour per meal are £5. The fixed costs of the restaurant are £1000 per month. Calculate the break-even number of customers per month. (4 marks)

Ah, give us a break...

You might be asked to calculate the break-even point or draw it on a graph, so make sure you can do both. Make sure you can also give examples of how the break-even point is used by businesses to make decisions, and learn some advantages and disadvantages of break-even analysis. Then give yourself a pat on the back and move on to the next page. Yippee...

Cash Flow Forecasting

Cash flow is money flowing in and out of a business. It's vital to have enough money to meet your immediate debts — otherwise the people you owe money to start getting very cross.

Cash Flow isn't the same as Profit

1) **Cash flow** is all the money flowing **into** and **out of** the business over a period of time, calculated at the **exact time** the cash **enters** or **leaves** the bank account or till.
2) **Profit** is calculated by recording all transactions that will **lead** to cash going **in** or **out** of the business either at that moment or at some point in the **future**. Selling something on credit counts as profit now, but it won't count as cash flow until the customer actually pays for it.

The Cash Flow Cycle is the Gap between Money Going Out and Coming In

1) Businesses need to **pay money out** for fixed assets (e.g. buildings, machinery and vehicles) and operating costs to fulfil an order **before** they **get paid** for that order. The money needed to run a business from day to day is called **working capital**. New firms **need money** to spend on start-up costs **before** they've made any sales at all.
2) This **delay** between money going out and money coming in is the **cash flow cycle**.

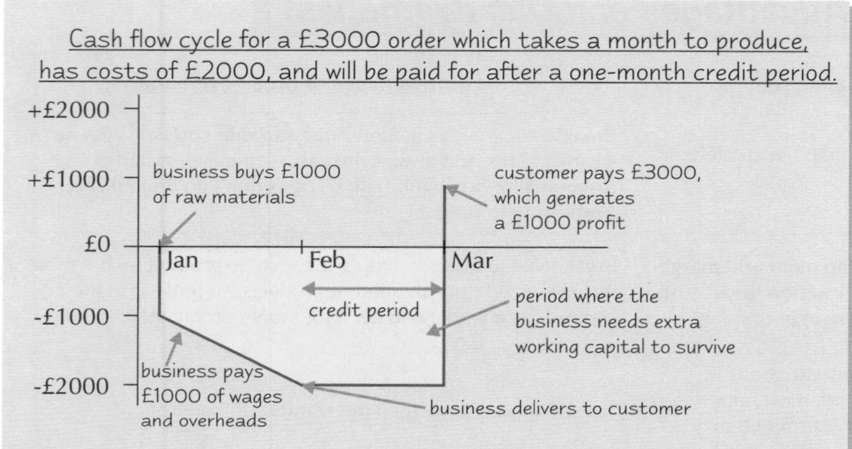

Bankruptcy is for sole traders/partnerships, and insolvency is for companies.

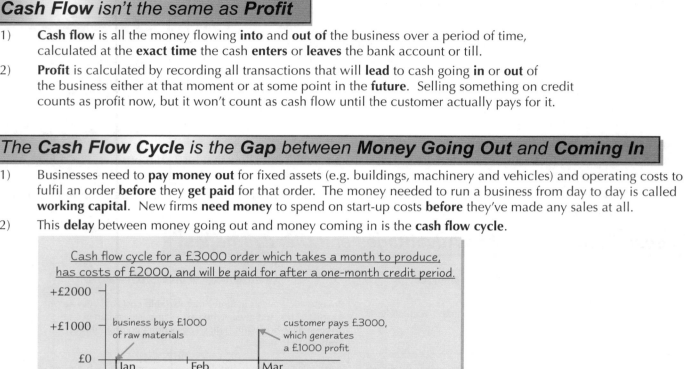

3) It's important to make sure there's always **enough money** available to pay **suppliers** and **wages**. Not paying suppliers and employees can be something of a **disaster**.
4) If a business **produces too much**, they'll have to **pay** suppliers and staff **so much** that they'll go **bankrupt** or **insolvent** before they have the chance to **get paid** by their customers. This is called **overtrading**.

Cash flow calculations are pretty much **the most important thing** to a business in the **short term**. Businesses need cash to survive. Looking at the **long term**, **profit** is important — making profit is the main objective for businesses.

Businesses have Various Canny Tricks to Improve cash flow

1) Businesses try to **reduce the time** between **paying** suppliers and **getting money** from customers. They try to get their **suppliers** to give them a **longer** credit period — and give their **customers** a **shorter** credit period. It's important to **balance** the need to manage cash flow with the need to keep suppliers and customers **happy** — you don't want customers to go elsewhere.
2) Businesses can try to hold less **stock**, so less cash is tied up in stock.
3) **Credit controllers** keep **debtors** in control. They set credit limits and remind debtors to pay up.
4) **Debt factoring** gives instant cash to businesses whose customers haven't paid their invoices. Banks and other financial institutions act as **debt factoring agents**. The agent pays the business about **80%** of the value of the invoice as an **instant cash advance**. The agent gets the customer to pay up, and then **keeps** about **5%** of the value of the invoice — debt factoring costs money and the agent needs to make a living.
5) **Sale and leaseback** is when businesses **sell** equipment to **raise capital**, and then **lease** (rent) the equipment back. That way, they get a big **lump sum** from the sale, and pay a **little** bit of money each month for the lease of the equipment. Of course, they don't get to own the equipment again unless they get enough cash to buy it back — and they have to pay the lease in the meantime.

Cash Flow Forecasting

Businesses make **Cash Flow Forecasts** to help them make decisions

1) **Cash flow forecasts** (also called cash budgets) show the amount of money that managers **expect** to **come into** the business and **flow out** of the business over a period of time in the **future**.
2) Managers can use cash flow forecasts to **make sure** they always have **enough** cash around to pay **suppliers** and **employees**. They can **predict** when they'll be **short of cash**, and arrange a **loan** or **overdraft** in time.
3) Businesses show cash flow forecasts to **banks** and venture capitalists when trying to get **loans** and other finance. Cash flow forecasts prove that the business has an idea of where it's going to be in the future.
4) **Established** firms base forecasts on **past experience**. **New** firms have no past data, so their forecast should consider the business' **capacity**, experiences of **similar firms** and customer behaviour trends shown by **market research**.

Here's how to **Construct** and **Interpret** a **Cash Flow Forecast**

Example: A new firm starts up with a loan of £18 000 and £5000 of capital. It expects to sell £5000 of goods in January, £35 000 in February, £35 000 in March and £40 000 in April. All customers will get a **one month credit period**. Wages and rent will cost £15 000 each month, and other costs are expected to be £5000 in January, £8000 in February, £2000 in March and £2000 in April.

	Item	**Jan**	**Feb**	**Mar**	**Apr**
Cash in	Sales revenue		£5000	£35000	£35000
	Other cash in	£18000			
	Total cash in	**£18000**	**£5000**	**£35000**	**£35000**
Cash out	Wages and rent	£15000	£15000	£15000	£15000
	Advertising/other costs	£5000	£8000	£2000	£2000
	Total costs	**£20000**	**£23000**	**£17000**	**£17000**
Net monthly cash flow	**Net cash flow**	**(£2000)**	**(£18000)**	**£18000**	**£18000**
	Opening balance	£5000	£3000	(£15000)	£3000
	Closing balance	**£3000**	**(£15000)**	**£3000**	**£21000**

This shows cash coming in from sales and from the initial start-up loan.

This shows cash going out to pay for the firm's costs.

Net cash flow = total cash in – total costs

The opening balance is money in the bank at the start, in this case £5000.

Closing balance = opening balance + net cash flow

The closing balance for last month is this month's opening balance.

April's sales revenue isn't included because it won't be paid until May, by the way.

Figures in brackets are negative.

According to this, the business will have £21 000 in the bank by the end of April. But it'll still owe £18 000 from the start-up loan ...

In the exam, they might ask you to fill in missing figures in a cash flow forecast, amend (change) it, draw a new one from scratch, or analyse it to say what financial position the business is likely to be in in the future.

Cash Flow Forecasting isn't always accurate

1) Cash flow forecasts can be based on **false assumptions** about what's going to happen.
2) Circumstances can **change suddenly** after the forecast's been made. **Costs** can **go up**. Machinery can **break down** and need mending. **Competitors** can put their prices up or down, which **affects sales**.
3) Good cash flow forecasting needs lots of **experience** and lots of **research** into the market.
4) A **false forecast** can have **disastrous** results. A business that runs out of cash can go **bankrupt** or **insolvent**.

Practice Questions

Q1 What's the difference between profit and cash flow?

Q2 Give two reasons why a cash flow forecast is useful to someone setting up their own small business.

Q3 If a company has total cash in of £8000 and total costs of £9500, what is its net cash flow?

Q4 If a company has an opening balance of £20 000 and its net cash flow is (£7000), what is the closing balance?

Q5 How can you work out a company's opening balance in any given month?

Answers on p.82.

Exam Questions

Q1 Examine the ways in which a business can improve its cash flow. (9 marks)

Q2 To what extent can a business successfully and accurately predict future cash flow? Explain your answer. (12 marks)

Dunno 'bout you, but cash flows through my wallet like water...

Cash flow is vitally important — without it, businesses can go bankrupt or insolvent. Make sure you know how to calculate the figures in the table on this page. It can be slightly tricky to start with, so go over it a few times until you really get it. Don't forget to learn the ways that businesses can improve their cash flow too. It's tricky but it'll be worth it in the exam.

Setting Budgets

Businesses make financial plans. They set targets for how much money they're going to make, and how much they're going to spend. Then they check to see how they've done. It sounds simple enough...

Questions about budgets in the exam will ask you to fill in missing figures or amend (change) a budget.

A **Budget** is a **Financial Plan** for the future

A **budget** forecasts **future earnings** and **future spending**, usually over a 12 month period. Businesses use different budgets to estimate different things. There are three types of budget:

1) **Income budgets** forecast the amount of money that will come into the company as revenue. In order to do this, the company needs to predict **how much** it will sell, and at what **price**. Managers estimate this using their **sales figures** from previous years, as well as **market research.**
2) **Expenditure budgets** predict what the business' **total costs** will be for the year, taking into account both fixed and variable costs. Since variable costs increase with output, managers need to predict what the output will be (based on how much they expect to sell).
3) The **profit budget** uses the totals from the income and expenditure budgets to calculate what the expected **profit** (or **loss**) will be for that year.

Budgets affect **All Areas** of the business

1) The expenditure budget forecasts **total** expenditure. This is broken down into **department** expenditure budgets — each department is allotted a certain amount of money to spend.
2) Department expenditure budgets are broken down into budgets for **specific activities** within the department.
3) **Budget holders** are people **responsible** for spending or generating the money for each budget. For example, the budget holder of the expenditure budget for marketing would be the head of the marketing department.
4) The **master budgets** help businesses understand their cash flow situation **as a whole**, and the department and activity budgets help local managers control and coordinate their work.
5) Budgets **set targets** that can be used to **control** or **motivate** staff, depending on management style.

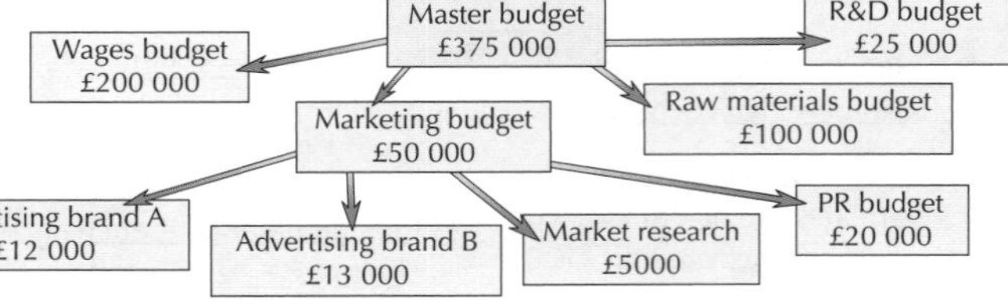

The **Budget Setting** process involves **Research** and **Negotiation**

1) To set the **income budget**, businesses **research** and **predict** how sales are going to go up and down through the year, so that they can make a good prediction of **sales revenue**.
2) To set the **expenditure budget** for **production**, businesses research how labour costs, raw materials costs, taxes and inflation are going to go up over the year. They can then figure out the **costs** of producing the volume of product that they think they're going to sell.
3) Annual budgets are usually agreed by **negotiation** — when budget holders have a say in setting their budgets, they're **motivated** to achieve them.
4) Budgets should **stretch** the abilities of the business, but they must be **achievable**. **Unrealistically** high income budgets or low expenditure budgets will **demotivate** staff. No one likes being asked to do the **impossible**.
5) Once they've agreed the budget, budget holders **keep checking** performance against the budget. This is called **variance analysis**. There's more about variance and variance analysis on p. 34-35.

Budgets have **Advantages** and **Disadvantages**

Benefits of budgeting

- Budgets help **control** income and expenditure. They show where the money goes.
- Budgeting forces managers to **review** their activities.
- Budgets let heads of department **delegate** authority to budget holders. Getting authority is **motivating**.
- Budgets allow departments to **coordinate** spending.
- Budgets help managers either **control** or **motivate** staff. Meeting a budget target is **satisfying**.

Drawbacks of budgeting

- Budgeting can cause **resentment** and rivalry if departments have to compete for money.
- Budgets can be **restrictive**. Fixed budgets stop firms responding to changing market conditions.
- Budgeting is **time-consuming**. Managers can get too preoccupied with setting and reviewing budgets, and forget to focus on the real issues of **winning business** and **understanding** the **customer**.

Setting Budgets

Budgets can be *Updated Every Year* or developed from *Scratch*

1) **Start-up businesses** have to develop their budgets **from scratch** (known as **zero budgeting**). This is difficult to do because they don't have much information to base their decisions on — they can't take into account the previous year's sales or expenditure. This means that their budgets are likely to be **inaccurate**.
2) After the first year, a business must decide whether to follow the **historical budgeting** method, or to continue using the **zero budgeting** method.

Historical budgets are updated each year

1) This year's budget is based on a percentage increase or decrease from last year's budget. For example, a business expecting 10% revenue growth might add 10% to the advertising, wages and raw materials purchasing budgets.
2) Historical budgeting is **quick** and **simple**, but it assumes that business conditions stay **unchanged** each year. This isn't always the case — for instance, a product at the introduction stage of its **life cycle** (see p.62) needs more money spent on advertising than one in the growth or maturity stages.

Zero budgeting means starting from scratch each year

1) Budget holders **start** with a budget of **£0**, and have to **get approval** to spend money on activities.
2) They have to **plan** all the year's activities, ask for money to spend on them, and be prepared to **justify** their requests to the finance director. Budget holders need good **negotiating** skills for this.
3) Zero budgeting takes much **longer** to complete than historical budgets.
4) If zero budgeting is done properly it's **more accurate** than historical budgeting.

Budgets affect how *Flexible* a business can be

1) **Fixed budgets** provide **discipline** and **certainty**. This is especially important fora business with **liquidity** problems — fixed budgets help control **cash flow**.
2) **Fixed budgeting** means budget holders have to stick to their budget plans throughout the year — even if market conditions change. This can **prevent** a firm reacting to **new opportunities** or **threats** that they didn't know about when they set the budget.
3) **Flexible budgeting** allows budgets to be altered in response to significant changes in the market or economy.
4) **Zero budgeting** gives a business more **flexibility** than **historical budgeting**.

Mary Lou had no problems with flexibility

Practice Questions

Q1 Name the three main types of budget that a business will set, stating what each tells you.

Q2 If a business has an income budget of £125 000 and a profit budget of £30 000, what is its expenditure budget?

Answer on p. 82.

Q3 State three benefits and three drawbacks of using budgets.

Q4 What is historical budgeting?

Q5 Explain the difference between fixed and flexible budgets.

Exam Questions

Q1 To what extent might fixed budgets help a manufacturer in the fast-changing computer software sector? (15 marks)

Q2 (a) Discuss the benefits that setting a budget will have for a new business. (6 marks)
(b) Discuss the problems that a new business might have in setting budgets for the first time. (9 marks)

I set myself a word budget today and I'm just about to run out...

Budgets are multi-purpose — they help businesses forecast their future spending, and they can help to motivate people, too. Luckily, you won't get marked on how good you are at budgeting in the exam — the examiners are only interested in how well you understand income, expenditure and profit budgets, why businesses use them, and how they set them.

Variances

Variance is the difference between actual and budgeted spend. Understanding variances helps managers control business performance, and it'll help you sail through your exams too, with a bit of luck.

Variance is the Difference between Actual figures and Budget figures

1) A variance means the business is performing either **worse** or **better** than expected.
2) A **favourable variance** leads to **increased profit**. If revenue's more than the budget says it's going to be, that's a favourable variance. If costs are below the cost predictions in the budget, that's a favourable variance.
3) An **adverse variance** is a difference that **reduces profits**. **Selling fewer items** than the income budget predicts or **spending more** on an advert than the expenditure budget for marketing allows is an adverse variance.
4) If £10 000 is spent on raw materials in a month when the budget was only £6000, the variance is £6000 – £10000 = –£4000, so there is a £4000 **adverse variance.**
5) Variances **add up**. For example, if actual sales exceed budgeted sales by £3000 and expenditure on raw materials is £2000 below budget, the variance is £3000 + £2000 = £5000, so there's a combined **favourable variance of** £5000. This is called **cumulative variance**.
6) Variances can be calculated for each budget each month, for each budget as a running total, and for groups of budgets as a monthly or running total variance:

(A) means an adverse variance.
(F) means a favourable variance.

	Jan Budget	Jan Actual	Jan Variance	Feb Budget	Feb Actual	Feb Variance	Cumulative Variance
Revenue	£100k	£90k	£10k (A)	£110k	£110k	£0	£10k (A)
Wages	£40k	£30k	£10k (F)	£40k	£41k	£1k (A)	£9k (F)
Rent	£10k	£10k	£0	£10k	£11k	£1k (A)	£1k (A)
Other costs	£5k	£6k	£1k (A)	£5k	£6k	£1k (A)	£2k (A)
Total costs	£55k	£46k	£9k (F)	£55k	£58k	£3k (A)	£6k (F)

Variances can be Bad — even when they say you're doing Better than Expected

1) When variances occur, it means that what has happened is **not** what the business was expecting. Businesses need to **know** about variances so that they can find out **why** they have occurred.
2) It's extremely important to spot **adverse** variances as **soon** as possible. It's important to find out which budget holder is responsible — and to take action to fix the problem.
3) It's **also** important to **investigate favourable variances**. Favourable variances may mean that the budget targets weren't **stretching** enough — so the business needs to set more **difficult targets**. The business also needs to understand **why** the performance is better than expected — if one department is **doing something right**, the business can **spread** this throughout the organisation.

Variances are caused by several factors — Internal and External

External Factors Cause Variance

1) **Competitor behaviour** and changing **fashions** may increase or reduce **demand** for products.
2) Changes in the **economy** can change how much workers' wages cost the business.
3) The cost of **raw materials** can go up — e.g. if a harvest fails.

Internal Factors Cause Variance

1) Improving **efficiency** (e.g. by introducing automated production equipment) causes **favourable** variances.
2) A business might **overestimate** the amount of money it can save by streamlining its production methods.
3) A business might **underestimate** the **cost** of making a change to its organisation.
4) Changing the selling price changes sales revenue — this creates variance if it happens after the budget's been set.
5) Internal causes of variance are a **serious concern**. They suggest that internal **communication** needs improvement.

Variances

Variance Analysis *means* ***Identifying*** *and* ***Explaining*** *variances*

1) Variance analysis means **spotting** variances and figuring out **why** they've happened, so that action can be taken to fix them.
2) **Small** variances aren't a big problem. They can actually help to **motivate** employees. Staff try to **catch up** and sort out small **adverse** variances themselves. Small **favourable** variances can motivate staff to **keep on** doing whatever they were doing to create a favourable variance.
3) **Large** variances can **demotivate**. Staff don't work hard if there are large favourable variances — they **don't see the need**. Staff can get demotivated by a large **adverse** variance — they may feel that the task is **impossible**, or that they've **already failed**.

Businesses *have to* ***Do Something*** *about variances*

When variances occur, businesses can either change what the **business** is doing to make it fit the budget, or change the **budget** to make it fit what the **business** is doing. There are three factors that they need to take into account to make this decision:

1) Businesses need to **beware** of chopping and changing the budget **too much**.
2) Changing the budget **removes certainty** — which removes one of the big benefits of budgets.
3) Altering budgets can also make them **less motivating** — when staff start to expect that management will change targets instead of doing something to change performance, they don't see the point in trying any more.

Businesses Try to Fix Adverse Variances

1) They can change the **marketing mix**. **Cutting prices** will increase sales — but only if the demand is price elastic (see p.68). **Updating** the product might make it more attractive to customers. Businesses can also look for a **new market** for the product, or change the **promotional strategy** — e.g. by advertising the product more or doing point of sales promotion.
2) **Streamlining production** makes the business more **efficient**, so this reduces costs.
3) They can try to motivate **employees** to **work harder**.
4) Businesses can try to cut costs by asking their **suppliers** for a **better deal**.

Businesses Try to Fix Favourable Variances

1) If the favourable variance is caused by a **pessimistic** budget, they set more **ambitious targets** next time.
2) If the variance is because of **increased productivity** in one part of the business, they try to get everyone else doing whatever was **responsible** for the improvement, and set higher targets in the next budget.

Practice Questions

Q1 Define variance.

Q2 If a business sets an expenditure budget of £15 000 for marketing, and the actual expenditure for marketing is £18 000, how much is the variance and what type of variance is it?

Q3 Why are variances a concern for businesses?

Q4 State two external factors and two internal factors that cause variance.

Q5 How do businesses deal with variances?

Answers on p.82.

Exam Question

Q1 (a) Using the figures in the table on p.34, calculate monthly and cumulative variances for March. Assume all budgets remain the same as February, and that actual sales are £120k, wages are £39k, rent is £11k and other costs are £5k. (10 marks)

(b) Explain what your answer to (a) suggests about the budget planning process for this company. (6 marks)

Variance is one of those words that looks odd if you stare at it enough...

Variance variance variance variance variance... ahem... anyway. As well as knowing what businesses do when they set a budget, you need to know what they do when the real-life results don't quite match up to what the budget says. They don't panic and run about shouting "beeble beeble" in the car park. They just sort it out so it doesn't happen next time.

Measuring and Increasing Profit

Businesses need to measure their profit to find out how successful (or unsuccessful) they are.

Profit** is **Not** the same as **Revenue

1) **Revenue** is the amount of money that a business receives from sales of its products (see p. 26). But they **don't keep** all of it — the business also has **costs**.
2) When the **costs** are **deducted** from its **revenue**, what is left is the **profit**.
3) If the business' **costs** are **greater** than its **revenue**, it will make a **loss** instead of a profit.

*Businesses want to **Increase** their profits*

1) Most businesses exist to make a **profit** — if a business makes large profits then it is **successful**. Even successful businesses want to **increase profits** and become **more successful**.
2) Businesses can **improve** their **profits** by increasing their **prices** (if the demand for their products is price inelastic — see p. 68) or **reducing** their prices to increase **demand** (if demand is price elastic). They could also try to reduce their **costs**, or use **marketing** to increase demand so that they sell more and make bigger profits.
3) Businesses **measure** their profits on a regular basis. They **compare** their profits from the current period (usually a year) to the profits from previous periods to measure their **progress**.
4) If profits go **down**, this is **bad news**, even if the business is still making large profits. For example, if a business makes a profit of £100 million in a year, this might sound like good news, but if the previous year's profits were £125 million then it's a **bad sign**.
5) This is why businesses work out the **percentage increase** or **decrease** in their profits from year to year — it makes it easy to see how well they're performing in comparison with other years.
6) If profits are decreasing, the business needs to investigate **why** this is happening and **take action** to resolve the problem.

In the exam, set your workings out like the formula.

The formula for measuring the **percentage change** in profit is:

$$\textbf{Percentage Change in Profit} = \frac{\textbf{Current Year's Profit} - \textbf{Previous Year's Profit}}{\textbf{Previous Year's Profit}} \times \textbf{100}$$

If a business makes a profit of **£20 000** in one year and **£30 000** the next year, the percentage change in profit is (£30 000 – £20 000) ÷ £20 000 × 100 = 50% — a **50% rise** in profits.

If a business makes a profit of **£10 000** in a year after having made a profit of **£15 000** in the previous year, the percentage change in profit is (£10 000 – £15 000) ÷ £15 000 × 100 = –33% — a **fall** in profits of **33%**.

*There are **Two Types** of profit — **Gross Profit** and **Net Profit***

1) **Gross profit** is the amount left over when the **cost of making the products** is taken away. You can calculate **gross profit** by subtracting **variable costs** from the **revenue**.

Gross Profit = Revenue – Variable Costs

2) **Net profit** takes into consideration not only the cost of actually producing each product, but also the **fixed costs** involved in running the business (for more on fixed and variable costs, see p. 26). You get the **net profit** by subtracting both **fixed costs** and **variable costs** from the **revenue**.

Net Profit = Revenue – (Fixed Costs + Variable Costs)

Polly hoped that her net profit would increase enough for her to be able to make a whole dress.

Example

Hannah's Hammers is a small company selling hammers with a floral design. The variable cost of producing each hammer is **£2**, and they are sold for **£5** each. Hannah also has fixed costs of **£15 000** a year.

If Hannah sells **10 000** hammers in a year, her **revenue** is 10 000 × £5 = **£50 000**.

Hannah's **gross profit** is £50 000 – (2 x 10 000) = **£30 000**.

Her **net profit** is £50 000 – (£15 000 + £20 000) = **£15 000**.

Measuring and Increasing Profit

Net Profit Margins show how Profitable a business or product is

1) Net profit margins measure the relationship between the **net profits made** and the **volume of sales**. They tell you what **percentage** of the selling price of a product is actually **net profit**.
2) Businesses can calculate their profit margins for **individual products**, or for the company **as a whole**.
3) The net profit margin is expressed as a percentage — the formula is:

$$\text{Net Profit Margin (\%)} = \frac{\text{Net Profit}}{\text{Revenue}} \times 100$$

4) It's best to have a **high** net profit margin, although it does depend on the type of business.
5) The net profit margin can be improved by **raising prices** or **lowering the cost of making the products** or (most importantly) the **fixed costs**. Raising prices might cause **demand** to **fall** though (see price elasticity of demand, p. 68), so **increasing** the net profit **margin** too much could end up having a **negative** effect on **profits**. Similarly, **reducing** the **cost** of making the products could be **risky** if it affects the level of **quality**.
6) A business can improve its overall net profit margin by **stopping** selling products with a **low net profit margin**.
7) If a business has a revenue of £60 000 and a net profit of £18 000, its net profit margin is: (£18 000 ÷ £60 000) × 100 = **30%**.
8) If the business manages to reduce its fixed costs the following year by £3000, and turnover stays the same, the new net profit will be £21 000, so the net profit margin will rise to (£21 000 ÷ £60 000) × 100 = **35%**

Return on Capital Employed (ROCE) is an Important Profitability Ratio

1) The **return on capital employed** (ROCE) is considered to be the **best** way of analysing **profitability**.
2) The **ROCE** tells you how much money is **made** by the business, compared to how much money's been **put into** the business. It tells you how good the business is at generating profits from money invested.
3) In order to calculate the ROCE, you need to know what the **net profit** is, **excluding** any profit made from **one-off activities** (e.g. if a business raises £700 by putting on a raffle, this **shouldn't** be included in the ROCE calculation).
4) You also need to know the figure for **capital employed**. Capital employed means all the money that has been **invested** in the business, so it refers to the money that has come into the business from **loans** and **shares**.
5) ROCE is expressed as a percentage — the formula for calculating it is:

$$\text{Return on Capital Employed (\%)} = \frac{\text{Net Profit}}{\text{Capital Employed}} \times 100$$

6) A good **ROCE** is about **20%**, but 10-15% is OK. It's important to compare the ROCE with the Bank of England interest rate at the time — if the return is less than the interest rate then the investors would have been better off putting their money in the bank.
7) A business can improve its ROCE by using part of its net profit to **pay off some debts** — this will reduce capital employed. Another way to improve the ROCE is by making the business more **efficient** to **increase net profit**.

Practice Questions

Answer on p. 82.

Q1 If a business makes a profit of £50 000 in 2006 and £52 000 in 2007, what is the percentage change in profit?

Q2 What is the formula for calculating Return on Capital Employed?

Q3 Give two ways in which Return on Capital Employed can be improved.

Exam Questions

Q1 Calculate the ROCE for a business with a net profit of £100 000 and capital employed of £40 000. (2 marks)

Answers on p. 82.

Q2 A business has a revenue of £2 million. Its gross profit is £750 000, and its fixed costs are £250 000.
(a) Calculate the net profit margin. (4 marks)
(b) Recommend what the business could do to improve the net profit margin. Explain why you're making this recommendation. (6 marks)

I'm just about 100% fed up with all these percentage calculations...

OK, I admit this hasn't been the world's most interesting page but this is all really important stuff, so make sure you get your head around it before moving on. You need to be able to calculate net profit margin and ROCE, so learn the formulas —you also need to understand what they actually mean for a business, and how businesses can improve their profitability.

Business Structures

The structure of a business depends on its size, its geographical distribution, the kind of product or service it offers, and the history and culture of the organisation.

Structure** and **Hierarchy** are shown by an **Organisational Chart

1) The traditional business structure is a series of levels, where each level has responsibility for, and authority over, the levels below. This is called a **hierarchy**.
2) An **organisational chart** sets out who has **authority** to make decisions, and who has **responsibility** for making them.
3) It shows who individual employees are **accountable** to — who is directly **above** them in the hierarchy.
4) It shows who employees are **responsible** for — who is directly **below** them in the hierarchy.
5) The chart also shows how the organisation is divided up. This chart is divided by **function**, e.g. into a production department, a marketing department etc., or it can be divided by **product** or **geographical area**.

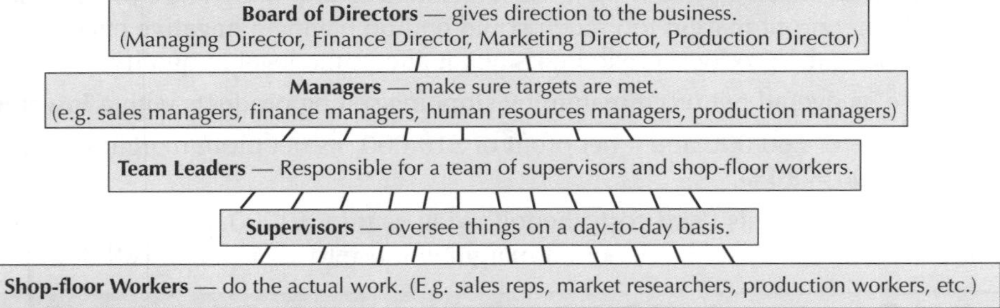

Board of Directors — gives direction to the business.
(Managing Director, Finance Director, Marketing Director, Production Director)
Managers — make sure targets are met.
(e.g. sales managers, finance managers, human resources managers, production managers)
Team Leaders — Responsible for a team of supervisors and shop-floor workers.
Supervisors — oversee things on a day-to-day basis.
Shop-floor Workers — do the actual work. (E.g. sales reps, market researchers, production workers, etc.)

Structures** can be **"Tall"** or **"Flat"

1) Organisations with **lots of levels** in their hierarchy are called "**tall**". They have a large number of people between the top and the bottom. Tall structures have a long **chain of command**. The chain of command is the path of **communication** and **authority** up and down the hierarchy.
2) If the structure is **too tall**, it affects **communication**. Messages take a **long time** to get from one end of the chain of command to the other, and they can get **garbled** on the way. **Decisions** take a long time to make, and there's a lot of **paperwork** to deal with.
3) "**Flat**" organisations only have a few levels in the hierarchy. People may be given more responsibility and freedom.
4) If the structure is **too flat**, then managers can get **overwhelmed** by too many people reporting to them.

A tall structure

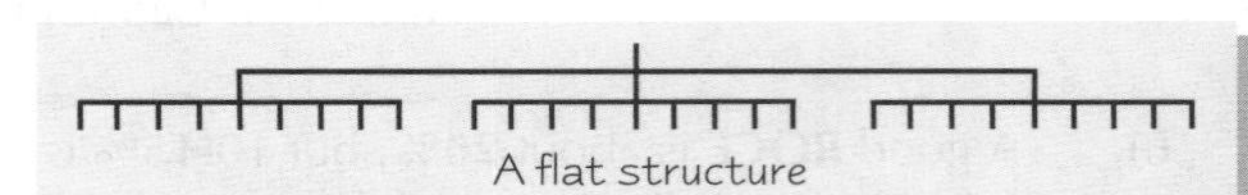

A flat structure

Structures** can have broad or narrow **Spans of Control

1) The **span of control** is the **number of people** who report directly to a manager. Managers in **flat** organisational structures have **wide** spans of control. This means they have a lot of workers answering to them.
2) Managers in tall structures have **narrower** spans of control — they aren't responsible for as many people. This allows them to **monitor** the people who report to them **more closely**.
3) If the span of control is **too broad**, managers can find it hard to manage **effectively**.
4) If the span of control is **too narrow**, workers can become **demotivated** — they may feel that they're being **micromanaged** (over-managed) by interfering bosses.
5) **Traditionally**, business experts thought it would be hard for a manager to keep a close eye on workers if the span of control was bigger than about 6 people. But if the workers are all doing the **same routine task**, they don't need as much close supervision — so a span of control of 10-12 people (or more) is fine.

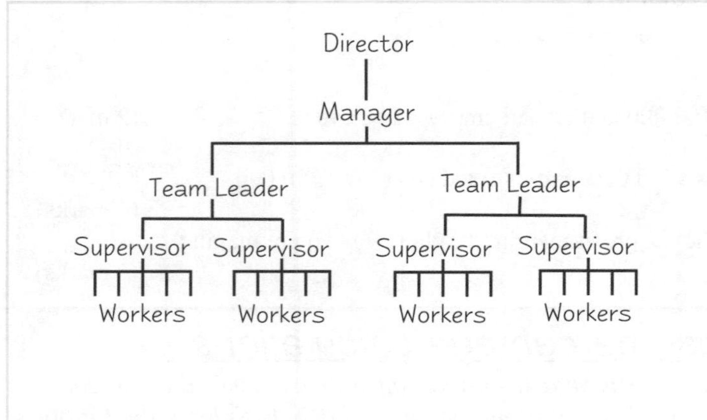

Business Structures

Centralised Structures keep Authority for decisions at the Top

In an organisation where decision-making is **centralised**, all decisions are made by **one person**, or one committee of **senior managers** right at the **top** of the business.

Advantages of Centralisation	Disadvantages of Centralisation
Business leaders tend to have plenty of **experience**.	Not many people are **expert** enough in **all aspects** of the business.
Managers get an **overview** of the whole business.	Excluding employees from decision-making can be **demotivating**.
Senior managers understand **central** budgeting restrictions and can make decisions to save the **whole business** money.	Decisions can take a **long time**. The organisation reacts **slowly** to change, and can end up a couple of steps behind its competitors.

Decentralised Structures share out the Authority to make decisions

1) Decentralisation **shares out authority** to more **junior** employees.
2) Giving responsibility for decision-making to people below you is called **delegation**.
3) **National** and **multinational** organisations **decentralise** decision-making and delegate power to **regional** managers.

Advantages of Decentralisation	Disadvantages of Decentralisation
Involvement in decision-making **motivates** employees.	Subordinates may not have enough **experience** to make decisions.
Employees can use **expert knowledge** of their sector.	**Inconsistencies** may develop between sectors in a business.
Decisions can be made more **quickly** without having to ask senior managers.	Junior employees may not be able to see the **overall situation** and **needs** of an organisation.

Delayering removes layers of hierarchy

Delayering is a key way in which a manager can **alter** the **structure** of a business. Changing the structure of the business can improve **performance** and increase **competitiveness**.

1) Delayering is when a business **removes** a layer of the hierarchy from its organisational structure — usually a layer of managers from somewhere in the **middle** of the hierarchy.
2) Delayering helps to **lower costs**. Cutting management jobs can save a lot of money in salaries.
3) After delayering, you get a **flatter** structure with **broader** spans of control. It's worth being careful not to **overdo** it. If a company is delayered to too great an extent, managers can end up **stressed** and overworked with **huge, vast-reaching** spans of control.
4) Delayering can give junior employees **enhanced roles** with more responsibility.
5) Some businesses use delayering as an **excuse** to cut jobs.

Zoë didn't hold back her feelings towards the company's plans to delayer.

Practice Questions

Q1 Why might a flat structure be popular with junior employees in a business?

Q2 What is meant by "span of control"?

Q3 Give two advantages of a centralised decision-making structure.

Q4 Give two disadvantages of a decentralised decision-making structure.

Exam Questions

Q1 A firm of management consultants have advised Douglas McLeod to delayer and flatten the structure of his business.
(a) What is meant by flattening the structure of the business? (2 marks)
(b) Discuss the factors that Douglas should think about before starting to delayer. (10 marks)

Q2 To what extent is a wide span of control desirable for a manager in a business? (10 marks)

Delayering — isn't that taking off your cardigan when it's warm...

Delayering can be a great way of simplifying things and saving money — if your middle managers are useless David Brent types, getting rid of them is the kindest thing to do, really. Both tall and flat structures have pros and cons — learn them in case you get asked to evaluate a particular kind of business structure, or in case you bump into an architect at a party...

Measuring Workforce Effectiveness

A business needs to measure the effectiveness of every resource used, and that includes its employees. People don't always like the idea of having their performance measured, but it's good for the business.

Human Resource Management (HRM) keeps the Workforce Flexible

Businesses need to be **flexible** enough to react in a competitive and changing environment. Change comes from consumer **demand**, new **technology** and new **laws**. **Competitors** are constantly joining and leaving the market. A flexible workforce tends to be an effective one, so HRM makes sure that the workforce is **adaptable** to these changes.

1) The main function of Human Resources is to ensure that the business has the **right number of employees** and that they're of the **right quality** in terms of **qualifications and skills**.
2) HRM plans how to **recruit** staff — where to advertise, how to interview, etc.
3) **Human resources strategies** can be **short-term** (e.g. recruiting part-time staff for Christmas sales in retailing) or **long-term** (e.g. anticipating growth or a change in production techniques).
4) Human resources departments also decide how to treat staff while they're working for the business — how to **use their skills**, how to **keep** them working for the company, how to **train** and **reward** them, and eventually how to **terminate** their employment.
5) The HRM department might also set up a **performance management system** to check that human resources are always being used to maximum efficiency. This system calculates performance based on **labour productivity**, **absenteeism**, and **labour turnover**.

Labour Productivity measures How Much each Employee Produces

It's important for companies to know how productive their workforce is, because changes in labour productivity can have a massive impact on the business. This is especially true in **labour-intensive** firms, where labour costs are a high proportion of total costs.

$$\text{Labour Productivity} = \frac{\text{Output per period}}{\text{Number of employees}}$$

Dave's productivity currently stood at 900 rabbits per hour.

The **higher** the labour productivity, the **better** the workforce is performing.
As labour productivity **increases**, labour costs per unit **fall**.

Example: A factory has 30 workers per shift working 3 shifts per day to produce 9000 DVD players per week.
Productivity = 9000 ÷ 90 workers = **100** DVD players per worker per week.

Ways to increase labour productivity

1) Labour productivity can be improved by **improving worker motivation** (see p.44-45).
2) **Training** can make workers more productive.

Businesses need to consider the Consequences of Increasing Productivity

1) Some companies **reward** increased productivity. Paying workers using a **piece rate** system (see p.45) encourages staff to produce more. Managers should take care that **quality** doesn't suffer in the process.
2) Increasing labour productivity means **redundancies** and **job losses** unless sales increase. Businesses need to **plan** for the consequences of improved productivity to avoid upsetting staff.
3) Businesses must **balance** productivity against things like product **quality** and long-term worker **motivation**.

Measuring Workforce Effectiveness

Absenteeism measures the Proportion of Time employees are Off Work

$$\text{Absenteeism (\%)} = \frac{\text{Number of staff days lost}}{\text{Number of working days}} \times 100$$

To calculate the number of working days, multiply the number of days that a company operates by its total number of employees and then subtract the number of days holiday it gives its staff.

1) Absenteeism is measured as a percentage. Obviously, **low** is best.
2) You have to analyse figures in the **context** of each industry. For example, **police** officers might have **higher** than average figures because of the dangers and stresses of the job, while **sales** people paid on commission have **lower** rates because they lose pay when off work.
3) **Causes** of absenteeism include poor **working conditions**, poor **relationships** with managers and other staff, **stress** or **disillusionment** with the job, and poor **motivation**.
4) Absenteeism **increases costs**. It results in **lost opportunities**, e.g. sales enquiries left unanswered.
5) There are several ways a firm might **reduce absenteeism**, depending on what's causing it. These might include **job enrichment** (see p.45), improving **working relationships**, improving **working conditions**, or **flexi-time**.

Labour Turnover measures the Proportion of Staff who Leave each year

$$\text{Labour Turnover} = \frac{\text{Number of staff leaving}}{\text{Average number of staff employed}}$$

Work out the part-timers as if they're fractions of a full-time employee. Two people who each work half a week = one person working a whole week.

1) The **higher** the figure, the larger the proportion of workers leaving the firm each year.
2) **External causes** of high labour turnover include changes in regional **unemployment** levels, and the growth of other local firms using staff with **similar skills**.
3) **Internal causes** of high labour turnover include poor motivation of staff, low wages, and a lack of opportunities for promotion. Staff will **join other firms** to increase their pay and job responsibilities.
4) A **poor recruitment** process which selects incompetent candidates will also increase labour turnover.
5) Increased **delegation**, **job enrichment**, higher **wages** and better **training** can reduce employee turnover.
6) Businesses need **some** labour turnover to bring new ideas in. Labour turnover of 0% means no one **ever** leaves.

Benefits of high staff turnover	Disadvantages of high staff turnover
Constant stream of **new ideas** through new staff.	Lack of **loyal** and **experienced** staff who know the business.
Firm can recruit staff who've **already been trained** by competitors — saves money.	Firm **loses** staff it has **trained**, often to direct competitors.
If sales fall, firm can reduce workforce through **natural wastage** rather than costly redundancy.	**Training costs money** and **productivity drops** while new staff get trained.
Enthusiasm of new staff influences other workers.	**Recruitment** costs are high.

Practice Questions

Q1 A company has low labour productivity. Make three suggestions that might help to increase its output.

Q2 A firm operates for 245 days per year. It has 56 full-time staff who get 25 days holiday each. In 2006, holiday aside, staff were absent for a total of 274 staff days. Calculate the firm's absenteeism.

Q3 State two benefits and two drawbacks of a high labour turnover percentage.

Q4 In 2007, 18 people leave a firm which employs an average of 600 staff. Calculate the firm's labour turnover.

Answers on p. 82.

Exam Questions

Q1 Explain why a major employer such as the NHS should be concerned about differing absenteeism percentages in different hospitals, and recommend what action they could take. (10 marks)

Q2 Evaluate potential problems if a firm were to change its production method to improve labour productivity. (6 marks)

I have a flexible workforce — they're always bending the rules...

They're all quite easy really, these equations. Problem is, the numbers alone don't really tell you anything. It's good to have high productivity if you're making something simple, like baked beans, but not necessarily if the product is complicated — a jet plane, for example. The same can't be said for absenteeism though — that's always a bad thing...

Workforce Planning

A good recruitment process means a company has the right number of people with the right skills to do the job.

The **Recruitment Process** can take a long time

There are seven key steps in a successful recruitment process:

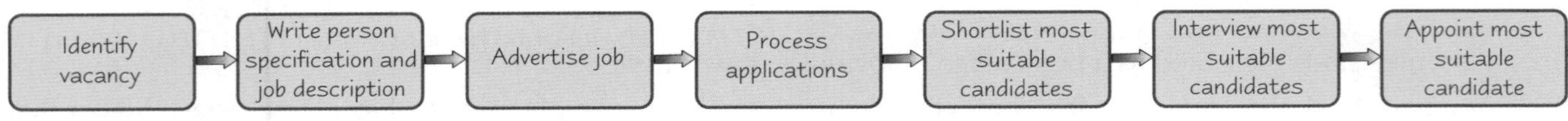

Identifying a vacancy

1) Businesses do an **internal audit** (check). They look at all the **jobs** in the organisation — what each job entails and what sort of **qualities** and **skills** are needed. They then see whether current staff **match** these requirements.
2) HRM departments ask **other experienced managers** for their **opinions** and **advice**.
3) **Past statistics** (backdata) are used to see if employee numbers have **risen**, **fallen** or **stayed the same**.
4) An increase or decrease in **demand** for a product means an increase or decrease in the **need for workers**.
5) HRM analyses the **current staff details** to see how many are likely to **leave** or **retire** in the near future.
6) The introduction of **new techniques** (e.g. automation) will alter the number of workers needed.

Businesses can recruit **Internally** or **Externally**

Internal recruitment is recruiting people who **already** work for the business. **External recruitment** recruits people from **outside** the company.

Advantages of **internal recruitment**	1) Managers **know** the internal candidates. 2) Internal candidates **know the business** and its objectives. 3) It's a **shorter** and **less expensive** process than external recruitment. 4) It **motivates** workers by encouraging them to go for promotion.
Disadvantages of **internal recruitment**	1) Internal promotion leaves **another vacancy** to be filled. 2) It can cause **resentment** among colleagues who aren't selected.
Advantages of **external recruitment**	1) External recruits bring in **fresh new ideas**. 2) External recruits bring **experience** from other organisations. 3) There's a larger pool of applicants to **choose** from.
Disadvantages of **external recruitment**	1) Managers **don't know** the applicant. 2) It's usually a **long** and **expensive** process. 3) External recruits usually need a longer **induction** process (see p.43).

External recruitment seemed to have worked for the German police force.

Businesses **advertise** vacancies to external applicants in national and local newspapers, specialist trade magazines, and through employment agencies or job centres. **Where** they advertise the job depends on the **type** of job, the **size** of the organisation and **where** the organisation operates.

Selection — getting the **Right People** for the job

It's obviously important to get the best possible candidate for a job. To have the best chance of getting this, the HR department **analyses** the vacancy and draws up a **job description** and a **person specification**.

1) The **job description** lists the tasks and responsibilities the person appointed will be expected to carry out. It may also state the job title, the location, the nature of the business and other details like salary and conditions (e.g. holiday entitlement, pension arrangements and so on).
2) The **person specification** outlines the ideal profile of the person needed to match the job description. It describes their **qualifications**, experience, interests and **personality**. It's important to know whether the candidate will fit into the **culture** and **atmosphere** of the business, as well as knowing whether they've got a GNVQ in Tourism, or if they can do SQL programming.
3) **Interviews** are the most common way of choosing candidates. Candidates can be interviewed **one-to-one** or by a **panel** of interviewers. Phone interviews are thought to be less effective than **face-to-face** interviews.
4) Some organisations use **assessment centres** to help them **test** candidates. Tests include **psychometric** testing which assesses personality fit, **aptitude** tests which find out how good the candidate is at job tasks, and **group exercises** which show how candidates interact with other people in various situations.

Workforce Planning

Employees need **Training** and **Development**

1) The **first day** or so on the job is usually spent learning the workings of the business, covering the health and safety issues, and meeting key personnel. This is the **induction** part of the human resources cycle.
2) Most new employees need some training — either to learn **new skills** or **improve** and **update** existing skills.
3) Training can be done **off-the-job** — e.g. studying part-time at a local **college**, a short one- or two-day **course** at a business training centre, or **studying at home** for a professional qualification.

On-the-job training can take several forms:

1) The **traditional** way is to sit the new trainee next to an **experienced worker**. The newbie watches and learns from the experienced worker, who is there to answer any questions about the job.
2) **Mentoring** is where the new employee is advised by an experienced worker who acts as **tutor** and guru.
3) **Coaching** gives the trainee **specialised** knowledge and skills, e.g. through **seminars** or **group sessions**. It is often offered **long-term**.
4) **Job rotation** is where the new person **moves around** the organisation and experiences **different jobs**.

This is rather endearingly called "sitting next to Nellie".

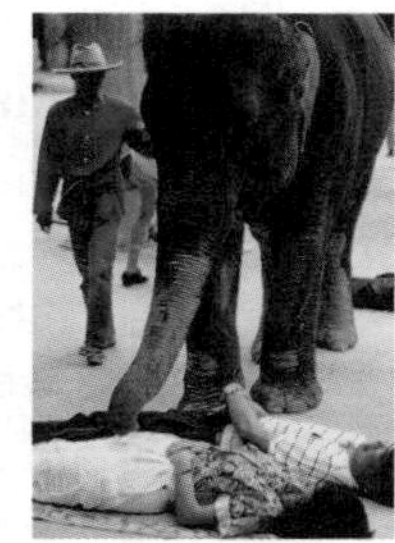

"Lying next to Nellie."

The **Right** kind of **Training** depends on the **Size** and **Type** of business

Advantages of **on-the-job** training	1) On-the-job training is **easy** to **organise**. 2) **Costs** of training tend to be **lower**. 3) Training is **specific** to the job in question.
Disadvantages of **on-the-job** training	1) **Trainer** and **trainee** are **not productive** during training hours. 2) The **trainer** may **not** be **skilled** in **communication** or may have other **weaknesses**. 3) **Bad** work **practices** can be **passed on** to the trainee. 4) **New ways** of **working** are **not introduced** into the company.

The job that the trainee is employed to do affects the type of training too.

Businesses should **evaluate** their training to see how it's **working**, using clear, measurable objectives. Managers should be able to **compare training costs** with the **financial gains** in overall performance using **cost-benefit analysis**.

Advantages of **off-the-job** training	1) Off-the-job training uses **specialist trainers**. 2) Training can be more **intensive**. 3) **New theories** and **practices** can be **introduced** to the business. 4) Training occurs **away from** the **distractions** of the job.
Disadvantages of **off-the-job** training	1) Off-the-job training is more **expensive**. 2) The trainee might **not** have **access** to **specific tools** used in their job. 3) The trainee is **off-site** and is **not productive**.

Practice Questions

Q1 Outline one advantage and one disadvantage of both internal recruitment and external recruitment.

Q2 Briefly explain the terms "job description" and "person specification".

Q3 Explain the difference between on-the-job training and off-the-job training.

Q4 List and describe three methods of on-the-job training.

Exam Questions

Q1 A major London hotel wants to recruit an experienced accountant.
Outline the procedures they may follow in the recruitment process. (9 marks)

Q2 Evaluate the advantages and disadvantages of internal and external recruitment for a retail organisation with 200 stores nationwide. (15 marks)

Internal recruitment — sounds painful...

Businesses can use up a lot of time and money on recruitment and training. They're worth doing properly though, because the additional costs tend to pay off in the long run. A well-chosen employee will work harder and stick around for longer (as long as they're being well trained!) so it'll be a while before they have to go through the whole process again. Phew.

Motivating the Workforce

Motivation is important in business — motivated employees get more done than non-motivated employees. For the past 150 years industrial psychologists and sociologists have tried to figure out what motivates workers...

1) Taylor and Scientific Management — people are in it for the Money

1) In the early 20th century, FW Taylor thought that workers were motivated by **money**. He believed workers would do the **minimum** amount of work if left to their own devices.
2) Taylor developed his theories through **work-study** — watching how people work. He did **time and motion studies**, timing work activities with a **stopwatch**. This allowed him to figure out the **most efficient** way to do a job, and then make sure every single worker did it that way. He favoured **division of labour** — breaking work down into a lot of **small repetitive tasks**. This approach is called **scientific management**.
3) Taylor believed in paying workers according to the **quantity** they produced — the most **productive** workers got a **better rate**. He believed that financial incentives would **motivate** workers and raise **productivity**.
4) Scientific management didn't go down well with workers. Increased productivity meant that **fewer workers** were needed — workers worried about losing their jobs.
5) There were other disadvantages, too — increased productivity could lead to a reduction in **quality**. **Supervisors** were needed to monitor efficiency and for quality control purposes.
6) Taylor's approach wouldn't work for modern businesses — it would be seen as **exploitation**. It also ignores the **demotivating** effect of doing very repetitive boring work.
7) However, aspects of Taylor's theory have survived — **piece rate pay** is based on his ideas, and the role of the **supervisor** still exists.

2) Mayo and Human Relations — people are motivated by Social Factors

1) Elton Mayo found that people achieved more when they got **positive attention**. Mayo was doing an experiment on productivity when he found that **all** workers taking part in the experiment became more productive. He worked out that this was because they liked the **social contact** that they got from the experiments, and they liked working in a **group**.
2) Mayo thought management should **pay attention** to workers as individuals, and **involve** them in decision-making. He thought that firms should try to make business goals compatible with workers' goals. This required a **democratic** style of management, as well as lots of **delegation** and good **communication**.
3) He also thought that workers should **socialise** together — outside work as well as at work.

3) Maslow's Hierarchy of Needs — people need Basics first

Maslow and Herzberg both believed that workers had needs which were specific to them as individuals.

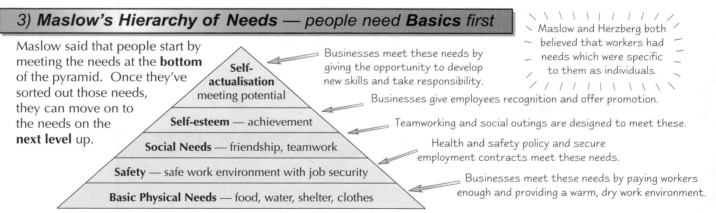

Maslow said that people start by meeting the needs at the **bottom** of the pyramid. Once they've sorted out those needs, they can move on to the needs on the **next level** up.

- **Self-actualisation** meeting potential — Businesses meet these needs by giving the opportunity to develop new skills and take responsibility.
- **Self-esteem** — achievement — Businesses give employees recognition and offer promotion.
- **Social Needs** — friendship, teamwork — Teamworking and social outings are designed to meet these.
- **Safety** — safe work environment with job security — Health and safety policy and secure employment contracts meet these needs.
- **Basic Physical Needs** — food, water, shelter, clothes — Businesses meet these needs by paying workers enough and providing a warm, dry work environment.

The pyramid **looks good** — but it isn't always **obvious** which level an individual is at.

4) Herzberg's Hygiene and Motivating factors — sort out a Good Environment first

In the 1960s, Frederick Herzberg interviewed accountants and engineers to find out what motivated and satisfied them at work. He identified two groups of factors which influenced the motivation of workers:

1) **Hygiene factors** are things like good **company policy**, **supervision**, **working conditions**, **pay**, and **relations** with fellow employees. They don't motivate as such, but if they **aren't good**, workers get **dissatisfied**.
2) **Motivating factors** are things like **interesting work**, personal **achievement**, **recognition** of achievement, and scope for more **responsibility** and personal **development**. These factors **do** positively motivate workers.

Motivating the Workforce

Financial Incentives are used to Reward and Motivate

Most people get paid a monthly **salary** or a weekly **wage**, but there are other kinds of financial motivation, too.

1) Workers who are paid a **weekly wage** get a set rate of so many **pounds per hour**. The more hours they work the more they get paid. There's a minimum wage — in 2007 it was £5.52 per hour for those aged 22 and over. Workers usually work a **fixed working week** of about 40 hours, and get paid more for any **overtime** they work.
2) Workers who get paid a monthly **salary** get a set amount per **year**, divided into 12 monthly payments. The salary isn't directly related to the number of hours worked — salaried employees work a minimum number of hours a week, and then as many hours as it takes to get the job done.
3) **Piecework** is where **production workers** are paid by **piece rate** — they get paid **per finished item** (or set quantity). The more the worker produces, the more they get paid.
4) Salespeople are usually paid **commission** — a **percentage** of the **sales** they achieve. Most sales staff get a low **basic salary** and earn commission on top of that, but some get commission only.
5) **Performance-related pay** gives more money to employees who meet their targets. Performance-related pay is linked to employee **appraisals** (interviews to find out how well an employee is doing). Some employees worry that they won't get a performance-related pay rise if they don't get on with the manager doing the appraisal interviews.
6) Employees may also get **fringe benefits**. These can include a **staff discount** for company products (common in retail, not so common in aircraft manufacturing...), employer contributions to employee **pensions**, private **medical insurance**, a company **car**, **profit-sharing** schemes or **shares** in the company.
7) Companies which have a **tall** structure are more likely to use **pay** to motivate people. **Communication** in tall structures can be **poor**, so it's **difficult** for them to use methods like **empowerment** and **consultation**.

Non-Financial Motivation — Jobs are Designed to be more Satisfying

Lots of businesses today design jobs to be motivating. A well-designed job has **varied job tasks** and gives employees some **control** over their work. It will also try to include as many of **Herzberg's motivating factors** as possible, e.g.:

1) **Job enlargement** gives the employee more work at the same level. It's also called **horizontal loading**.
2) **Job enrichment** gives workers more **challenging** work, and the **training** they need to do it. It gives employees more responsibility for organising their work and solving problems. It's also called **vertical loading**.
3) **Teamworking** puts workers into small teams and lets them organise their own work. In recent years, many firms have begun organising employees into teams, which is why organisational structures often include **team leaders**.
4) An organisation with a **flat** structure might **not** want to introduce **teamworking**, because having **team leaders** introduces an **extra** level of **hierarchy** and makes the structure taller.
5) **Empowerment** gives people more **control** over their work, and a greater role in **decision-making** — **quality circles** let groups of workers from various departments meet to suggest **improvements** to productivity and quality.
6) Organisations with a **flat** structure tend to be better at focusing on the **needs** of the **individual**, so they might motivate people through job **enlargement** or **enrichment**. **Communication** is **easier**, so staff are often involved in **decision-making** — **delegation** and **empowerment** are common.

Practice Questions

Q1 Give a brief description of Taylor's views on motivation.

Q2 Put the following needs in ascending order according to Maslow's hierarchy: friendship, job security, achievement.

Q3 Briefly explain the term "fringe benefits".

Q4 List and explain three non-financial motivators.

Exam Questions

Q1 A coffee-shop owner has a workforce made up of women with children, and part-time students. Explain how he could best increase motivation levels among his staff, giving reasons for your choices. (10 marks)

Q2 Colin is a checkout clerk in a supermarket, Jane is a travelling sales representative and Mike is a bricklayer. Say whether each person is likely to be paid by piece rate, hourly rate or commission, and explain why. (15 marks)

Sandwiches with Mayo increase productivity — no, really, they do...

It's the social factor, you see — people like eating them together. Right, back to the point... the theories of motivation. You won't be tested on who said what, but the ideas might well come in handy for giving examples of how managers today could increase the motivation of their workforce. Believe it or not, people aren't just in it for the money — no, really...

Capacity Utilisation

Changes in capacity utilisation affect a firm's ability to meet targets and impact on its break-even point and profit levels.

Capacity is Maximum Output with the Resources Currently Available

1) The **capacity** of an organisation is the **maximum** output that it can produce in a given period without buying any more fixed assets — machinery, factory space, etc.
2) Capacity depends on the **number of employees** and how skilled they are.
3) Capacity depends on the **technology** the business has — what **machinery** they have, what state it's in, what kind of computer system they have, etc.
4) Capacity depends on the kind of production **process** the business uses.
5) The amount of **investment** in the business is also a factor.

Check out the capacity on that...

Capacity Utilisation

Capacity utilisation is how much **capacity** a business is **using**. The following formula can be used to calculate it:

$$\text{Capacity Utilisation (\%)} = \frac{\text{Output}}{\text{Capacity}} \times 100$$

Example: a hotel with half its rooms booked out has a **capacity utilisation** of **50%**. A clothing factory with an output of 70 000 shirts per month and a maximum capacity of 100 000 shirts is running at **70%** capacity utilisation.

90% Capacity Utilisation is better than 100% Capacity Utilisation

High capacity utilisation is better than low capacity utilisation. However, 100% capacity utilisation has drawbacks.

1) Businesses have to consider all their **operational targets** when they plan their capacity usage. **Cost** isn't the only thing to think about — it might not be possible to operate at 100% capacity and keep **quality** levels high.
2) The business may have to turn away potential **customers**.
3) There's no **downtime** — machines are on **all the time**. If a machine has a problem, it'll cause delays as work piles up waiting for it to be fixed. There's no time for equipment maintenance, which can reduce the life of machinery.
4) There's no **margin of error**. Everything has to be perfect first time, which causes **stress** to managers. **Mistakes** are more likely when everyone's working flat out.
5) The business can't **temporarily increase output** for seasonal demand or one-off orders.
6) If output is greater than demand, there'll be **surplus stock** hanging about waiting to be sold. It's not good to have valuable **working capital** tied up in stock.

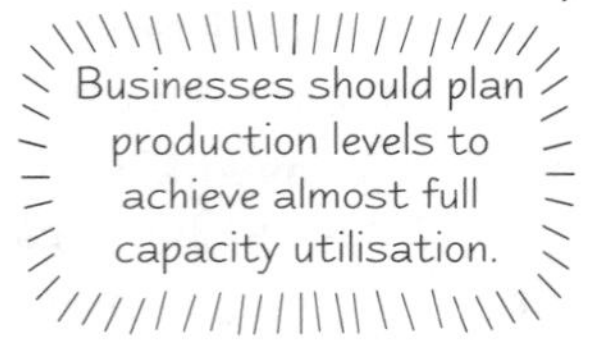

Businesses should plan production levels to achieve almost full capacity utilisation.

Firms can Increase their Capacity if they reach 100% capacity utilisation

Firms which are operating at full capacity don't just stop accepting new orders. They have ways of **increasing** their **capacity** so that they can **match** their **output** to **demand**. The best way to do this depends on whether the rise in demand is expected to be **temporary** or **long-term**.

1) Businesses can use **more capacity** by using their facilities for **more** of the **working week**. They can have staff working in two or three **shifts** in a day, and on weekends and bank holidays.
2) Businesses can buy **more machines**, if they can afford them (and the staff needed to operate them).
3) Businesses can **increase** their **staff levels** in the long run by recruiting new permanent staff. In the short run they can employ **temporary staff**, **part-time staff**, or get their staff to work **overtime**.
4) Businesses can also increase their capacity utilisation by increasing **productivity**. They can reorganise production by reallocating staff to the busiest areas, and they can increase employee **motivation**.

Firms can respond to unexpected Rises in Demand by Subcontracting work

1) **Subcontracting** is when a firm uses its **facilities** to do work on behalf of **another business**. E.g. a manufacturer of detergent might make detergent for a **supermarket** and package it with the supermarket's own label.
2) Companies can **subcontract** work to other businesses in **busy periods**. This means they can meet **unexpected increases in demand** without increasing their own capacity and having the costs of extra staff and facilities all year round.

Capacity Utilisation

Under-utilisation is Inefficient and increases Unit Costs

Low capacity utilisation is called **under-utilisation**. It's **inefficient** because it means a business is **not** getting **use** out of **machines** and **facilities** that have been paid for.

1) Under-utilisation increases costs because it causes fixed costs to be spread over less output, so unit costs increase.
2) Higher capacity utilisation creates **economies of scale**, which means a **decrease** in **variable costs**.

$$\text{Unit cost} = \frac{\text{Total Costs}}{\text{Output}}$$

You'll need to learn this as they often ask you to calculate unit costs in the exam. For more on unit costs, see p. 27.

Example: A chocolate factory's total costs are £7200 a month. In November, the factory output 18 000 chocolate bars, giving a unit cost of £0.40. In December, absenteeism caused output to fall to 16 000 bars, meaning that the unit cost rose to £0.45.

Firms with Low Demand should try to Reduce Capacity

Sometimes firms have **too much capacity** and **not enough demand** for their product, which leads to **under-utilisation.** When this happens, they'll **first** try to **increase demand**, but if that doesn't work, they need to **reduce capacity**.

1) Businesses stimulate demand by changing the **marketing mix**. They can change the **promotion** of a product, or change its **price** or its **distribution** (see p.59-71 for more on the marketing mix).
2) Businesses can also fill spare capacity by **subcontracting** work for other firms (see p.46). It's better to make goods for a **competitor** and make a bit of money than it is to leave **machinery** sitting around doing **nothing**.
3) If a business can't increase demand for their product, they need to **reduce their capacity** by closing part of their production facilities. This is called **rationalisation** (or **downsizing**). It's become popular with large firms who want to stay competitive by cutting their production costs.
4) Businesses can reduce capacity in the **short term** by stopping **overtime** or reducing the length of the working week, allocating staff to **other work** in the business, and by not renewing **temporary contracts**.
5) Businesses can reduce capacity in the **long term** by not **replacing** staff as they retire (natural wastage), making staff **redundant**, and by **selling off** factories or equipment.

Firms have to consider how their Capacity Needs will Change over Time

1) Demand **changes** over time, so firms must think about demand in the **future** as well as the current demand.
2) The key to **long-term** success is planning **capacity** changes to match long-term changes in demand, but this can be tricky. You can use market research to help predict future demand, but it's not 100% certain. There's always an element of risk.
3) **Short-term** changes in **capacity utilisation** provide **flexibility**. Firms should be flexible and **temporarily** increase existing capacity utilisation if an increase in demand isn't expected to continue **long-term** — e.g with seasonal goods like Christmas crackers, goods heading towards decline in their life cycle, and one-off special orders.
4) **Long-term** solutions end up giving **lower unit costs** — as long as **predictions** of demand turn out to be **true**.

Practice Questions

Q1 Calculate capacity utilisation for a restaurant that has 65 seats but only 42 people dining each night.

Q2 Give three ways in which a firm can increase its output to meet an increase in orders.

Q3 Calculate how much it costs to produce one shirt, if a factory is making 450 a month and has total monthly costs of £1600.

Q4 Explain what is meant by "rationalisation".

Answers on p. 82.

Exam Questions

Q1 Discuss why 95% capacity utilisation is considered better for a firm than 100%. (4 marks)

Q2 Analyse how a manufacturer of fashion clothing should expand their business if recent growth has led to capacity utilisation reaching 100%. (10 marks)

She cannae take any more, Jim...

Capacity utilisation crops up elsewhere. Under-utilisation is a consequence of low demand. When a business launches a product, capacity utilisation starts out low and then builds up as demand for the new product increases. It really is very much worth your while to know how businesses take action to get their capacity utilisation to around the 90% mark.

Quality

Increased competition means that firms now compete through quality as well as price.
High quality increases revenues and reduces costs.

Good Quality products and services Meet Customer Needs

1) Products have to be **fit** for the **purpose** they're made for. For example, the quality of a tin-opener is judged by how well it opens tins.
2) The **customer's opinion** of quality is the most important one. Businesses should use **market research** to check customers are satisfied with product quality.

High Quality Increases Profits

1) In the **dark old days**, managers thought quality improvements **increased costs**, so they only went for **slight** quality improvements which wouldn't cost very much.
2) Enlightened managers think of the **opportunity cost** of **not** having a great quality product. They go for high quality as a way of actually **reducing costs** and increasing revenue.

Quality improvements reduce costs:

1) Less **raw materials** and less **worker** and **machinery** time get used up by **mistakes.**
2) You don't need as much **advertising** and **promotional** gubbins to persuade **shops** to stock high quality goods.
3) You don't need to spend as much on **marketing** to attract **new customers.**
4) You need fewer **customer care staff** because there aren't as many **complaints** to deal with.
5) There are fewer **refunds** and fewer claims on **warranties.**

Quality improvements increase revenue:

1) You don't need to **discount** prices to sell **damaged stock** when there isn't any damaged or "seconds" quality stock.
2) You have greater price flexibility — high quality products allow for **premium pricing.**
3) Quality is a way of differentiating your product from the competition — it can function as a **unique selling point (USP).**
4) High quality products improve the **image** and **reputation** of the business.
5) Quality goods and services make it easy to keep **existing customers.**
6) A good reputation for quality brings in **new customers.**

Self-checking can be more Motivating than Inspection

1) The traditional **quality control** approach assumes that errors are **unavoidable**. It says that the best you can do is to **detect errors** and **put them right** before customers buy the products.
2) Traditionally, **quality control inspectors** checked other people's work. This has drawbacks — inspectors are additional staff and need to be paid, and employees feel distrusted and demotivated.
3) **Quality assurance** is a more modern approach to quality control. With quality assurance, workers check their own work. This is called **self-checking**. **Empowering** employees to check the quality of their own work can be highly **motivating**.
4) Under a self-checking system, it's **everyone's responsibility** to produce good work. Everyone should try to get it **right first time**. Workers can **reject** components or work in progress if they're not up to standard. They don't pass the poor quality off as **someone else's problem**. Workers are responsible for passing on good quality work in progress to the next stage of the production process.
5) **Training** is really important for quality assurance. Workers have to be trained to produce good quality products and services. New recruits get this as part of their **induction**. Experienced workers might need **retraining** from time to time.
6) Workers must be **motivated** and **committed** to quality for quality assurance schemes to work.
7) The ultimate aim of quality assurance is to create a culture of **zero defects**.

Quality

Total Quality Management is the Ultimate version of Quality Assurance

1) **Total Quality Management** (TQM) means the **whole workforce** has to be committed to quality improvements. The idea is to **build quality** into every department and not let quality get squeezed out.

2) With TQM, every employee has to try to **satisfy customers** — and everybody that they work for must be thought of as a customer, even fellow employees. So both **external** customers that the business sells things to, and **internal** customers within the business, must receive a quality service.

3) It takes **time** to introduce TQM — workers need **training** so that they see quality as their responsibility. This can be **expensive** and **disrupt production** in the short-term. It can also seem like a lot of extra work, which can be **demotivating** for employees. Some companies that use TQM motivate their staff by **rewarding** quality.

Quality Awards are Evidence of High Standards

1) **BS 5750** is an award given out by the **British Standards Institution** to firms with good quality assurance systems which meet the industry standard. **ISO 9000** is the **European** quality award. It's equivalent to BS 5750.
2) To get the award, a business must set **quality targets**, make sure their production process **achieves** these targets, and continually **monitor** production quality. This process can **cost money**.
3) The British Standards Institute **don't care** too much what the business' quality targets actually are, only that they meet the **industry standard** and have systems in place to meet their own targets.
4) BS 5750 and ISO 9000 can be used in **marketing** to win the trust of customers.

They couldn't understand what had happened to their quality award.

Practice Questions

Q1 Give two reasons why high quality reduces costs.

Q2 What's the difference between quality control and quality assurance?

Q3 What must a business do in order to get a BS 5750 award?

Exam Questions

Q1 Examine the potential costs and benefits of obtaining ISO 9000 certification. (8 marks)

Q2 The Managing Director of Ropey Textiles decides to introduce Total Quality Management to the business. Explain why employees may be resistant to TQM, and suggest how it might be successfully introduced. (10 marks)

AS Examiners — the ultimate quality control inspectors...

It's pretty obvious that good quality is important in business. People don't like paying for things that aren't any good. There are different ways to go about making sure that products and services are of good quality — one important difference is between quality control inspections of finished products and quality assurance systems for the whole production process.

Customer Service

Providing good customer service is one thing that makes businesses competitive in the long term. If a business is committed to providing good service, it needs to spend a lot of money and time developing a quality culture.

Customers **Expect** good service from a **Company**

Basically, customer service means providing a service or product in the way that has been promised.

1) **Customer service** is the **actions** that a business takes to **keep** its **customers happy**. Customer service can be part of the sales process **before**, **during**, or **after** the sale itself.

2) Having a customer service **philosophy** means admitting to mistakes and dealing with complaints — customers like companies to admit when they're wrong, explain the problem and make amends. An important part of the process is making **customer service** part of the organisation's **culture**, and ensuring that all **employees** work hard to provide **excellent** levels of **customer service**.

3) Knowing the customer is **vital** to good customer service. A company has to know what its customers **want** and **expect** in order to be able to provide it — that's why **market research** (p.12) and **feedback** are so important. Companies can get feedback through guestbooks, questionnaires, **secret shoppers** (customers who are paid to use a service to provide feedback on it) and emails.

4) The way companies deliver customer service is **changing**. Email and chat systems make it easy for customers to speak to experts at **any time**, and call centres can handle **hundreds** of customers per hour. These developments have also made senior management more **directly involved** in customer services — in some cases (e.g. service stations) you can directly telephone the **manager** to complain.

Good Customer Service gives companies a **Competitive Advantage**

Providing good customer service uses up **time** and **money**. There are plenty of reasons why many companies think it's still **worth** making the **effort**, though...

1) Good customer service can provide a **USP** (Unique Selling Point, see p.60).
2) Customers can now shop 24 hours a day, online or by phone, and expect to be able to buy products **quickly** and **easily**. Since many companies provide identical products at similar prices, most customers will go to one that offers high levels of **service** that are **consistently delivered**.
3) New products, services and technological improvements can be copied by the competition, but a good **service reputation** is **hard** to **duplicate**.
4) Companies that provide added value and superior customer service can **charge more** than their competitors.
5) **Long-term customers** buy more, take less company time, bring in new customers and are less price sensitive (put off by price rises). Companies now look at customers in terms of their **LTV** (Lifetime Value) to the company.
6) **Satisfied customers** are the best **advert** for the company as they spread its reputation by **word of mouth**.

In a world dominated by Chip and Pin technology, giving customers the chance to sign for goods was a unique customer service.

Customer Service

Different Types of Business offer Different Types of Customer Service

The way in which a business provides service depends on what type of business it is.
However, most businesses offer some form of these three basic aspects of customer service:

1) Products and services need to be **customer-focused** and provide **value** for money.
2) Businesses have to treat customers as individuals with **different needs**.
3) **After-sales service** — following up with after-sales support such as maintenance.

Companies who want to get a **competitive advantage** from customer service often try to **go beyond** the types of service listed above. **How** they go about this depends on what type of business they are:

1) Businesses such as shops, where the customer comes **face to face** with staff, are likely to invest in **staff training**. **Extended opening hours** and **home delivery** might also improve customer satisfaction.
2) **Online** and **telephone retailers** don't deal with the customer face to face, so they have to find other ways of giving good customer service. Some have customer service **call centres** that are open **long hours**. Others offer **next-day** or **free delivery** or are more **flexible** about **returning** goods.
3) **Business to Business (B2B)** companies (see p.57) focus their customer service efforts on building **long-term relationships** with their **clients**, often by providing spare parts or maintenance. This is because businesses that sell to businesses usually have a **few clients** who each spend **lots** of **money**, whereas firms that sell to private customers have a lot of customers each spending relatively small amounts of money.

Research, Training and Quality Management all Improve Customer Service

Companies are always trying to monitor and improve the level of customer service that they offer.
They do this by investing in market research and training and by introducing quality management systems.

1) **Market research** involves gathering and analysing information about customers through **customer surveys** and **questionnaires**. Managers can use this information to help them **understand** the **market** and make sure products and services meet the **customer's needs.** Look back at page 12 for more on market research.

2) Staff should be **knowledgeable** about the product or service they are selling. Companies use **training** to make sure employees have this knowledge. Training can also be used to ensure that staff have a **positive attitude** towards the customer.

3) **Quality systems** ensure that products and services are **produced** and **sold** at an acceptable **standard** and **quality**. Firms can use methods of **quality assurance** such as **Total Quality Management** (TQM, see p.49) to create a quality culture and make sure all employees are contributing in some way to customer service targets. Alternatively, they might introduce **quality standards** such as ISO 9000 (see page 49).

Quality culture.

Practice Questions

Q1 How would you define customer service?

Q2 Why is it beneficial for a company to have long-term customers?

Q3 What factors contribute to high levels of customer satisfaction?

Q4 How can a company benefit from satisfying customer needs?

Exam Question

Q1 a) Discuss the alternatives a company has for developing its customer service. (10 marks)

b) Analyse the benefits it might gain as a result of improving its customer service. (6 marks)

All our writers are currently busy — please continue to hold...

When you've been waiting for someone to answer your call for an hour, it's easy to feel like companies don't care about customer service at all. But it costs them as much to win one new customer as it does to keep five existing ones. So, believe it or not, they're usually doing everything in their power to keep you sweet. Make sure you learn how they do it.

Suppliers

It's not called a supply chain for nothin' — every business in the chain needs to pull their weight, or production just doesn't happen...

Producing **High Quality** products **Depends** on **Good Suppliers**

A company's **performance** is often **linked** to the activities and performance of its **suppliers**.

1) A **supply chain** consists of the group of **firms** that are involved in **all** the various **processes** required to make a **finished product / service** available to the customer.
2) The chain **begins** with the provider of **raw materials** and **ends** with the firm that sells the **finished product**.
3) The members of a supply chain will **vary** depending on the type of product/service, but will typically include **suppliers**, **manufacturers**, **distributors** and **retailers**.
4) **All** the **members** of the supply chain need to **function efficiently**. If any of them are unreliable, the product won't be on the shelves when it needs to be, or the quality will be poor, which reflects badly on the company producing it.

"We should be able to get those components to you by 1952."

Companies need to consider **Price** and **Reliability** when **Choosing** a **Supplier**

The most **effective suppliers** are those who offer products or services that **match** (or **exceed**) the **needs** of your business. So when you are looking for **suppliers**, it's best to be **sure** of your **business needs** and what you want to achieve. The most important factors to consider are:

Price	The **total cost** of acquiring the product. Firms have to decide **how much** they are willing to pay and whether **cost** is their **first priority**. If they want to cut down the time it takes to serve customers, suppliers that offer faster delivery will rate higher than those that compete on price alone.
Payment Terms	Companies need to know **how much** they need to pay, **how** it has to be paid and **when** it should be paid by. **Small suppliers** may only be able to offer **30 days' credit**, as they often have poor cash flow. Some **larger firms** may be able to offer as much as **120 days'** credit.
Quality	The **quality** of supplies needs to be **consistent** — customers associate **poor quality** with the business they buy from, not their suppliers.
Capacity	Businesses need to select **suppliers** who are able to **meet** any **peaks** in **demand** for particular products / services.
Reliability	If **a supplier** lets a **firm** down, that firm may not be able to supply its **own** customers. Suppliers need to **deliver on time**, or give plenty of **warning** if they can't.
Flexibility	**Suppliers** need to be able to **respond easily** to **changes** in a company's **requirements**. Efficient production relies on suppliers who can provide extra (or fewer) supplies at **short notice**.

Companies build **Relationships** with their **Suppliers**

A **strategic working relationship** is one where both companies in the relationship can get **long-term benefits** from **working together**. There are several ways for companies to build strategic working relationships with their suppliers:

1) **Linked Networks** — **shared IT systems** such as inventory (stock) control management allow both the company and its supplier to view stock levels, so they both know in plenty of time when more supplies will be needed. This can improve **efficiency**, cut **costs**, and improve **customer value**.
2) **JIT (Just-in-Time) Systems** — these are becoming a popular way of managing operations. The goal of JIT systems is to have only the **right amounts** of **materials** arrive at precisely the **times** they are **needed**. Because supplies arrive just as they are needed you don't need a big warehouse, and there's **less waste**.
3) **Shared Costs** — if a business and its supplier are producing similar goods, there's a good chance they'll be able to save money by sharing **specialist equipment** and storing their goods in the same **warehouse**.

Suppliers

A Well-managed Supply Chain can Improve Operational Performance

1) If a business **works** closely with the **right suppliers**, there's a good chance that **operational performance** will **improve**.
2) **Productivity** will **increase**, which causes **costs** to **fall** (for more on the link between these two, see p.40).
3) Also, a business with an **efficient supply chain** is in a much better position to meet its customers' expectations.

Mr MacDonald and Mr Paulin had spent three days choosing a supplier for a new stapler.

1) A company's buyers need to make sure that they **only buy** the **supplies** that the **company** really **needs** — they mustn't be wowed by slick sales pitches.

2) They also need to understand the difference between a **strategic supplier**, who provides goods or services that are essential to the business — such as high-value raw materials, and a **non-strategic supplier** who provides low-value supplies such as office stationery. It's important to spend **more time** selecting and managing **strategic suppliers** than non-strategic suppliers.

3) It's often easier, and generally more **cost-effective**, for businesses to **limit** the number of **sources** they buy from. However, it's **dangerous** to have just **one supplier** because if there are ever problems with that supplier, the business has nowhere to turn.

4) It's always worth having an **alternative supply source** ready to help in difficult times. This is really important for suppliers who are essential to the success of the business.

Practice Questions

Q1 Give three types of company that you would expect to find as part of a supply chain.

Q2 Why would a business choose a JIT method of production?

Q3 What is the difference between a strategic supplier and a non-strategic supplier?

Q4 Why is it risky for a business to rely on a single supplier?

Exam Questions

Q1 Alpha Ironmonger Ltd is looking for a supplier of beef to use in its new range of beef pies. Discuss the factors it should consider before deciding which one to choose. (8 marks)

Q2 Mr Brown, director of Browns Brushes Ltd, wants to improve his relationship with his suppliers. Discuss the ways in which he could achieve this. (8 marks)

Supply me to the moon, let me sing among the stock...

If you're a business, the relationship with your supplier might be the best one you'll ever have. Or the worst. If your suppliers do what they're supposed to when they're supposed to, there's a good chance that the production process will all run to plan. If they're late, or just don't deliver, production stops, staff have absolutely nowt to do — it's a disaster, basically...

Technology in Operations

Most modern businesses rely heavily on technology, from automated production lines to computer systems. Technology can make a firm more cost-effective and efficient, but it needs constant updating and maintenance.

Businesses use Two main types of Technology

The main technologies that companies use in day-to-day operations are:

1) **Robotic Engineering** — using robots as part of the manufacturing process.
2) **Computer Technology** — computers are used by businesses in lots of different ways. Product development, business communications and finance departments all depend heavily on IT systems.

Using Robots can Reduce Staffing Costs

1) **Robots** are mostly used to replace human staff for **tasks** which are **dangerous**, **repetitive** or **boring**.
2) **Factories** and **production plants** often use **automated pickers** to take goods from the production line and pack them into boxes. It's usually **cheaper** and **faster** for robots to do this job instead of humans.
3) Companies that are planning to replace human workers with robots need to weigh up the **advantages** of using robots against the **demotivating effect** that it is likely to have on staff.

Advantages of using Robots	1) Company needs **fewer employees**, so staff **costs fall**. 2) Robots are generally more **accurate** — human error is eliminated. 3) Robots are more **reliable** than human workers. 4) Robots can be used for **tasks** that could be **unsafe** for **humans**, e.g. bomb detection.
Disadvantages of using Robots	1) Some staff may **lose** their **jobs**, which can be **demotivating** for colleagues. 2) **Incorrect programming** can lead to **errors** being made. 3) **High initial cost** involved in **purchasing** robot. 4) **Maintenance** costs can be **expensive**.

Luke claimed to be developing a new robot. His colleagues thought he was just playing chess.

IT helps make Companies more Efficient

1) **Computer-aided design** (CAD) uses computers to design new products, or make alterations to existing products. CAD produces 3D mock-ups on screen — managers don't have to wait for a **prototype** (model) to be built before they know what the product will look like. This can also be useful for marketing things like new kitchens.
2) **Computer-aided manufacture** (CAM) uses computers to produce a product, usually involving **robots** or 'computer-numerically controlled' (CNC) machines — automatic lathes which form a material into a finished product from a computer design. CAM is often combined with the CAD process — products are designed on computer, and the design data fed straight into the production machine. This is called **CAD/CAM**.
3) Computers make **stock control** easier. Holding stock information in a database makes it much easier to monitor when you need to order new stock. In retailing this is often combined with **Electronic Point of Sale (EPOS)** systems that rely on barcodes to record which products are being purchased by customers. This means stocks can be re-ordered automatically. Having a good stock control system makes it easier for companies such as supermarkets and big retailers to move to a **just-in-time** supply system (see p.52).
4) **IT** helps with **budgetary control**. The finance department can easily compare current expenditure levels with original budgets using **spreadsheets**.
5) Spreadsheets allow managers to investigate "what if?" scenarios. They can calculate the impact of **potential changes** in expenditure or sales, which makes **decision-making** easier.

IT helps make Communication Faster and more Effective

Information can be shared **within** the **company** using an **intranet**. Businesses communicate with other **businesses** and with **customers** by **fax**, **email** and the **internet**.

1) Email is a fast and efficient method of communicating, both internally and externally.
2) The **internet** allows businesses to reach a **larger customer base**, and do business **24 hours a day**. Customers can check a business' **website** for information rather than phoning a helpline or sending a letter in the post.

Technology in Operations

Marketing departments use **Technology** to gather **Information** about **Customers**

Many companies now use **technology** to gather **information** about the **lifestyles** of their **customers** and the **products** that they **buy** or are likely to buy. This helps them to make sure that **promotions** are **targeting** the right people and will actually cause **sales** to **increase**.

1) Lots of supermarkets offer **loyalty cards** which give customers money back according to how much they spend. One **benefit** for the supermarket is that it allows them to form a **database** of customer names and addresses which they can then use to create **mailing lists** for **direct marketing** campaigns.
2) **Loyalty cards** also tell the supermarkets what **products** a particular customer is **buying**. This means they can send out **offers** which **relate** to the kind of products that the person buys **most often**.
3) **Social networking websites** are another way that businesses can use technology to find out more about customer likes and dislikes. People who use these sites often list information about themselves, including the type of **music** they like, where they go on **holiday**, what **car** they drive etc. Companies who advertise on these sites can make their adverts visible only to the people who are **likely** to **buy** their product — this is **cheaper** and more **effective** than targeting everyone who uses the website. **Search engines** like Google™ often use targeted advertising — they show adverts that are **relevant** to the topic the user searched for.

Firms need to consider the **Advantages** and **Disadvantages** of **Technology**

Most companies invest a lot of money in technology. Technology is beneficial if it leads to:

1) **Increased productivity** — machines can often do tasks quicker than humans can.
2) Improved **quality**.
3) **Reduced waste** through more effective production methods.
4) More **effective** and **efficient delivery** of goods and services to the customer.
5) More **effective marketing** campaigns that target the right customers.
6) More productive **staff utilisation** — staff can be transferred to more urgent or complicated tasks.
7) **Reduced** administrative and financial **costs**.
8) **Better communications** both internally and externally.

However, introducing new technology or updating older systems can create problems:

1) **Initial costs** of technology may be **high**.
2) Technology requires **constant updating** in order to stay current, which can also be **expensive**.
3) New IT systems may create an **increased** need for **staff training**.

Practice Questions

Q1 What is meant by CAD? How can a business use it?

Q2 Give two advantages and two disadvantages of using robots.

Q3 How can social networking websites be beneficial to marketing departments?

Q4 Give two advantages and two disadvantages of using technology in business.

Exam Question

Q1 (a) Identify three areas where technology may be utilised in a company. (3 marks)

(b) Discuss how technology can be used in each of these areas to benefit the company. (12 marks)

If these pages are repetitive and boring — they're the work of a robot...

Reading through this lot is enough to make you wonder how businesses ever coped before technology came along. You need to know the two main types of technology that businesses use today, as well as the benefits and pitfalls of using technology. Robots might be cheaper than humans, but they tell lousy jokes, don't flirt, and are no good at making tea...

Effective Marketing

Marketing is "the management process responsible for identifying, anticipating and satisfying consumer requirements profitably." Well, that's what the Chartered Institute of Marketing says — I suppose they'd know.

Marketing identifies customer Needs and Wants

1) Marketing finds out what customers **need and want**. Marketing also tries to **anticipate** what they'll want in the future so that the business can get **one step ahead** of the market.
2) Marketing tries to ensure that the business supplies **goods and services** that customers **want** in order to **make a profit**. It's mutually beneficial — the customer gets something they want, the business makes a profit.
3) Marketing covers **research**, **analysis**, **planning** and the "**marketing mix**". The "marketing mix" is all the decisions a business makes about promoting and selling a product.
4) Most larger businesses have a specialised **marketing department** — but marketing affects all departments.

Marketing is important in a Competitive Environment

1) Companies selling goods in a competitive environment rely on **marketing** to help them **obtain** a **share** of the **market**.
2) Once they have a customer base, marketing (especially **market research**) helps them come up with **new products** and make sure that their **customers** don't **shop elsewhere**.
3) Companies invent **unique selling points** (USPs) for their products to persuade customers to buy their products rather than products from a competitor (there's more on USPs on p.60).
4) **Marketing** helps make sure that **customers** stay **loyal** to a particular **brand** (see p.64 for more on branding).

High Disposable Income increases the Need for Marketing

1) **Disposable income** is the amount of money that consumers have left to spend **after** they have paid **taxes** and **pension** contributions. It tends to go up and down depending on whether the economy is strong or weak.
2) When consumers have **lots** of disposable income, they start to **buy things** they **wouldn't usually** buy — such as luxury and designer goods.
3) Manufacturers of these types of product all want to attract a **share** of this new group of customers, so they **increase** the amount that they spend on **marketing**.
4) This extra spending on marketing causes sales to rise, which leads to an **increase** in **revenue**.
5) The combination of increased revenue and a wider market means companies might consider **new forms** of **advertising** which target a bigger group of people — e.g. a national women's magazine, or billboards.
6) However, an increase in disposable income can also lead to a **decrease** in demand for **cheaper**, lower quality **products**. Manufacturers of these products might spend **more** on **marketing** to win back market share.

Globalisation and Brand Awareness can affect Marketing Strategy

1) In general, **globalisation** is **good** for **large companies**, because it allows them to sell their product all over the world. **Coca-Cola®** and **McDonald's** are examples of very successful **global brands**.
2) The global market has led to **customers** being very **brand aware**. Companies often **market** major brands **differently** from the way that they market lesser-known products.
3) Successful brands, such as Cadbury, often choose to **advertise** the **brand name**, rather than a specific product. The advantage of this is that it **increases** the sales of **all** their products, not just one in particular.
4) The producers of **successful** brands tend to have a lot of **influence**. This makes it easier for them to persuade **retailers** to install special point of sale displays (for more on point of sale, see p.65) and gives them access to extremely high profile forms of advertising, such as **product placement** in films.
5) Some consumers **dislike** buying from large, **global companies**, because they feel that they are impersonal or too powerful. This has led some companies, such as HSBC, to adopt **marketing** campaigns which **emphasise** their ability to adapt to the **local** environment.

Effective Marketing

Marketing can be aimed at Large or Small Groups of Consumers

Mass marketing is a way of trying to make sure that **as many** customers **as possible** see a particular product. **Niche marketing** tries to sell to a **smaller**, more **specific** group of people. More on niche and mass markets on p.8 and p.10.

Advantages of Niche Marketing

+ Niche marketing **only** targets people who are likely to be **interested** in the product in question. So although it only reaches a small group of consumers, there is a good chance they will want to buy the product.
+ Because it only targets a very limited group of customers, niche marketing is **cheaper** than mass marketing.

Disadvantages of Niche Marketing

– Some companies selling to a niche market are forced to set a **high price** for their product. This is because their low levels of production prevent them benefiting from **economies of scale**.
– Another disadvantage of niche marketing is that identifying a niche can be **expensive**, as well as **time-consuming**.

Advantages of Mass Marketing

+ The most obvious advantage of mass marketing is that it allows companies to reach a **huge audience**.
+ Producers of mass market products save money because of **economies of scale**. These savings can be passed on to consumers, allowing firms to **compete** on **price**.

Disadvantages of Mass Marketing

– A mass marketing strategy is unlikely to make customers feel that a product meets their **exact needs**. **Market share** can **decrease** as niche products break the market into smaller segments.
– Mass marketing is **expensive**, as it relies on **widespread forms** of promotion, such as TV advertising.

Companies can use Marketing to target Customers or Other Businesses

The growth of the internet has created many new types of business. Two of the most important of these are **business-to-business** (B2B) companies, and **business-to-consumer** (B2C) companies.

With a name like B2C they would never have reached the top 40, even without the pink trumpet.

1) B2B companies sell to other **businesses**. They usually sell **services**, such as help with recruitment, or **telecommunications** and **computer products**.
2) B2C businesses, such as Amazon.com®, sell goods **directly** to the **public** via the internet.
3) B2B marketing tries to **build** a **long-term relationship** with the consumer. It emphasises **after-sales service**.
4) B2C companies use **discounts**, **advertising** and other **promotions** to persuade people to **spend money**.

Practice Questions

Q1 What is meant by "disposable income"?
Q2 Give three ways in which increased brand awareness has changed the way that businesses market goods.
Q3 What kind of services and products do B2B businesses usually sell?

Exam Questions

Q1 Explain how changes in disposable income can increase the need for marketing. (5 marks)

Q2 Justify why a business selling tie-dye T-shirts should consider a niche marketing strategy. (4 marks)

Maybe I'll find a niche, crawl into it, and stay there forever...

You might feel like you can't get away from all this marketing stuff — companies probably feel that way too. When customers are spending more money, companies need marketing to persuade them to spend it on their products. When they spend less, marketing tries to tempt them to keep buying. If only consumers weren't such a fickle bunch...

Managing a Range of Products

There's a lot to think about before bringing a new product onto the market. Businesses need the right mix of new, growing and mature products to survive in the long-term. And the wrong product can be a pricey mistake.

Businesses need a Variety of Products — a Mixed Product Portfolio

1) A **product line** consists of related products with similar characteristics, uses or target customers.
2) The **product mix** is the **combination** of all the **product lines** that a business produces.
3) Businesses aim to have a **product mix** that contains a variety of different products, all at different stages of the product life cycle (see p.62). That way if one product fails, the business should still be able to depend on the others.

The product mix is also called the product portfolio.

The Boston Matrix is a model of Portfolio Analysis

The Boston Matrix compares **market growth** with **market share**. Each **circle** in the matrix represents **one product**. The **size** of each circle represents the **sales revenue** of the product.

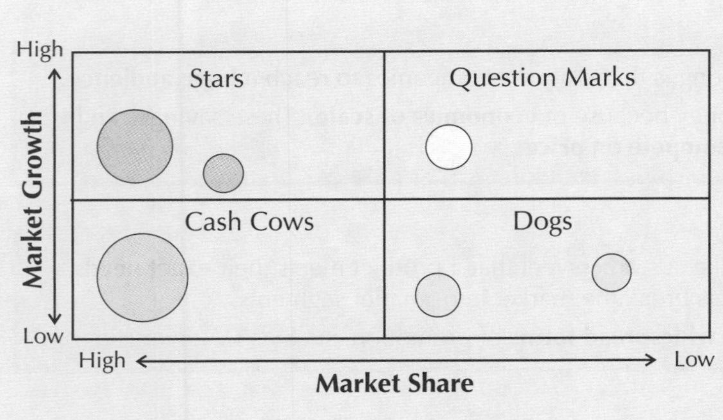

1) All **new products** are **question marks** (sometimes called **problem children** or **wildcats**) and they have small market share and high market growth. These aren't profitable yet and could succeed or fail. They need **heavy marketing** to give them a chance. A business can do various things with question marks — **brand building, harvesting** (maximising sales or profit in the short term) or **divestment** (selling off the product).

2) **Stars** have high market growth and high market share. They're in their profitable **growth** phase and have the most potential. They're future cash cows.

3) **Cash cows** have high market share but low market growth. They're in their **maturity** phase. They've already been promoted and they're produced in high volumes, so costs are low. Cash cows bring in plenty of **money**.

4) **Dogs** have low market share and low market growth. They're usually pretty much a lost cause. If they're still profitable, e.g. a chocolate bar that is still popular, but no longer growing, the business will **harvest profit** in the **short term**. If the product is no longer making a profit it can be **sold off**.

Jack had low growth — so he tried standing on two legs to make himself look taller.

The Boston Matrix is a useful tool

1) The Boston Matrix lets a business see if it has a good balanced **product portfolio**. A balanced product portfolio means that a business can use money from its **cash cows** to **invest** in its **question marks** so they can become **stars**. Because the products are all related in this way, it's important to take them all into account when making decisions.
2) The Boston Matrix **can't** always **predict exactly** what will happen to a product. A product's **cash flow** and **profit** may be **different** from what the matrix suggests (e.g. a dog may have strong cash flow and be profitable despite falling sales).

Managing a Range of Products

The Marketing Mix — Product, Price, Place, Promotion

The marketing mix describes the **factors** that firms consider when **marketing** a product. It's often known as **the 4 Ps**.

1) The marketing mix is the combination of factors that **affect a customer's decision** to buy. The **price** has to be right, the **product** has to be right, the product must be distributed to the right **places**, and it has to be **promoted** in the right way. **Market research** helps companies put together a marketing mix that works.

A marketing mix with factors which work well together is called an integrated marketing mix.

2) The factors in the marketing mix have to **work together**. E.g. if a company develops a very exclusive product, which it then distributes to shops all over the country, then the easy availability of the product could cause it to lose its exclusivity, which might discourage people from buying it. But businesses also have to **compromise** — it would be unusual for a **niche product** produced by a small firm to have a high enough marketing budget to allow for TV adverts, promotional pricing and point-of-sale displays, so the **marketing department** has to **decide** which of these they think will be **most effective**.
3) A business has to be **realistic** when it's putting together its marketing mix. E.g. a business that's based in Alaska might not be able to include next-day delivery to the rest of the world in its mix.

The Marketing Mix is influenced by the Marketing Environment

The marketing mix needs to be **constantly reviewed** if a product is going to be successful in the long term, because the environment that surrounds the marketing mix changes all the time.

1) The **marketing environment** is made up of many **different forces** which influence the marketing mix. These forces might be **legal**, **financial**, **technological** or **political**.
2) It can be hard for companies to **predict** changes in the marketing environment. Most companies **react** to changes by **adapting** their marketing mix.
3) Companies might change their marketing mix as a result of new **market research**.
4) **Political** forces include **government taxes** — the government can raise or lower tax on things like cigarettes and alcohol in its annual **budget**.
5) **Legal** forces are designed to prevent **monopolies** (see p.72) and to **protect** the consumer. They stop companies from charging excessive prices or manufacturing **products** that could be dangerous, e.g. clothing made of flammable fabric.

Cindy thought the 4 Ps were Party, Party, Party, Party.

6) Advances in **technology** have two main effects. They influence the **type of products** that a company can offer and also cause **customers' aspirations** to change.
7) **Financial** or economic forces affect both **consumer** and **company** spending. In times of prosperity, both consumers and businesses spend more, whereas a **weak economy** (high interest rates, high unemployment etc.) causes consumers to cut back and forces businesses to cut costs, too.
8) **Social** factors, like an increasing number of pensioners, or more workers from Eastern Europe affect **demand** and **consumer spending** patterns.
9) Some changes in the marketing environment are **harmful** to certain companies, but **beneficial** to others. In the 1990s, when sales of beef were affected by BSE, sales of other meats rose as people changed their **buying habits**.

Practice Questions

Q1 What can a business do to its question marks to turn them into stars?

Q2 What is meant by "marketing mix"?

Q3 Give examples of ways in which changes in technology might influence the marketing mix.

Exam Questions

Q1 Discuss the usefulness of the Boston Matrix to a biscuit manufacturer. (10 marks)

Q2 A crisp manufacturer has just carried out market research which shows that consumers now want luxury crisps for dinner parties. Suggest how the firm might change its marketing mix in reaction to this. (8 marks)

Cash cows bring in plenty of money — but piggy banks do that too...

There's a lot for businesses to plan before they launch a new product — they have to be as sure as they can be that the product they've spent time and money on won't be a flop. Once it's gone from 'question mark' to 'cash cow,' they need to keep an eye on the marketing environment, and adjust the marketing mix to make sure the product stays profitable.

Marketing Mix: Product

Many marketing experts think that the product is the most important element of the marketing mix. Not everyone agrees, but companies do need to develop new goods and services in order to keep on being successful.

New Products can be great for a business

There are three main reasons why it is worthwhile for companies to develop new products:

1) New products can bring in **new customers**.
2) They give a **competitive** advantage.
3) They allow companies to maintain a **balanced product portfolio**.

Competition and Technology can inspire New Products

Most new products come about for one of three reasons:

1) **Technological developments** mean that a company can now offer the customer something that it couldn't offer before, e.g. a DVD player instead of a video player.
2) A company might develop a new product in response to one which has been launched by a **competitor**, e.g. lots of companies developed bagless vacuum cleaners after the launch of the Dyson™.
3) Somebody within the company (usually the owner or a manager) identifies a **gap in the market**. See page 12 for more on identifying gaps in the market.

There are Three Types of New Product

A product is considered to be 'new,' if it fits into one of the following categories:

1) **Innovative** — innovative products are completely original. Products such as Sony's Walkman® or 3M's Post-it® notes originally fitted into this category.
2) **Imitative** — these are products which copy innovative products once they have become successful. For example, there are now loads of different makes of portable CD player or sticky notes.
3) **Replacement** — a new model of an existing product is developed and the old one is phased out.

1) In order to create **innovative products**, companies have to spend lots of money on **research and development (R&D)**.
2) They also need a **proactive** approach to product development. This happens when a firm is attempting to be a **leader** and **create the market**. This strategy is **high risk**, but also carries the **highest potential rewards**.
3) The alternative approach to product development is for firms to be **reactive**. A reactive firm markets **imitative** and **replacement products**. Smaller companies usually take this approach, as they have less money to invest in R&D.

Companies with innovative products often protect their ideas using patents. See p. 8.

New Products need a Unique Selling Point (USP)

Every successful new product, whether it be innovative, imitative or a replacement for an existing product, needs to have something that **differentiates** it from the **competition**. This is known as a **Unique Selling Point** or a **Unique Selling Proposition (USP)**.

1) Products have **tangible benefits** and **intangible benefits**. Both can be used as USPs.
2) **Tangible benefits** can be **measured**. Products with tangible benefits that could be used as USPs are things like low-calorie pizza, energy-efficient fridges and savings accounts with high rates of interest.
3) **Intangible benefits** are things that can't be measured. They are based on concepts such as reputation and product image. E.g. Beauty products market themselves as making the consumer feel good, certain makes of car are perceived as being reliable, and some fashion brands are seen as 'cool.'

Jim had read the whole manual, but he still couldn't find his computer's USP.

4) A product's tangible and intangible benefits are important, but there are other things the consumer considers. These might be things like **customer service**, **money-back guarantees**, and availability of **spare parts**.

Marketing Mix: Product

New Product Development includes Several Stages

1) **Ideas stage** — Market researchers look for a **gap in the market**, and figure out how a new product can best meet customer needs. The business does **research and development** (R&D) and analyses **competitor** products.

2) **Screening stage** — The business analyses the idea for the new product to see if it's **easy to market**, and to see if it'll make a **profit**. Market researchers find out what **consumers think** about the potential new product. A **prototype** (model) might be made to find out what the new product will really look like in real life.

3) **Product development stage** — The prototype is turned into a saleable product. The **functional design** of the product (its **structure** and how it **works**) and the **formal design** (its **appearance**) are tuned up and made as good as possible.

The relative importance of formal and functional design depends on the product and the market.

4) **Value analysis** — The business tries to make the product good **value** for money. They look at the economy of **making, warehousing** and **distributing** the product to make sure the whole process will be **efficient** and give value for money — for the **business** and for the **consumer**.

5) **Testing** — Just before launch, the product may be tested. A small batch of **pilot products** are made, and market research investigates **customer reactions** to them. If the public like it, the **production line** is tooled up to make the product. All systems are go — the business **launches** the product.

Most new products Fail — it's better to fail Sooner rather than Later

New product development is **expensive**. **Limited money** often puts the brakes on development. Sometimes it turns out that the product is **too expensive** to make and wouldn't be profitable.

Products that survive long enough to reach the market can create **new problems** over time:

1) **Fixed-asset** purchases often increase, because companies need new machines, factories etc. to produce the new product.
2) **Revenue expenditure** also tends to increase — the company needs to purchase materials to make the new product, and if it needs to employ extra staff, it has to pay their wages, too. This all affects the company's **liquidity** (the amount of cash it has available to use).
3) It can be difficult for firms to create **customer confidence and loyalty**. Lots of customers will buy a new product once, but it can be hard to get them to make repeat purchases. This is especially true for firms which are still young.

In the first few months of their life, the business spends much more on new products than they bring in in revenue This tends to even out over time.

Practice Questions

Q1 There are three types of new product. What are they called?

Q2 What is the benefit for a company of having a product with a unique selling point?

Q3 What are the stages of new product development?

Exam Questions

Q1 Explain why a small company which is new to the market might prefer to launch an imitative, rather than innovative, product. (4 marks)

Q2 Sam and Bob want to open a luxury chocolate shop, and want to make sure their product is unique. Explain what is meant by a USP and give four examples of USPs they could use for their product. (5 marks)

Most new products fail — sounds like they could do with a revision guide...

Launching a product sounds easy — if you can't come up with your own idea, you can just imitate someone else or replace something that exists already. It's tougher than it looks though, which means that, of all the crazy new product ideas that people come up with every day, only a tiny proportion ever live to see the shelves...it's quite a sad story really.

Marketing Mix: Product

All products are born with no sales at all. If they're looked after, they grow into big strong products with lots of sales, then they get married and have lots of spin-offs ... er, maybe.

Products have a Life Cycle

The product life cycle shows the **sales** of a product over **time**.

It's useful for planning **marketing strategies** and changing the **marketing mix**.

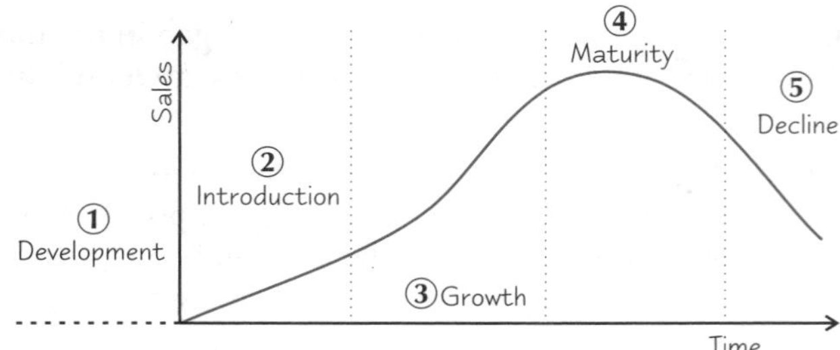

1 — Development

1) The **research and development** (R&D) department **develop** the product.
2) The **marketing** department does **market research**.
3) The **costs** are **high**, and there aren't any sales yet to cover the costs.
4) Development has a **high failure rate**. This is because there's often **not enough demand**, or because the business can't make the product **cheaply** enough to make a profit.

2 — Introduction

1) The product is **launched**, either in one market or in several markets. It's sometimes launched with **complementary** products — e.g. the PlayStation® was launched with games.
2) The business often **promotes** the product heavily to build sales — but businesses need to make sure they've got enough **resources** and **capacity** to **meet the demand** that promotions create.
3) The **initial price** of the product may be **high** to cover **promotional costs**. This is called **skimming** (see p.67).
4) Alternatively, the price can start off **low** to encourage sales. This is **penetration pricing** (see p.67).
5) Sales go up, but the sales revenue has to pay for the high **fixed cost** of development **before** the product can make a **profit**. The business usually ditches products with disappointing sales after this stage.
6) There aren't many **outlets** for the new product.
7) Competition may be **limited** (if it's an **innovative** product).

3 — Growth

1) Sales grow fast. There are **new customers** and **repeat** customers.
2) **Economies of scale** mean the price of manufacturing a unit goes down the more you make, so **profits rise**.
3) **Competitors** may be attracted to the market. Promotion shows **differences** from the competitors' products.
4) The product is often **improved** or **developed**.
5) Rising sales encourage **more outlets** to stock the product.

4 — Maturity

1) **Sales** reach a **peak** and profitability increases because **fixed costs** of **development** have been **paid for**.
2) At **saturation** (when the market is full and has reached maximum growth) sales may begin to drop, depending on the product. Sales are more likely to drop for long-lasting products that customers do not need to replace regularly. The price is often reduced to stimulate **demand**, which reduces profits.
3) There aren't many new customers. **Competition** within the industry becomes fierce — again sales might **suffer**.

5 — Decline

1) The product doesn't **appeal** to customers any more. **Sales fall** rapidly and profits decrease.
2) On the other hand, the product may just stay profitable if **promotional costs** are **low** enough.
3) If sales carry on falling, the product is **withdrawn** or **sold** to another business (selling a product to another company is called **divestment**).

Marketing Mix: Product

Extension Strategies keep a product Going Strong for Longer

Extension strategies try to prolong the life of the product by changing the **marketing mix**. They include:

1) **Product development** — businesses **improve**, reformulate or **redesign** a product. They can change the design of **packaging** to make it look more up to date, or make **special editions** of the product. This can also give a **new focus** to existing **marketing** campaigns.
2) **Market development** — businesses can find **new markets** or **new uses** for existing products, for example by aiming a product at a new market **segment** (e.g. selling baby oil and baby powder for adult use).
3) A business can change the way the product's **distributed** — by selling through the **internet**, selling through **supermarkets** or convenience stores, etc.
4) A business can change the way the product's **priced**.
5) A business can change the way they **promote** the product — by running a new **ad campaign**, for example.

Decline isn't inevitable — it's usually caused by products becoming obsolete, changing consumer tastes or poor marketing. Quality products with excellent original design (e.g. Cadbury's Dairy Milk) can carry on selling for **decades**.

Cash Flow Depends on the Product Life Cycle stage

Cash flow is the difference between **money coming in** and **money going out**. Money comes in from **outside investment** (especially at the start of the life cycle) and from **sales** (mostly later on). Money goes out as **fixed** and **variable costs**. If more money comes in than goes out, cash flow is **positive**. If more goes out than comes in, cash flow is **negative**.

1) At the **development** stage, cash flow is likely to be **negative**. Money is being spent on research and development and there aren't any sales to cover costs.
2) At **introduction**, cash flow is still **negative**. The product is likely to have **cost more** than it makes in sales.
3) As the product goes into the **growth** phase, **cash flow perks up**. Promotion costs should go down, and at the same time sales should be increasing.
4) When the product is in the **maturity** phase, cash flow is **positive**. Sales are **high** and unit **costs** are **low**.
5) In the **decline** phase, sales fall and this might lead to cash flow becoming **negative** again.

The Product Life Cycle stage affects Capacity Utilisation

1) **Capacity** is the **maximum amount** of a product that a business can produce at a particular point in time.
2) **Capacity utilisation** is **how much** of the capacity a business is using.
3) Before a business launches a product, it has to work out how many it'll need to make to fulfil **demand** at the **peak** of the life cycle. It should have those **production resources** in place at the **beginning** of the product life cycle — it's less upheaval than installing new production line machinery every few weeks to keep up with demand.
4) **Capacity utilisation** at **introduction** is **low**.

See p.46-47 for more on capacity utilisation.

Practice Questions

Q1 What are the stages of the product life cycle?

Q2 What are extension strategies?

Q3 What happens to cash flow during the growth stage of a product's life cycle?

Q4 Why does profitability increase in the maturity phase of the product life cycle?

Exam Questions

Q1 Describe what happens to cash flow during a product's life cycle. (5 marks)

Q2 To what extent are declining sales inevitable for products? (10 marks)

No product can live for ever — except maybe the wheel...

There's a lot to learn on these pages, I'll give you that. If you take it step by step, it's fairly straightforward though — it really just goes through the different stages in the life cycle of a product. And if you know the product life cycle inside out, it won't be so hard to learn the other bits mentioned here about extension strategies, cash flows and capacity utilisation.

Marketing Mix: Promotion

Promotion — basically it means using advertising, branding, sales promotion and PR to sell more products.

Promotion is part of the **Marketing Mix**

1) Promotion is designed either to **inform** customers about a product or service, or to **persuade** them to buy it.
2) **Promotional objectives** include increasing **sales** and **profits**, and increasing **awareness** of the product.
3) All promotion has to get the customer's **attention** so that they can be informed or persuaded about the product.

Many companies choose to **Advertise** through the **Media**

1) Advertising is **non-personal communication** from a business to the public.
2) Ads are used to **promote goods and services** — and also to promote a firm's **public image**.
3) Advertising uses various **media** including print, film, TV, radio, billboards (also called hoardings) and the internet. There are adverts on buses, on bus stops, on the pavement — almost **everywhere**.
4) The choice of media depends partly on the **number of target customers** and the number of **readers** or **viewers** who'll **see** the ad. Ideally, a business wants its adverts to be seen by as **much** of the target market as possible.
5) Advertising **costs** a business **money**. The cost of an advertising campaign must be **worth it** in terms of the **extra sales** it creates. TV adverts at prime viewing times are very expensive. Ads shown when fewer people are watching are cheaper, but have less impact, as they don't reach as many people.
6) The **impact** of an ad is very important. Just as the impact of a TV ad varies depending on what time it is shown, the impacts of ads in other types of media vary too. An advert that covers a two-page spread in a magazine has much more impact that a single page, or a small ad stuck in the classified section at the back.
7) **Specialist media** are used to advertise specialist products to **niche markets**. For example, a manufacturer of fish hooks would do better to advertise in a monthly fishing magazine than in the Daily Telegraph newspaper.
8) **Mass media** are mainly used to advertise **mass market consumer** products and services. However, **business** equipment like computer systems and stationery are advertised on **TV** these days, so it's not right to say that mass media advertising is **only** for consumer products.
9) There are **legal constraints** on advertising some products. E.g. companies are not allowed to suggest that alcohol can make people socially or sexually successful. Cigarette advertising is banned altogether.
10) The **Advertising Standards Agency (ASA)** regulates advertising in the UK. It makes sure that advertisements **do not mislead**, do not cause **serious or widespread offence** or **harm**, are **socially responsible** and have regard for **fair competition**.

The TV remote — scourge of TV advertisers everywhere. People are changing channel when the ads come on, the FIENDS...

Advertising changes during a **Product Life Cycle**

See p.62-63 for more on product life cycles.

1) Products are often heavily advertised at **launch**. If a product is completely **new** to the market, the adverts are **informative**. They tell customers about the product.
2) During the **growth** phase, advertising **differentiates** between brands. It persuades consumers that the product is different from and better than the competitor products. The objective of advertising in the growth phase is to **maintain** or **increase market share**.
3) When a product is at the **mature**, **saturation** phase, consumers need to be **reminded** of it. If the manufacturer has an **extension** strategy, they can use advertising to inform consumers about, say, any **improvements** they've made to their product.

Branding is a key aspect of **Product Image**

Branding can be very useful when it comes to advertising — not only does it give a product an identity, but it differentiates it from the competition.

1) **Homogenous** (generic) products are the same no matter which business sells them. Brands are **unique**.
2) Brands are important because customers pay a **premium price** for them, and customers are **loyal** to them. Brands have a specific **brand image** — a good brand has a lot of **intangible benefits** for the customer.
3) Brands can be **individual** products — like Sprite® or Daz or KitKat®. They can also be "family brands" which cover a **range** of products, like Heinz or NIKE.
4) Packaging is important because it helps to **distinguish** the product, e.g. the Coca-Cola® bottle. Packaging also helps to give a good **image** of a product. Packaging isn't important for all products though, e.g. those in industrial markets. A box of **fancy chocolates** needs attractive packaging, but a bulk order of **printer toner** doesn't.

Marketing Mix: Promotion

Not All promotion involves *Advertising*

1) Manufacturers often offer **sales promotions**. These are things like **special offers**, e.g. "buy one get one free" (**BOGOF)**, competitions, free gifts, **sponsorship** and **trade-ins**. Sales promotions can be aimed straight at the **customer** to **raise awareness** or **increase sales** of a product. Manufacturers also aim sales promotions at the **retailer** to encourage them to **stock** more of their products.
2) **Merchandising** means ensuring that retailers are displaying a company's products as effectively as possible. Some merchandisers offer retailers **point of sale displays** (e.g. special colourful racks with the company logo).
3) **Direct mail** means **mailshots** sent out to customers. The customer usually hasn't **asked** to receive them. Businesses that keep information about their customers on a database can **target** their direct mail to particular consumer groups. Direct mail that is untargeted ("**junk mail**") can sometimes be a **waste of money**, because it often just gets thrown away.
4) **Personal selling** or **direct selling** is personal communication between a **salesperson** and a customer. Personal selling can involve sales assistants in shops as well as travelling salespeople and phone salespeople.
5) **Event sponsorship** makes consumers aware of a firm and its product. It also gives the firm a good image.
6) **Direct Response TV Marketing** encourages consumers to contact the advertiser directly to purchase a product they have seen advertised on television. **Shopping channels** are an example of this kind of promotion.

PR gets Businesses or Products *Good Publicity* in the *Media*

Public relations (PR) is a key form of promotion. Many companies have **specialist PR departments**.

1) PR involves **liaising** with the **media**, writing **press releases**, and answering **enquiries** from the press.
2) PR departments write **brochures**, **newsletters** and **leaflets** giving information about the company.
3) Public relations deals with things like **product launches**, **conferences** and other **special events**.

The *Promotional Mix* reflects *Product*, *Budget* and *Competitor Activity*

1) Businesses use a **mixture** of methods to promote products. The combination of promotional techniques that a business uses to promote a product is called the **promotional mix**. The main elements in the mix are often **personal selling** and **advertising**. Other methods have a supporting role.
2) The promotional mix depends on: the **product** itself, the **market**, **competitor activity**, the **product life cycle** (see p.62-63) and the **budget** available.
3) In general, **inexpensive**, **simple** products purchased by the **consumer** are promoted by **advertising**.
4) **Expensive** and **complex** products are more likely to be promoted by **personal selling**. So are products or services sold in the **industrial market**.
5) **Consumer durables**, for example **cars** or **washing machines**, are often sold by a combination of **advertising** and **personal selling**. TV, print and billboard adverts **attract the buyer** into the showroom, where the salesperson moves in for the kill.
6) Manufacturers use different methods to sell their product to a **retailer** than to sell it to the **final customer**. Businesses often use **salespeople** to get **shops** to stock their product, and **advertising** to persuade **customers** to buy the product in the shops.

Practice Questions

Q1 What two things is promotion designed to do?

Q2 In which phase of the product life cycle does advertising stress differences with competitor products?

Q3 What is meant by "PR"?

Exam Questions

Q1 Discuss how a business might change its advertising according to a product's position in its life cycle. (4 marks)

Q2 Analyse how a manufacturer of breakfast cereal could promote its product, if it did not want to advertise. (10 marks)

We want people to buy our product — that's why we tell them to BOGOF...

When it comes to promotion, it's all in the mix. You'll need to suggest which combination of methods would best suit a firm, and why. It's important to consider budget too — most companies can't afford to have David Beckham in their ads.

Marketing Mix: Price

The basics rules of pricing are obvious — a firm needs to price its product so that it covers its costs but is still affordable for the consumer. Products often change price at different stages in their life cycle.

Pricing **Strategy** is a **Long-term** plan — **Tactics** only work in the **Short-term**

1) Pricing **strategies** are the way in which a company plans to price a product for the **medium** to **long-term** future.
2) Price **skimming** and **penetration** pricing are both pricing **strategies**.
3) Price **tactics** are **short-term** measures which are introduced in response to particular **issues** or **problems**.
4) **Loss leaders** and **psychological pricing** are two types of **tactics** companies often use.

Price Discrimination means charging **Different Customers Different Prices**

When a company sells its product at different prices to different groups of consumers, this is called **price discrimination**.

1) Price discrimination often occurs when consumers are **buying a service in advance**. Hotel rooms, air travel and rail tickets are all examples of this. Prices change as the **departure date gets nearer**. They can also change according to the **day** or **time** that a customer wants to travel.

Cheap theatre tickets — one reason why it's great to be old.

2) Other companies might vary prices according to the **age** or **social status** of their customers. **Theatres, cinemas** and **theme parks** sell tickets at different rates to **OAPs, students, under-16s** and **families.**

3) The advantage of price discrimination is that it allows companies to **respond quickly to changes in demand**. If demand is high at a particular time, prices rise, and if demand is low, prices go down. It also allows firms to offset some of the costs of having **excess capacity**.

4) Companies need to make sure it's possible to **separate out the different markets** before using price discrimination. Building merchants, e.g. Ridgeons, sell to businesses at lower prices, so they need to be able to tell the difference between their trade and private customers. Otherwise they might sell to private customers at trade prices by mistake.

Existing Products can be either **Price Leaders** or **Takers**

Strategies for existing products:

1) A **price leader** is an existing brand that's in such a **powerful position** within the market that it sets the price, and other businesses follow. Rival businesses know that consumers see the price leader as **the** brand of tea bags or baked beans, so they'll have to price their own rival product a tiny bit lower or nobody will buy it.
2) **Competition** reduces prices. In very competitive markets, **buyers dictate the price**, and sellers have to **take whatever price** the buyer is willing to pay — this is called **price taking.** E.g. milk producers selling to supermarkets are **price takers.**
3) **Predatory pricing** is when a business **deliberately lowers prices** to force another business **out of the market** — e.g. a large nationwide company might target a successful but small local competitor by lowering their prices in that area until the small competitor **goes out of business**. Prices can stay high in all other areas, so the business will lose little money overall, and once the competitor has gone they will **raise** their prices again.
4) **Competitive pricing** is when companies **monitor** their **competitors' prices** to make sure that their own prices are set at an equal or lower level. **Supermarkets** and **department stores** often use this method. Some stores will **refund the difference** in price if you are able to find a product cheaper somewhere else.

Marketing Mix: Price

Psychological Pricing and Loss Leaders help to attract More Customers

Businesses use certain **tactics** to ensure they make profitable sales. For example:

1) **Psychological pricing** bases the price on customers' **expectations** about what to pay. For instance, a high price may make people think the product is high quality, and £99.99 seems better than £100 even though it's only 1p difference.
2) **Loss leaders** are products sold at or below cost price. These products may well **lose money**, but the idea is that they'll make a profit for the business indirectly anyway, e.g. by enticing customers into the shop where they'll probably buy full-priced items too. The loss leaders can be widely advertised to encourage this. This tactic can work well in **supermarkets**, where customers will usually buy lots of other items as well as the loss leader.

Companies use Promotional Pricing Strategies when launching New Products

1) **New and innovative products** are often sold at **high prices** when they first reach the market. This is known as **skimming**, or **creaming**. Consumers will pay more because the product has **scarcity value**, and the high price boosts the **product's image** and increases its appeal. New **technological products**, such as computers, tend to be priced using this method. Prices are then dropped quite considerably when the product has been on the market for a year or so.
2) **Skimming** is a good strategy to use if a company can **protect its product** to make sure competitors don't launch an imitative product at a lower price. They might use **patents** or **trademarks** to stop other people copying their idea.
3) **Penetration pricing** is the opposite of skimming. It means launching a product at a **low price** in order to **attract customers** and gain **market share**. It is especially effective in markets which are **price-sensitive**.
4) **Penetration pricing** works best for companies that can benefit from **economies of scale** (e.g. lower costs) when manufacturing large quantities of a product.

Several Factors affect Demand for a product

1) The **price of the product** affects demand. As the price goes up, demand tends to go down. As the price goes down, demand goes up.
2) The **price of similar products** affects demand. When one manufacturer increases its prices, demand for **cheaper competitor products** tends to **rise**.
3) **Customer income** affects demand. When people have **more money to spend**, there's more demand.
4) **Seasonality** affects demand. E.g. the demand for soft drinks is greater in the **summer**.
5) Successful **marketing** stimulates demand.

No one was sure which was falling faster — Jim, or demand for tiny swimming trunks.

Practice Questions

Q1 What is meant by "pricing strategy"?

Q2 What is the difference between a price leader and a price taker?

Q3 What kind of products tend to be sold using the skimming method?

Q4 Give three examples of factors other than price which affect demand.

Exam Questions

Q1 Analyse why a hotel might benefit from pricing its rooms according to a strategy of price discrimination. (6 marks)

Q2 A small company is launching a new brand of fruit juice. Suggest which pricing methods it should consider, and explain why. (6 marks)

Skimming and creaming — both ways of milking profits...

When it comes to pricing, most companies use a cost-based method and throw in the occasional bit of promotional pricing to keep consumers interested. The key point to remember is that price isn't the only thing that bothers customers — a lot of people would rather buy high quality chicken nuggets than cheap ones made of scrawny bits of chicken neck.

Marketing Mix: Price

OK, so price isn't the only thing that affects demand, but it can certainly have a pretty major impact. Just how big or small that impact is depends on the price elasticity of demand.

Price Elasticity of Demand shows how Demand changes with Price

1) **Price elastic** products have a **large percentage change in demand** for a **small percentage change in price**.
2) **Price inelastic** products are the opposite — there's a **small percentage change in demand** for a **big percentage change in price**.

They won't ask you to do this calculation in the exam. They'll give you the elasticity coefficient and you'll just need to use it to say how price change affects revenue.

Price elasticity of demand = $\frac{\text{\% change in quantity demanded}}{\text{\% change in price}}$

Example: A price **rise** of **10%** results in a **30% reduction** in demand.

Price elasticity of demand = $\frac{-30\%}{+10\%} = -3$ Price **elastic**, because the price elasticity of demand is **more than 1** (ignoring the minus sign).

Basically, as price goes up demand falls, and vice versa.

Example: A price **reduction** of **20%** results in a **5% increase** in demand.

Price elasticity of demand = $\frac{+5\%}{-20\%} = -0.25$ Price **inelastic**, because the price elasticity of demand is **less than 1**.

This is called the elasticity coefficient.

3) Price elasticity of demand is **always negative**, so ignore the minus sign. This is because a positive change in price causes a negative change in demand, and a negative change in price causes a positive change in demand.
4) If the price elasticity of demand is **greater than 1** (ignoring the minus sign), the product is **price elastic**. If the price elasticity of demand is **less than 1**, it's **price inelastic**. So, –3 is price elastic and –0.25 is price inelastic.

Price Elasticity affects Revenue and Profit

1) **Sales revenue** = **price** of product × **quantity sold**. Price elasticity shows how price affects sales revenue.
2) If demand is **price elastic**, a **price increase** will make **sales revenue go down**. The **% decrease in sales** will be **more** than the **% increase in price**.
3) If demand is price **inelastic**, a rise in **price** will make **sales revenue go up**. The % decrease in sales isn't big enough to offset the % increase in price.
4) If demand is **price elastic**, a firm can **increase revenue** by reducing price, which then greatly increases the number of sales. **But profit = revenue – cost**, and more sales often mean **higher costs**. The **profits** will only increase if the **rise in revenue** is **more** than the **rise** in **costs**.
5) If demand is **price inelastic**, **decreasing** the **price** will make **sales increase** slightly. Sales **revenue goes down** because the price has fallen and only a few more units have been sold.

Price change	PED more than 1 (elastic)	PED equal to 1	PED less than 1 (inelastic)
Increase in price	Sales revenue decreases	Sales revenue doesn't change	Sales revenue increases
Decrease in price	Sales revenue increases	Sales revenue doesn't change	Sales revenue decreases

This table shows how price changes affect sales revenue.

Example: A company makes scarves and sells them for £11. Annual sales are 9600 scarves. The product's elasticity coefficient is –2.5. If they increase the price to £12.10, calculate the change in revenue.

Current revenue: £11 x 9600 = £105 600

% change in quantity demanded: 10% change in price x 2.5 elasticity coefficient = 25% decrease

25% of 9600: 9600 x 0.25 = 2400 **New sales**: 9600 – 2400 = 7200 **New revenue** = 7200 x £12.10 = £87 120

Change in revenue: £105 600 – £87 120 = £18 480 decrease in revenue

It can be Hard to Work Out price elasticity of demand

1) Estimating price elasticity of demand is **difficult** because price isn't the **only** factor affecting demand. An increase in demand for ice cream could be partly down to **hot weather** and/or a good **advertising** campaign.
2) Businesses use **primary market research** (see p.12) to ask people if they'd buy a product for a **higher** or **lower price**. This can give a good idea of the relationship between **price** and **demand**.
3) However, the values used in price elasticity calculations may be wrong. The calculations are often based on **estimates** of percentage change in price and demand, or on **unrepresentative** data. The market may have **changed** since the data was collected and the market research itself may be unreliable or inaccurate.

Marketing Mix: Price

Price elasticity of demand **Depends** *on* **Ease** *of* **Switching Brands**

1) If a consumer can **easily switch** to a **competitor** product, the demand will be **price elastic**. This will result in customers jumping ship and buying the **competitor's product** instead.
2) Businesses try to **differentiate** their products to create **brand loyalty**. **Loyal** customers won't switch even if the price goes up, so this makes the demand **less** price elastic.
3) It's easier for customers to switch if they can **compare prices** and find cheaper alternatives. The **internet** makes it easier to switch and **increases price elasticity**.
4) People tend not to switch to alternatives in the **short term**. They **take time** to get **fed up** with a product.
5) **Product types** tend to be **price inelastic**, but individual **brands** tend to be **price elastic**. For example, **petrol** sales are **inelastic** because all cars need fuel. The sales of an **individual company's petrol** are **elastic** because motorists can easily go to a **cheaper filling station**.

Income Elasticity *of* **Demand** *shows how* **Demand** *changes with* **Income**

When people earn **more money**, there's **more demand** for some products.
Funnily enough, there's **less demand** for other products.

$$\text{Income elasticity of demand} = \frac{\text{\% change in quantity demanded}}{\text{\% change in real incomes}}$$

Example: A **rise** in income of **10%** results in a **5% increase** in demand.

$$\text{Income elasticity of demand} = \frac{+5\%}{+10\%} = +0.5$$

Change in <u>real income</u> means change in income, taking into account how prices have changed (usually increased) over the same period.

1) **Normal goods** have a **positive income elasticity of demand** that's **less than 1**. This means that as **income rises**, the **demand** for normal goods **rises** — but at a **slower rate** than the increase in income.
2) **Luxury goods** have a **positive income elasticity of demand** which is **more than 1**. This means that the **demand for luxury goods** grows **faster** than the increase in income.
3) In a business sense, "**inferior**" goods are cheaper 'value' products — taking a **coach** instead of the **train**, for example, or eating a **cheaper supermarket value brand** of baked beans because you can't afford **Heinz baked beans**. Inferior goods have a **negative income elasticity of demand** — **demand falls** when **income rises** and **demand rises** when **income falls**.

Elasticity *helps a business make* **Choices**

1) **Price elasticity** helps a manufacturer **decide** whether to **raise** or **lower** the price of a product. They can see what might happen to the sales, and ultimately what will happen to sales revenue.
2) **Income elasticity** helps a manufacturer see what'll happen to sales if the **economy** grows or shrinks.

Practice Questions

Q1 If a product has an elasticity coefficient of –0.9, is it elastic or inelastic?

Q2 Give two reasons why it can be difficult to calculate price elasticity.

Q3 What kind of products become less popular when there's an increase in income?

Answer on p. 82.

Exam Questions

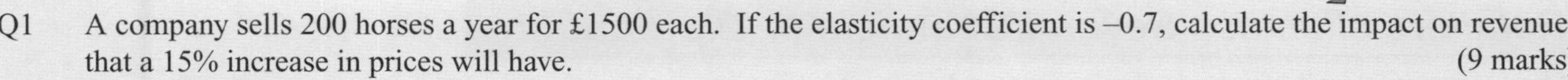

Q1 A company sells 200 horses a year for £1500 each. If the elasticity coefficient is –0.7, calculate the impact on revenue that a 15% increase in prices will have. (9 marks)

Q2 Explain why product differentiation reduces elasticity of demand. (3 marks)

Rubber prices are usually the most elastic...

The clues are in the names with these two — price elasticity shows how much price influences demand, and income elasticity shows how much demand is affected by income. The method for working out changes in revenue using the elasticity coefficient has quite a few steps, so make sure you get your head round each and every one of them...

Marketing Mix: Place

Distribution is important. This is the "place" part of the marketing mix. If a product can't get to the marketplace, no one can buy it. Needs go unfulfilled, companies don't make profits, anarchy reigns...

*It's **Vital** to get the **Product** to the **Consumer***

A **channel** of **distribution** is the route a product takes from the producer to the consumer. A product usually passes through **intermediaries** on the way from producer to consumer — e.g. **retailers**, **wholesalers** and **agents**.

1) **Retailers** are **shops** who sell to consumers. They're usually the **final stage** in the distribution channel. Tesco, Argos and Amazon.co.uk® are **retailers**. Retailers can be physical shops or online "e-tailers".
2) **Wholesalers** buy products cheaply in **bulk** and **sell them on** to **retailers**. Wholesalers make life **easier** for retailers and manufacturers:
    - Wholesalers **buy** goods from manufacturers in bulk and **sell** them in **smaller quantities** to **retailers**. This is called "**breaking bulk**" — a wholesaler takes the goods off the manufacturer's hands and **pays** for the whole lot. Manufacturers don't have to **wait** for customers to buy the goods before they see any cash.
    - Wholesalers make distribution **simpler**. Without a wholesaler, the manufacturer would have to make **separate deliveries** to lots of retailers, and send each and every retailer an **invoice**. Selling to one wholesaler cuts down the paperwork and the number of journeys.
    - Wholesalers can **store more goods** than a retailer can — they act as the retailer's storage cupboard.
3) **Agents** act on behalf of **manufacturers**. See below for more about the role of an agent.

*There are **Different Channels** of **Distribution***

Channels of distribution have different levels. It's more expensive, but sometimes necessary, to have a **multi-layered** channel.

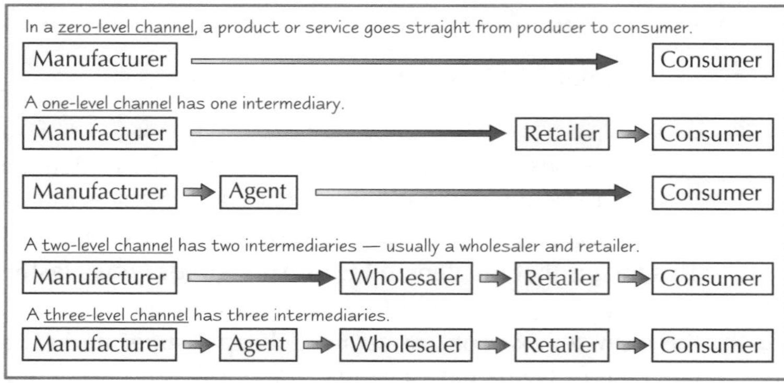
In a zero-level channel, a product or service goes straight from producer to consumer.
Manufacturer
Consumer
A one-level channel has one intermediary.
Manufacturer
Retailer
Consumer
Manufacturer
Agent
Consumer
A two-level channel has two intermediaries — usually a wholesaler and retailer.
Manufacturer
Wholesaler
Retailer
Consumer
A three-level channel has three intermediaries.
Manufacturer
Agent
Wholesaler
Retailer
Consumer

Direct Selling: Manufacturer → Consumer

Accountants, electricians and hairdressers sell their **services** direct to the consumer. The **internet** has made it **easier** for producers of goods to sell **direct** to the consumer. Direct selling is now very popular, and is done through door-to-door sales, TV shopping channels, telephone sales and mail-order catalogues.

Indirect Selling: Manufacturer → Retailer → Consumer

Large supermarkets buy goods in bulk direct from the manufacturer and have them delivered either straight from the manufacturer or via their own warehouses.

Indirect Selling: Manufacturer → Wholesaler → Retailer → Consumer

This is the **traditional** distribution channel used for **fast moving consumer goods** (known as FMCG).

Direct Selling through an agent: Manufacturer → Agent → Consumer

An agent is like a sales representative, except they are not employed by the company whose goods they sell. They get commission (a percentage of the value of the goods they sell) instead of being paid a salary. Ann Summers lingerie is sold by **agents** through **party plans** — people invite friends to their **home** and an **agent** sells the goods **at the party**. Some **mail-order catalogues** (e.g. Avon) use agents who place orders on behalf of other people and collect payments from them.

Retailers** often use **Several Channels** of **Distribution

Many firms now sell goods via the internet. Having an online store can affect the way a company distributes goods.

1) Stores which **only** sell **online** may have **cheaper costs**, because they use a **single** channel of distribution. However they can have **problems** establishing **brand loyalty**.
2) Companies such as supermarkets and fashion retailers which have high street stores as well as an internet store are using a **multi-channel strategy**. This may lead to added costs if they are supplying goods from different warehouses, but it also allows them to target a wider market.
3) For small firms, a low-cost option is to sell goods using **auction sites** or **electronic marketplaces** (e.g. eBay™).

Over a third of the UK population now uses the Internet for shopping.

Marketing Mix: Place

Businesses choose a **Channel** of **Distribution** to **Suit Their Needs**

The choice of distribution channel is a compromise between cost, ease and control.

1) It's **more profitable** to **sell direct** to the customer. Each intermediary (party) in the distribution chain takes a **slice of profit** from the manufacturer — wholesalers and retailers have to make money too. Businesses that **sell direct** can offer their product at a **lower price** than **retailers** at the end of a long distribution chain.
2) On the other hand, it's **easier** to use **intermediaries**. It'd be a hassle to distribute a small amount of product to lots of little shops. It's easier to sell to a **wholesaler** who can deliver products from several manufacturers in a single delivery. Using a wholesaler gives a manufacturer the chance of more **market coverage**.
3) The **fewer intermediaries** in the distribution chain, the more **control** a manufacturer has over how its products are sold. It has more say in the **final selling price** and how the product is **promoted**.
4) UK **retail trends** have **changed** in recent years, as retailers have found **cheaper** or **more effective** ways of distributing their products. **Out-of-town retail parks**, **concessions** (shops within shops), and **mail-order catalogues** have **cheaper overheads** than high street stores and can sometimes offer customers other **benefits**, such as **free parking**. **Factory outlets** allow firms to make a return on **imperfect goods** (seconds) or **last season's stock**.

There are no real hard and fast rules about which distribution channel a business might choose, but there are a few trends.

Short Distribution Channels	Long Distribution Channels
Industrial products	Consumer products
Few customers	Many customers
Customers concentrated in one place	Customers widely spread out
Expensive, complex goods	Inexpensive, simple goods
Infrequent sales	Frequent sales
Bulky products	Small products
Bespoke (made to measure) products	Standard products
Services	Goods

Businesses set **distribution targets**. They might set a target of £X worth of sales through supermarkets, or selling to more retail outlets in a particular area of the country. Businesses can use a number of **different strategies** to **achieve** their distribution targets, e.g. offering discounts to particular retailers, or using advertising in trade magazines.

Different Distribution Strategies suit different products

1) **Everyday groceries** and **convenience** items need to be distributed as **widely** as possible. Consumers want to be able to buy things like a newspaper, a pint of milk and a bar of chocolate at a convenient local shop. They don't want to travel 20 miles to a "Pints Of Milk R Us" superstore.
2) **Luxury** goods don't need to be widely distributed. Manufacturers of luxury goods like to sell them in a small number of **exclusive** shops — it's about **quality**, not quantity.
3) Specialist goods like electrical products need to be distributed to **specialist** shops. Consumers like to be able to **compare** several different kinds of computer or CD player before buying, and often need specialist advice and assistance when choosing what to buy.

Practice Questions

Q1 What is the role of a wholesaler?

Q2 Name two types of distribution channel.

Q3 What kind of distribution channel is traditionally used for FMCG?

Q4 What kind of distribution strategy is needed for everyday groceries?

Exam Questions

Q1 Analyse the different factors a firm must consider when deciding on an appropriate channel of distribution. (8 marks)

Q2 Evaluate internet sales as a distribution channel for luxury consumer goods. (7 marks)

I'm a new product — get me out of here...

Distribution can seem like a mundane, boring thing. Yes, it is all about warehouses full of cardboard boxes, fleets of trucks going from A to B and little men popping catalogues through your letterbox. But on the other hand it's a vital part of the wondrous marketing mix. Where you can buy something is a big factor in deciding whether to buy it.

Improving Competitiveness

Competition is good for the consumer, but not so great for businesses. Companies are always trying to improve their competitiveness and steal market share from their competitors — usually by changing their marketing mix.

Competition is Beneficial to the Consumer

Most businesses operate in a **competitive market**. A competitive market is one where there are lots of companies selling products which are roughly the same. As far as the customer is concerned, competition is good news:

1) It forces **prices down**.
2) It tends to **improve** customer **services**.
3) It **improves** the **quality** of goods on offer.

The amount of Competition depends on the Market Conditions

Not all markets are structured in the same way. Some markets have **loads of firms** competing for the same group of consumers, while other markets are made up of just a **few companies**:

1) A **monopoly** is a **market** which has only **one organisation** providing a product or service.

2) The **government** can **intervene** to **stop** companies ending up with a high degree of **monopoly** (i.e. massive market share). This is because a company with a monopoly might **exploit** its **customers** by charging high prices, or **use resources inefficiently**.

3) Nonetheless, **some companies** in the UK do have a **high degree of monopoly**. These include train companies (because there is often only one company operating on each route) and utility companies. The government uses **regulators** to make sure that these companies don't act unfairly.

The Board Game Professors — they've all got high degrees in Monopoly.

4) When there are a few **dominant businesses** in a market, this is called an **oligopoly**. E.g. 4 major supermarket chains dominate the UK groceries market.

5) Other markets consist of **many businesses**, all of whom **know** what **price** the market is charging for a particular product, but are **too small** to **influence** it. This is **perfect competition**. Businesses in this kind of market survive by offering personal and specialist services and attempting to create **niche markets** (see p.8).

The Market Conditions affect the Marketing Mix

1) **Monopolies** have it easy when it comes to the marketing mix — they get to **decide** what **price** they want to charge for their product (within reason) and **don't** really have to worry too much about **marketing**.
2) **Oligopolies** can seem very competitive, as firms operating in this type of market **spend a lot** on their **marketing mix**. However, if one firm cuts prices, all the others usually will too, which means they tend to **compete** on things other than price, such as **special offers** or **advertising**.
3) Where there's **perfect competition**, companies have to **accept** the **price** set by the market. **Marketing isn't** really **possible**, so companies have to be efficient and keep **costs low**.

It's Hard for New Companies to enter the Market

Firms which have a lot of financial and marketing power can create **barriers to entry**. These are **obstacles** which make it **hard** for **new businesses** to **establish themselves** in the market.

1) Creating **high consumer loyalty** means **customers** are **unlikely** to **switch** to a new product which has just entered the market. Businesses establish customer loyalty by **investing** heavily in **advertising** and **branding** (see p.64).
2) **High set-up costs** (such as the cost of **machinery** or **premises**) can also deter new firms from trying to enter the marketplace. This is because they would have to raise very **high** levels of **investment** in order to fund the start-up and they know that they **won't** be able to **recover** this **investment** if they're not successful and choose/are forced to leave the market. Industries with high set-up costs include aviation (airlines) and pharmaceuticals (medicines).

Improving Competitiveness

Changing the *Marketing Mix* can help to make a business *More Competitive*

Markets are **dynamic**. This means they are **constantly changing**. New competitors enter the market and failed ones leave, new improved products and services are introduced and aggressive marketing ploys are used.

1) In order to **remain profitable**, companies need to keep **reviewing** their **marketing mix**, taking into account the actions of competitors and other changes in the marketplace.
2) For a company to stay profitable, it needs to stay **competitive**. A business is competitive if it has something that **customers want** or **need** that **other** similar **businesses don't** have.
3) A company can **improve** its **competitiveness** by **changing** any one of the four elements in the **marketing mix**. They can improve the **quality** of the **product**, reassess their methods of **promotion**, use new **pricing strategies**, and reconsider channels of distribution.
4) Having a **unique product** is a key weapon in beating off the competition. Companies invest heavily in **branding** and **design** and protect their products with **patents** to keep the competitors at bay. See p.8 for more on patents.
5) **Technological advances** are another reason why companies might change the mix. Widespread **internet** access has meant that many firms have **changed** their **method of distribution**.

To find out more about USPs, see p.60.

Not all ways of *improving Competitiveness* involve *Marketing*

Changing the marketing mix is not the only way of improving competitiveness. Firms can **improve** their **profitability** by **reducing costs**, or they can improve the **quality** of their **service**.

1) Many firms attempt to increase competitiveness by **reducing** their **fixed costs** (see p.26). They may choose to **rationalise** their staffing (see p.47), as staff costs are often their biggest fixed cost. Other ways of reducing fixed costs include switching to **cheaper utility providers** and **cheaper** sources of **raw materials**. Some firms may also **cut back** on **research** and **development**.

Rob wondered if being naked would improve his chances in the swimming competition.

2) Businesses can also improve their competitiveness by improving the **quality** of their **customer service**. Good customer service increases **consumer loyalty** and also encourages customers to **recommend** the **business** to **other people**. Ways of improving customer service include setting **higher standards** for **recruitment** and **training** (for more on these two, see p.42-43).

Practice Questions

Q1 What is meant by a monopoly?

Q2 What is meant by "perfect competition"?

Q3 Why would high set-up costs dissuade a business from entering a market?

Q4 How can a business use non-marketing methods to improve its competitiveness?

Exam Questions

Q1 A luxury hotel in the Lake District has just discovered that a five-star spa hotel is opening just down the road. Discuss how it could make sure it maintains its current market share once the competitor opens? (8 marks)

Exterminate! Exterminate!

It's a cut-throat existence out there in the business world. Threats exist in every type of market, not just in the highly competitive ones. These challenges force businesses to keep changing and updating their services or products, which is ultimately a good thing for the consumer. It's like that saying — what doesn't kill your business can only make it stronger.

Understanding Statistics

There are loads of statistics involved in running a business, so you need to be able to understand what they all mean.

Businesses produce lots of **Statistics**

1) Businesses have a lot of **figures** — e.g. figures for sales, costs, revenues and profit, and market research data.
2) Businesses often deal with **large numbers** — e.g. profits for a small business could be thousands or tens of thousands of pounds (thousand can be written as "k", so 15k means 15 thousand pounds). Big businesses might have very large numbers for sales or revenue figures — millions (a thousand thousand, or 1 000 000) or even billions (a thousand million, or 1 000 000 000).

   Remember that negative numbers can be shown by brackets in cash flow forecasts and variance tables.

3) Businesses need to understand what their figures **mean** so that they know how well the business is **performing**, and can forecast how well it will perform in the **future**. In order to understand the data and be able to use it, they present it in a way that makes it **easy** to understand.

Diagrams make data **Easier** to **Understand**

1) **Pie charts** are used for showing **market share**. Each **1% share** is represented by a **3.6°** section of the pie (because there's 360° in a circle and 360 ÷ 100 = 3.6). Pie charts are **simple to use** and **easy** to **understand**. They can be created quickly using **spreadsheets**.

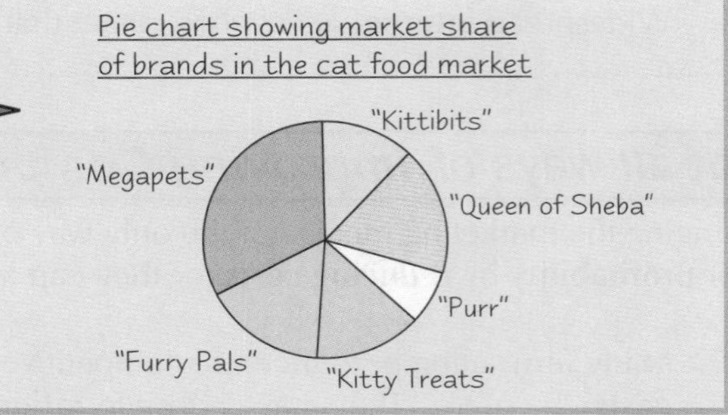

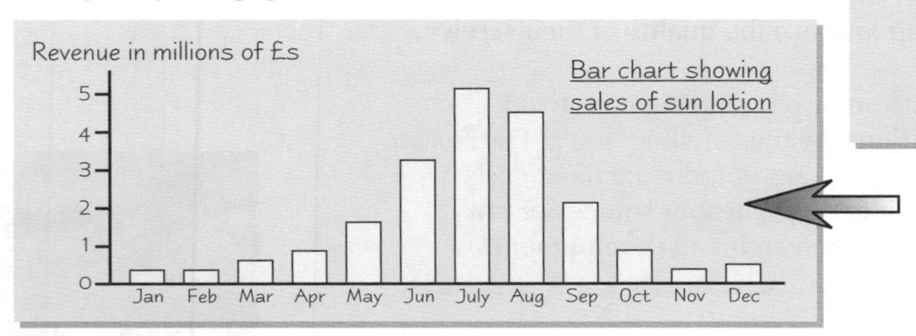

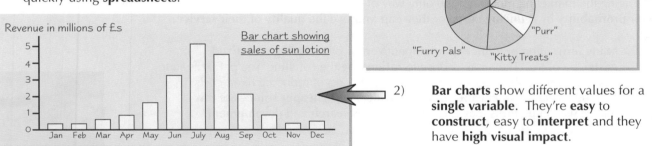

2) **Bar charts** show different values for a **single variable**. They're **easy** to **construct**, easy to **interpret** and they have **high visual impact**.
3) A **histogram** looks quite similar to a bar chart. However, in a histogram the **area** of each block is proportional to the value of the variable measured (not just the height), and there are no gaps between the blocks. So a histogram is different from a bar chart because the bars can vary in both **width** and **height**. Histograms are suitable for comparing variables with **large ranges**.
4) A **pictogram** is a bar chart or histogram where the bars are **pictures** — logos or images. Pictograms are often used in **corporate brochures** — e.g. Cadbury might use pictures of their choccie bars in their sales charts.
5) **Line graphs** plot one variable against another — e.g. sales against time. **More lines** can be added on to show **more variables** — they should be in different colours to keep the graph easy to read.

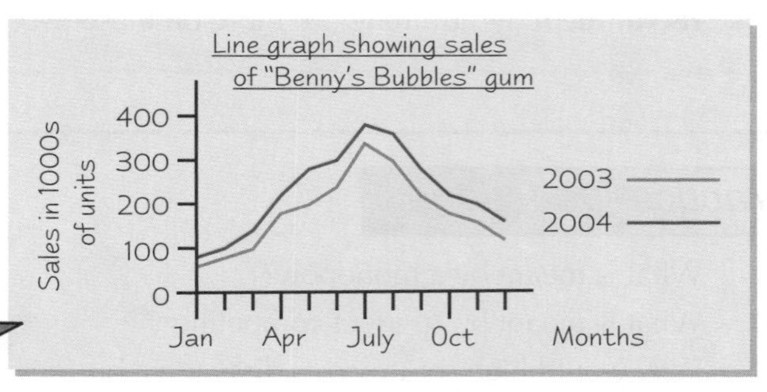

Diagrams can be **Misleading**

1) Graphs and charts can sometimes give a **false impression** of what is actually going on.
2) If the scales on a graph don't start at **zero**, it can be difficult to see what they show and the meaning can be distorted — e.g. the graph on the right seems to show that the profit has **tripled** between 2004 and 2007, but actually it has only gone up by **10%**.

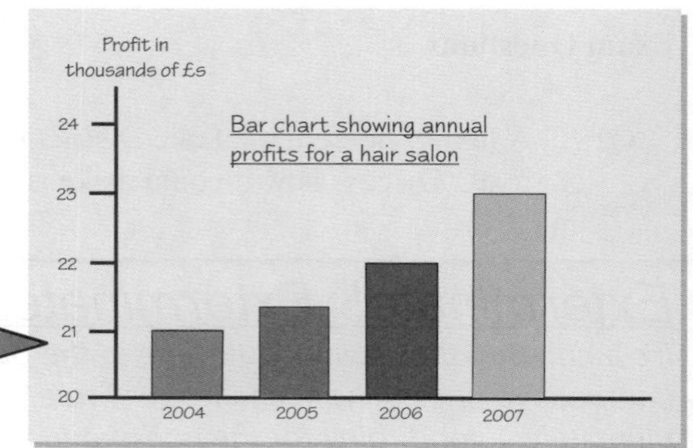

Understanding Statistics

You need to be able to Analyse Data and Graphs

1) As well as being able to read graphs and charts, you need to be able to **analyse** them.
2) This means you need to be able to say what you think is the **important bit** of the chart — e.g. an upward trend in sales, or a big market share.
3) You need to be able to say what you think is **causing** it, and what the potential **effects** might be — e.g. a **decrease** in market share might have been caused by the arrival of a new **competitor**, so the **marketing** budget will have to be **increased** to try to get the market share back.

Data is clustered around an Average — Mean, Median or Mode

1) The **mean** is found by **adding together** all numbers in a data set and **dividing** the total by the **number of values** in the data set. Shops often calculate the mean spend per customer as the starting point of a marketing campaign aimed at increasing customers' spending per shop visit.

Example: 10 customers spend £5.90, £27.98, £13.62, £24.95, £78.81, £16.99, £13.20, £9.95, £2.58 and £14.96.

Mean spend = $\frac{5.9 + 27.98 + 13.62 + 24.95 + 78.81 + 16.99 + 13.20 + 9.95 + 2.58 + 14.96}{10} = \frac{208.94}{10}$ = £20.89

2) The **median** is the **middle** value in a data set once all the values are put in **ascending order** — e.g. a business might rank all salespeople by the revenue they've generated over the past month, then identify the **median** and pay everyone above this position a bonus for good performance.

Example: 15 sales people generate revenue of £1200, £1350, £1400, £1500, £1600, £1750, £1900, £1950, £2100, £2200, £2340, £2400, £2450, £2500 and £2950.
Median sales revenue = the middle number, which is the 8th number = £1950

3) The **mode** is the **most common number** in a data set. Marks & Spencer might check the modal dress size when planning their shop displays so that the mannequins would reflect the most common body size among British women.

Example: 15 women have the following dress sizes:
10, 12, 16, 14, 12, 14, 8, 18, 16, 14, 12, 14, 10, 14, 16.
Modal dress size = 14

Obviously M&S would need a much bigger sample than this.

Extensive market research had gone into finding the perfect mannequin to represent today's average British woman.

The Range of Data is Important as well

1) **Range** means the **difference** between the **largest** and the **smallest** in a group of numbers.
2) Averages can be a bit misleading. The **mean** of a **small range** of values is likely to give a **true picture** of the data, but the **mean** of a **large** range of values would give a number somewhere in the middle of the range — this wouldn't show that some of the values were actually really big or really small.
3) A **standard deviation** shows the **spread** of a set of values around the average. You don't have to know how to work out a standard deviation. All you need to know is that a **large** standard deviation means the numbers in the original data set are **spread out**, and a **small** standard deviation means they're **clumped close together**.
4) A **confidence level** is another statistical trick. It indicates how **accurate** a conclusion is likely to be. A confidence level of 95% means managers can assume the prediction would be correct 19 times out of 20.

Understanding Statistics

Businesses work out **Percentage Changes** in figures

1) Businesses work out **percentage** increases or decreases in figures like sales volumes, revenue, profit and market share in order to see how performance is **progressing** over time. By looking at percentage changes over a number of months or years, they can see **trends** in the business' performance.
2) The **formula** for working out percentage change is:

$$\text{Percentage change} = \frac{\text{new figure} - \text{previous figure}}{\text{previous figure}} \times 100$$

E.g. if sales of umbrellas have gone up from 9 000 to 11 000, the percentage increase in sales is (11 000 – 9 000) ÷ 9 000 × 100 = 22.2%.

3) It's important not to underestimate large changes in figures even if they only produce a small percentage change — e.g. an increase in revenue of £2 million shouldn't be overlooked even if it's only a 3% increase.

Index Numbers show **Changes** in data over time

1) **Index numbers** are a simple way of showing percentage changes in a set of data over time.
2) Businesses take a set of data showing revenue/ profits etc. over a number of years, and make the earliest year the **base year** — the value for the base year is set as 100, and the figures for the following years are shown relative to this figure. E.g. the table below shows the index numbers for revenue for an Italian restaurant:

Year	Total Revenue	Revenue Index (2003 = 100)
2003	£17 000	100
2004	£19 550	115
2005	£21 250	125
2006	£22 440	132
2007	£24 650	145

To work out the revenue index for any year, take the total revenue from that year, divide it by the total revenue in the base year and multiply it by 100, e.g. for 2006:

$$\frac{22\,440}{17\,000} \times 100 = 132$$

3) The main advantage of indexing is that it makes it easy to see trends within the business.

Businesses **Forecast** what **Future** data will be

1) Businessses use data from the past to predict how the business will perform in the future — e.g. if revenue has been going up by around 5% a year for eight years, they might forecast a 5% rise for the coming year.
2) Forecast figures are only estimates though — many factors inside and outside the business might influence how it performs, so it's impossible to be certain that the forecast will be accurate.

Practice Questions

Q1 Why can graphs and charts sometimes be misleading?

Q2 Explain the difference between the "mean", "median" and "mode" of a set of data.

Q3 What do index numbers show?

Exam Questions

Q1 Discuss how statistics can hinder as well as help decision-making. (10 marks)

Q2 Explain what is meant by "confidence level." (2 marks)

There are lies, damned lies and statistics...

Statistics can be very helpful but they can also be biased. If you're given a table or graph as part of an exam question, watch out for things like how the axes are labelled, whether the axes start at zero, and whether important info is left out. Remember that businesses often use graphs and charts to put their facts and figures in as good a light as possible.

Get Marks in Your Exam

These pages are meant to get you familiar with how the exam's set out, so that when you turn up on the day, you'll know exactly what to expect from each paper.

If you know what to expect, there won't be any nasty surprises...

The AS-Level is broken down into Two Exams

1) The Business Studies AS is made up of **two exams** — Unit 1 and Unit 2.
2) Each exam tests a **different** set of **topics** that you'll have covered during the year. Make sure you revise the right set of topics for each exam.
3) The two exams don't have exactly the same **style** of **questions** — so practise answering the different types of questions that can come up.

Unit 1 is about Starting a Small Business

Unit 1's made up of two topics — **Starting a Business** and **Financial Planning**. These cover the basic requirements of starting a small business. In the financial planning section you have to do calculations, and understand what they show.

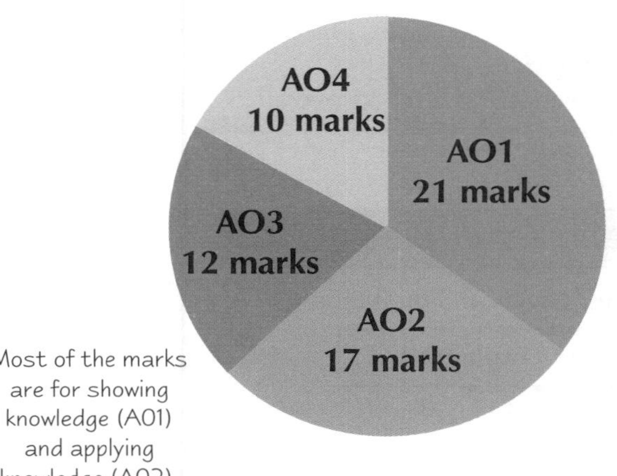

Most of the marks are for showing knowledge (AO1) and applying knowledge (AO2).

1) Unit 1 is made up of two sections — both based on an **unseen mini case study**.
2) The exam lasts for 1 hour 15 minutes and there are 60 marks available. So, allowing for reading time, you need to achieve **a mark almost every minute**. Use that as a guide as to how long to spend on each question.
3) Section 1 consists of around six short-answer questions, worth between 2 and 6 marks. You'll have to do some calculations in this section (see the box below for the ones you need to learn).
4) Section 2 is made up of fewer questions, but they need extended answers and so are worth more marks.

Calculations to learn for Unit 1

Fixed, variable and total costs	Market size, Market share and Market growth	Revenue
Break-even analysis	Contribution	Gross and net profit

Unit 2 is about Running a Business

Unit 2 has four main sections — **Finance**, **People in Business**, **Operations Management** and **Marketing and Competition**. Although its focus isn't just on small businesses, Unit 2 does have links with Unit 1, so don't forget about those topics when you're revising.

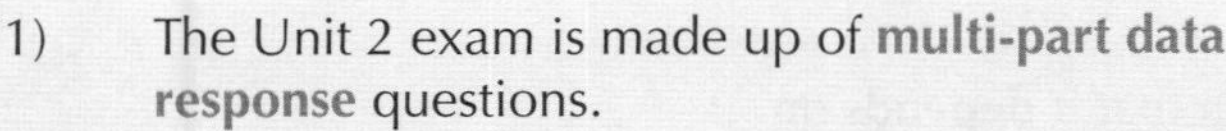

1) The Unit 2 exam is made up of **multi-part data response** questions.
2) You'll have 1 hour 30 minutes and there are 80 marks available, so again you should be aiming to achieve about a mark a minute.
3) There will usually be two sections, with each section based on a different case study. There will be a range of short-answer and extended questions in each section, so don't spend too long on one section.

On this paper half the marks are for analysis and evaluation.

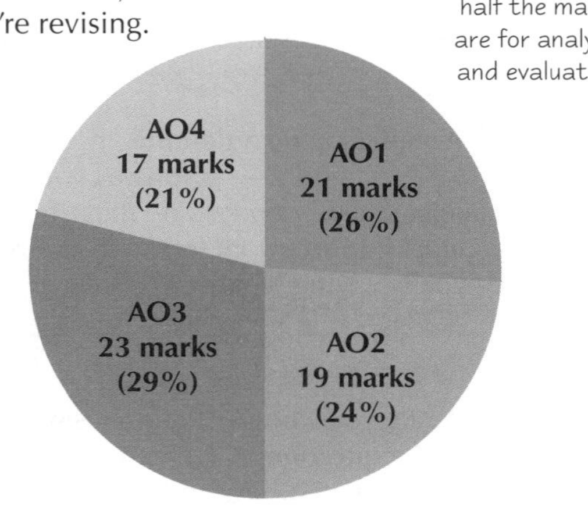

Calculations to learn for Unit 2

Variance	Unit costs	Labour productivity and Labour turnover
Return on capital	Net profit margins	Capacity utilisation

Get Marks in Your Exam

These pages explain how the exams are marked. Basically, the marks are divided up into four different skills — AO1, AO2, AO3 and AO4, and the more skill levels you hit, the more marks you get. Bit like pinball really...

You get marks for AO1 (showing knowledge) and AO2 (applying knowledge)

AO1 and AO2 questions usually start with words like "**State**" or "**List**".

1) **AO1** marks are for **content** and **knowledge**.
2) This means things like knowing the **proper definitions** for **business terms**.
3) You'll only get about 2 marks for AO1, whether the question is a short one worth 2 marks, a shortish one worth 6 marks or a long one worth 15 marks.

To make sure you'll get marks for content, always give definitions of terms you're using, or formulas if you're doing a calculation.

1) **AO2** marks are for **application** — applying your knowledge to a situation. This means thinking about the **type of business** in the **question**, the product or service it's selling, and the type of market it's in.
2) Numerical **calculations** are also marked as **application**.
3) AO2 is also worth 2-3 marks, but questions which want you to demonstrate AO2 will be expecting you to demonstrate AO1 too, so they'll be worth between 4 and 6 marks overall.

You'll get more marks when you Analyse (AO3) and Evaluate (AO4)

AO3 marks are for **analysis** — thinking about benefits, drawbacks, causes, effects and limitations.

Analysis questions usually start with words like "**Analyse**", "**Examine**" or "**Explain why**".

1) Use your knowledge to **explain** your answer and give **reasons**.
2) If there's data, say what the figures **mean**, talk about what might have **caused** them and say what **effect** you think they will have on the business in the **future**.
3) For top marks, write about **context** — compare a situation with the industry as a whole, or with a competitor.
4) Consider **both sides** of the **argument** — you can only get **limited** analysis **marks** by looking at **one side**.

AO4 marks are for **evaluation** — using your **judgement**.

Evaluation questions usually start with words like "**Evaluate**", "**Discuss**", "**Justify**" or "**To what extent**".

1) **Weigh up** both sides of the argument — consider the **advantages** and **disadvantages** and say which **side** of the argument you think is **strongest**.

2) You don't need a **definite** answer. You can point out that it **depends** on various factors — as long as you say **what the factors are**, and say **why** the right choice depends on those factors. Use your judgement to say what the **most important factors** are. The most important thing is to **justify** why you're saying what you're saying.

3) Relate your answer to the **business described in the question** and to the **situation in the question**. Give reasons why **this business** would make a particular decision, and how and why **these particular circumstances** would affect their decision. For example, there's no point saying that Mr Richards might consider floating his business on the stockmarket if he only has a turnover of £280,000 a year — it's just not a realistic choice for a company of that size.

It floats — but not on the stockmarket.

Get Marks in Your Exam

*They give marks for **How You Write**, too*

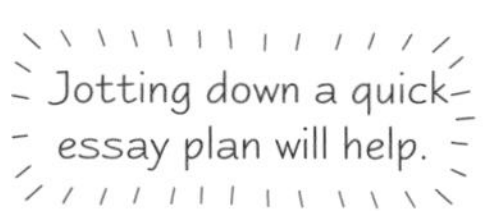

1) You have to use the **right style** of writing and **arrange relevant information clearly** — write a **well-structured essay**, not a list of bullet points. You need to use **specialist vocabulary** when it's appropriate, so it's well worth **learning** some of the **fancy terms** used in this book.
2) You have to write **neatly** enough for the examiner to be able to read it. You also need to use good **spelling**, **grammar** and **punctuation** to make your meaning **crystal clear**. Don't worry, you won't lose marks for spelling errors — but if your handwriting, grammar, spelling and punctuation are **so** far up the spout that the examiner **can't understand** what you've written, **expect problems.**
3) Out of the whole paper, you only get **2** or **3** marks for written communication — but remember that if the examiner can't **read** or **understand** your writing, you won't get the **other marks** either.

Dudley got no marks for his "Boston Matrix in Mime".

The Examiner** will try to show you **How Much to Write

1) The examiner does try to help you by telling you how many marks each question is worth and by giving you an idea of how much you need to write.
2) They usually provide about **two lines** for every mark — so for a question worth two marks you'll get four lines.
3) Generally, if the question is worth 2 or 3 marks then you just need to show your business studies knowledge. Give a short answer and move on quite quickly.
4) For a 12 to 15 mark question you need to show analysis and evaluation. You'll have to write much more for these questions. They usually expect you to make a decision, or have an opinion and be able to justify it. There's rarely a right or wrong answer to this sort of question, so just convince the examiner that your opinion is valid by explaining your reasons.

*Don't forget to include **All** the **Skills** in **Extended Answer Questions***

1) When you come up against a long question (worth, say, 15 marks), **don't jump** straight to the **evaluation** stage. The examiner will be looking for **evidence** of the **other skills**, too.
2) So, if they ask you how Mr Frimble can increase his profits, and you think he should either increase his mark-up or make some staff redundant, you need to:

    1) **Define** what is meant by mark-up and redundancy (this will get you your **AO1** marks).
    2) Explain how mark-up/redundancy are **relevant** to the type of **business/product** that Mr Frimble owns/produces (for **AO2** marks).
    3) Give the **advantages** and **disadvantages** of each method of increasing profits (for **AO3** marks).
    4) Finally, for the **AO4** marks, **weigh up** both sides of the argument and **decide** if Mr Fimble should increase his mark-up or make some staff redundant (you might decide he needs to do both).

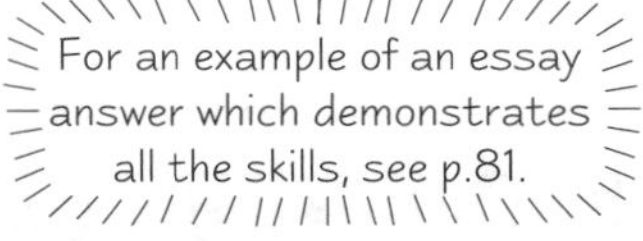

For an example of an essay answer which demonstrates all the skills, see p.81.

It's exam time — let's get down to business...

These pages should take some of the surprise out of your exams. You don't need to know this upside down and back to front like you do the actual business studies stuff. What you do need to know is what the examiners actually want to see from you — not just that you know the facts, but also that you understand and can put to use what you've learnt.

Do Well in Your AQA Exam

Here's an example of the kind of case study and questions you may get in Unit 1.

Crinkle Cakes Ltd

Janet Jones had always enjoyed pottering around in her kitchen, and took great pride in the fact that friends and family used to ask her to bake cakes for birthdays and special occasions. However, it was only when one of her friends insisted on paying her £10 for a cake that she first thought of it as a way of making a living.

Eight years on and what had been Janet's sole trader business has grown into a medium-sized private limited company. Although she still plays an important day-to-day role in the business, it is no longer based in her kitchen. The business now operates out of premises equipped with machinery which allows them to produce 50 cakes per hour.

The business operates in a very competitive market which is dominated by two national bakeries. It also faces competition from a long-established local firm, which has an excellent reputation in the area. Janet believes that in order to ensure the long-term survival of the business she needs to look at ways in which Crinkle Cakes Ltd could compete more effectively, and achieve its objective of increasing both sales and market share. Money is tight though, since the premises and machinery were obtained using finance which is still being paid off.

Janet had always hoped to see her cakes on the shelves of the big supermarkets, but so far Crinkle Cakes has been unable to secure a deal to supply any of the major chains. The main reasons the supermarkets gave for not stocking Crinkle Cakes products were that they had a very narrow product range (selling only whole cakes rather than multi-pack slices or individual portions), and that their cakes were priced higher than competing bakeries.

Janet and her marketing director Stephen Simms have spent a considerable amount of time looking at ways to address these issues. Stephen did some market research, and he presented Janet with the results (see Appendix 1).

Meanwhile, Janet spoke to the operations manager in order to discuss costs. Crinkle Cakes had originally aimed at prices no more than 10% higher than supermarket own-brand prices. The reality though is somewhat different (see Appendix 2). Controlling costs is a real headache due to big fluctuations in the price of raw materials, such as flour. This all gave Janet plenty to think about.

Appendix 1
Results from Market Research (Percentage of People Asked)

Product	Purchased weekly	Purchased monthly	Purchased rarely	Never purchased
Family-sized cake	2	8	62	28
Multi-pack, e.g. slices	55	23	14	8
Individual portions	67	17	10	6

Appendix 2
Recommended Retail Price of Competitors' Products

Company	Family cake	Multi-pack	Individual Portions
Crinkle Cakes Ltd	£5.29	-	-
Local Competitor	£5.09	-	£0.59
National Competitor	£4.49	£1.39	£0.55
Market Leader	£4.99	£1.39	£0.60
Supermarket Own Brand	£3.99	£1.19	£0.49

*An **Example Question and Answer** to give you some tips:*

The business referred to in the article is a private limited company. Outline TWO features of a private limited company. (4 marks)

A private limited company belongs to its shareholders, who have to be part of the company. The shares cannot be bought by the public and won't be quoted on the stock exchange.

The shareholders of a private limited company have limited liability, which means that they are not personally responsible for the debts of the business. The only money they can lose is the money they have invested in the company.

Both features outlined here are to do with ownership, but there are plenty of other things you can say about private limited companies. Other points that could have been made include the fact that private limited companies don't have a minimum share capital requirement and that they tend to be quite small family-run businesses.

Do Well in Your AQA Exam

An **Example Extended Question and Answer** to give you some tips:

Suggest a marketing strategy that might ensure that Crinkle Cakes Ltd can continue to compete within their competitive market. (15 marks)

Any marketing strategy is based around the idea of the marketing mix. This is more commonly referred to as "the four Ps" of product, price, place and promotion. In order to develop a marketing strategy it is necessary to examine each of these four factors in turn.

There are a number of factors that need to be examined if Crinkle Cakes wish to improve the product aspect of their marketing. At present they appear to produce mainly family cakes, which 28% of customers never buy according to the research findings in Appendix 1.

In addition this has meant that few supermarkets have shown a willingness to sell Crinkle Cakes' products. As such I would recommend that they sell a wider range of cake sizes. In addition to the full cakes they could introduce a multi-pack containing cake slices, aimed at families, and single-slice packs, perhaps aimed at single people or impulse purchases. This would widen their target market, since they are likely to be purchased by a different type of consumer. One final alteration that Crinkle Cakes could make to their products is to introduce a range of new cake flavours, though this may require further market research.

The price that Crinkle Cakes charge for their products is stated in the case study to be higher than their competitors' prices, yet they also indicate that the target price should be no more than 10% above the own-brand products. If they adopt this strategy then the figures given in Appendix 2 show that Crinkle Cakes' prices would be lower than their main three competitors. The strategy should be continued to pursue the objective of increasing sales and market share. However, the study states that the costs of raw materials have prevented this, so steps to control costs would have to be taken to make this possible. Controlling costs is also important while the business is still paying off the cost of its premises and machinery.

As far as place is concerned, Crinkle Cakes must take steps to get their products into the major supermarkets. This should be possible if they make the changes to the product size already discussed.

The case study does not give any detail about what promotion has taken place. Advertising could be a problem, due to the financial constraints of having to raise finance from within. As such, the company may wish to investigate methods of sales promotion involving tie-ups with other companies. This might be particularly useful if new products are to be launched. The company may also wish to use publicity and public relations to raise brand awareness in a more cost-effective way than advertising.

In conclusion, there are a number of recommendations, as outlined, which Crinkle Cakes Ltd should consider in order to make improvements to their marketing mix, and to achieve the objectives that they have set themselves.

Stating knowledge is fine, but don't waste too much time

A02: Links knowledge about marketing mix to business in question (2 marks)

Apply your suggestions to the business in question

It's fine to say you don't think change is needed as long as you explain why

A03: Considers possible risks/ problems (2 marks)

Referring to financial restrictions is always a good idea

A04: Makes vague attempt at overall evaluation (1 mark)

A01: Refers to, and defines, marketing mix (2 marks)

Make use of information in the case study

A04: Makes a sensible recommendation after considering evidence (1 mark)

Don't waste time repeating the case study, just refer to it

A02: Links issue of price to business in question (1 mark)

A03: Considers consequences of financial decisions (1 mark)

This is a little vague

A04: Makes a sensible recommendation after considering evidence (1 mark)

Summarising your ideas is a good idea, but make your recommendations clear

This is a reasonably good answer and would get about **11 marks**. It considers a range of marketing options and applies them to the business in the case study. It also makes excellent use of the **information provided** by the examiner. This answer has been set out sensibly with a separate paragraph for each aspect of the marketing mix.

The conclusion is poor and doesn't add anything to the answer. It would've been better if it had made clear which aspects of the marketing mix should be changed as a priority. Remember that the examiner is looking for **evaluation**, and one way of doing this is to explain why it might be better to take one course of action instead of another.

Answers to Numerical Questions

Section One — Starting a Business

Page 11 — Understanding Markets

Practice Questions

Q2 Market share (%) = sales ÷ total market size × 100
= 30 000 ÷ 150 000 × 100 = 20%

Section Two — Financial Planning

Page 27 — Costs, Revenues and Profits

Exam Questions

Q2 (a) Maximum of 6 marks available
[1 mark for each correct start/finish point of each line]

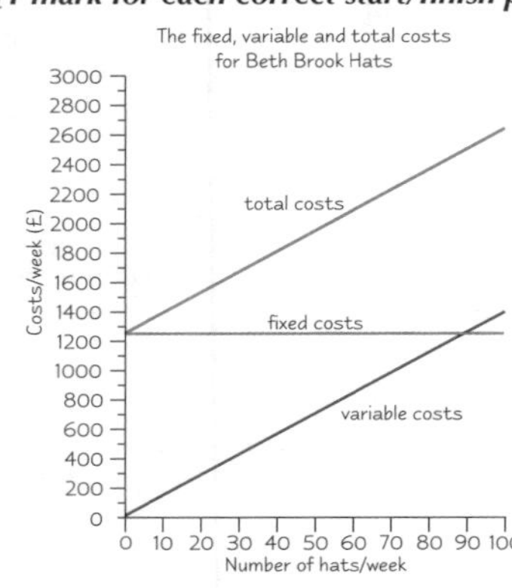

(b) Maximum of 4 marks available.
Costs at 60 hats per week = fixed costs + variable costs ***[1 mark]***
= 1260 + (60 × 14) = £1260 + £840 = £2100 ***[1 mark]***
Revenue = selling price × quantity sold
= £50 × 60 = £3000 ***[1 mark]***
Profit = revenue – costs = £3000 – £2100 = £900 ***[1 mark]***

Page 29 — Break-Even Analysis

Exam Questions

Q2 Maximum of 4 marks available.
Contribution per unit = selling price per unit– variable costs per unit ***[1 mark]*** = £13 – £5 = £8 ***[1 mark]***
Break-even point = fixed costs ÷ contribution per unit ***[1 mark]***
= £1000 ÷ 8 = 125 customers ***[1 mark]***

Page 31 — Cash Flow Forecasting

Practice Questions

Q3 Net cash flow = total cash in – total costs= £8000 – £9500 = (£1500)
Q4 Closing balance = opening balance + net cash flow
= £20 000 + (£7000) = £13 000

Page 33 — Setting Budgets

Practice Questions

Q2 Profit budget = income budget – expenditure budget
Expenditure budget = income budget – profit budget
= £125 000 – £30 000 = £95 000

Page 35 — Variances

Practice Questions

Q2 Variance = £15 000 – £18 000 = (£3000)
so there is a £3000 adverse variance

Exam Questions

Q1 (a) Maximum of 10 marks available

	Feb cumulative variance	Mar budget	Mar actual	Mar variance	Mar cumulative variance
Revenue	£10k (A)	£110k	£120k	£10k (F)	£0
Wages	£9k (F)	£40k	£39k	£1k (F)	£10k (F)
Rent	£1k (A)	£10k	£11k	£1k (A)	£2k (A)
Other costs	£2k (A)	£5k	£5k	£0	£2k (A)
Total costs	£6k (F)	£55k	£55k	£0	£6k (F)

Page 37 — Measuring and Increasing Profit

Practice Questions

Q1 Percentage change in profit
= (current profit – previous profit) ÷ previous profit × 100
= (£52 000 – £50 000)
÷ £50 000 × 100 = 4%

Exam Questions

Q1 Maximum of 2 marks available.
ROCE = net profit ÷ capital employed × 100 ***[1 mark]***
= £100 000 ÷ £40 000 × 100 = 250% ***[1 mark]***

Q2 (a) Maximum of 4 marks available.
Net profit = gross profit – fixed costs ***[1 mark]***
= £750 000 – £250 000 = £500 000 ***[1 mark]***
Net profit margin = net profit ÷ revenue × 100 ***[1 mark]***
= £500 000 ÷ £2 000 000 × 100
= 25% ***[1 mark]***

Section Three — People in Business

Page 41 — Measuring Workforce Effectiveness

Practice Questions

Q2 Absenteeism
= Number of staff days lost ÷ number of working days × 100
Number of working days = number of days company operates × number of staff – staff holidays
= 245 × 56 – (25 x 56)
= 12320
Absenteeism = 274 ÷ 12320 × 100 = 2.22%
= 2% (to nearest whole percentage).

Q4 Labour turnover
= Number of staff leaving ÷ average number of staff × 100
= 18 ÷ 600 × 100 = 3%

Section Four — Operations Management

Page 47 — Capacity Utilisation

Practice Questions

Q1 Capacity utilisation = output ÷ capacity × 100
= 42 ÷ 65 × 100 = 65% (to nearest whole percentage).

Q3 Unit cost = total costs ÷ output
= £1600 ÷ 450 = £3.56

Section Five — Marketing and Competition

Page 69 — Marketing Mix: Price

Exam Questions

Q1 Maximum of 9 marks available.
Sales revenue = price of product × quantity sold ***[1 mark]***
Sales revenue = £1500 × 200 = £300 000 ***[1 mark]***

Percentage change in quantity demanded
= percentage change in price × elasticity coefficient ***[1 mark]***
= 15% × 0.7 elasticity coefficient = 10.5% decrease ***[1 mark]***.

10.5% of 200 (current sales) = 200 × 10.5 ÷ 100 = 21 ***[1 mark]***.
New sales = 200 – 21 = 179 ***[1 mark]***.
New price = £1500 × 115 ÷ 100 = £1725 ***[1 mark]***.
New revenue = £1725 × 179 = £308 775 ***[1 mark]***.
Change in revenue = £308 775 – £300 000 = £8775 increase ***[1 mark]***.

A2-Level

Business Studies

Exam Board: AQA

Functional Objectives and Strategies

Here's a nice short section to start with. It's all about functional objectives and strategies — that might sound a bit scary, but it's not too bad really. Here goes...

Corporate Objectives are objectives for the Whole Business

1) All businesses have **objectives**. Objectives are things that the business wants to **achieve**. **Corporate objectives** are general objectives that refer to the business as a **whole**, e.g. an objective to become the first-choice supplier of ready meals for UK supermarkets.
2) Setting corporate objectives is fairly **straightforward** for a sole trader or partnership business — the owner or owners know what they're trying to achieve. The planning process for a **limited company** is usually more **complicated** because the managers and directors have to make decisions on behalf of the shareholders (more on corporate objectives on p.164).

Functional Objectives contribute to the Company's Corporate Objectives

1) **Functional objectives** (sometimes called **departmental objectives**) are the objectives of each **department**. They're more **detailed** than corporate objectives, and they are **specific** to each department. E.g. to increase sales per salesperson from 10 to 13 orders a day within the next 2 years is a sales objective, and to increase the net profit margin from 15% to 22% within the next 2 years is a financial objective.
2) Businesses need to set **functional objectives** that will help them **achieve** their **corporate objectives**. Whenever a corporate objective is set, **all** the managers in the business have to look at how their department can help to achieve the objective, and set **functional objectives** that will **contribute** to achieving the corporate objective.
3) The table shows some common **corporate objectives**, and the **functional objectives** that help businesses to achieve them:

Corporate objective:	Functional objectives:
1) **Increase profits**	• **Minimise costs** (e.g. cut costs by 10% over 12 months) — this could be a functional objective for **all departments**. • **Increase sales** (e.g. by 20% over 12 months) — this would be a functional objective for the **sales** department, and it would also involve the **marketing** and **research and development** departments.
2) **Increase customer satisfaction**	• **Reduce** the number of **faulty products** (e.g. by 5% over 12 months) — a functional objective for the **production** department. • **Reduce** the number of **customer complaints** (e.g. by 5% over 12 months) — this would be a functional objective for the **sales** department, and any other departments that deal directly with customers.
3) **Improve staff motivation**	• **Reduce the staff turnover rate** (e.g. by 10% over 3 years) — a functional objective for the **human resources** department. • **Increase wage and salary rates** (e.g. by 2% more than the rate of inflation for each year of service) — a functional objective for the **finance department**.

4) Functional objectives **aren't** the last stage of setting objectives — **team managers** within a department might set objectives for their **team** based on the functional objectives of the whole department, and **individual staff members** might even have their own **personal objectives**.
5) E.g. if the sales department has a functional objective to increase sales by 10% over 12 months, the telesales team might have an objective to increase sales from 500 to 550 a week. An experienced telesales operative's objective might be to increase their sales from 20 to 25 a day, and a less experienced operative might be set an objective to increase their daily sales from 15 to 16. Short-term or small-scale objectives like these are called **tactical objectives**.

Functional Objectives and Strategies

Objectives are used to form *Strategies*

1) A **strategy** is a **plan of action** developed to achieve an objective. Strategies can only be formed once a business has decided what its **objectives** are.
2) **Corporate strategies** are developed to achieve **corporate objectives**. These can involve **several departments**.
3) **Functional strategies** are developed to achieve **functional objectives**. Each department has its own functional objectives, so functional strategies only involve **one department**. E.g. if the HR department's objective is to reduce staff turnover by 5%, the functional strategy to achieve this might be to increase staff training.
4) A **strategic gap** is when the results from the strategy that has been developed **aren't** expected to **achieve** the stated **objective**. E.g. if the objective is to increase sales by **10%**, and the strategy is to use a TV advertising campaign, which is only expected to increase demand by **8%**, there's a **strategic gap**. When a strategic gap is identified, managers must either **alter the objective** or develop more **supporting strategies** to achieve the original objective — e.g. they could do a 2-for-1 promotion in addition to the advertising campaign to increase demand further.

Objectives should be *Specific, Measurable, Agreed, Realistic* and *Timely*

To be effective, an objective should be '**SMART**' — specific, measurable, agreed, realistic and timely.

Specific	**Vague objectives** like "to improve quality" **don't** really tell staff what they're supposed to be aiming for. Making them more **specific**, e.g. "to reduce the number of items produced that have defects", means that the business is more likely to **achieve** them.
Measurable	If the objective **isn't measurable**, the business **won't know** if it's achieved it or not. E.g. "to increase turnover by 5%" is a measurable objective, but "to improve the business" isn't.
Agreed	Everyone who's going to be involved in **achieving** the objective needs to **know** about it and **agree** to it. E.g. if the objective is to increase sales, the sales manager and salespeople will all need to agree to it.
Realistic	There's no point setting objectives that are **too ambitious**, e.g. tripling sales within 12 months, or achieving a 95% market share. **Impossible objectives** just **demotivate** staff.
Timely	There should be a **specific timeframe** that the objective has to be achieved in. E.g. the objective might be to increase turnover by 5% within 12 months. If there's **no time limit**, staff won't see the objective as **urgent** — they might think they don't need to worry about achieving it because as long as it gets done at some time in the future then it doesn't matter.

Practice Questions

Q1 What's the difference between corporate objectives and functional objectives?

Q2 What is the purpose of functional objectives?

Q3 What are corporate strategies?

Q4 What does SMART stand for in the term 'SMART objectives'?

The exam questions in this book won't be exactly like the ones that you'll get in your exam, because we haven't got room to add the case studies and tables of data. But they'll still be really good practice.

Exam Question

Q1 Discuss the importance of the SMART criteria for setting objectives. [8 marks]

This all seems pretty DUMB to me...

That's section one over already — brilliant. No such luck with section two I'm afraid — that one's a whopping thirty pages. There's lots to learn here before you get onto that though, so don't go skipping over it. Make sure you know objectives and strategies forwards, backwards and upside down — knowing the basics will really help you with the rest.

Understanding Financial Objectives

Here's where the real fun starts — it's finance time.

Financial Objectives are what the business wants to Achieve financially

1) **Financial objectives** are **financial goals** that a business wants to achieve. Businesses usually have **specific targets** in mind, and a **specific period of time** to achieve them in. E.g. a business might have an objective to increase its profits by 10% within three years.
2) Businesses might have objectives about **return on capital employed** (**ROCE**):

$$\text{ROCE (\%)} = \frac{\text{gross profit}}{\text{capital employed}} \times 100$$

Return on capital employed measures how **efficiently** the business is running — it tells you how much money the business has made compared to how much money's been put into the business. A ROCE of about 20-30% is good, so if the business' ROCE is lower than that, it might aim to **increase** it. See p. 101 for more on ROCE.
3) Businesses might aim to **improve** their **cash flow**. Even **profitable** businesses can fail if they don't have enough cash to pay their debts when they're due. Businesses can improve their cash flow by getting their debtors to pay them **promptly** and using **debt factoring** (see p. 107) if payments to the business are taking a long time. Holding **less stock** and not taking more orders than the business can fulfil also improves cash flow.
4) Another financial objective might be to **minimise costs** — if the business still sells the same number of products at the same price, this will **increase** its overall **profits**. See below for how businesses can minimise their costs. Businesses have to be careful that cutting costs doesn't reduce the **quality** of their products or services — otherwise sales might drop, and they'd end up with **lower profits** instead of higher profits.
5) Limited companies and PLCs might aim to **increase returns** for their **shareholders**. Businesses usually pay out around a third of their net profit to shareholders as **dividends**. To increase dividends, they can either pay out a **bigger percentage** of the net profit as dividends (but this means there's less money left to reinvest in the business) or **increase profits**.

Businesses try to Minimise their Costs

1) A business' **profit margin** is the proportion of **revenue** from each sale that is **profit**. E.g. if a bottle of shampoo costs £1.20 to produce and sells for £3.50, the business makes a profit of £2.30 (66%) on each bottle sold.
2) Businesses can **increase** their **profit margins** by either **increasing** their **prices** or **reducing** their **costs**. Most businesses try to keep their costs as **low** as possible in order to benefit from large profit margins without putting their prices up (since this is likely to **reduce demand** for their products).
3) **Minimising costs** is particularly important for businesses operating in very **competitive markets**. They're forced to keep their prices **low** in order to compete, so the only way for them to increase their profits is by cutting costs.
4) Businesses can cut the average cost of making a product by producing in **large quantities** so that they can benefit from **economies of scale** (see p. 134). Other ways of cutting costs include switching to **cheaper suppliers** (or negotiating cheaper deals with existing suppliers), cutting **staffing levels** or taking on less experienced staff who don't need to be paid as much.

Costs influence Business Decisions

1) Before they make a decision, businesses usually consider the **costs** involved. Businesses tend to focus on the **internal costs** (the costs the business has to pay) because they have a direct impact on the business' **profits**.
2) Cutting costs **doesn't** always mean that a business' **profits** will **increase**. If cutting costs **reduces** the **quality** of the company's products or services, it could end up causing a **fall** in **profits**. E.g. a food company might change to a cheaper type of packaging to cut costs, but if the new packaging is prone to leaking, the company's reputation could suffer and sales will probably fall.
3) When making **decisions** about which raw materials to use, which supplier to use, which staff to employ, etc, businesses **don't** just look at the cost. They also consider other **issues** depending on the company's **aims**, **culture**, etc. E.g. a health food company that prides itself on having **knowledgeable staff** to advise customers **won't** want to reduce costs by cutting back on **staff training**, because this would go against its basic aims and principles.

Understanding Financial Objectives

Internal and *External* factors influence *Financial Objectives*

Businesses have to make sure that their financial objectives are **realistic** and **achievable**. There are several factors that influence a company's **ability** to **achieve** its objectives, and managers need to take these factors into account when they set financial objectives.

Internal factors influencing financial objectives

1) **The overall objectives of the business.** E.g. a company with a strong **environmental** standpoint might be more interested in minimising its carbon footprint than in maximising its profits.
2) **The status of the business.** **New** businesses might set **ambitious** targets for revenue because they're trying to grow quickly and establish themselves in the marketplace. **Established** companies might be satisfied with **smaller** increases in revenue if they're not actively trying to grow.
3) **Employees.** E.g. if a business has a **high turnover of sales staff**, an objective to dramatically increase revenue might be **unrealistic** because well-trained, experienced staff are needed to encourage customers to spend more.

External factors influencing financial objectives

1) **The availability of finance.** **Cash flow** targets might depend on how easy or difficult it is for the business to get **credit**.
2) **Competitors.** If **new competitors** enter the market, or **demand** for existing competitors' products **increases** (due to a marketing promotion or price reduction, etc), a business might set an objective to **cut costs** in order to be more competitive.
3) **The economy.** In a period of economic **boom**, businesses can set **ambitious** ROCE and profit targets. In a **downturn**, they have to set more **restrained** targets, and they might also set targets to **minimise costs**.
4) **Shareholders.** Shareholders usually want the best possible **return** on their investment — this might put pressure on businesses to set objectives to increase **profits** or **dividends**.

Businesses and *Shareholders* use *Financial Data* to make *Decisions*

1) Businesses can **compare** their company accounts and financial ratios (see p. 88-103) with the same financial data from **previous years** to see whether the business is performing better or worse than in the **past**, and to see whether there are any **trends** in the data.
2) If possible, businesses also **compare** their financial data with the same data from **other businesses** to see how well they're performing compared to their **competitors**.
3) Looking at the financial data also helps businesses assess their **financial position** and see what they need to **improve** on (e.g. cash flow) — they can then set objectives to improve their financial position.
4) Potential **shareholders** look at the financial data of businesses when they're deciding where to invest . They use shareholders' ratios (see p. 104) to assess which companies will provide a **good return** on their investment.

Practice Questions

Q1 What is a financial objective?

Q2 List three ways that businesses can minimise their costs.

Q3 Why might cutting costs not lead to an increase in profits?

Q4 Why might a business look at its financial data over time?

Exam Question

Q1 Discuss the internal and external factors that influence the financial objectives of a business. [4 marks]

There are too many objectives here — I object...

A nice couple of pages to ease you in gently to this lovely long finance section. There's nothing too tricky here, but make sure you still learn it as well as you can, because if you can master the basics then it'll be much easier to understand some of the more complicated stuff in the rest of the section. Once you're sure you've got it, turn over for company accounts.

Company Accounts: Balance Sheets

Luckily, you don't need to be able to draw up a balance sheet for your A2 exam. You still need to be able to understand and analyse them though, so keep reading to find out how.

Balance Sheets *are lists of* ***Assets*** *and* ***Liabilities***

1) Balance sheets are a **snapshot** of a firm's finances at a **fixed point in time**.
2) They show the value of all the business' **assets** (the things that belong to the business, including cash in the bank) and all its **liabilities** (the money the business owes). They also show the value of all the **capital** (the money invested in the business), and the source of that capital (e.g. loans, shares or retained profits) — so they show where the money's **come from** as well as what's being **done** with it.
3) The '**net assets**' value (the total fixed and current assets minus total current and non-current (long-term) liabilities — see next page) is **always the same** as the '**total equity**' value — the total of all the money that's been put into the business. That's why they're called balance sheets — they **balance**.

Sally soon realised that balancing isn't as easy as it looks.

Interpreting *balance sheets —* ***Here's How It All Looks***

ABC Company Ltd
Balance Sheet as at 30 March 2009

Premises			£100000
Machines			£10000
Vehicles			£15000
Total non-current assets			£125000
Inventories (stock)		£20000	
Receivables (debtors)		£10000	
Cash in the bank		£5000	
Total current assets		£35000	
Payables (creditors)	(£20000)		
Overdraft	(£2000)		
Dividends	(£10000)		
Unpaid tax	(£1000)		
Total current liabilities		(£33000)	
Net current assets			£2000
Non-current liabilities (long-term loans)			£55000
Net assets			£72000
Share capital			£60000
Reserves			£12000
Total equity (shareholders' funds)			£72000

Balance sheets show the financial state of affairs on one particular day.

Raw materials and finished products — things the business has spent money on, but not sold yet.

Value of products sold but not paid for yet. Money owed to the business. See p. 89.

Money owed by the business.

Dividends (see p. 104) not yet paid to shareholders.

This is the working capital available to pay for day to day spending. See p. 91-92.

The value of non-current assets includes depreciation (see p. 93) — it's what they're worth now, not when the business bought them.

Brackets mean a negative number.

Net current assets = current assets – current liabilities

Net assets = net current assets + non-current assets – non-current liabilities. See p. 89.

These two figures ALWAYS balance.

The figure for reserves takes into account depreciation — it's an expense on the income statement, so the net profit has already had depreciation deducted (see p. 94). Depreciation is taken into account in 'net assets', so if it wasn't included here, the figures wouldn't balance.

Company Accounts: Balance Sheets

Assets are things the *Business Owns*

1) Businesses can use **capital** to buy **assets** that will generate more revenue in the future — this is **investment**.
2) Assets (like machinery and stock) provide a **financial benefit** to the business, so they're given a monetary value on the balance sheet. Assets can be classified as **non-current assets** (fixed assets) or **current assets**.
3) **Non-current assets** are assets that the business is likely to keep for **more than a year**, e.g. property, land, production equipment, desks and computers. The '**total non-current assets**' value on the balance sheet is the **combined value** of all the business' non-current assets.
4) Non-current assets often **lose value** over time, so they're worth less every year. This is **depreciation** — see p. 93. Businesses should factor in depreciation to give a **realistic** value of their non-current assets on the balance sheet.
5) **Patents** can also be classed as **fixed assets** on the balance sheet. A patent gives a business the right to use a new **invention** or **product**, and **prevents** other businesses from using the same invention or making the same product without permission for 20 years. Businesses can **sell** patents to other companies, so they are an asset on the balance sheet.
6) When one business buys another, the buyer might pay more for the business than just the value of its **assets**, because it has a good **reputation**, good **location** or established **customer base**, etc. The extra money is included on the buyer's balance sheet as a **fixed asset**, called **goodwill**.
7) **Current assets** are assets that the business is likely to exchange for cash **within the accounting year**, before the next balance sheet is made. Current assets include "**receivables**" (or "debtors" — money owed to the business by other companies and individuals) and **inventories** (or "stock" — products, or materials that will be used to make products, that will be sold to **customers**). All the current assets are added together to give the '**total current assets**' value on the balance sheet.
8) The business' **current and non-current assets** are added together, then current and non-current liabilities (see below) are deducted to give the figure for '**net assets**' on the balance sheet.

Liabilities are *Debts* the *Business Owes*

1) **Current liabilities** are **debts** which need to be paid off within a year. They include **overdrafts**, **taxes** due to be paid, money owed to **creditors**, and **dividends** due to be paid to shareholders. **Total current liabilities** are **deducted** from total fixed and current assets to give the value of 'assets employed'.
2) **Non-current liabilities** are debts that the business will pay off over several years, e.g. mortgages and loans.

Bad Debts are debts that debtors *Won't Ever Pay*

1) **Ideally**, every debt owed by debtors to the business would be paid. **Unfortunately**, the **real world** isn't like that. Most debts get paid eventually, but some debtors **default** on their payments — they **don't pay up**.
2) Debts which don't get paid are called "**bad debts**". These bad debts **can't** be included on the balance sheet as an **asset** — because the business isn't going to get money for them.
3) The business **writes off** these bad debts, and puts them as an **expense** on the profit and loss account. This shows that the business has **lost money**.

> It's important to be **realistic** about bad debts.
>
> The business shouldn't be **over-optimistic** and report debts as **assets** when it's unlikely that they're ever going to be paid. On the other hand, they shouldn't be **too cautious** and write debts off as **bad debts** when they could make the debtors pay up.
>
> - Being **over-optimistic** results in an asset valuation that's **too high**.
> - Being **overcautious** results in an asset valuation that's **too low**.

Company Accounts: Balance Sheets

Balance Sheets show the **Short-Term Financial Status** of the **Company**

1) The balance sheet shows you how much the business is **worth**.
2) **Working capital** (net current assets) is the amount of money the business has available in the short term. It's calculated by subtracting **current liabilities** from **current assets**. See p. 91-92 for more on working capital.
3) **Suppliers** are particularly interested in **working capital** and **liquidity**. They can look at the balance sheet to see how **liquid** the firm's assets are, as well as how much working capital the firm has. The more liquid the assets, the better the firm will be at **paying bills**. This helps them decide whether to offer the business supplies on **credit**, and how much credit to offer.
4) The balance sheet shows **sources of capital**. Ideally, **long-term loans** or **mortgages** are used to finance the purchase of fixed assets. A well managed business wouldn't borrow too much through **short-term overdrafts**, because overdrafts are an expensive way of borrowing.

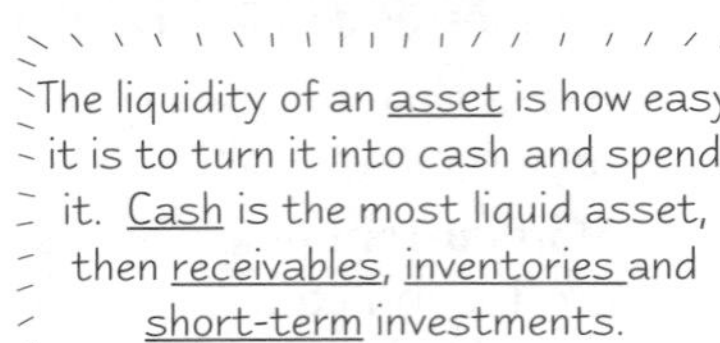
The liquidity of an asset is how easy it is to turn it into cash and spend it. Cash is the most liquid asset, then receivables, inventories and short-term investments.

By **Comparing Balance Sheets** you can see **Long-Term Trends**

1) Comparing this year's balance sheet to previous years' accounts lets you pick out **trends** in company finances. Looking at the "bottom line" over several years shows you how the business is **growing**.
2) A **quick increase** in **non-current assets** indicates that the company has invested in property or machinery. This means that the company is investing in a **growth strategy**, which may increase its profit over the medium term — useful information for shareholders and potential shareholders, who want to see more profit.
3) Increases in **reserves** also suggest an increase in **profits** — good news for shareholders.
4) Looking at several balance sheets together also shows **trends** in how the business has **raised** its **capital**. It's risky to suddenly start **borrowing** a lot, in case interest rates rise. A company with a high value of loan capital and a relatively low value of share capital or reserves would be in trouble if the Bank of England put **interest rates** up.

The monks loved nothing better than to compare balance sheets.

Practice Questions

Q1 Which two figures on a balance sheet are always equal?

Q2 What's the difference between current and non-current assets?

Q3 Give two examples of current liabilities and two examples of non-current liabilities.

Q4 Why would suppliers be interested in a business' balance sheet?

Exam Questions

Q1 The balance sheet of Joanne's hairdressing salon shows £400 inventories (stock), £50 receivables (debtors), £150 cash, and current liabilities of £120. Evaluate the short-term financial position of Joanne's business. [4 marks]

Q2 Explain how balance sheets can be used to show long-term trends. [6 marks]

All this revision's making me feel a bit unbalanced...

Balance sheets can seem weird. If you look at it as where the money's from, and what the firm's done with it, you can see why it balances. You won't have to draw a balance sheet in the exam, but you might need to use a balance sheet to assess a company's performance, so make sure you learn it well.

Company Accounts: Working Capital

If you enjoyed those pages on balance sheets, you'll probably like working capital even more. Maybe.

Working Capital is the Finance available for Day-To-Day Spending

1) Working capital is the amount of **cash** (and **assets** that can be easily turned into cash) that the business has available to pay its **day-to-day debts**. The more working capital a business has, the more **liquid** (able to pay its short-term debts) it is. See p. 98 for liquidity ratios.
2) Working capital is the same as **net current assets** on the balance sheet (see p. 88) — the amount left over when you subtract **current liabilities** (e.g. overdraft, payables (creditors) and tax due to be paid) from **current assets** (i.e. cash, receivables (debtors) and stock):

Working capital = current assets – current liabilities

3) Working capital is important for businesses. As well as generating sales, the business must make sure it **collects money** quickly to get **cash** to pay its liabilities. Businesses **can't survive** if they don't have enough working capital . They need to make sure that they don't **tie up** too much of their working capital as inventories or receivables — businesses **can't** use inventories or receivables to pay their current liabilities until they're turned into **cash**.

Businesses need Enough Cash but Not Too Much

1) Businesses need **just enough** cash to pay short-term debts. They shouldn't have too much cash, because spare cash is great at **paying off debts**, but lousy at **earning money** for the business.
2) To make money, the business needs **non-current assets** that make sales possible (e.g. machinery that produces products).
3) The amount of cash a business needs depends on several factors:

Factors affecting how much cash a business needs:

1) Businesses with **high sales volumes** tend to have **high costs** compared to the price of their products (they don't need a big **profit margin** because they're selling large numbers of products) so they need **more cash**.
2) The more **credit** a business offers, the more **cash** it needs to fend off a **cash flow crisis**.
3) The longer the **cash flow cycle/operating cycle** (see diagram) the more cash a business needs. E.g. supermarkets have a short operating cycle because they don't hold stocks (inventories) for long, and they don't have to wait for payment on credit.

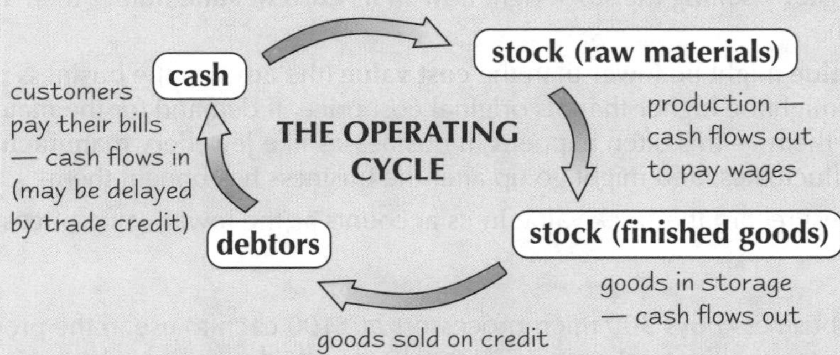

4) **Inflation** increases the costs of wages and buying and holding stock, so firms need more cash when inflation is high.
5) When a business **expands**, it needs more cash to avoid **overtrading**. Overtrading means producing so much that the business can't afford to pay its **suppliers** until it gets paid by its **customers**.

Company Accounts: Working Capital

Businesses also need finance for **Capital Expenditure**

1) **Fixed capital** (or **capital expenditure**) means money used to buy **non-current assets** (fixed assets). These are things used over and over again to produce goods or services for sale — e.g. **factories** and **equipment**.
2) Businesses need capital expenditure to **start up**, to **grow** and to **replace** worn out equipment. They must **set aside** enough **money** to stop **non-current assets** from **wearing out**, and then they can **decide** how much **money** to invest in **growth**. This is called **allocating capital expenditure**.
3) You'll find **capital expenditure** on the balance sheet (see p. 88-90) as **non-current assets**.

Businesses have to **Control** their **Debtors (Receivables)**

1) A business needs to control its **debtors** (people who owe money to the firm). It's important that businesses make sure that their debtors pay them **on time**.
2) A company might sell millions of pounds worth of goods, but if it doesn't make sure that **payment** has been received, there'll be **no money coming in**. That means that the business is **no better off** in terms of cash flow than if it had sold nothing at all.
3) The business still has to **pay** wages, loan repayments, etc. whether its debtors have paid up or not, so businesses have to control debtors to remain in a **liquid** position.

Karen and Rita spent many a long hour in the debtor control room.

Businesses have to **Control** their **Stock (Inventories)** too

1) A business needs to hold suitable volumes of **stock** (raw materials and unsold products) to allow it to satisfy the demands of the market.
2) A business holding **too little stock** will **lose sales** as it won't be able to supply enough goods to the market to meet demand.
3) A business with **too much stock** has money tied up in stock instead of **working** for the company. It would be better to use the money to pay debts or wages, or invest it in new projects.
4) Businesses **predict** what the **demand** for their products will be in order to make sure that they have a suitable level of stock. See p. 131 for more on sales forecasting.

Stock is **Valued** at **Cost** or at **Net Realisable Value**, whichever's **Lower**

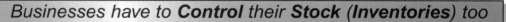

1) Accounting conventions say that stock values must be **realisable**. The **net realisable value** is the amount the company could get by **selling** the stock right now in its **current state** (rather than after it's been used to make a finished product).
2) The **realisable value** might be **lower** than the **cost value** (the amount the business **paid** for the stock). Or the net realisable value might be **higher** than its original cost price, if demand for the materials has increased since the business bought them — this often happens in businesses like **jewellery manufacturers**, as the price of gold and precious stones fluctuates, and might go up after the business has bought them.
3) The company must record the stock value in its accounts as the **lower** value of **cost** and **net realisable value**.

Example

A computer business buys 300 microprocessors at £100 each to use in the production of laptop computers, so the total cost is £30 000. Later, the business updates the specification of the laptops and can't use the microprocessors it originally bought, so it has to sell them. In the meantime, technology has moved on and there are more advanced, faster microprocessors on the market. There's little demand for the old microprocessors, and the business would only be able to sell the old stock for £40 each (£12 000 altogether). The business has to record the value of the stock as £12 000 in its accounts, rather than the £30 000 it originally paid.

Company Accounts: Depreciation

Assets Depreciate — they Lose Value over Time

1) Most assets **lose value** over time — the **longer** the business has them, the **less** they're **worth**. E.g. if a business has been using a piece of machinery for six months, it won't be worth as much as it was when it was new, even if it's still in good condition.
2) Assets lose their value for three main reasons — they suffer **wear and tear**, they may **break down**, and they become **old fashioned** when new models or inventions come onto the market.
3) The **drop in value** of a business asset over time is called **depreciation**.
4) Although most assets depreciate, sometimes it can work the other way round and assets can **increase** in value. E.g. **property** can increase in value over time because property prices tend to rise.

Derek wondered if this meant the factory wouldn't increase in value after all.

Accounts reflect the Depreciation of assets

1) Businesses **calculate depreciation** each year to make sure that an asset's **value** on the **balance sheet** is a **true reflection** of what the business would get from **selling** it.
2) Building depreciation into each year's accounts **avoids** the fall in value hitting **all at once** when the business **sells** the asset. E.g. by depreciating a piece of machinery over 10 years, a business can take a tenth of the **fall in value** of the equipment (the difference between what the asset cost to buy and what managers think they'll be able to sell it for when they finish using it) into account each year. Without depreciating the asset, the business would be **understating its costs** (and therefore overstating its profits) for each year until it got rid of the asset, which would then show up as a **huge cost** on the accounts. Spreading out the cost of the depreciation over several years is a truer reflection of the situation and allows the business to make **comparisons** between financial years more easily.
3) The **amount lost** through depreciation is recorded on the **income statement** (see p. 94-96) as an **expense**. It's unusual because it isn't a cash expense — it's a recognition of the money that's been put into the asset that the business can't ever get back.

Practice Questions

Q1 How do you calculate working capital?

Q2 Why can too much working capital be a problem for a business?

Q3 Why do businesses need to control their debtors?

Q4 What does 'net realisable value' mean?

Q5 What is depreciation?

Q6 Why do businesses depreciate their assets each year?

Exam Question

Q1 Discuss the main factors that affect how much working capital a business needs. [8 marks]

Is London the working capital of England...

There's loads to learn here. It's all about balance — you don't want too much working capital, but on the other hand you don't want too little. The same goes for stock. Then there's debtors to chase up, and depreciation to take into account too. Don't forget the bit about net realisable value, and the difference between working capital and capital expenditure.

Company Accounts: Income Statements

The income statement is a pretty handy collection of financial information. Potential investors can use it to see how well the business is performing, and businesses can use it to compare their performance to their competitors' (see p. 87).

Income Statements show Revenue and Expenses

1) The income statement (also known as a profit and loss account) shows how much money's been **coming into the company** (**revenue**) and how much has been **going out** (**expenses**).
2) Revenue is **sales income** from selling goods and services. This includes **cash payments** and sales on **credit**.
3) If **revenue** since the business published its last income statement has **increased** by **more than** the rate of **inflation** (see p.168), it's often a sign that the company is **healthy**.
4) Expenses are all the business' **costs**.
5) Revenue includes any sales that were made on credit — they're included in the accounts even though the customers haven't paid for the goods yet.

Profit = Revenue – Expenses (and there are different categories of profit...)

1) **Gross profit** is **revenue** minus the **cost of sales** (see p. 95).
2) **Net profit** is **gross profit** minus **indirect costs**. Indirect costs (**overheads**) are all the costs that aren't directly related to how much the business produces (e.g. office rent, rates, interest payments and depreciation — see p.93).
3) **Operating profit** takes into account all revenues and costs from **regular trading**, but not any revenues and costs from **one-off** events such as the sale or purchase of another business. It only covers activities that are likely to be **repeated** year on year. If a company's **gross profits** are **rising** but its **operating profit** is **falling**, it usually means the company is **not controlling** its **costs**.
4) **Net profit before tax** covers **all revenues and costs**, including those from **one-off events**.
5) **Net profit after tax** is what's left after corporation tax has been paid.
6) **Retained profit** is what's left from net profit after tax, once **share dividends** have been paid to shareholders.

One-off profit is Low Quality — Sustained profit is High Quality

1) Profit can be "**high quality**" or "**low quality**", depending on whether it's likely to carry on into the future.
2) Profit from **one-off events** like the sale of part of the business is considered to be **low quality**.
3) **Operating profit** is **high quality**, because it's probably going to carry on being made year on year.
4) **Shareholders** like **high quality** profit, because they want profit to continue into the future. Future profits mean future dividend payments and happy shareholders.

One-offs aren't always low quality.

Company Accounts: Income Statements

The *Income Statement* is *Three* accounts in *One*

The income statement is made up of three separate parts — the trading account, the income statement, and the appropriation account.

1) The **trading account** works out **gross profit** — revenue minus direct costs.
2) The **income statement** subtracts overheads (indirect costs) to work out **operating profit**, and adds one-off sources of revenue to get **net profit**.
3) The **appropriation account** shows what's done with profits — it's either paid to the government as **tax**, **distributed** between shareholders, or **kept** in the business (as **retained profit**) to invest in future activities.

Here's what the *Income Statement* looks like

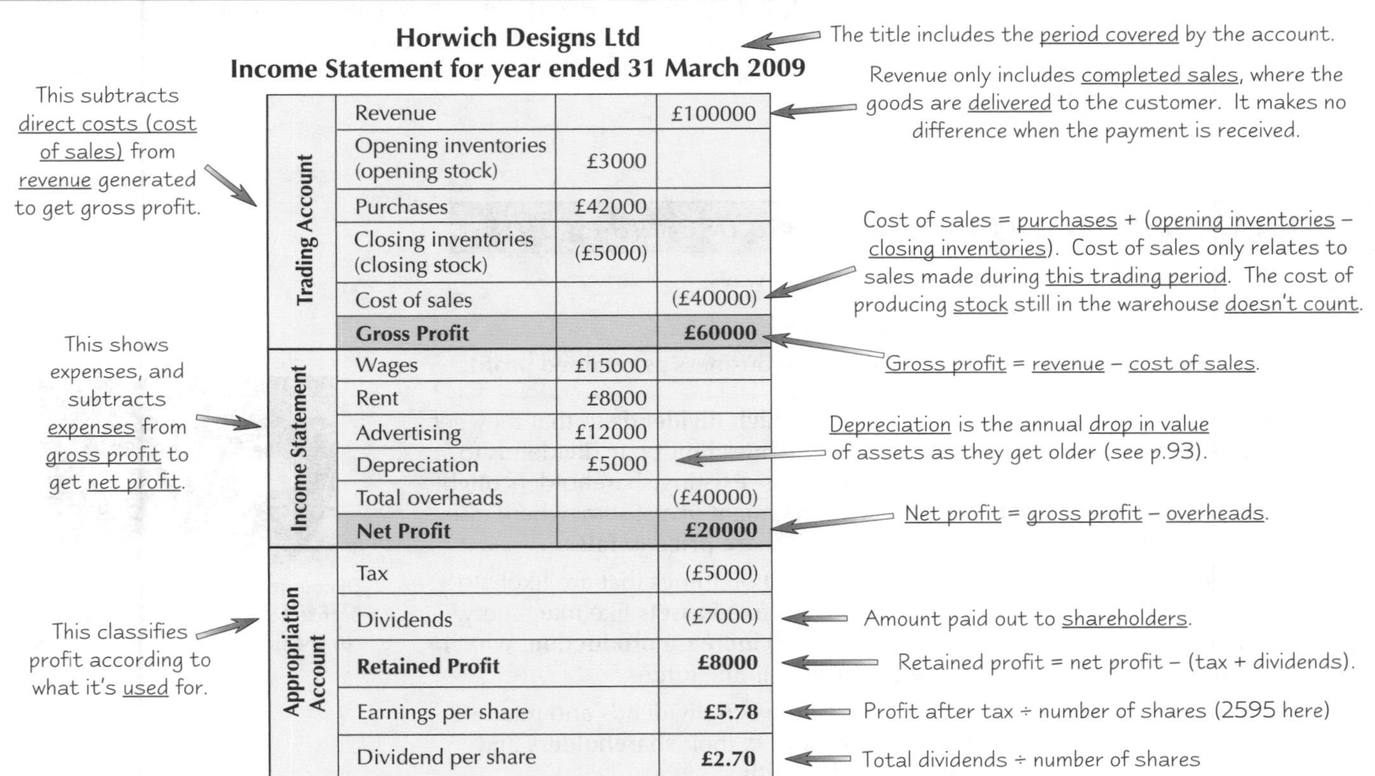

Horwich Designs Ltd
Income Statement for year ended 31 March 2009

Trading Account	Revenue		£100000
	Opening inventories (opening stock)	£3000	
	Purchases	£42000	
	Closing inventories (closing stock)	(£5000)	
	Cost of sales		(£40000)
	Gross Profit		**£60000**
Income Statement	Wages	£15000	
	Rent	£8000	
	Advertising	£12000	
	Depreciation	£5000	
	Total overheads		(£40000)
	Net Profit		**£20000**
Appropriation Account	Tax		(£5000)
	Dividends		(£7000)
	Retained Profit		**£8000**
	Earnings per share		**£5.78**
	Dividend per share		**£2.70**

The title includes the period covered by the account.
Revenue only includes completed sales, where the goods are delivered to the customer. It makes no difference when the payment is received.
This subtracts direct costs (cost of sales) from revenue generated to get gross profit.
Cost of sales = purchases + (opening inventories – closing inventories). Cost of sales only relates to sales made during this trading period. The cost of producing stock still in the warehouse doesn't count.
Gross profit = revenue – cost of sales.
This shows expenses, and subtracts expenses from gross profit to get net profit.
Depreciation is the annual drop in value of assets as they get older (see p.93).
Net profit = gross profit – overheads.
This classifies profit according to what it's used for.
Amount paid out to shareholders.
Retained profit = net profit – (tax + dividends).
Profit after tax ÷ number of shares (2595 here)
Total dividends ÷ number of shares

Practice Questions

Q1 What's the difference between profit and cash?

Q2 What is net profit?

Q3 What are the three accounts that make up the income statement?

Q4 How is the cost of sales calculated in the income statement?

Exam Question

Q1 Explain the terms "high quality profit" and "low quality profit". [4 marks]

32p and a stick of chewing gum — that's what I call low quality profit...

Let's just say I wouldn't recommend busking if you're trying to make your fortune. Especially if you're tone deaf. There's no time for busking anyway — there's too much to learn. You don't need to be able to produce income statements, but you do need to know what they mean, so don't skip them. There's more on income statements over the page — hurray.

Company Accounts: Income Statements

Income Statements calculate *Profits* over a period of *Time*

1) Income statements should cover one whole accounting year. An income statement that covers **less than 12 months** can be **misleading**. High Street retailers can generate **half their annual revenue** in the lead-up to **Christmas** — an income statement ignoring this period won't give an **accurate picture** of the business.

2) Sometimes income statements cover a little **more** or a little **less** than a year — e.g. when a business changes its accounting year from Dec-Dec to Apr-Apr, it'll have one set of accounts that cover a short period between the end of the old accounting year and the beginning of the next one (Dec-Apr).

3) Income statements usually contain the **previous year's data** as well, for **easy comparison** to see what's changed. Some companies provide the previous five years' data as well. It's useful for spotting **trends** in turnover, costs and profits, and helps whoever's looking at the accounts to see what kind of a **financial position** the business is in.

Profit Utilisation is *How* a business uses its *Profits*

1) Businesses can use their **profits** in **two** main ways:
   - they can pay **dividends** to shareholders.
   - they can keep the profit in the business as **retained profit**.
2) **Shareholders** want companies to pay them **high dividends** so that they get a **good return** on their investment. If companies **don't** pay dividends to their shareholders, or pay very **low** dividends, existing shareholders might **sell** their shares, and potential shareholders might invest somewhere else instead — this would cause the company's **share price** to **fall**.
3) **Retaining profit** allows the business to **spend** on things that are likely to **increase** their profits in the future — buying **fixed assets** like machinery, business premises, etc allows the business to **increase production**, which could lead to **increased revenue** and **profits** in the future.
4) Companies usually try to find a **balance** between dividends and retained profit — they pay a proportion of their profit to their **shareholders** and **reinvest** the rest in the business to fund **growth**.

Of course, you could always use your profits to send your HR department to the Caribbean. They'd love that.

PLCs are *Legally Required* to publish their accounts

1) PLCs (public limited companies) have to **publish** their accounts so that they're available to **anyone** who wants to look at them — that includes shareholders, potential shareholders and competitors.
2) Most PLCs put as **little** information as possible in their income statements, because they don't want to give their **competitors** too much information about their performance — especially if their competitors could **use** that information to improve their own performance.
3) Private limited companies and businesses with unlimited liability have to **produce** accounts, but they **don't** have to publish them. Small businesses are allowed to produce **less detailed** accounts than larger private limited companies or PLCs.

Company Accounts: Limitations

Accounts are Useful for Decision-Making

1) Accounts can be really useful for comparing a business' current performance to its **competitors' performance**, and to its own performance in the **past** — they make **trends** in the business' financial performance clearer.
2) They can also help managers to make **decisions** — e.g. directors might decide to **reduce dividends** and retain more of their profits to invest in the business if their accounts show that the business' growth has been slow.

Accounts Don't Contain anything Non-Numerical

1) Company **accounts only** contain **financial data** about a company. This is **useful** for **potential investors**, but it **ignores** a lot of **qualitative** (non-numerical) **data** that potential investors should also take into account.
2) **Internal factors** that **don't appear** on accounts include the **quality** of staff and products, the company's **market share**, future **sales targets**, **productivity** levels, the firm's impact on the **environment** and **customer satisfaction**.
3) **External factors** like the **economic** or **market** environment aren't reflected in the accounts either. Accounts don't tell you anything about what a **competitor** might do next, or what legislation the government might pass. The development of **technology**, or potential changes to the **location** of the business (e.g. a new rail link) don't appear in the accounts. You'd need to analyse all these **external factors** to see how they might affect the business.

The Income Statement doesn't tell you Everything

1) The **income statement** is useful for assessing the performance of the company, but it isn't the be-all and end-all.
2) It doesn't include any information about **external factors** such as **market demand**, which would be useful in forecasting **future turnover** and **profit**.
3) It doesn't include any information about **internal factors** such as staff morale, which would be useful in determining **productivity** and therefore **profitability**.
4) In times of **inflation**, the income statement isn't so useful, because inflationary rises in price distort the true value of turnover.
5) The income statement can be **deliberately distorted**, by bringing forward sales from the next trading period and including them as part of this trading period.

The Balance Sheet Doesn't tell you Everything, either

1) The **balance sheet** is a statement about one point in the **past**, which may not help predict the **future**.
2) The balance sheet doesn't give any clues about the **market** or the **economy** that the business is trading in.
3) Balance sheets value some intangible assets (e.g. a brand recently purchased by the company), but they don't value intangible assets like **staff skill**, **staff motivation** or **management experience**.
4) If bad debts are included in the balance sheet as an asset, the accounts will be misleading — see p. 89.
5) It's best to look at the income statement and the balance sheet **together** to get the best idea of a business' finances.

Practice Questions

Q1 Why can income statements that cover less than 12 months be misleading?

Q2 Why do PLCs often put as little detail as possible in their income statements?

Q3 Give two examples of non-numerical external factors that affect businesses but don't appear on their accounts.

Exam Question

Q1 Evaluate the usefulness of income statements for assessing a company's financial position. [6 marks]

Accounts never tell me anything — I can't get them to say a word...

There's nothing too taxing here, which makes a nice change from most of the section. You still need to learn it though — when you're reading through you might think it's all a bit obvious, but it's funny how your mind can go blank in an exam as soon as you get a question like 'Why shouldn't shareholders rely solely on accounts to make investment decisions?'

Financial Ratios

Ratios turn final accounts into easy-to-understand numbers. You can use them to compare firms and to compare a firm's performance over time — brilliant.

Liquidity Ratios show How Much Money is available to Pay The Bills

1) A firm without enough **working capital** (see p. 91) has poor **liquidity**. It can't **use** its assets to **pay** for things when it needs them.
2) The **liquidity** of an asset is how easily it can be turned into **cash** and used to **buy** things. **Cash** is **very** liquid, **non-current assets** such as **factories** are **not liquid**, and stocks (inventories) and money owed by debtors (receivables) are in between.
3) A business which doesn't have enough **current assets** to pay its liabilities when they are due is **insolvent**. It either has to quickly find the money to pay them, give up and **cease trading**, or go into **liquidation**.
4) **Liquidity** can be **improved** by decreasing stock levels, speeding up collection of debts owed to the business, or slowing down payments to creditors (e.g. suppliers).
5) **Liquidity ratios** show how **solvent** a business is — how able it is to pay its debts. There are **two** liquidity ratios you need to know — **acid test ratio** and **current ratio**.

1) The Acid Test Ratio = Current Assets (excluding stock):Current Liabilities

1) The **acid test ratio** compares **current assets (excluding stock**, or inventories) to current liabilities. It shows how much of what a business owes in the short term is covered by its current assets. It doesn't include stock, because it isn't always easy to sell stock in time to pay off debts.

$$\text{Acid test ratio} = \frac{\text{Current assets} - \text{Stock}}{\text{Current liabilities}} \quad \text{(written as a ratio } x:1\text{)}$$

For example: $\frac{£30\,000 - £7000}{£32\,000} = 0.71875:1$

2) A ratio of 1:1 is ideal — it shows **both** amounts are the **same**. A value much **more** than this means the business has **money lying around** that they could use more profitably if they invested it elsewhere. A ratio of less than 1:1 means the business doesn't have **enough** current assets to **pay its bills.** A ratio of 0.8:1 shows a firm has only 80p of current assets for every £1 of current liabilities it owes. Not good...

Arthur definitely passed the acid test — he looked hot in lemon yellow.

2) The Current Ratio = Current Assets (including stock):Current Liabilities

1) The **current ratio** compares **current assets (including stock**, or inventories) to current liabilities.

$$\text{Current ratio} = \frac{\text{Current assets}}{\text{Current liabilities}} \quad \text{(expressed as a ratio } x:1\text{)}$$

For example: $\frac{£30\,000}{£32\,000} = 0.9375:1$

The current ratio is also called the working capital ratio.

2) In reality, the business probably couldn't **sell off** all its stock. It'd also need **additional capital** to **replace** stocks — the current ratio should be **higher** than 1:1 to take account of this. 1.5:1 or 2:1 is considered ideal.
3) A value much below 1.5:1 suggests a **liquidity problem** and that it might struggle to meet its current liabilities. See above for **ways** that a company can **improve** its **liquidity**.

Financial Ratios

Efficiency or Performance Ratios show how Efficiently the firm is working

1) Efficiency ratios show managers and shareholders **how well** the business is using its **resources**.
2) There are **four** important efficiency ratios — **asset turnover** ratio, **inventory turnover** ratio (stock turnover ratio), **receivables days** ratio (debtor days ratio) and **payables days** ratio (creditor days ratio). They show how efficiently the business is using its **assets**, and how well managers are controlling **stock**, **debtors** and **creditors**.

1) Asset Turnover Ratio = Sales Revenue ÷ Assets

1) The asset turnover ratio compares the **sales revenue** a business makes to the value of its **total assets**:

$$\text{Asset Turnover ratio} = \frac{\text{Sales Revenue}}{\text{Assets}}$$

For example: $\frac{£40\ 000}{£200\ 000} = 0.2{:}1$

2) The asset turnover ratio shows how much **sales revenue** a business is making from every pound's worth of its **assets**. **Non-current assets** (like **machinery**) help the business operate efficiently, and so make lots of sales (turnover or revenue), so a firm with a lot of non-current assets should have a large turnover. A low asset turnover ratio could suggest that the business **isn't** using its non-current assets **efficiently**, so its assets aren't generating as much turnover as they should. It could also mean that the firm has **too many current assets** (e.g. its stock levels are too high).
3) What counts as a **good** asset turnover ratio depends on the type of business. E.g. manufacturing businesses will have lots of **machinery** and **stock**, so they're likely to have a **low** asset turnover ratio. Businesses that provide **services** don't usually have as many assets, so they should have a **higher** asset turnover ratio. You can tell if an asset turnover ratio is good by comparing it to **similar businesses** — comparisons across industries **don't work**.
4) Managers should **compare** the asset turnover ratio to **previous operating periods**, to see if the firm is **improving** its efficiency month after month, or year after year.
5) Businesses can improve their asset turnover ratio by **getting rid** of under-used **non-current assets**, or holding **less stock** (since surplus stock doesn't generate revenue).
6) Operating machinery to **full capacity** helps fixed assets generate the maximum amount of revenue. There are **problems** with this though — machinery operating at its limit is more likely to break down and need **expensive repairs** or replacement.

2) Inventory Turnover Ratio = Cost of Sales (per year) ÷ Average Stock Held

1) The inventory turnover ratio (stock turnover ratio) compares the **cost** of all the **sales** a business makes over a year to the **average value** of **stock** that it holds.
2) You need to know the **cost price** of everything the business has **sold**, i.e. what the products cost the firm to make. **Stock** is valued at **cost price**, so you need **sales** at cost price too. You'll find **cost of sales** on the **income statement** and **stock held** is on the **balance sheet**.

$$\text{Inventory Turnover ratio} = \frac{\text{Cost of Sales}}{\text{Cost of Average Stock Held}}$$

For example: $\frac{£160\ 000}{£8000} = 20{:}1$

3) This ratio tells you **how many times** a year the business **sells all its stock**. A fruit and veg stall might sell their entire stock every day, which would give a stock turnover ratio of 365. A property developer who took 4 months to do up and sell each house would have a ratio of 3. Businesses operating **JIT production** have a **very high** ratio.
4) When you analyse this ratio, you need to judge if the business has **enough stock** to **fulfil orders**, but **not too much stock** to be **efficient**. Holding twice the stock needed might not be an efficient use of funds.
5) The inventory turnover ratio can be improved by **holding less stock**, or **increasing sales**. Easier said than done...
6) **Aged stock analysis** lets managers make sure that old stock gets sold before it becomes **obsolete** and **unsaleable**. It lists all stock in **age order**, so the manager can **discount** old stock and cut down orders for slow-selling stock.

Financial Ratios

3) Receivables Days Ratio = Average Receivables ÷ Total Credit Sales × 365

1) The receivables days ratio (debtor days ratio) compares the **average amount owed** to a business by its **debtors** to the value of the **total sales** that it gives buyers credit for:

$$\text{Receivables Days ratio} = \frac{\text{Average Receivables}}{\text{Total Credit Sales}} \times 365$$

For example: $\frac{£1500}{£50\,000} \times 365 = 10.95$ days

You'll find 'receivables' on the balance sheet as a current asset. Average receivables is the average amount of money owed to the firm by its debtors (not the average number of debtors) over the trading period. Divide it by the value of all the credit sales over the period.

2) 'Receivables days' is the number of days that the business has to **wait to be paid** for goods it supplies on credit.
3) It's best to have **low** receivables days, because it helps with **cash flow** and **working capital**. What makes a good receivables days ratio depends on the type of business. **Retailers** tend to get paid **straight away** unless they offer credit on items such as TVs or fridges. **Medium size businesses** usually take **70-90 days** to get invoices paid.
4) You can **compare** receivables days ratios with previous months or years to look for **trends**. An **upward trend** may be because the business has offered **longer credit terms** to attract more customers. However, if it isn't monitored, the business may be heading for **cash flow problems**.
5) **Aged receivables analysis** lets managers **control receivables days**. Unpaid accounts are listed in order of how long they've been unpaid. The ones that are **most overdue** are **targeted** first for repayment.
6) **Asset turnover**, **inventory turnover** and **receivables days** are all measures of **activity** — they tell you how **effectively** a business is using its **resources** to generate **revenue**.

4) Payables Days Ratio = Average Payables ÷ Total Credit Purchases × 365

1) The payables days ratio compares the **average amount** the business **owes** to its **creditors** to the value of the **total purchases** that it makes on credit:

$$\text{Payables Days ratio} = \frac{\text{Average Payables}}{\text{Total Credit Purchases}} \times 365$$

For example: $\frac{£300}{£7000} \times 365 = 15.64$ days

'Payables' is a current liability on the balance sheet. Average payables is the average amount of money that the business owed to all its creditors over the trading period. Divide it by the cost of all purchases the business made on credit.

2) This is the number of days the firm takes to **pay** for goods it buys on credit from **suppliers**.
3) You can establish a **trend** over a period of time and use this trend to analyse the efficiency of the firm. For instance, if the trend is upwards it may suggest the firm is getting into **difficulties paying** its suppliers. This might be OK, but if the suppliers get the hump and decide they want to be paid **now**, it's a **problem**.

Practice Questions

Q1 How do you work out the current ratio and acid test ratio?

Q2 What does the asset turnover ratio show?

Q3 Which would have the higher inventory turnover ratio, a Porsche dealer or a shoe shop?

Q4 What's the difference between the receivables days ratio and the payables days ratio?

Exam Questions

Q1 A company is owed an average of £5000 by its trade customers and sells an average of £20 000 of goods on credit each year. What can you say about its debt collection using receivables days analysis? [6 marks]

Q2 Comment on the efficiency of a firm that generates revenue of £750 000 using £2 000 000 in assets. Last year its asset turnover ratio was 0.25:1. Is the business more or less financially efficient this year than last year? [6 marks]

Oh look, what a lot of "lovely" ratios...

Being totally honest, these ratios are a bit of a pain in the backside. They're all really similar so it's tricky to know which one to use when. Don't worry too much about remembering the formulae, because you'll get a formula sheet in the exam if you need one — but make sure you're clear on what each one's for. Don't be tempted to rush this, even though it's a bit tedious.

Financial Ratios

If you were worried that you'd got to the end of financial ratios, you'll be pleased to know there's still three more pages of them to go — phew. First up, profitability ratios — they show profit margin.

Gross Profit Margin (%) = Gross Profit ÷ Revenue × 100

1) The **gross profit margin** measures the relationship between the gross profit and the value of sales. It's expressed as a percentage, calculated by:

$$\text{Gross Profit Margin (\%)} = \frac{\text{Gross Profit}}{\text{Revenue}} \times 100$$

Gross profit = revenue – cost of sales.
Revenue = value of sales.

2) What counts as a good gross profit margin depends on the **type of business**. A business with a high asset turnover (e.g. a bakery) can afford to have low gross profit margin.
3) The ratio can be **improved** by **increasing prices** or **reducing** the direct **cost of sales**.
4) Also, a business can improve its overall gross profit margin by **stopping** selling products with a **low gross profit margin**.

Net Profit Margin (%) = Net Profit ÷ Revenue × 100

1) The **net profit margin** takes **overheads** (indirect costs) into account. The ratio is again expressed as a percentage:

$$\text{Net Profit Margin (\%)} = \frac{\text{Net Profit}}{\text{Revenue}} \times 100$$

Net profit = gross profit – indirect costs.

2) It's best to have a **high** net profit margin, although it does depend on the type of business, like the gross profit margin.
3) It's useful to **compare** net profit margin with gross profit margin over a **period of time**. A business with a **declining net profit margin** compared to gross profit margin is having trouble with its **overheads**.
4) Net profit margin can be improved by **raising revenue** or **lowering** cost of sales or (most importantly) **overheads**.

Return on Capital Employed (ROCE) is the most Important profitability ratio

1) The **return on capital employed** (ROCE) is considered to be the best way of analysing profitability. It's expressed as a percentage, calculated by:

$$\text{Return on Capital Employed (\%)} = \frac{\text{Operating Profit}}{\text{Total Equity + Non-current Liabilities}} \times 100$$

The operating profit is on the profit and loss account, and the total equity and non-current liabilities are on the balance sheet. There are several ways of calculating this ratio, but this method will get you through the exam.

2) The **ROCE** tells you how much money is **made** by the business, compared to how much money's been **put into** the business.
3) A decent **ROCE** is about **20-30%**. It's important to compare the ROCE with the Bank of England interest rate at the time, because this tells investors whether they'd be better off putting their money in the bank.
4) ROCE can be **improved** by **paying off debt** to reduce non-current liabilities, or by making the business more **efficient** to **increase operating profit**.
5) ROCE is just one measure of **return on investment**. Another important one is the **average rate of return** (see p. 110).

Financial Ratios

Gearing shows *Where* a business gets its *Capital* from

1) **Gearing** is another really important ratio. It shows **potential investors** where a business' finance has come from — what **proportion** of its finance comes from **long-term loans** (debt) rather than **share capital** or **reserves** (equity).
2) Gearing is calculated using information from the lower part of a **balance sheet** (see p. 88) — the part that shows where the money comes from. To work out the gearing, divide the amount of finance that comes from **long-term loans** by the **total amount** of finance in the company (from loans, shares and reserves):

$$\textbf{Gearing (\%)} = \frac{\textbf{long-term loans}}{\textbf{total equity + non-current liabilities} \text{ (see p. 88)}} \times \textbf{100}$$

3) A gearing **above 50%** shows that **more than half** of a business' finance comes from **loans** — the business is **high-geared**. A gearing of **below 50%** shows it is **low-geared**, because **less than half** of the finance comes from loans.

Gearing shows how *Vulnerable* a business is to *Changes* in *Interest Rates*

1) The more the business is **borrowing**, the harder they'll be hit by a rise in interest rates. How much **borrowing** a business can do depends on its profitability and the value of its **assets** — the more assets the business can offer as **security**, the more money it will be able to borrow.
2) Gearing is a crude **risk assessment** that an investor can use to help decide whether to buy shares in the company. The more the firm borrows, the **more interest** it will have to pay — this may affect **profits** and the **dividend** paid to shareholders. The more the firm borrows, the more **risk** there is that the investor won't get much dividend.

Looks pretty high geared to me.

Example

A firm has gearing of 11% — it's **low-geared**.

- This tells you that **most** long-term funds come from **shareholders**, not loans.
- This could be a sign that the firm is **risk averse** — it doesn't want to run the risk of spending too much money on interest payments.
- Because the firm doesn't have to spend its profits on interest payments, it can **withstand** a **fall** in profits more easily than a highly geared firm, since the firm can easily choose to **reduce** dividend payments to shareholders, unlike loan repayments, which have to be made.

Example

Another firm has gearing of 72% — it's **high-geared**.

- This tells you that **most** long-term funds come from **loans**.
- It's obvious that the firm is willing to take **risks** — if profits fall, or interest rates rise, the business still has to keep up with the **loan repayments** or it could **lose** the **assets** the loans are secured on (e.g. business premises).
- The company may be high-geared in order to fund **growth** (see next page), or because its directors don't want outside shareholders to **own** a large part of the business, and so they prefer to borrow money rather than sell shares.

Financial Ratios

High Gearing has Risks and Rewards for Businesses

High gearing is **risky** for businesses, but some businesses are willing to take the risks that come with high gearing because of the **potential rewards** it can bring:

Rewards of high gearing for businesses

1) One benefit of **borrowing** money for the business is extra **funds** for expansion. Ideally, the loan is invested in projects or technology which **increase profits** by more than enough to pay off the loan repayments. **High gearing** can be attractive during a **growth phase**. A firm that's trying to become the market leader, and has growing profits along with a strong product portfolio, may decide to borrow heavily in order to **fund expansion** and gain a **competitive advantage**. This will **increase** the firm's **gearing**. During times of **growth**, there is plenty of **profit** even after they've paid the loan interest and repayments, so high gearing can be good for the business.
2) When interest rates are very **low**, high gearing is less risky because interest payments are lower.

Risks of high gearing for businesses

1) The **risk** to the business of borrowing money is that it might not be able to afford the **repayments** — it might not make enough profit to pay back the **loan** and **interest**.
2) Taking out loans can be **risky** even when interest rates are low, because they might **go up** later and the business will still be committed to making the **repayments**.

High Gearing has Risks and Rewards for Investors too

1) The reward (of investing money in the business) for the **lender** or **shareholder** is **interest** for lenders or a share **dividend** for shareholders (often paid out twice a year). Shareholders can also sell their shares at a **profit** if the share price goes up. Since high gearing can lead to high profits for businesses, shareholders might expect to see **large dividends** and a **big increase** in the share price compared to a low-geared company.
2) The **risk** to the **shareholder** of high gearing is that the business may **fail** if it can't afford to keep up with loan repayments. When a business goes into **liquidation**, lenders will probably get the money they're owed, but the shareholders could lose most or all of the money they've invested in the business.

Practice Questions

Q1 How is the gross profit margin calculated?

Q2 Give an example of when it's not a problem to have a low gross profit margin.

Q3 What does ROCE stand for?

Q4 What does ROCE tell you about a business?

Q5 What's meant by "high gearing"?

Exam Questions

Q1 A business has sales revenue of £2 million. Its gross profit is £750 000, and its overheads are £250 000.
(a) Calculate the net profit margin. Answer on p.203. [3 marks]
(b) How might the business improve its net profit margin? [5 marks]

Q2 Evaluate the risks of investing in a business which has high gearing. [6 marks]

Low gearing is also helpful when driving uphill...

More ratios — good old AQA sure knows what makes A level students happy. You can probably guess what I'm going to say — learn what each ratio is for, and be prepared to use them in the exam. Exam questions might ask for a specific ratio analysis, or you can get marks for choosing to use them yourself if you're asked to assess a business' financial position.

Shareholders' Ratios

Shareholders use ratios to see how much dividend they'll get, and to see how the business is performing.

Investors use Ratio Analysis to decide where to invest

1) **Investors** use several share-related financial ratios when making decisions about where to invest their money. These ratios are called **shareholders' ratios**.
2) **Dividends** are paid out to shareholders once or twice a year, out of the company's profits. **Ratios** help an investor to see the **rate of return** to expect — what proportion of its profits a company pays out in dividends.
3) Investors would also expect to see the price of their shares **increase** over time. A return on investment caused by a rise in the share price is called a **capital gain**.
4) Some investors want **short-term profits** which give them a quick return through **dividends**. Shareholders' ratios are most useful for these investors.
5) Other investors want a **long-term return** through **capital gain**. They'd want the company to invest profits in growth instead of paying them out as dividends.

What it's all about...

Dividend Per Share = Total Dividend ÷ Number of Shares

1) **Dividend per share** is usually stated at the foot of the **income statement** appropriation account (see p.95).
2) The amount of profit set aside for dividend payment is simply divided by the number of shares issued.
3) The resulting figure is usually expressed as a number of **pence**. Say the dividend per share is 9.5p and you own 1000 shares — you'd get a dividend cheque for £95.
4) Shareholders looking for **short-term return** want the dividend per share to be as **high** as possible. Shareholders looking for **long-term return** through capital gain might be happy with a **low** dividend per share.
5) It's pretty much OK for a company with a **low share price** to have a low dividend per share — shareholders can afford to **buy more shares** to get the dividend return they want.
6) It's the directors' decision how much profit they set aside for dividend payments, by the way. But if the shareholders don't like it, they can vote at the AGM to sack the directors and bring in a new lot.

$$\text{Dividend Per Share} = \frac{\text{Total Dividend}}{\text{Number of Shares Issued}}$$

Dividend Yield (%) = Dividend Per Share ÷ Price Per Share × 100

1) **Dividend yield** is a comparison between the cost of the shares and the dividend received. It's expressed as a percentage and calculated by:
2) Shareholders looking for **short-term return** want a **high dividend yield**.
3) Dividend yield and dividend per share can both be improved by increasing the proportion of profits that are paid out as dividends.
4) Dividend yield depends on share price — which can go up and down, depending on business performance.

$$\text{Dividend Yield (\%)} = \frac{\text{Dividend Per Share}}{\text{Price Per Share}} \times 100$$

Example: Johan buys **100 shares** at **500p** each, and the dividend per share is **15p**.

$$\text{Dividend Yield (\%)} = \frac{15}{500} \times 100 = 3\%$$

3% really **isn't very good** for a short-term return. If he wants short-term profit, Johan ought to be looking at **other forms of investment** to see if he could earn more profit elsewhere — e.g. a savings account at the local bank.

Dividend Cover = Net Profit ÷ Dividend Paid Out

1) **Dividend cover** allows you to see how many times a company could pay the dividend from its profits. It's calculated by:
2) So, if the dividend cover is 2 then the company is paying out **half** of its earnings as a dividend. This might be rather **attractive** to an investor.

$$\text{Dividend Cover} = \frac{\text{Net Profit After Tax}}{\text{Total Dividends}}$$

Value and Limitations of Ratios

***Ratio Analysis** has its **Limitations** — just like the final accounts do*

All financial **ratios** compare two figures from the **accounts**, and give you a raw **number** as an answer.

Ratios don't take account of any **non-numerical factors**, so they don't provide an absolute means of assessing a company's financial health. They have several limitations that you must be able to evaluate in your exam answers:

1) **Internal strengths**, such as the quality of staff, don't appear on the accounts, so they won't come up in ratios.
2) **External factors**, such as the **economic** or **market** environment, aren't reflected in the accounts. When the market's very **competitive**, or the economy's in a **downturn**, it's OK for ratios to suffer a bit.
3) **Future changes** such as technological advances or changes in interest rates can't be predicted by the accounts, so they won't show up in the ratios.
4) Ratios only contain information about the **past** and **present**. A business which has **just started** investing for growth will have lousy ratios until the investment **pays off** — that doesn't mean it's not worth investing in.

Example of how ratio analysis can't predict changes in external factors

- Harry is interested in **investing** in XYZ Ltd. **Ratio analysis** indicates that XYZ is **performing strongly** and gives a **good rate of return** for the investor, so he decides to **buy 1000 shares**.
- Later that day, Harry talks to Sarah, who says **new EU health and safety legislation** will **ban XYZ** from making any more of its products from next year onwards. XYZ Ltd must now either **diversify** into another product/service or **close**.
- Harry doesn't feel so clever about his investment now. XYZ Ltd will need **time** and **money** to **reinvest** in a new production line so **profits will be very scarce** for the next few months. Worse still, XYZ Ltd may go **bankrupt** and he'd have shares with **no value at all**. What a nightmare.

*When **Comparing** ratios, compare **Like with Like***

1) It's important to **compare** today's ratios with ratios for the same business over a period of time, to spot trends. These comparisons over time need to take account of **variable factors** — things which change over time, such as **inflation**, accounting procedures, the business activities of the firm and the market environment. These things won't always stay the same over the period that you're looking at.
2) It's also useful to compare ratios with **other businesses**, either in the same industry or in different industries. It's important to **compare like with like**. Other firms may **differ** in size, objectives and product portfolio. They may do their **accounts** differently, e.g. they may have their financial year end in a different month.

Practice Questions

Q1 Why might a shareholder not automatically want as high a dividend per share as possible?

Q2 Dividend yield is a better measure of performance than dividend per share. Why is this?

Q3 Give a brief outline of two non-numerical factors that should be taken into account when doing ratio analysis.

Q4 Why might comparisons of today's ratios with last year's ratios be misleading?

Exam Questions

Q1 Net Profit: £500 000 Profit after tax: £300 000
Dividend per share: 6p Shares issued: 100 000
a) From the above information calculate the dividend cover. [3 marks]
b) If the share price is 300p, calculate the dividend yield. [2 marks]

Answers on p.203

Q2 Outline two external factors that should be taken into account when analysing financial ratios. [8 marks]

Q3 Ratio analysis gives information about the past.
Discuss what value ratio analysis has in predicting future performance. [12 marks]

Limitations of ratios — well, they can't do cartwheels for starters...

It's not possible to make 100% solid conclusions from ratio analysis alone. You need to use other data from several sources alongside ratios. It's important to consider the market that the business is trading in, and what its competitors are doing. Also, bear in mind that using data from the past isn't always a great way to predict the future. Stuff changes.

Selecting Financial Strategies

All businesses need finance, and they have to decide what's the best way to get it. Sources of finance have to be suitable for the type of business, and for what the business wants to spend the finance on.

All businesses need *Finance*

1) All businesses need enough **fixed capital** (see p. 92) to buy the non-current assets (fixed assets) they need to produce their products. If they don't have enough fixed capital, businesses **can't grow** because they can't buy extra machines, larger premises, etc.
2) They also need enough **working capital** (see p. 91) to pay day-to-day bills and expenses. Otherwise the business **won't survive**.
3) There are several different ways that businesses can raise finance. They have to decide which source of finance is **most suitable**, depending on **how much** finance they need, what they want to **spend** the money on, and **how long** they need it for.
4) Not all types of finance are available to all businesses, so the source of finance also depends on what's **available** to the business, not just what managers and directors prefer.

Finance can be *Internal* or *External*

1) **Internal** finance is capital raised **within** the firm by doing things like cutting costs or putting **profits** back into the business (see below).
2) **External** finance is capital raised **outside** the firm. Businesses can raise external capital in several ways, including **selling shares**, getting an **overdraft** or getting a **loan** from a bank or a venture capitalist (see p. 107 for more).

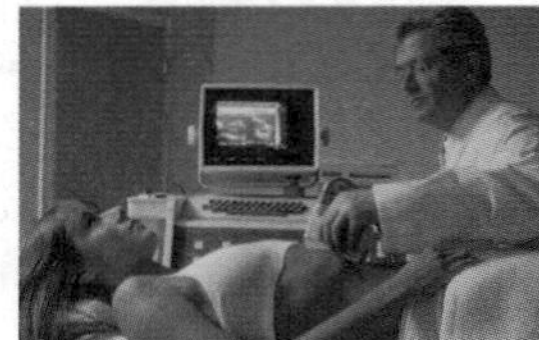

Unfortunately, Helen's scan didn't show any evidence of internal finance — just another baby.

There are *Three Main Ways* to raise *Internal Capital*

Retained profit

1) **Profit** can be retained and built up over the years for **later investment**.
2) The main **benefit** of using profit for investment is that the business doesn't have to pay **interest** on the money. **Not all businesses** can use this method though — they might not be making enough **profit**.

Rationalisation

1) **Rationalisation** is when managers **reorganise** the business to make it more efficient. They can do this by **selling** some of their **assets** (e.g. factories, machinery, etc) to generate capital.
2) Businesses don't need to pay **interest** on finance they raise by selling their assets.
3) The main **drawback** to selling assets is that the business **no longer owns** the asset. Also, assets like cars and computers **lose value** over time, so the business won't get back as much as it paid for them.

Squeezing working capital

1) A business can find some internal capital by **squeezing working capital**. They do this by reducing the amount of **stock** they hold, **delaying** payments to **suppliers** and **speeding up** payments from **customers**.
2) The main advantage of raising finance in this way is that it can be done **quickly**. However, the amount of capital a business can get from tightening its belt like this is **limited**.

Selecting Financial Strategies

External Finance can increase *Working Capital* in the *Short Term*

Trade credit

1) **Trade credit** is where there's a **delay** between a business **receiving** raw materials or stock and **paying** for them.
2) The main advantage of trade credit is that the business gets to **keep** its money for **longer**.
3) Suppliers **won't** always give trade credit to new businesses or businesses that might have trouble paying.

Overdrafts

1) **Overdrafts** are where a bank lets a business have a **negative** amount of money in its bank account.
2) Overdrafts are **easy to arrange** and **flexible** — businesses can borrow as **little** or as **much** as they need (up to the overdraft limit) and they only have to pay **interest** on the amount of the overdraft they actually use.
3) The main disadvantage of overdrafts is that banks charge **high rates** of **interest** on them.

Debt factoring

1) **Debt factoring** is when banks and other financial institutions take **unpaid invoices** off the hands of the business, and give them an instant **cash** payment (of less than 100% of the value of the invoice).
2) The **advantage** of this for businesses is that they can **instantly** get money they are owed.
3) The **disadvantage** of debt factoring is that the debt factoring company **keeps** some of the money owed as a **fee**.

External Finance is used for *Medium-Term Needs* (1-5 years)

1) **Loans** have lower interest charges than overdrafts, and are repaid in monthly instalments. The drawback is that banks need **security** (usually **property**) for a loan, which they can **sell** if the business doesn't repay the loan.
2) **Leasing** is when a business **rents** fixed assets like cars and office equipment instead of **buying** them. It means paying a smallish amount each month instead of a lot of money all in one go. Businesses can easily **upgrade** equipment or vehicles they're leasing. In the **long run**, leasing works out **more expensive** than buying, though.

External Finance can be used for *Long-Term Projects* (up to 25 years)

1) **Debentures** are special kinds of long-term **loan** with **low fixed interest** rates and **fixed repayment dates**. As with bank loans, the main drawback is that they're **secured** — usually against property.
2) **Grants** are money from local government and some business charities. The good thing about grants is that businesses don't have to pay them back — it's **free money**. However, businesses usually only qualify for a grant if they're creating **new jobs**, setting up in **deprived** areas or being started by **young people**.
3) A limited company can sell **shares** in the business. The advantage of this for the business is that they **don't** have to pay the money back. The disadvantage is that the shareholders **own** part of the business, so the business has to give them a share of the **profits** (called a dividend) and allow them to vote on some issues.
4) **Venture capitalists** provide capital by giving loans and by buying shares. The advantage is that venture capitalists may provide **business advice** as well as cash. The disadvantage is that applying for funding is a **long** and **complicated** process. Also, selling shares to venture capitalists means that they **own** part of the business.

Practice Questions

Q1 What is internal capital?

Q2 Give three examples of long-term sources of external finance.

Exam Question

Q1 Discuss the advantages and disadvantages of using overdrafts for short-term finance. [6 marks]

Internal finance — selling one of your kidneys...

Finding suitable sources of finance might not be the most exciting topic in the world, but it's really important for businesses. Nearly all businesses set out to make a profit, and if they can't get enough money to pay for day-to-day survival, they won't last very long at all. Make sure you're clear on all the different ways that businesses can raise internal and external finance.

Cost and Profit Centres

Businesses can look at sales budgets and production budgets for the whole of the business — or they can look at one part of the business in isolation and work out how much money it's spending, and how much it's making.

Managers set **Budgets** for **Parts** of the **Business** — **Cost** and **Profit Centres**

1) Cost and profit centres are just a **way to work out budgets** for a particular **part** of a business. With a **cost centre**, you can set a **cost budget**, and with a profit centre, you can work out **costs** and **revenues** and set a budget for how much profit you want that part of the business to **make** over a year.
2) **Cost centres** are parts of a business that directly **incur costs**. The business can identify costs, measure them, and **monitor** them against a **mini-budget** that applies just to that part of the business.
3) **Profit centres** are parts of a business that directly **generate revenue** as well as costing money. The business can work out the **profit** or **loss** they're making by subtracting the **costs** from the **revenues**.
4) The IT department of a business is an example of a **cost centre**. Managers can work out the **costs** of IT technicians' wages and new computer upgrades. They **can't** work out the **revenue** that the IT department earns, because they **don't charge** other departments for providing IT support.
5) A chain of shops can treat **each shop** as a **profit centre**. The business owner can work out the **profit** for each shop separately using the **costs** of stock, rent and staff wages for each shop, and the **sales revenue** for each shop.
6) Manufacturers can treat each **product line** as a profit centre. Individual **brands** can also be profit centres. You can figure out how much they cost, how much they make, and then **set a budget** based on how much you **think** they're going to cost and how much you think they're going to make next year.

How is Hairdressing doing as a profit centre?
We're radically "trimming" costs and "restyling" price structure.
Nice.

Cost and profit centres have several **Uses**

① Financial decision making

1) Overall profit figures don't tell senior managers exactly **where** profits are being made. Cost and profit centres let managers **compare** the costs of different parts of the business. Then they can try to make the less cost-efficient parts **more efficient**.
2) Managers can use **profit centres** to help them **set prices** — once they know the cost, they can set the price so that they'll make a **profit**.

② Organisation and control

1) Managers can use cost and profit centre information when they want to change the **organisation** of the business. They can focus on the **profitable** areas and might get rid of **unprofitable** shops or products.
2) Managers can set **cost limits** and **profit targets** to coordinate staff and get them to **focus** on specific activities. They can link **pay** and **bonuses** to meeting **profit targets** and keeping costs down in each department, team or shop.

③ Motivation

1) Each cost or profit centre has its own budget, so **junior managers** and **employees** have the opportunity to control budgets in individual centres.
2) **Profit share** schemes mean employees and managers within profitable profit centres can earn **bonus** payments, but this can backfire if profits aren't as good as expected — staff could end up less motivated instead of more motivated.

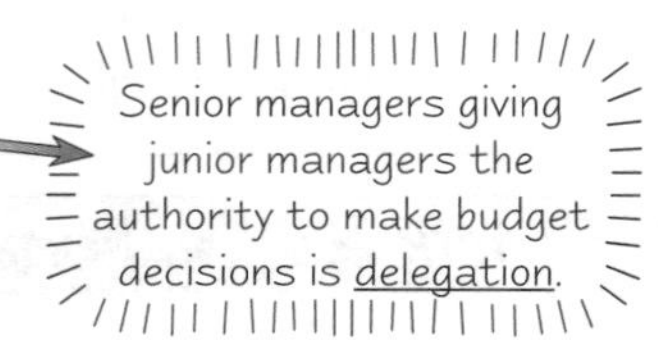

Senior managers giving junior managers the authority to make budget decisions is delegation.

Example: When British Airways came under intense pressure from budget airlines, the company realised they had to **cut costs** to compete. They calculated costs, revenues, profit and loss for each **route**. Managers **closed** the **loss-making** routes and put money toward **increasing** the services on the more **profitable** routes. The marketing department were set targets intended to motivate them and generate more customers for these routes. Company performance started to improve.

Cost and Profit Centres

Businesses **Define** cost and profit centres in **Different Ways**

Depending on the type of business, cost and profit centres can be defined by:

1) **Product** — e.g. a high street **clothing** company might monitor costs and revenues for each product, so it could work out how much **profit** or **loss** different lines of clothing contributed to the business.
2) **Factory** — e.g. **car manufacturers** use their different factories as cost and profit centres, so they know what percentage of costs and profits each factory represents to the business. This information is useful if the business needs to **downsize** — they can close the **least profitable** factories.
3) **Location** — e.g. **supermarkets** that know how much profit (as well as how much revenue) each **store** generates for the business will find it easier to choose areas with **profitable** stores for expansion.
4) **Person** — e.g. businesses with a sales force will usually monitor **each sales person** as a profit centre. Sales people are very **expensive** to employ — so a business wants to make sure none of them are **costing** the business **more** than they generate in profit.

Cost Centres must include **Indirect Costs**

When businesses calculate the cost of a **cost centre**, they have to remember to include **indirect costs** (e.g. **managers' salaries** and rent on a shop or factory), not just the **direct costs** that are involved in making each product (like the cost of raw materials).

Cost and profit centres have **Advantages** and **Disadvantages**

Advantages of cost and profit centres	Disadvantages of cost and profit centres
Managers can easily spot the successful and unsuccessful parts of the business.	Giving junior employees responsibility for setting budgets can be too much for them to handle. They'll need financial training first.
Local managers can make decisions to suit their cost or profit centre. They can set prices for the local market.	It can be hard to divide a business into cost and profit centres. Sharing out the costs of overheads like rent is particularly tricky.
Meeting targets on a local level can be more motivating than working towards a distant national target.	There's rivalry between cost and profit centres in a business. If it goes too far, it can be a problem — branches could be more concerned with beating each other's profits than with customers.

Cost and profit centres don't suit all businesses. Leaders who like to **make all the decisions** won't be happy about **delegating responsibility** for budgets. Businesses without **good junior staff** won't be able to **handle** cost and profit centres. It often isn't worth working out cost and profit centres for a business which just sells **one kind of product**.

Practice Questions

Q1 What is a cost centre?

Q2 Would the maintenance department be a cost centre or a profit centre?

Q3 Give two reasons for using cost and profit centres.

Q4 State three types of profit centre that a business might use.

Q5 Give two drawbacks of using profit centres.

Exam Questions

Q1 Why might a small business owner decide not to establish cost and profit centres for their business? [6 marks]

Q2 Tanya Richards owns and manages four beauty salons, and runs each salon as a profit centre. She also has a small office where she and her assistant look after all the admin, accounting and marketing for the business.
(a) Why does Tanya run her office as a cost centre, not as a profit centre? [4 marks]
(b) To what extent might running the salons as profit centres motivate Tanya's staff? Explain your answer. [11 marks]

Need profits — go to the local profit centre...

Cost and profit centres are especially good for businesses like banks, supermarkets and manufacturers — it makes a lot of sense to divide those businesses up into individual bank branches, individual stores and individual product lines. Don't go thinking that profit centres and cost centres are opposites — it's just that you can't measure profit for a cost centre.

Investment Decisions

Investment appraisal helps businesses decide what projects to invest in, in order to get the best, fastest, least risky return for their money.

Investment** decisions must balance **Risk** and **Return

1) Businesses often need to **invest** in order to achieve their **objectives** — e.g. if a firm's objective is to **increase sales** by 25% over three years, they'll need to invest in extra **staff** and **machinery** so that they can make the extra products they hope to sell.
2) Any situation where you have to **spend** money in the hope of **making** money in the future is **risky**, because there's always the possibility that you **won't** make as much money as you expect. Businesses like the **risks** to be **low** and the **return** (profit) to be **high**.
3) When companies are making strategic **decisions** about how to **invest** their money (whether to launch a new product, take on more staff, relocate their call centre, etc) they gather as much **data** as possible so that they can work out the **risk** and **reward** involved.
4) There are **two** main **questions** that businesses try to answer to enable them to make good investment decisions:
   - **how long** will it take to get back the money that they spend?
   - how much **profit** will they get from the investment?
5) There are **four methods** that businesses can use to help them **answer** these questions and decide whether investments are a good idea: **average rate of return** (see below), **payback period calculation** (p. 111), **discounted cash flow** (p. 113) and **internal rate of return** (p. 114).
6) These **investment appraisal methods** assess how much **profit** a project is going to make, and how **fast** the money will come in. The faster money comes in, the less risk in the long run.
7) All of the methods are **useful**, but they're only as good as the **data** used to calculate them.

Average Rate of Return** (ARR) compares **Yearly Profit** with **Investment

1) **Average rate of return** (ARR — sometimes called Accounting Rate of Return) compares the **average annual profit** with the level of investment.
2) The higher the ARR, the more **favourable** the project will appear.
3) ARR is expressed as a **percentage** and calculated by: → $\frac{\text{Average Annual Profit} \times 100}{\text{Investment}}$

Example:

	Investment	Year 1	Year 2	Year 3	Year 4	Year 5
Project A — net cash flow	(£10M)	£4M	£5M	£6M	£7M	£5M
Project B — net cash flow	(£8M)	£3M	£3M	£4M	£6M	£6M

The pirate accountants were very fond of the average rate of return.

Project A (£10M investment) has a profit of (£M) 4 + 5 + 6 + 7 + 5 – 10 = **£17M**.
Average annual profit is £17M divided by the five years = **£3.4M**
ARR = £3.4M / £10M investment × 100 = <u>34%</u>
Project B (£8M investment) has a profit of (£M) 3 + 3 + 4 + 6 + 6 – 8 = **£14M**
Average annual profit is £14M ÷ 5 years = **£2.8M**
ARR = £2.8M / £8M investment × 100 = <u>35%</u>

All other things being equal, the managers would choose project B because it has a higher ARR, just. Just. By a whisker.

Advantages of Average Rate of Return:	It's easy to calculate and understand. It takes account of all the project's cash flows.
Disadvantages of Average Rate of Return:	It ignores the timing of the cash flows. It ignores the time value of money (see p. 112).

Investment Decisions

Payback measures the **Length of Time** it takes to **Get Your Money Back**

1) The **payback period** is the time it takes for the project to make enough money to pay back the **initial investment**.
2) The **formula** for calculating the payback period is:

$$\frac{\text{Amount invested}}{\text{Annual profit from investment}}$$

   For example, a £2 million project that has an **annual profit prediction** of £250,000 will reach payback in 8 years (£2 million ÷ £0.25 million = 8).
3) Managers **compare** the payback periods of different projects so that they can choose which project to go ahead with — managers usually want to get their money back as soon as possible, so they prefer a **short payback period**.

There are **Advantages** and **Disadvantages** to **Payback Period Calculation**

Calculating the payback period can be helpful, but it has drawbacks too:

Advantages of Payback Period Calculation

1) It's **easy** to calculate and understand.
2) It's very good for **high tech** projects (technology tends to become **obsolete** fairly quickly, so businesses need to be sure that they'll get their initial investment back before the products **stop** generating a return) or any project that might not provide **long-term** returns.

Disadvantages of Payback Period Calculation

1) It **ignores cash flow** after payback. E.g. two projects (project A and project B) might both have a payback period of three years, but project A will continue to provide a profit of £20 000 a year after the payback period, while project B won't provide any more profit after it's payback period — project A is clearly the **better investment**, but payback period calculation **doesn't** take this into account.
2) It **ignores** the **time value** of money (see p. 112).

Practice Questions

Q1 What are the two questions that businesses ask about potential investments?

Q2 Give two disadvantages of average rate of return.

Q3 Give two disadvantages of payback period calculation.

Q4 What does ARR take into account that the payback period calculation doesn't?

Exam Questions

Answers on p.203

Q1 A business is investing in a new product. The initial investment is £200 000. The product will generate a revenue of £320 000 over 8 years, with total costs of £40 000 over 8 years. Calculate the average rate of return on the investment. [5 marks]

Q2 Priya owns a donut shop. She's thinking of buying a new donut-making machine, costing £5000. She estimates that it will generate an extra profit of £1500 per year. Calculate the payback period for the new machine. [3 marks]

'Revenge of the Business Studies students 2: Payback'...

These aren't the most interesting couple of pages in the world, but investment appraisal techniques are really useful for businesses, and they could come in quite handy in your Business Studies exam if you get a question on them. So stick with it until it's all practically tattooed on your brain, and then turn over for... more on investment appraisals (sorry).

Investment Decisions

More investment appraisal methods I'm afraid. Stick with them though because they're really important.

The **Future Value** of cash inflow depends on **Risk** and **Opportunity Cost**

If someone offers you £100 cash in hand now or in one year's time, you'd do best to take it **now**. **Risk** and **opportunity cost** both **increase** the longer you have to wait for the money, which means that it's **worth less**. This is called the **time value of money**.

1) There's a **risk** that the person would never pay you the £100 after a year had gone by.
2) In a year's time the money would be worth less due to **inflation** — a general rise in prices over time. You wouldn't be able to buy as much stuff with that £100 as you could today.
3) There's an **opportunity cost** — if you had the money now you you could **invest** it instead of **waiting** for it. A high interest account would beat the rate of inflation and the £100 plus interest that you'd end up with in a year's time would be worth **more** than the £100 in your hand today, and much more than the £100 would be worth to you in a year.
4) You could invest **£100** in an account giving you **3% interest**, and you'd get **£103** at the end of the year. If you invested **£97.09** in an account giving you 3% interest you'd get **£100** at the end of the year. So, if you assume that you'd get an interest rate of **3%** if you invested the money, the value of **£100** paid to you at the **end of the year** would be the same as **£97.09 today**.

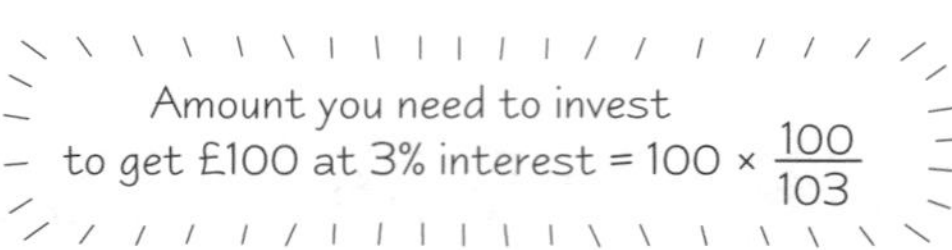

Amount you need to invest
to get £100 at 3% interest = 100 × $\frac{100}{103}$

A payment after a year or two, or three, is **always worth less** than the **same payment** made to you **today**.

Discounting adjusts the value of **Future Cash Inflows** to their **Present Value**

1) **Discounting** is the process of **adjusting the value of money** received in the **future** to its **present value**. It's done so that investors can **compare like with like** when they look at the cash inflows they'll receive from projects. £4 million this year **isn't the same** as £4 million in five years' time, and it's not wise to **pretend** that it is the same.
2) **Discounting** can be seen as the **opposite** of **calculating interest**.

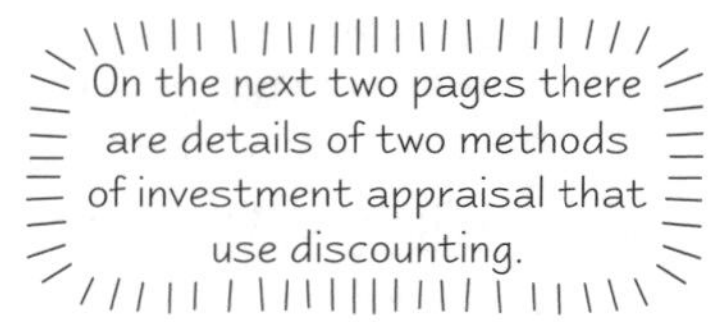

On the next two pages there are details of two methods of investment appraisal that use discounting.

3) It's done by **multiplying** the amount of money by a **discount factor**. This discount factor is like the opposite of a bank interest rate. Discount factors are **always less than 1**, because the value of money in the future is always less than its value now.
4) **Discount factors** depend on what the **interest rate** is predicted to be. **High** interest rates mean that the future payments have to be **discounted a lot** to give the correct present values. This is so that the present value represents the **opportunity cost** of not investing the money in the **bank** where it'd earn a nice **high interest rate**.

Year	0	1	2	3	4	5
Discount Factor for 10% interest	1	0.909	0.826	0.751	0.683	0.621
Present Value of £1000	£1000	£909	£826	£751	£683	£621

Year 1 discount factor = 100/110 = 0.909. Year 2 discount factor = $(100/110)^2$ = 0.826. Year 3 discount factor = $(100/110)^3$ = 0.751. It's like compound interest in reverse. You don't need to be able to work discount factors out yourself though — you'll be given them in the exam if you need them.

5) As you might expect, when **interest rates** are predicted to be **low**, the future cash inflow needn't be discounted so much. There's less opportunity cost.

Investment Decisions

Discounted Cash Flow allows for Inflation and Opportunity Cost

1) **Discounted cash flow** (DCF) is an investment appraisal tool that takes into account the **changing value** of money over **time** (because of **inflation** and the **opportunity cost** of not investing in something else instead).
2) **Discount factors** (see p. 112) are used to calculate the **net present value** (NPV) of the project. This is the value of the project assuming all future returns are discounted to what they would be worth if you had them **now**, which is **always** less than their face value (because of inflation and lost interest).
3) The **discount factor** applied is based on the **rate of interest** the business could get at the bank instead of doing the project. Don't forget that if you have to work out NPV in an exam, you'll be **given** the **discount factors**, so you **don't** need to worry about how to work them out — phew.
4) If you end up with a **negative NPV**, that means that the business could get a better return by putting their money into a **savings account** rather than going ahead with the project. Businesses will usually only go ahead with projects with a **positive NPV** — projects that are going to **make them money**.
5) The **downsides** of discounted cash flow are that it's a bit **hard to calculate**, and that it's hard for businesses to work out what the **discount factor** ought to be, because they don't know what the bank interest rates are going to be in the future. The longer the project is set to last, the harder it is to predict the discount factor.

Here's an Example of Discounted Cash Flow

Project A has an initial investment of **£10M**, and **project B** has an initial investment of **£8M**.
The **expected rate of interest** is **10%**.
The discount factors are: **0.909** (year 1), **0.826** (year 2), **0.751** (year 3), **0.683** (year 4) and **0.621** (year 5).

Project A	**Cash inflow**	**Discount Factor (10%)**	**Present Value**
Year 1	£4M	0.909	£4M × 0.909 = £3 636 000
Year 2	£5M	0.826	£5M × 0.826 = £4 130 000
Year 3	£6M	0.751	£6M × 0.751 = £4 506 000
Year 4	£7M	0.683	£7M × 0.683 = £4 781 000
Year 5	£5M	0.621	£5M × 0.621 = £3 105 000
Total Present Value of Cash Inflows			£20 158 000
Net Present Value (total minus Investment)			-£10M = **£10 158 000**
Project B	**Cash inflow**	**Discount Factor (10%)**	**Present Value**
Year 1	£3M	0.909	£3M × 0.909 = £2 727 000
Year 2	£3M	0.826	£3M × 0.826 = £2 478 000
Year 3	£4M	0.751	£4M × 0.751 = £3 004 000
Year 4	£6M	0.683	£6M × 0.683 = £4 098 000
Year 5	£6M	0.621	£6M × 0.621 = £3 726 000
Total Present Value of Cash Inflows			£16 033 000
Net Present Value (total minus Investment)			-£8M = **£8 033 000**

The £27M that project A will generate is worth £20 158 000 now. Taking into account the original investment of £10M, that's a return (profit) of £10 158 000 over 5 years — 101.6%.

Project B will earn the company £22M — worth £16 033 000 now. The original investment's £8M, so that's a return of 100.4%.

Working out the NPVs shows that **both** projects are **worthwhile**, because both have a **positive NPV**.
Project A gives a **slightly better** return than **project B**.

Practice Questions

Q1 How do you calculate the net present value of a cash inflow?

Q2 What does it mean if a project has a negative net present value?

Exam Question

Q1 Explain the concept of the time value of money. [4 marks]

Discounts? Brilliant — I love a bargain...

Another tricky couple of pages here. It's nearly the end of the section though, so try to summon up the energy to learn these two pages, and then there's just two more to go. Discounting future income is a bit of a weird concept to get your head around at first, but it really makes sense for businesses to do it, so keep going over it until you're sure you've got it.

Investment Decisions

There's just one more investment appraisal method to learn, then a few other bits and bobs about investment decisions, and then that's section two over — phew.

Internal Rate of Return (IRR) works out Several NPVs

1) **Internal Rate of Return** (IRR) is concerned with the **break-even rate of return** of the project.
2) It uses **discounted cash flow** (see p. 113) to produce **several net present values** for each project, using **slightly different discount factors**, until they get an **NPV** of **zero.** An NPV of **zero** means that their money **wouldn't increase or decrease** in value — the investment would **break even**. The discount rate that gives an NPV of zero is called the **internal rate of return**.
3) Managers then need to work out whether the **bank interest rates** are likely to be **higher** than the **internal rate of return** — if they are then they might as well put the money in the **bank** instead of investing it in the project, since this will give them a **better return**.
4) Managers can also set their own "**criterion level discount rate**" which is their **minimum rate of return**. Projects which have an **internal rate of return** lower than this criterion level don't get the go-ahead.
5) Calculating the IRR is **really hard**, and there's a lot of repetition involved. It's best done by **computer**. Luckily, you **don't** need to know how to calculate it for the exam — just what it is and how it helps businesses make investment decisions.

Advantages of Internal Rate of Return:	It allows you to set the **required rate of return**. It allows for the **time value of money**.
Disadvantages of Internal Rate of Return:	The calculation requires **computers**. Some managers find it **hard** to get their heads around it.

Non-Numerical, Qualitative factors also affect Investment Decisions

The investment decisions made by managers are based upon a wide range of numerical data and quantitative methods. But managers must also put the decisions into a **qualitative** context, based on internal factors and market uncertainty.

Business Objectives and Strategy can Influence Investment Decisions

1) An investment appraisal recommended purely on financial data **may not fit in** with the **objectives** of a firm. Many businesses will only make an investment if the project will **help them achieve** their objectives.
2) For example, a business which aims to produce **low cost products** for a large mass market (e.g. teaspoons) would be unlikely to invest **as much** in **research and development** as a high-end technology business.
3) **Human resources investment** takes away from short-term profit, so a firm with the objective of **maximising profit** for shareholder dividends would be unlikely to invest too highly in staff development. On the other hand, a business which aims to produce **high quality**, high-tech products would invest in **skilled staff**.

Corporate Image can Influence Investment Decisions

1) **Good corporate image** brings **customer goodwill** and **loyalty** in the long term, and the firm may consider this more important than **short-term rate of return** on investment. Investment decisions that create bad publicity and damage customer loyalty will damage the bottom line in the **long term**.
2) A firm with a green, **ecologically friendly** image would avoid investments that would damage the environment. Some firms incorporate environmental costs into their investment appraisals.

Phil had spent all morning perfecting his corporate image.

Industrial Relations can Influence Investment Decisions

1) Investments which result in a **loss of jobs** may be turned down, even if they show a good rate of return.
2) **Loss of jobs** affects **staff morale**. Cost of **redundancy payments** should be factored into the decision. Trade unions may **strike** over the job losses, which would affect **productivity**. **Corporate image** may also be damaged.

Investment Decisions

There's Always Risk and Uncertainty involved in Investments

1) Businesses can use all the investment appraisal methods on the last few pages, but that **doesn't** mean that a **new project** will necessarily be successful just because they expect it to be — there's **always** a **risk** involved in investing in a new project.
2) All investment appraisal methods are based on **predictions** made by the business about how much **income** they can generate from investments. It's very **difficult** to **accurately** predict what's going to happen in the future, so businesses **can't** always **rely** on their predictions. E.g. a business might work out that the **payback period** of a machine is four years, based on a predicted income from the investment of £8000 a year — but the investment could easily end up only generating £3000 a year, so their payback period calculation would be **completely wrong**.
3) Market environments are always **uncertain**. Circumstances might change **unexpectedly**, and this could have a negative impact on the business. **Exchange rates** may alter, **sales** may decrease, **customers' tastes** may change, **competitors** may become stronger, the **cost** of **raw materials** may increase, etc. Any change in the **circumstances** that businesses based their investment **predictions** on can mean that their predictions are **no longer valid**. E.g. if a business works out the net present value of a project based on an interest rate of 6%, but the interest rate actually goes up to 9%, their net present value results will be **inaccurate**.
4) Every firm has a **different attitude** to **risk** — some firms are happy to take big risks that might lead to big financial rewards, but other firms prefer to play it safe and go for less risky investments.

Investment Appraisal methods can Reduce Risk

1) Although investment appraisal methods **aren't** 100% foolproof, it's still **less risky** for businesses to make investment decisions with the help of investment appraisal methods than without them.
2) **Investment appraisal methods** can give a business a pretty good **idea** of whether an investment is likely to be **worthwhile** or not. E.g. if they calculate that the **payback period** for a project is going to be **75 years**, it's probably not worth going ahead with it — their **estimates** of future income are unlikely to be **so far wrong** that they've overestimated the payback period by 70 years.
3) As long as businesses use **sensible predictions** (e.g. not using an interest rate of 30% when 3% is more likely), investment appraisal methods are a **helpful** tool for deciding which projects to invest in.

Wearing protective headgear is another way of reducing risk.

Practice Questions

Q1 Give one advantage and one disadvantage of IRR.

Q2 How do industrial relations influence investment decisions?

Q3 Why can't businesses rely completely on their predictions?

Q4 How do investment appraisal methods reduce risk?

Exam Question

Q1 Discuss the qualitative factors that affect investment decisions. [8 marks]

Ow, my head hurts...

You won't need to be able to work out IRR in the exam, but you still need to know why businesses use it. Learn everything on these pages and then that's it — the end of the whole Financial Strategies and Accounts section. Congratulations. You might need a bit of a lie down now to recover from all this accounting before you move onto the next section.

Marketing

If you can think back as far as last year, you'll remember that marketing made up a big chunk of AS. And here we are on marketing again. It's like you've never been away. Everyone should be familiar with the stuff on these pages, but don't rush or skip them — learn them properly.

The Role of Marketing is to Identify and Satisfy customer Needs and Wants

1) Marketing ensures that the business supplies goods and services that the customer **wants**, in order to achieve a **competitive advantage** (see p.183) over other firms. It's **mutually beneficial** for the business and the customer — the customer gets something they like and the business achieves higher profit levels.
2) Remember, marketing covers **market research**, **market analysis**, **market planning** and the "**marketing mix**" — the four big Ps of product, price, promotion and place (distribution).

Objectives and Strategies set out Marketing Aims and Directions

1) **Marketing objectives** are what the marketing department uses to say **exactly** what it's **hoping to achieve**.
2) For many companies, the key marketing objectives are **increasing profit levels** and **gaining market share**.
3) Other marketing objectives might include **creating** and **maintaining** a strong **brand ID**, helping the company to **grow**, making sure a particular product **survives** when a rival product enters the market, or helping the business to **cut costs**, e.g. by switching from expensive television ads to a cheaper online marketing campaign.
4) Objectives can be **qualitative** (e.g. **non-numeric** plans for brand image, product quality, product development) or **quantitative** (**specific figures** for market share, sales revenue, market penetration and profitability).
5) **Marketing strategies** say who the company's **target market** is, and how they're going to use the **marketing mix** to **achieve** their marketing **objectives**.

Marketing Objectives are Influenced by things Inside and Outside the Business

INTERNAL FACTORS

CORPORATE OBJECTIVES — The marketing department has to make sure its activities fit in with the company's **overall goals**. For example, if the business has set a **corporate objective** of **improving profits** in the **short term**, there's no point in the marketing department focusing on an innovative **new product** idea that still needs to be developed and is **two years** away from being **launched**.

FINANCE — The finance department allocates the marketing department's **budget**. This affects what the marketing department is able to do. If the budget is **cut** then marketing objectives may need to be **scaled down**.

HUMAN RESOURCES — **Workforce planning** (p.152-153) identifies how many **staff** the marketing department needs. If the marketing objectives involve lots of **different activities**, the marketing department will need a **lot** of staff to get them all done. If the business has decided to **reduce** staffing levels, marketing might have to set **less ambitious** objectives.

OPERATIONS — The production department can only produce **so many** units in a certain **time** period. A marketing objective of increasing market share that involves increasing sales by giving away **free samples** in magazines will only work if production have the **spare capacity** to make them.

EXTERNAL FACTORS

MARKET — The **state** of the **economy** has a big impact on marketing objectives. An economic **boom** is a good time to try to increase **sales volumes** since **income levels** are generally higher. In a **recession** the marketing department is more likely to set an objective of maintaining **market share**. For more about the business cycle, go to p.166.

TECHNOLOGY — Changes in technology affect some businesses more than others. In markets where technology changes **rapidly**, the objectives of the marketing department tend to be more focused on **sales** and **price**, because new technology causes prices to rise or fall very fast. For example, the price of **DVD players** has **fallen** rapidly since the launch of **Blu-Ray**™. This isn't necessarily a bad thing — DVD players still have a high share of the market because they're now so cheap. However, it does mean that the marketing department of a DVD player manufacturer will have to reassess sales objectives and pricing strategies to ensure that they aren't left with **unsold stocks**.

COMPETITORS — The actions of competitors affect marketing, particularly in a highly **competitive** market. If a competitor is focused on **low prices**, then the marketing department may alter their objectives so customers see them as **price competitive**. For example, Tesco launched their "Real Baskets" advertising campaign in 2009, in direct response to Asda's "Saving you money every day" campaign.

Marketing

The **Law** directly affects the **Marketing Objectives**

The Government regulates businesses to make sure they act in the **public interest**. It has a direct impact on marketing.

1 — Product

- Some products are **plain illegal** under UK law, e.g. handguns.
- The **Sale of Goods Act** means that goods must be **"fit for purpose"** and **"of satisfactory quality"**.

2 — Price

- **Predatory pricing** (cutting prices to force a competitor out of business) is illegal in the EU and in the US.
- Firms can't **fix prices** — they can't **agree** with their **competitors** to all charge the **same price** for a particular **item.**
- Consumers must be **told** the **price** before they buy — e.g. pubs must display drink prices.

3 — Place / Distribution

- Some products can only be sold in certain places by certain people — e.g. some medicines.
- **Licences** are required to sell some products, e.g. **alcohol** or firearms.
- **Sunday trading** is limited.

4 — Promotion

- The **Trade Descriptions Act** regulates promotion. Businesses can't lie about their products.
- **Offensive adverts** can be **banned**. The Advertising Standards Authority regulates adverts.
- Advertising of some products is **restricted**. **Prescription medicines** can't be advertised at all and there are very few places where **tobacco** products can be advertised. Advertising of alcoholic drinks is also restricted.
- **Advertising hoardings** need planning permission.

Businesses analyse their current situation using **SWOT**

SWOT stands for **strengths**, **weaknesses**, **opportunities** and **threats**. It's a tool that allows a business to consider both **internal** and **external** factors. It tells managers **where the business is** in terms of its strengths and weaknesses, and the opportunities and threats that the market currently offers. It can also help formulate marketing **objectives**.

1) The business must identify its **strengths** and **weaknesses** in a **factual** and **objective** way. For example, a bakery's **strengths** might include the fact that it's the only place in town that offers freshly made sandwiches. A **weakness** might be that it's located down a dark, dingy side alley, away from other shops.
2) The **external** environment provides the **opportunities** the business wants to exploit and the **threats** that might prevent success. So the bakery would see the opening of a new call centre with 500 employees as an opportunity, but the introduction of a low price lunch menu by a local restaurant as a threat.
3) SWOT lets the business know where it has a **competitive advantage** over its rivals. Marketing departments can use the opportunities section of the analysis to highlight ideas for **product development** and **market expansion**. Threats to the business may highlight **competitor brands** which can affect the business's market share.

Strengths
Weaknesses
Opportunities
Threats

Practice Questions

Q1 Name two internal and two external factors that influence marketing objectives.

Q2 What does SWOT stand for?

Exam Questions

Q1 Jo Porter has just opened a pub on her local village high street.
How would government legislation affect the way she can market her business? [8 marks]

Got a high-risk marketing situation? Call in the SWOT team...

When it comes to marketing, different companies prioritise different things — most want to increase sales, but some value things like brand ID too. Marketing departments are influenced by lots of different factors within the business and they have to consider things like the economy and the law too. Make sure you learn all this stuff so you understand what marketing is.

Marketing Analysis

Market analysis is essential — it tells firms how big the market is, if it's growing or shrinking and about their market share.

Market Classification leads to Market Analysis

1) **Market classification** tells businesses which market they are operating in. It involves **identifying** a **market's characteristics**. Markets can be classified by:

- **Geography** (local, national, international)
- **Nature** of the product (agricultural, technological)
- **Seasonality** (seasonal or year-round)
- **Development** level (new, growing, saturated)
- Product **destination** (trade, private consumers)

2) Companies **don't always spot** all the **markets** they could be in — they might have been supplying a product to industrial customers for so long that they don't notice that private customers might be interested in it, too.
3) **Marketing** can also be a **problem** for firms that operate in several markets. They often need to use **different marketing activities** to target **different markets**. They also need to be able to **afford** to carry out a variety of marketing activities **simultaneously**.

Once a business **identifies** which market it's operating in, it can begin **analysing** that market. Analysis of the chosen market allows businesses to set **marketing objectives** and **strategies** (see p. 116) that determine the business's future **marketing plan**. Market analysis can be **quantitative** or **qualitative**.

Market Analysis helps companies Segment the Market

Different groups of customers have different needs. **Analysing** different **segments** of a target market allows a firm to **focus** on the needs of **specific groups** within that market. A market can be segmented in several ways:

Income — **luxury products** are usually aimed at **high income** groups.
Age — firms can target products at specific **age groups** — pre-teens, teens, 25-35 year olds, the over 55s etc.
Gender — e.g. chocolate companies target some bars at **women** (e.g. Flake) and some at **men** (e.g. Yorkie®).
Geographical region — some products have a **regional market** — e.g. Welsh cakes, haggis.
Amount of use — for example, **mobile phone** suppliers market differently to **heavy** and **light** users.
Ethnic grouping — new **ethnic minority** digital **TV channels** make it easier for firms to target ethnic groups.
Family size — e.g. Large **"family packs"** of breakfast cereal, loo roll etc. are aimed at large families.
Lifestyle — **busy young workers** often buy microwaveable **ready meals**, so this kind of item is often aimed at them.

Quantitative Analysis has Advantages and Disadvantages...

Quantitative analysis uses **numerical data** such as sales figures, client databases and sampling. It looks at **who** buys a product and **how much** they buy. It is used to determine things like the **market share** and the way the market is **segmented**. **Large samples** of raw data, such as customer databases, can be analysed using **IT**.

Advantages

1) Quantitative analysis is **quick** to obtain — questions are usually numbers or yes or no answers.
2) It is also fairly **quick to analyse** using specialist computer software programs (see p. 123).
3) Trends can be **extrapolated** from numerical data to influence marketing forecasts. This kind of forecasting is usually quite **accurate** as many **trends** are fairly **consistent** over time.

Disadvantages

1) Data used may be **out of date** in a constantly changing market or there might not be **enough data**.
2) There can be problems of interpretation if there is **too much data** or some data is **irrelevant**.
3) **Random variations** in results can make it difficult to draw conclusions.
4) **Trends** don't always follow the **same pattern** — they can be affected by **unexpected events.**

Marketing Analysis

...and so does Qualitative Analysis

Qualitative analysis uses **non-numerical data** such as focus groups and in-depth interviews. It looks at the **human motivation** behind product choice — why people choose to buy certain products. It considers **thoughts** and **opinions** to work out how different consumer groups behave. It uses a **smaller** but more **detailed** sample of information.

Advantages

1) Analysis focuses on the **needs of the consumer**.
2) It helps companies to learn more about the preferences and **behavioural trends** of their market segments. They can use this information to **target** their market more effectively.
3) Some managers might feel **more comfortable** working from data provided by a **human** rather than processed by a **computer package**.

Disadvantages

1) Collecting and analysing the data is **time-consuming**. Answers can't be analysed using a computer.
2) Conclusions must be drawn using **subjective human judgement** so can be **unreliable**. The results of the research depend on the **skill** of the person doing the research.
3) Qualitative analysis uses **small samples**, so the data might not be **representative** of the whole population.

Market Analysis tells firms about Market Size and Growth

1) **Market analysis** is when a company **looks closely** at **market conditions**. It's useful for **planning**.
2) **Market size** is the **total sales** in the market — the **volume of sales** (**units** sold) or the **value of sales** (total **revenue**).
3) Businesses need to know if the market is **growing** (i.e. demand is increasing) or **shrinking** (i.e. demand is decreasing). The formula for market growth is:

$$\text{Market growth (\%)} = \frac{\text{New market size} - \text{old market size}}{\text{Old market size}} \times 100$$

4) In a **growing** market, **several** firms can **grow easily**. In a **shrinking** market **competition** can be **heavy** — there are fewer customers to go around. Firms can **diversify** or they may want to **get out** of the market altogether.

Market Analysis tells firms about Market Share

1) Market share is the **percentage** of sales in a market that is made by **one firm**, or by **one brand**. It's calculated using this formula:

$$\text{Market share (\%)} = \frac{\text{Sales}}{\text{Total market size}} \times 100$$

2) E.g., if **1 out of 4** PCs bought was a Dell, this would give Dell a **25% market share** (in terms of volume). If **£1 in every £10** spent on perfume was a Chanel purchase, this'd give Chanel a **10% market share** (in terms of value).
3) It's important to look at **trends in market share** as well as trends in sales revenue. Letting your market share go down is not good — it means that **competitors** are **gaining an advantage** over you.

Example: Say the computer gaming market has grown by **15%** from one year to the next. A software company would not be happy if they'd only increased their game sales by **5%** from £200 000 to £210 000 — they're failing to grow at the **same rate** as the market, so their **market share** has gone down.

Practice Questions

Q1 Give six ways that the consumer market can be segmented.

Q2 What is the formula for working out market growth?

Exam Questions

Q1 What are the advantages and disadvantages of using quantitative methods to analyse a market? [8 marks]

I wish market analysis involved actually going to the market...

Market analysis involves handling data and looking at lots of numbers — but at least there are fancy software programs which can help analyse it for you. Using IT can be useful and saves time but businesses have to work out if it's worth it in the long run. There's no point investing in fancy new software if they don't have enough data to make it worthwhile.

Marketing Data Analysis

Businesses have a lot of mathsy techniques for analysing data, and you need to know how they work.

Time Series Analysis looks at data over Time

1) **Time series analysis** is used to reveal **underlying patterns** by recording and plotting data over time, for example the recording of **sales** over a year.
2) Time series analysis can be used for **sales forecasting** and monitoring **production output**. It can also be used to look for **links** between **sales** and **marketing activity** and to spot **fluctuations** in the **economy** that might indicate a boom or bust period.
3) **Trends** are the long-term movement of a variable, for example the sales of a particular product over a number of years. Trends may be **upward**, **constant** or **downward**, but there are usually **fluctuations** around the trend.
4) **Seasonal** fluctuations repeat on a **regular** daily, weekly or yearly basis, e.g. the use of electricity over a 24-hour period, or the sale of ice lollies over a year.
5) **Cyclical** fluctuations are repetitions over a **medium-term** period, often many years. The business cycle of boom and bust has a cyclical pattern.
6) **Random** fluctuations have **no pattern** to them. They also include the results of **major disturbances** like **war**, changes of government and sudden **unpredictable events** like the outbreak of foot and mouth disease.

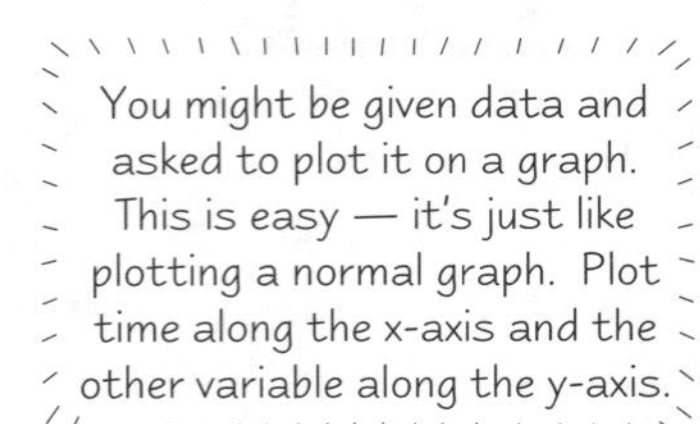

You might be given data and asked to plot it on a graph. This is easy — it's just like plotting a normal graph. Plot time along the x-axis and the other variable along the y-axis.

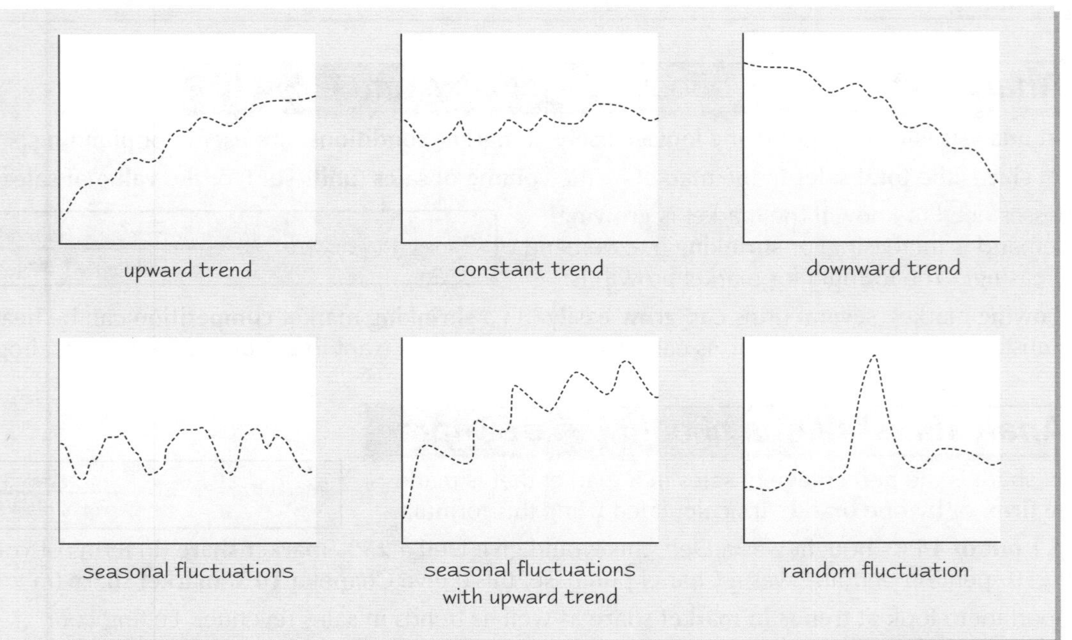

Time Series Analysis is Useful for making Short-term Plans

1) Managers can use time series analysis when making **decisions**.
2) It's often used at the end of the decision-making process to help weigh up the **costs** and **benefits** of different courses of action, e.g. to see whether decreasing the price of a product or introducing a "buy one get one free" offer would have a greater impact on sales.
3) It's best to use time series analysis as a **tactical forecasting** method, e.g. to make **short-term** predictions.
4) It's most useful in fairly **stable** environments, e.g. where the **size** of the **market** or the number of **competitors** is **unlikely** to **change** much.

Marketing Data Analysis

Correlation shows how Closely two Variables are Related

1) **Correlation** is a measure of how **closely** two variables are **related**, for example the age of customers and their income. Correlation may be **strong**, **weak**, or there may be no apparent correlation at all.
2) You can draw a **line of best fit** through a set of correlated points — the line should be as **close** as possible to **all** the **points** on the graph.

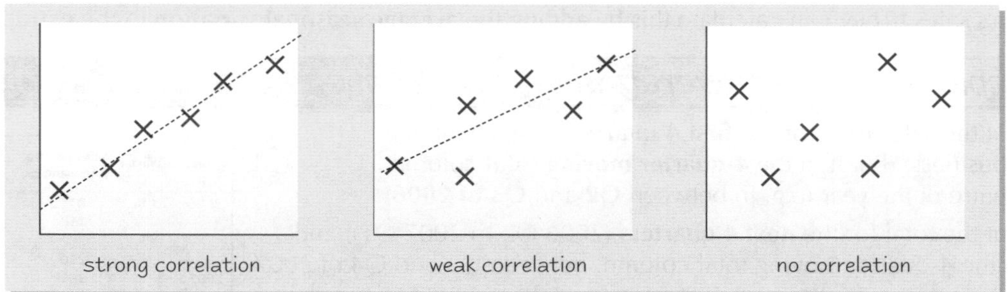

3) It's a **useful tool**, but correlation **doesn't prove** cause and effect. **Other variables** may be important — e.g. there might be strong correlation between an increase in marketing activity and ice-cream sales, but if the marketing coincided with a spell of hot weather, it's hard to say which factor had more impact.
4) If there's a **correlation** between two variables, managers might assume that the trend will **carry on**. They can **extrapolate** the graph — draw a **line of best fit** and then keep the line going to **project** the trend **further** along the **x-axis**. For example, if the graph shows the **cost** of **car repairs** against the number of **miles driven**, the line can be extrapolated to show that the **higher** the **mileage**, the **higher** the **cost** of repairs.
5) Extrapolation relies on **past trends** remaining **true**. Unfortunately, the **pace of change** in the market can be very fast, so extrapolations from the past don't always predict the future very accurately — it's best to use it for predicting just a **few months** ahead because customer desires and technology constantly change.
6) **Sudden unexpected events** are the biggest pitfall for extrapolation. Changes in the market due to things like **new technology** make extrapolation from past data look completely useless.

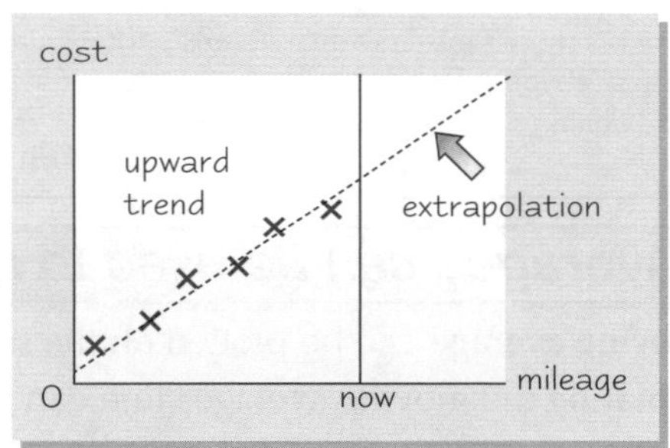

Practice Questions

Q1 What is time series analysis?

Q2 What is a trend?

Q3 What can cause random variations in time series analysis data?

Q4 What is correlation?

Q5 What is extrapolation?

The answer to this question is on p.203.

Exam Question

Q1 Draw a line graph for the sales data below. [6 marks]

Jan	170	Apr	280	Jul	190	Oct	170
Feb	195	May	350	Aug	130	Nov	160
Mar	160	Jun	250	Sep	150	Dec	185

A little less extrapolation, a little more action please...

Extrapolation is all about identifying a trend and then predicting what will happen next. It's important for businesses to look at past performance because it will give them a good idea of how a product will sell in the future. But don't forget, it's not 100% reliable — sudden events can really throw a spanner in the works and mess up your marketing strategy.

Marketing Data Analysis

Moving averages is a quantitative method of analysis which shows businesses the general underlying trend.

Moving Averages Smooth Out **Seasonal** and **Cyclical Fluctuations**

1) Moving averages are used to **smooth out** data which either contains **seasonal variations** or is **erratic**. The moving average **gets rid** of **fluctuations** to reveal the underlying trend, which can be **extrapolated** on a graph.
2) It's useful to know the general trend, but sometimes companies need a more **accurate** figure for a particular season's sales. They can calculate this by **adding** the **average seasonal variation** to the **extrapolated figure**.

An example of **Moving Averages** — pay attention because it's **Tough**

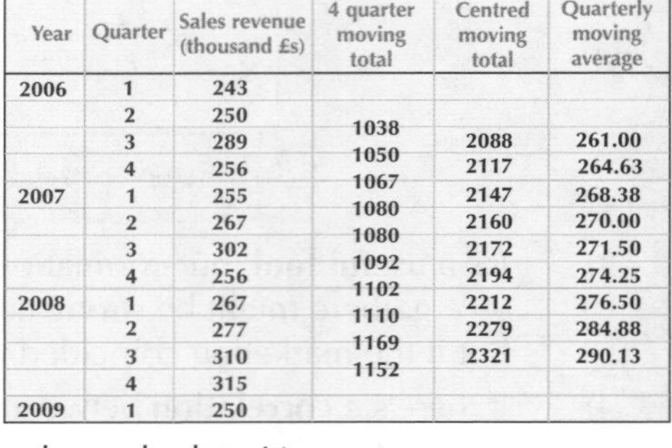

Year	Quarter	Sales revenue (thousand £s)	4 quarter moving total	Centred moving total	Quarterly moving average
2006	1	243			
	2	250	1038		
	3	289	1050	2088	261.00
	4	256	1067	2117	264.63
2007	1	255	1080	2147	268.38
	2	267	1080	2160	270.00
	3	302	1092	2172	271.50
	4	256	1102	2194	274.25
2008	1	267	1110	2212	276.50
	2	277	1169	2279	284.88
	3	310	1152	2321	290.13
	4	315			
2009	1	250			

1. Work out the sales total for the **first 4 quarters** (e.g. a whole year of business). Put it in the **4-quarter moving total** column, in the centre of the year (e.g. in between **Q2** and **Q3 of 2006**).
2. Work out the total for the **next 4 quarters** (2006 Q2 to 2007 Q1), and put it in the 4-quarter moving total column, between Q3 and Q4 of 2007. **Repeat** this process for the next 4 quarters, and the next, 'til you're done.
3. Add the first two **4-quarter moving totals** together and put the answer in the **centred moving total column**, in the 2006 Q3 row. **Repeat** for the rest of the 4-quarter totals.
4. **Divide** the **centred total** by **8** and put the value in the **quarterly moving average** column in the 2006 Q3 row (bang in the **middle** of the **data** you used to calculate it).
5. **Repeat** this process for the other **centred moving totals** to get your quarterly moving averages.
6. **Plot** the quarterly moving averages on a **graph**. Always **plot** the quarterly moving average in the **middle** of the quarters that it relates to — e.g. the quarterly moving average for the **2006 Q1** to **2007 Q1** should be plotted in line with **2006 Q3**. You should end up with a fairly **smooth line**.

You calculate a centred moving total as well as a 4-quarter moving average so that your midpoint always lines up exactly with one of the quarters. If you just used a 4-quarter moving average it would be halfway between two quarters, which wouldn't be as useful because you couldn't compare it directly with one of the quarters. If you were calculating the moving average for an odd number of periods, e.g. 3 months or 9 months, you wouldn't need to do this extra step.

Moving Averages can be used to **Predict Future Trends** and **Variation**

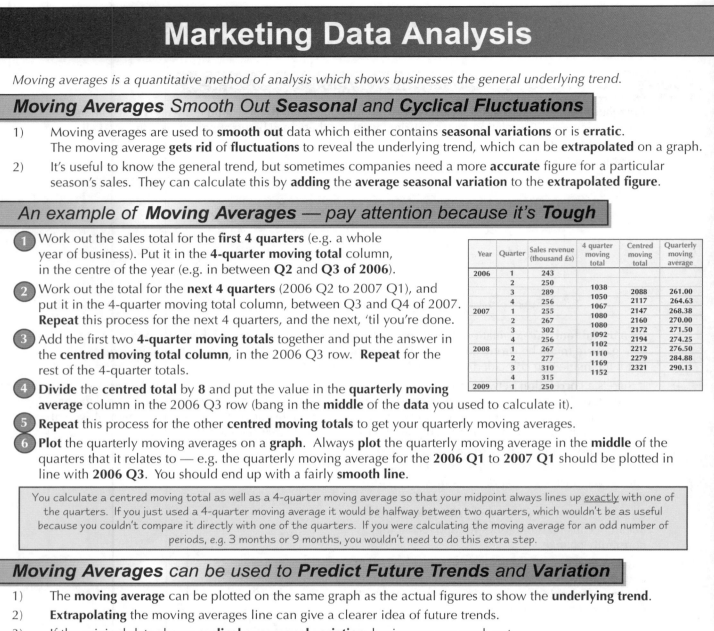

1) The **moving average** can be plotted on the same graph as the actual figures to show the **underlying trend**.
2) **Extrapolating** the moving averages line can give a clearer idea of future trends.
3) If the original data shows **cyclical** or **seasonal variation**, businesses can work out the **cyclical** or **seasonal deviation** to predict future figures **more accurately**.
4) The **cyclical** (or **seasonal**) **deviation** is the **average deviation** from the **moving average** for each point during the cycle. You work it out by calculating the **average difference** between the actual figure and the moving average for each Q1. See p.199 for how to calculate averages.
5) **Cyclical/seasonal deviation** can be included in the **extrapolation** of the graph to give a more accurate idea of what will happen in the future. E.g. the cyclical deviation for Q1 in the data in the example above is –11.4, so the predicted figure for each future Q1 would be 11.4 units below the trend line.
6) Moving averages can be really **useful** for businesses, but the trends they identify are only reliable if the business is operating in a **stable environment**.

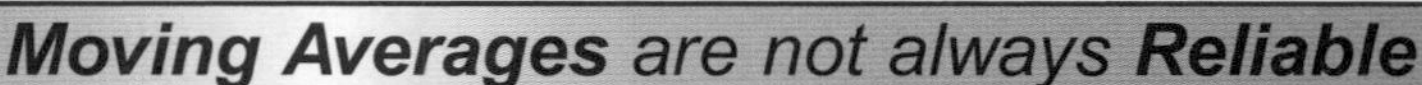

Moving Averages are not always **Reliable**

1) Moving averages are difficult to work out over **long periods** without using computer software.
2) They aren't useful at all in **unstable conditions** because random fluctuations can make predictions inaccurate.
3) The **past** isn't always a good basis for predicting the future — just because a product has performed well in the past doesn't mean it always will. Moving averages don't take into account the **changing consumer** market. They should be **combined with qualitative data** which informs managers about behavioural trends.
4) More **recent data** should be **weighted** — that means it will affect the analysis more than older data. The more recent the raw data, the more **relevant** the market analysis will be for future marketing objectives.

Marketing Data Analysis

IT can be used to help Analyse Markets

Most companies use **software** to do their marketing analysis. The **advantages** of this are:

1) Doing calculations **by hand** requires a lot of **concentration** — just one mistake affects the accuracy of the calculations and the reliability of the trends identified. By using IT, businesses can **reduce** the risk of **errors** being made.

2) Computers can **compare** moving-average trends from **different periods** at the touch of a button.

3) Computers can process much **more data** than humans can. It would be incredibly **time consuming** for a **human** to calculate moving averages or do other kinds of time series analysis on the huge amount of data that a **large firm** generates.

Little did Susan know that Mike was more loyal to his supermarket than he was to her.

4) IT can also be used to gather information for marketing analysis at the **point-of-sale**. For example, supermarket **loyalty cards** can provide information about the kinds of people who shop in a particular store or the products they're buying most often. There's more about this on p.184.

5) Lots of different companies now provide marketing analysis software. This makes it easier for a business to find a program that fits its **needs** exactly. For example, marketing analysis software allows managers to investigate "**what if?**" scenarios. They can calculate the impact of **potential changes** in expenditure or sales. The **price** of the software **falls** if the software providers are **competing** with each other on **price**.

Analysing marketing Data can be Difficult

Businesses might face **problems** when they're trying to analyse marketing data:

1) **Random variations**, more than one **correlation** in a set of data or **no** apparent **correlation** at all (see p.121) can make it hard for businesses to draw any useful conclusions from marketing analysis.
2) Buying **software** can be **expensive**. If a new version of the software is released and the business decides to **upgrade**, it costs even more money.
3) Staff need to be **trained** to use the software, which might be **expensive** and **time-consuming**. If the company **upgrades** their software at any point, further training might be needed.
4) There's a risk that having software that can deal with loads of data will lead to the company valuing the **quantity** of information over its **quality**. A business might produce lots of pretty graphs, but if nobody's drawing **conclusions** about what the **trends** mean for the company they're not useful at all.
5) Companies with lots of data might find that their **computer systems** aren't up to the job of **handling** it, e.g. if it takes too long to upload all the information. If this happens, they might have to **outsource** (see p.155) their marketing analysis to a **specialist company** or stick to analysing just a **proportion** of the available data.

Practice Questions

Q1 What are the benefits of using IT to carry out market analysis?

Exam Question

Q1 a) Calculate the quarterly moving averages for the sales revenue data below (figures are in thousands). (14 marks)

2006		2007		2008		2009	
Q1	630	Q1	621	Q1	602	Q1	589
Q2	567	Q2	578	Q2	550		
Q3	552	Q3	543	Q3	502		
Q4	678	Q4	600	Q4	560		

The answers to these questions are on p.203.

b) Plot the quarterly moving average trend line on a graph. (4 marks)

These moving averages can reach quite a speed on level ground...

Those moving averages are hard to get your head round, but not impossible. You'll need to really make sure that you genuinely, honestly follow all the steps for calculating them. Don't kid yourself that you get it if you don't. Read the hints for each step, and you can understand it. Honest. It's doable. Don't be tempted to skip it, because it may be in the exam.

Selecting Marketing Strategies

Once a business has gathered and analysed the data, it's time to choose the best marketing strategy.

*There are **Low Cost** and **Differentiation** marketing strategies...*

1) **Low Cost** strategy calls for the **lowest cost** of **production** for a given level of quality.
2) In a **price war**, the firm can maintain profitability while the competition suffers losses.
3) If **prices decline**, the firm can **stay profitable** because of their low costs.
4) A very **broad market** is needed for this strategy — preferably a **global** market, with huge production facilities to take advantage of **economies of scale**.

Differentiation

1) **Differentiation** strategy requires a product with **unique attributes** which consumers value, so that they **perceive** it to be **better** than rival products.
2) A unique product has 'added value' so the business can charge a **premium price**.
3) However, competitors might try to **copy** the product, or consumer **tastes** could **change**.

Of course, low cost and unique aren't always mutually exclusive...

*...and **Market Penetration, Diversification** and **Development** strategies, too*

1) **Market penetration** means trying to **increase** your **market share** in your **existing market**. E.g. if a company makes washing powder and currently has 25% market share, it might try to achieve 30% market share using **sales promotions**, **pricing strategies** and **advertising**. This strategy works best in a **growth market**. It **doesn't work well** in **saturated markets**, where demand for the product has stopped growing.
2) **Diversification** means selling **new products** to **new markets**. Diversification is a **very risky** strategy. It's used when a business really needs to reduce their dependence on a **limited product range** or if **high profits** are likely.
3) **Product development** is selling **new products** to **existing markets**. It's used when the market has good **growth potential** and the business has high market share, strong R&D (see p.136-137) and a good **competitive advantage**.
4) **Market extension** (or **market development**) can be done through **repositioning.** This means that a business focuses on a **different segment of the market**. They need to **research** the target market segment and work out how they can **adapt** their product to suit the needs of a different set of consumers. This might involve creating a new advertising campaign or promotion which **targets** a different audience.
5) **Market extension** can also be done by **expanding** into new markets to exploit the same market segment in a different country. Some businesses join forces with similar companies **abroad**, combining **local knowledge** with a product that has already proved **successful** in Britain. Or they can take over a **competitor company** abroad, which expands their customer base and eliminates some of the competition.

*Ansoff's Matrix is used for **Strategic Decisions***

1) **Ansoff's matrix** is used when a firm's **objective** is to **grow**. It shows the **strategies** that can be used to **achieve growth** according to how **risky** they are, which helps managers make decisions about which strategy to use.
2) The **advantage** of Ansoff's matrix is that it doesn't just lay out potential strategies for growth — it also forces market planners to think about the **expected risks** of moving in a certain direction.
3) One **disadvantage** of the matrix is that it fails to show that **market development** and **diversification** strategies also tend to require **significant change** in the **day to day workings** of the company.
4) **Product development** is less risky, but it works best for firms that already have a strong **competitive advantage**.
5) **Market penetration** is the **least risky** strategy of all — so **most firms** opt for this approach.
6) Some people believe that Ansoff's matrix **oversimplifies** the **options** available for growth. For example, **diversification** doesn't have to be **completely unrelated** to what the business does currently. It might be a **safe option** to diversify by moving into your **supplier's business**, as you know there's a **guaranteed market** for that product.

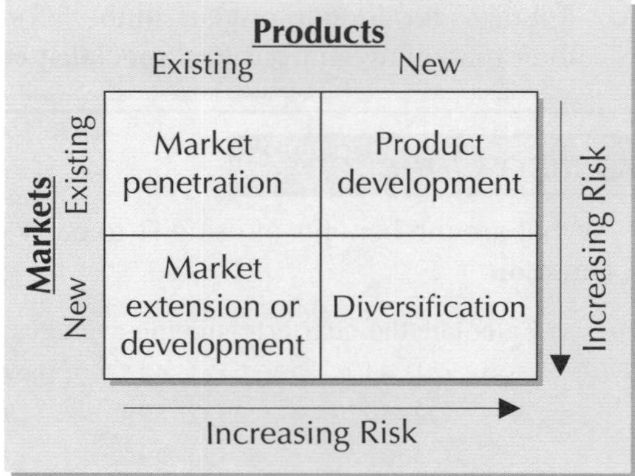

Selecting Marketing Strategies

There are *Fewer Strategies* for *Expanding* into *International Markets*

1) **Not all** the **strategies** that are shown on Ansoff's matrix are **suitable** if a company wants to **expand abroad**.
2) If a company chooses to **grow internationally**, this means it's entering a **new market**. So you can only use one of the strategies that involves **new markets** — either **market extension / development** or **diversification**.
3) It's **safest** and **most common** for companies expanding internationally to use a **market extension** or **development** option. It's less risky because the business doesn't need to develop a new product — their existing product is already successful. For example, **fast food restaurants** tend to use this option.
4) In theory, companies could also use a diversification strategy when expanding into international markets. But, because **diversification** is a **risky** strategy and **expanding internationally** is **already risky**, it's **very unlikely** that a firm would decide to launch a completely new product in a foreign market that's also completely new to them.

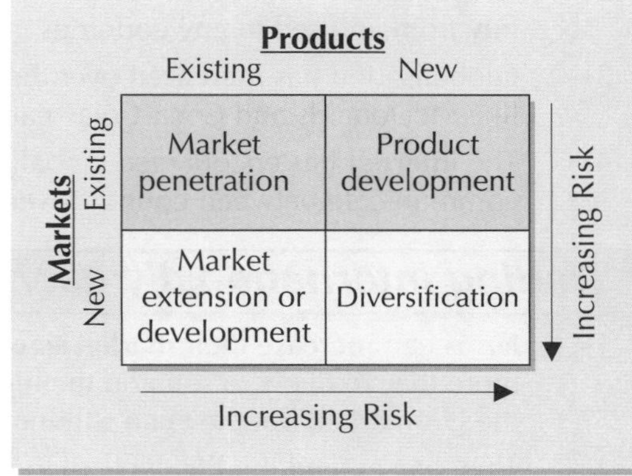

5) It's more common for a firm to expand overseas either by **exporting** goods or by allowing a **foreign firm** to produce their products under **licence** (e.g. someone else makes the product, but it's the original company's name on the packet). The manufacturer then pays the original company a set amount for every product sold.

Case Study: KFC® International Market Development

KFC®'s expansion from the USA market to the UK market is an example of **market development**. KFC® began operating in the USA in 1952 and extended their market by opening an outlet in Preston, UK in 1965. This was the **first American fast food chain** to open in the UK. There are now over 750 outlets across the UK and Ireland. These outlets were run as a **franchise** by an **independent company**, KFC GB Ltd, until it was bought by PepsiCo in 1986. The success of the market extension from the USA to the UK means that the UK is now used as a **training centre** for KFC® franchises for the European market.

Ansoff's matrix shows that KFC®'s market extension strategy is the result of taking an **existing product**, their fast food business model, and developing it in a **new market**, the UK. This is a **safer** option than **diversification**, particularly since the UK had no other fast food chains in 1965 so there was **no competition**.

Practice Questions

Q1 What is a low cost marketing strategy?

Q2 What is differentiation?

Q3 Explain the difference between repositioning and new market strategies.

Q4 What are the four areas of Ansoff's matrix.

Q5 What are the two safest marketing strategies for international expansion?

Exam Question

Q1 Louisa and Bob McKenzie run a company that makes organic porridge. The product has been doing well in the UK and Louisa and Bob are considering launching it internationally. Explain what kind of strategy they're most likely to use, giving reasons for your choice. [6 marks]

Ansoff's Matrix — bet Keanu wouldn't want to star in that one...

Marketing strategies probably won't save the world but they can be pretty useful for businesses who want to plan for the future. And knowing about them won't help you win the war against intelligent robotic lifeforms or help you escape from virtual reality but they just might come in useful when you're sitting your A2 Business Studies exam, so get learning.

International Markets

Trading in lots of different countries sounds like fun, but there's quite a lot to it.

Gina was very pleased with her latest purchase from the globe market.

Globalisation *is the creation of a* ***Global Market***

1) **Globalisation** is when businesses operate in lots of **countries** all over the world.
2) Globalisation means that companies can be **based** anywhere in the world, and can **buy** from and **sell** to any countries in the world.
3) Globalisation has **increased** over the last few decades — huge multinational **brands** like McDonalds and Coca-Cola® can be found almost **anywhere** in the world.
4) The **internet** has encouraged globalisation because it allows businesses to communicate between countries very quickly and cheaply.

Trading Internationally *offers businesses* ***Benefits***

1) Firms can **increase** their **market size** by selling existing products to **new countries** — the bigger the market, the more they're likely to sell and the higher their **revenue** will be. E.g. supermarkets like Tesco have nearly saturated the UK market, but they can still increase the size of their market by opening stores in other countries, like China.
2) They can **extend** the **life cycle** of their products by launching them in **new countries** as the product enters **maturity** in its home market or if **foreign competitors** begin to gain market share in the UK. This is common with cars — businesses can sell models that are old-fashioned in the UK to developing countries like India.
3) Businesses can **reduce costs** by getting their **raw materials** from countries with the **cheapest** prices.
4) They can also **manufacture components** in **overseas** countries where labour is cheaper, before putting the final product together in the UK. This is called **global sourcing**.
5) **Relocating** factories, etc to **developing countries** with lower wage rates than the UK also **reduces costs**.
6) **International growth** leads to **economies of scale**, which reduces the cost per item of products.
7) If the UK economy is in **recession**, businesses can secure revenue by **exporting** to a **growing economy**.

Businesses look for ***Opportunities*** *in* ***Developing Markets***

1) Because **developing markets** are usually many years **behind** developed economies, products that appear old in a developed economy can be offered as **new** in a developing economy.
2) This means firms are able to **lengthen** the **product life cycle** and **increase** sales **revenues** for existing products.
3) Developing economies like Brazil, India, China and Russia represent significant opportunities for businesses from developed countries because of their **large populations** and recent **economic growth**. E.g. many **tobacco manufacturers** based in developed economies have experienced recent **growth** by launching old established brands in developing markets, although many people consider this **unethical** (see next page).

Political Changes *can make international trade* ***Easier*** *or* ***Harder***

1) **Tariffs** (import taxes) **discourage** international trade. **Removing** or **reducing** tariffs between countries makes international trade **easier** and **cheaper**. Since the **World Trade Organisation** was set up in 1995 to encourage international trade, the proportion of imports worldwide that are **tariff-free** has risen to more than **50%**.
2) **Quotas** are **limits** on **imports** that one country places on another. Countries sometimes use quotas as a way of trying to **protect** their own economies and jobs — this is called a **protectionist policy**. **Removing** (or **reducing** the number of) quotas between countries **encourages** international trade.
3) Since the **UK** joined the **European Union** in 1973, British **exports** to EU countries have **increased** because there are **no quotas** or **tariffs** within the EU. **Imports** from other EU countries to Britain have also **increased**. EU countries also **manufacture** to increasingly **common standards**, which makes trade more **straightforward**.
4) **Trade** between **eurozone** countries has also **increased** in recent years. It has been made easier by the **common currency**, the euro. There's more about how the euro affects trade between eurozone countries on p. 174.
5) **Trading blocs** are when groups of countries agree to **remove trade barriers** (e.g. tariffs) between them. E.g. MERCOSUR (Brazil, Argentina, Paraguay, Uruguay and Venezuela) is a South American trading bloc. Trading blocs make trade between **member countries easier**, but **discourage** trade between the bloc countries and **other countries**.
6) **Trade embargoes ban trade** with a particular country. E.g. the USA has had an embargo against Cuba since 1962.

International Markets

International Trade involves *Ethical Considerations*

1) **International trade** offers businesses lots of opportunities to **make money** — **selling** their products **abroad** can increase their **turnover** by increasing the size of their market, and **buying raw materials abroad** or relocating **production** abroad can **cut costs**. However, there are also **ethical factors** involved in international trade, and businesses need to consider these when they make decisions about trading internationally.
2) Some companies with factories abroad might **exploit foreign workers** to cut their costs (see p.140). This kind of behaviour is very unethical, and can lead to consumers **boycotting** the company if its unethical practices come to light.
3) Businesses might take into account the **damage** that their activities might do to the **environment**. Getting **raw materials** from abroad is often **cheaper**, but **transporting** them from one country to another, often by plane, causes **pollution**. **Distributing** finished products to other countries also causes **pollution**. E.g. around 95% of the fruit sold in the UK comes from other countries.
4) **Tobacco companies** can make huge profits by selling **cigarettes** in **developing countries**, but many people think that this is unethical because people in developing countries often **don't know** about the **health risks** associated with smoking, so they can't make an **informed decision** about whether or not to smoke. Also, people in developing countries often **earn very little**, and cigarettes are **expensive** in comparison with their income, so if they get **addicted** to smoking they end up spending a **large proportion** of their **income** on cigarettes. Smoking-related **illnesses** can also **overwhelm** the **health system** of developing countries.
5) **Weapons manufacturers** can make money by selling **missiles** and other **weapons** abroad, but selling weapons to **oppressive regimes** or countries that are seen as a **security threat** is unethical. Governments place **restrictions** on which countries companies can sell weapons to.

There are Other Issues involved in International Trade

1) Businesses have to pay to **transport** the goods they want to buy from, or distribute to, other countries. Transporting goods **internationally** can be very **expensive**.
2) Businesses have to make sure that they're **aware of** and **follow** the **laws** of the countries they operate in — they can't just assume that employment laws, etc, will be the same everywhere. They also have to comply with all **customs laws** — e.g. some products, like fresh fruit, can't be transported across international boundaries without permits.
3) Businesses trading internationally will have **higher** business **travel costs** as employees will need to travel to the various locations the business trades in. Travel costs can be reduced by the use of ICT such as email, telephone conferencing and video conferencing.
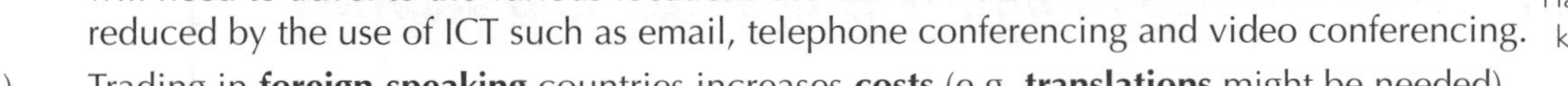
4) Trading in **foreign-speaking** countries increases **costs** (e.g. **translations** might be needed).
5) Fluctuations in **exchange rates** make the cost of international trade **unpredictable**, so it's difficult for businesses to accurately **forecast** revenue and profits.

Harry's boss was keen to keep staff travel costs as low as possible.

Practice Questions

Q1 What is globalisation?

Q2 What are: a) tariffs? b) quotas? c) trading blocs?

Q3 How does international trade affect the environment?

Q4 Why does trading in foreign-speaking countries increase costs?

Exam Question

Q1 Explain how international trade can extend the life cycle of a product. [4 marks]

I always thought an embargo was some kind of embarrassing illness...

Globalisation's quite an interesting one — some people hate the fact that city centres around the world are all starting to look alike, while other people find it comforting that wherever they are in the world, they can always find a McDonalds or a Starbucks. Whatever you think about it, you need to learn all the issues affecting businesses that trade in other countries.

Marketing Planning

So, you've got your marketing strategy. Good for you. But you're not done yet — you need to know how to put the strategy into action — you need a plan.

The Marketing Plan *says what the* Marketing *department's* Going To Do

1) A **marketing plan** is a document that gives details of all the **activities** that are going to take place in the marketing department to turn the **marketing strategy** into **reality**.
2) It also explains the **background** to the marketing strategy and says how **budgets** will be **spent**.
3) The information in the marketing plan is **useful** for **marketing staff**, because it lets them know **what** they'll be doing and **when**. **Other departments** use it too though, such as **HR** and **Production**.
4) It also ensures that the product meets the customer's needs in terms of **specification**, **price**, **availability** etc. The **finance department** are also involved — the product needs to make a **profit**.

All Marketing Plans *contain the* Marketing Objectives *and* Strategy

Marketing plans don't all contain exactly the same information. A **small business** might just produce an **informal document**, while **large businesses** usually write the marketing plan in the style of a **formal report**. Nearly all marketing plans will contain the sections listed below:

Objectives	• The marketing plan states the company's **corporate objectives**, and says how the **marketing objectives** will help to achieve them.
Budgets	• The plan contains detailed budgets with the **expected costs** of each product, department or marketing activity.
Sales Forecast	• It also says how many **sales** or how much **revenue** the business expects to make if the marketing plan is followed.
Marketing Strategies	• This section of the plan describes the **strategies** that will be used to **achieve** the **marketing objectives**.

Some companies include other sections, too — e.g. an **action plan**, saying **when** each **activity** will happen and **how long** it will take, or details of how they plan to **control** the activities to make sure everything stays **on time** and **on budget**.

The Marketing Plan *is affected by* Internal *and* External Factors

Internal Factors

1) The company's **product range** affects the marketing plan. For example, if they have **one** very **successful** product or already have an extremely **wide range** of products, they might not want to diversify further.
2) A successful marketing plan needs to consider the firm's **strengths** and **weaknesses** — so most marketing planners start by looking at the results of the business's SWOT analysis (see p.117).
3) A firm's marketing activities will be restricted by how much **finance** they have available.
4) **Human resources** are important too. The company needs to have staff with the right skills, or recruit some.
5) **Operational issues** also affect the marketing plan — the business needs to be sure it's capable of **producing** enough to keep up with extra demand. Otherwise, potential customers will end up **disappointed**.
6) The **current marketing mix** has an effect on the marketing plan. The business will probably want to incorporate some elements of the **existing mix** into the new plan.

External Factors

1) It's important to think about **competitors**. Firms need to consider their **competitors' sales** and **market share** and their **future plans** — if a rival is planning a TV campaign, it might be sensible for them to have one too.
2) The **state of the economy** has an impact too — if there's a economic downturn, some companies spend more on marketing, others spend less. It depends on the company and the product.
3) Companies look at the **market**. For example, the **increase** in **superbugs** created a **new market niche** — businesses started developing **personal hygiene kits** for patients to take into hospital with them.

Marketing Planning

The marketing planning Process is Cyclical

1) **Marketing plans** give a fairly **long-term** view of what the marketing department's planning to do.
2) The plan is dependent on **market** and **environmental circumstances** remaining roughly the **same** as they were when the plan was **written**. E.g. if the plan was written in a period of economic boom, and after several months, the economy shows signs of weakening, the **plan** will probably need to be **changed**.
3) Companies need to **constantly** review what's happening in the **market** and what their **competitors** are doing, to make sure the **marketing plan** stays **relevant**. If something's **changed**, they might need to develop **new marketing objectives** and **strategies** and a **new marketing plan** so that the company can still achieve its corporate objectives. The diagram below shows how the steps of marketing planning are **cyclical**:

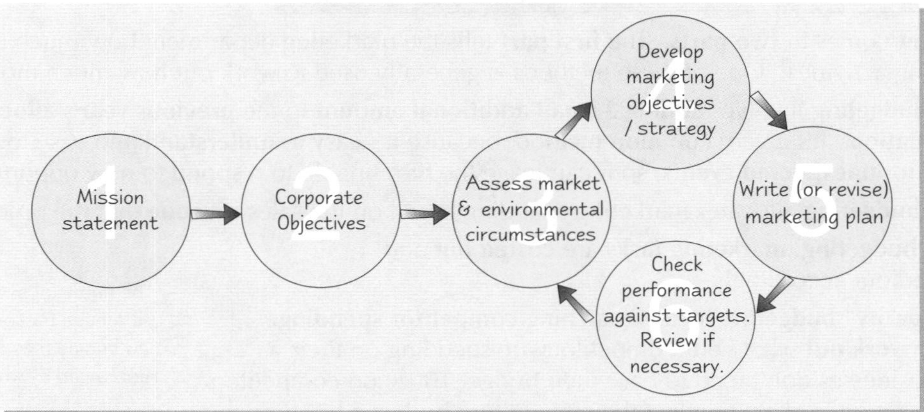

Marketing Plans can be Hard to Put into Practice

1) Having a marketing plan is great if all the **other departments** in the company are **willing** to do **what** the marketing department **wants** them to do, **when** they want them to do it. But it's not so great if, say, marketing wants the production department to print 200 000 promotional leaflets in July, but the production department knows it will be swamped with other work and won't have time to do it.
2) It's also hard to have a successful marketing plan if the company is in a market where the **circumstances change** so **fast** that the plan is **out of date** almost as soon as it's written.
3) The plan won't work if it doesn't look far enough **ahead** — it's supposed to be a **long-term** view. If marketing **confuse** short-term **tactics** with long-term **strategy**, it's hard for people to see what the **overall goals** are. And if people aren't sure what they're trying to achieve, they might **not** be very **motivated**.
4) **Bureaucracy**, or a **corporate culture** which **doesn't value cooperation**, can make it hard to have a successful plan.

Practice Questions

Q1 Give one example of how a department other than marketing might benefit from a marketing plan.

Q2 What four sections do nearly all marketing plans include?

Q3 Explain the cycle that a company needs to go through during the marketing planning process.

Exam Questions

Q1 Sophie and David Barton have just set up a company selling a new variety of pink tomato and need to write a marketing plan. Discuss the internal and external factors that they will have to consider when writing their plan. [8 marks]

Q2 Explain the difficulties that a business might encounter when trying to implement a marketing plan. [6 marks]

Marketing planners must feel like they're going round in circles...

Whatever you're doing, it's good to have a plan, and that's especially true for revision. If you don't have one yet, grab some felt tips and paper and make one. You can waste three hours that way...ok, I'm joking, but you do have time to scribble down a quick timetable before getting back to learning the stuff on these pages — just don't colour it in...

Marketing Budget

The marketing budget specifies the finances available for spending on marketing activities, and contains sales targets. Sales targets aren't plucked out of thin air — they're based on a forecast.

Marketing Departments do a **Marketing Audit** before Setting a Budget

1) Directors often do a **marketing audit** before they set a marketing budget. This allows them to find out what's **changed** with their **customers** and **competitors** since the last budget.
2) For example, they might have gained **market share** since the last budget or they might have lost some of the market to a competitor. **Customer demographics** (see p.118) might have changed, e.g. the target market might be getting older or have less disposable income.

Marketing Budget **Part One: Expenditure** Budget

The **marketing budget** comes in **two parts**. The **first part** tells the marketing department how much they can afford to **spend** on marketing activities. One of these methods is generally used to work out how much money is available:

1) **Incremental budgeting** involves adding a **small additional amount** to the **previous year's allocation**, to take account of **inflation**. It's a very **common** method, because it's **easy** to **understand** and easy to **do**. However, it doesn't allow for **unexpected events**, so it can leave the firm unable to respond to new opportunities or threats.
2) **Sales-related budgeting** allocates marketing spending based on the **sales revenue** that the product will generate.
3) In **task-based budgeting**, **marketing tasks** are **costed out** and finances shared out accordingly.
4) "**Competitor parity**" **budgeting** means matching **competitor spending**. It's **difficult** to **work out** what your competitors are spending on their marketing. Businesses don't tend to base their budget 100% on competitors — competitor action is likely to affect the expenditure budget a bit, though.

The financial state of the business is a huge factor. Small firms and new businesses are more likely to be restrained by what they can afford.

Marketing Budget **Part Two:** Marketing **Objectives**

1) The second part of the marketing budget contains the **targets** that the marketing department is aiming to meet, e.g. **increase sales** of a particular product by 15%.
2) The budget also gives the **sales targets** that need to be met in order to achieve the marketing objectives. Businesses set their sales targets by looking at past figures and **extrapolating** (see next page).
3) Sales targets also depend on **market conditions** — the **business cycle** and **competitor** actions can affect demand.
4) The **financial position** of the business and the **expenditure budget** are a factor. Spending a lot on marketing a product means that you'd expect it to **sell** pretty well.

Budget Setting has its **Pitfalls**

1) It's best if directors **consult** with the **managers** of each department when setting the budget — they **resent** not being involved in setting targets.
2) On the other hand, departmental managers shouldn't have too much control over budget setting, because they might set targets that are **easily reached**, or ask for more money than they need so that they won't **overspend**. Managers' **egos** are a factor as well — they may see a large budget as an indicator of **status**.
3) Preparing budgets can be very **time consuming**, especially when there's lots of negotiation.
4) Basing an **expenditure budget** purely on **financial position** has its drawbacks. It means that the business spends a **lot** on marketing when sales are **high**, and **less** on marketing when sales are **low** — when it needs it **most**.
5) With **incremental budgeting**, departmental managers may be tempted to spend the **whole budget** to make sure they get at least the same amount in next year's budget. This isn't a cost-effective way to behave.

Marketing Budgets need to be **Justified** by the **Product**

1) Budgets need to be justified in relation to the finances available, and the likely **return**. A product with a **high predicted rate of return** will earn itself a **bigger expenditure budget**.
2) **Product portfolio analysis** is used to determine which products should be supported by extra spending and which should be "milked" to provide revenue for other marketing activities.
3) Budgets also vary, depending on their stage in the **product life cycle**. Marketing expenditure is likely to be high during the **launch** and **growth** phases of a product, or when **extension strategies** are being used.

Marketing Budget

Sales Forecasting aims to Predict the Future

1) **Sales forecasting** predicts the **future sales** of a product using **quantitative** and **qualitative** data analysis (p. 118-119). This allows managers to set **sales targets**. Sales **performance** can be measured against those targets.
2) Sales forecasts help the **finance** department to produce **cash flow** forecasts — once they know how much the business is expected to sell, they can work out how much money is expected to come in.
3) Sales forecasts also help **production** and **human resources** departments to prepare for the expected level of sales. They can make sure that they have the right amount of machinery, stock and staff (see p. 150).

Extrapolation and Test Marketing are Quantitative Forecasting techniques

1) **Backdata** is **data from the past**. Sales backdata from last year can be used to predict likely sales for this year.
2) **Extrapolation** (see p.121) is a great way of predicting sales as long as trends stay **constant**. When there's a major upheaval in the market (rare, but it does happen), extrapolation can produce **misleading figures**.
3) Managers also use **market research data** to predict future sales.
4) **Test marketing** can be used to provide sales forecasts. The product is launched within a limited geographical area. Test marketing gives **accurate data**, and should be a **reliable** indicator of wider **demand**. Managers can **learn lessons** from the test marketing exercise and apply them to the full scale national launch.
5) On the other hand, test marketing allows **competitors** to see the product before the full launch.

Qualitative methods include Intuition and Brainstorming

1) **Intuition** is a particular **individual's feeling** about how well a product is going to sell. The individual usually **knows** lots about the **product** in question — e.g. they might be in charge of **product development**.
2) Some companies also ask their **sales staff** about their **hunches** because they're in **constant contact** with **customers** and know which **products** are **selling well**.
3) **Brainstorming** is when a **group** of people are asked to give as many **ideas** about something as they can in a **fixed** period of **time**. It's often used when a company is planning to **change** its **strategy.**
4) It's also possible to forecast sales based on **experience**. This means considering the **life cycle** of other, **similar products** that are **already available**. It's especially useful for **new firms** who don't have any **backdata**.
5) **Panel consensus** methods involve a panel of experts discussing an issue until they reach an agreement about it. It's more accurate than just asking one person for their views, but still carries a big risk of error.

For advantages and disadvantages of quantitative and qualitative techniques, see p.118-119.

Practice Questions

Q1 Explain the four ways budgets can be allocated.

Q2 Give three potential problems with setting budgets.

Q3 How do sales forecasts help other departments?

Q4 Give two examples of quantitative techniques for forecasting sales.

Exam Questions

Q1 Gary Snowdon is setting next year's budget for his firm. He plans to use the incremental method. Explain to him what the disadvantages of using this method might be. [8 marks]

Q2 Sue Roberts has been selling cashmere dog blankets for a year. She wants to forecast sales for the year to come, but hasn't decided whether to use a quantitative or qualitative method. Explain which method(s) you think it would be best for her to use, making sure you justify your decision. [12 marks]

More dodgy film ideas — how about 'The Hunch Backdata of Notre Dame'

Bet you got to the end of the last page and thought we'd forgotten to give you any words of wisdom to finish it off. But no, here it is, in all its glory, purely for your learning pleasure. Well, as much pleasure as you can possibly squeeze out of the fact that you now need to learn all the stuff on budgets and techniques that's been covered on the last two pages.

Operational Objectives

This section might sound complicated, but actually, it's not. 'Operations' is just a fancy word for the real reason businesses exist in the first place — to make stuff.

Operational Objectives** are **Targets** set by particular **Departments

A company meets its corporate objectives (p.84) by breaking them down into **smaller objectives**. These help each **individual department** know what it's supposed to be doing. Operational objectives might be linked to:

QUALITY — This type of objective is likely to involve either **maintaining** or **improving** levels of quality. For example, a company might aim to ensure that **95%** of their products last **five years** or longer, or they might aim to **reduce** the number of **customer complaints** that they get in a month.

COST — Many firms aim to **cut costs**, especially if they compete on **price**. Depending on the type of company, there are different ways of doing this. Costs can be cut in a particular **department** (e.g. HR might be asked to cut the costs of recruitment) or the costs of an individual **product** can be reduced (e.g. an airline might stop offering meals on a particular route).

VOLUME — Volume objectives often involve **increasing** the **amount** of goods or services that a company is producing. For example, a hotel might aim to have more rooms full on weeknights, or a football stadium might aim to fill more seats on match days. However, a company might also set an objective to ensure that **volume** doesn't **exceed demand**, e.g. if it knows people buy fewer healthy choice ready-meals at Christmas, it might reduce production in December.

EFFICIENCY — Efficiency objectives aim to make **better use** of **resources** in order to reduce costs and increase profit. This might mean increasing **capacity utilisation** (increasing output so it's closer to the maximum amount of goods the firm could produce with current levels of staff and machinery) or taking steps to improve **labour** and **capital productivity** (how much output a particular worker or piece of machinery generates in a set time period).

INNOVATION — Companies can set their **Research & Development** (R&D) department innovation targets, e.g. a car manufacturer might set an objective to produce the world's first pollution-free car by 2015. These objectives can be **hard** to **achieve**, as unexpected problems often occur.

ENVIRONMENT — **Pressure** from **customers** and the **government** often leads to firms setting environmental objectives, such as cutting **carbon emissions** or using a greater number of **recycled** raw materials.

***Operational Objectives** are influenced by **Internal** and **External** Factors*

INTERNAL

- **Nature of the Product**: a computer technology firm is likely to have very different targets to a family-run bed and breakfast. The **computer technology company** is likely to focus on **innovation** whereas the **B & B** may be trying to increase its **capacity utilisation** by having lots of rooms full.
- **Availability of Resources**: many businesses would like to **increase output** but are limited by whether they have enough **resources**. For example, it won't be possible to produce 50 handpainted dolls houses in 3 days if the company only employs five carpenters.

EXTERNAL

- **Competitors' Performance**: many firms set targets in **reaction** to their **rivals' actions**. For example, if a rival gains market share, you would also probably try to increase your share of the market to make sure they don't overtake you (or leave you even further behind). **Competition** from **abroad**, e.g. China, is forcing companies to set stricter **cost** and **efficiency** objectives.
- **Demand for Product**: businesses should try to make sure that **output** is not higher than **demand** (see above).
- **Changing Customer Needs**: e.g. if customers indicate that they'd like a firm to behave more ethically this can affect **cost** and **environmental** goals.

Operational Objectives

Production is all about turning Inputs into Outputs

1) Production means taking a set of **raw materials** and turning them into something the consumer **wants** or **needs**.
2) It generally refers to the **whole process**, from **obtaining resources** right through to **checking** the finished product for quality and **delivering** it to the customer.
3) Production can also be used to describe a company supplying a **service**, rather than a physical product.

Remember the Five common Methods of Production

You've seen these five different **production methods** at AS level. Here's a reminder:

Job production	Production of one-off items by skilled workers.
Flow production	Mass production on a continuous production line with division of labour.
Batch production	Production of small batches of identical items.
Cell production	Production divided into sets of tasks, each set completed by a work group.
Lean production	Streamlined production with waste at a minimum.

It was clear that the builders had misunderstood what was meant by "lean production".

Other Departments have an impact on Production

1) The **finance** department decides **how much money** can be spent on equipment and wages.
2) The **marketing** department tells the operations managers what customers want, and what they're willing to **pay** for it. Marketing will also say **when** the goods need to be produced to hit the market at the right time.
3) The **human resources** department is in charge of organising employees. They need to know how many employees are needed, what skills they need, and whether they'll need training.
4) These relationships go **both ways**. The marketing department can **ask** the production department to produce a large amount, but the production department has to say if it's **possible** or not.

Production needs to consider other Factors and Decisions

1) A business' **production method** has an effect on the **type** of **decisions** that managers are likely to make. Equally, managers can make **decisions** that have a **big impact** on the **production** department.
2) It's **hard** for some businesses to **grow** if they're committed to using **job production**.
3) If they decide to try to increase **market share**, a company might choose either to **increase production** or to switch **production methods** so that it can manufacture a **new product** alongside its existing range.
4) In periods of economic **downturn**, **survival** is often a company's main aim. In these periods, the company is unlikely to invest in **new machinery** or switch **production methods**. They might even have to consider **closing** a factory for a **few weeks** or temporarily **shutting down** certain areas of production.
5) A business that's trying to **increase** its long-term **profitability** might well switch to **batch** or **flow** production. If it's trying to improve its short-term **cash flow**, it probably won't invest in **new capital** (machinery).

Practice Questions

Q1 Identify six types of operational objective.

Q2 How does the finance department have an impact on production?

Q3 How might the production department respond to a decision to try and increase market share?

Exam Question

Q1 Explain how external factors influence the operational objectives of a business. [6 marks]

Cell production — an egg and a sperm combine to form a new cell...

Oops, no, sorry, wrong book. That's GCSE biology (which sounds more interesting, actually). The good news about the stuff on these pages is that, although it may be a bit dull, it's not that difficult. Make sure you learn the six different types of operational objective and the factors that influence operational objectives, and don't forget the five production methods.

Operational Objectives: Scale and Resource Mix

Not only do businesses have to decide what's the best size for them to be, they also need to work out if they want more machines than people. Or more biscuits than cake.

Economies of Scale mean bigger is Cheaper

Economies of scale mean that as **output increases**, the **cost** of producing **each item** goes down. **Internal** economies of scale increase efficiency **within** an individual firm. There are different types of internal economies of scale:

Technical	Technical economies of scale are related to **production**. Production methods for large volumes are often more **efficient**. Large businesses can afford to buy better, more advanced **machinery**, which might mean they need fewer staff, and wage costs will fall.
Specialisation	Specialisation economies of scale are linked to **employees**. Large businesses can employ managers with **specialist skills** and separate them out into specialised departments, which means the work is usually done more **quickly** and is of a higher **quality** than in non-specialised companies.
Purchasing	Purchasing economies of scale are to do with **discounts**. Large businesses can negotiate discounts when buying **supplies**. They can get bigger discounts and longer **credit periods** than their smaller competitors.
Financial	Financial economies of scale happen when companies **borrow money**. Large firms can borrow at **lower** rates of **interest** than smaller firms. Lenders feel **more comfortable** lending money to a big firm than a small firm.
Marketing	Marketing economies of scale are related to **promotional costs**. The cost of an ad campaign is a **fixed cost**. A business with a large output can share out the cost over more products than a business with a low output.
Risk-bearing	Risk-bearing economies of scale involve **diversification** into several different **markets** or catering to several different **market segments**. Large firms have a greater ability to bear **risk** than their smaller competitors.

External Economies of Scale make a Whole Industry or Area more efficient

External economies of scale happen when industries are concentrated in **small geographical areas**.

1) Having a large number of **suppliers** to choose from gives economies of scale. Locating near to lots of suppliers means firms can easily negotiate with a range of suppliers, which tends to increase quality and reduce prices.
2) A good skilled local **labour supply** makes an industry more efficient. This is most important in industries where training is **expensive** or takes a long time. For example, software development firms in California's "Silicon Valley" know that plenty of people who are qualified to fill their vacancies **already** live within driving distance.
3) Firms located in certain areas can benefit from good **infrastructure** — e.g. an airport, a motorway or good rail links. E.g. Dublin's tourist industry had a massive boost in profits after Ryanair started **cheap flights** to Dublin.

Diseconomies of Scale — being bigger can be Bad News, too

Diseconomies of scale make unit costs of production rise as output rises. They happen because large firms are harder to manage than small ones. They're caused by poor **motivation**, poor **communication** and poor **coordination**.

1) It's important to keep all departments working towards the **same objectives**. Poor coordination makes a business **less efficient**. In a big firm, it's hard to **coordinate** activities between different departments.
2) **Communication** is harder in a big business. It can be **slow** and **difficult** to get messages to the right people, especially when there are **long chains of command**. The **amount** of information circulating in a business can increase at a faster rate than the business is actually growing.
3) It can be hard to **motivate** people in a large company. In a **small** firm, managers are in **close contact** with staff, and it's easier for people to feel like they **belong** and that they're working towards the same aims. When people **don't feel they belong**, and that there's **no point** to what they're doing, they get **demotivated**.
4) Diseconomies of scale are caused by problems with management. Strong **leadership**, **delegation** and **decentralisation** can all help **prevent diseconomies** of scale and keep costs down.

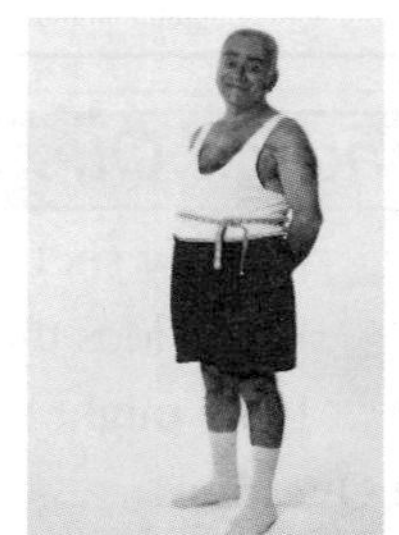

Being bigger was very bad news for Jerry — his wife banned him from eating pies.

Operational Objectives: Scale and Resource Mix

Businesses need to have the **Right Mix** of **People, Machines** and **Materials**

1) A successful business must have a **suitable combination** of **materials**, **machinery** and **people**. How hard it is to get this right depends on the **complexity** of the product and the number of **production stages**.
2) The **design** of the product affects the mix — e.g. freshly squeezed orange juice has just one component (oranges), but a car has hundreds. The **higher** the number of **components**, the more **complicated** the product is to produce, so the **harder** it is to get the correct mix of people, machines and materials.
3) Businesses can have problems getting the right mix if there's a **shortage** of suitably skilled **labour**. For example, at the moment there's a very limited supply of **care assistants**, **geologists** and **vets** in the UK.
4) Businesses are also limited by their **finances**. Most companies would have the **latest technology** if they could **afford** it, but in reality **smaller firms** can rarely afford to keep updating their machinery.

A **Capital-Intensive** firm has **Lots** of **Machinery**

1) A **capital-intensive** business uses more **machinery** and relatively few **workers**. The **car industry**, which tends to use robot-operated production lines, is one example of a capital-intensive industry.
2) **Larger** firms tend to be more **capital-intensive** than smaller companies. E.g. the Morgan Motor Company makes a small number of hand-built sports cars using lots of **labour**, whereas BMW uses more **robots** and machinery.
3) A rise in the **cost** of **labour** can also cause companies to **switch** to a **capital-intensive** method of production.

Advantages of Capital-intensive Production	Disadvantages of Capital-intensive Production
Usually works out **cheaper** than manual labour in the **long term**.	High **set-up** costs.
Machinery is often **more precise** than human workers, which might lead to more **consistent quality** levels.	If machinery **breaks down**, it can lead to long **delays**.
Machinery is able to work **24/7**.	Machines are usually only suited to one task, which makes them **inflexible**.
Machines are **easier** to **manage** than people.	If workers are worried that they might be replaced by machines, the fear of job losses can cause **motivation** to **decrease**.

A **Labour-Intensive** firm is very **People-Heavy**

1) A **labour-intensive** firm uses more **workers** and less **machinery**. For example, the **NHS** is very labour-intensive.
2) In countries where labour is relatively **cheap** (e.g. China) **labour-intensive** methods of production are common.

Advantages of Labour-intensive Production	Disadvantages of Labour-intensive Production
People are **more flexible** than machines and can be **retrained** if the company needs new skills.	It's **harder** to **manage** people than machines.
Labour-intensive methods are **cheaper** for **small-scale** production.	People can be **unreliable** — they may have days off through sickness.
Labour-intensive methods are also **cheaper** where **low-cost labour** is available, e.g. China and India.	People can't work without **breaks** or **holidays**.
Workers can **solve** any **problems** that arise during production and suggest ways to **improve quality**.	**Wage increases** mean that the cost of labour can increase over time. It can be difficult to forecast wage increases caused by inflation.

Practice Questions

Q1 What are external economies of scale?

Q2 Describe three types of diseconomy of scale.

Q3 Give two advantages of capital-intensive production methods and two advantages of labour-intensive methods.

Exam Question

Q1 Explain the different types of economy of scale a business might benefit from if it takes over a rival firm. [10 marks]

Economy of scales — when snakes wear the same skin 2 years running...

Economies and diseconomies of scale are pretty important to businesses. Think of it as a balancing act (scales, balancing act — geddit?) — firms benefit from being big, but if they get too big, the balance goes wrong and their size actually ends up costing them money. It's a bit like in Goldilocks — they can be too big or too small, but they want to be just right.

Operational Strategies: Innovation

Launching new products involves a lot of time at the drawing board.

Research and Development comes up with New ideas, products and processes

1) Research and Development (R&D) does **technical research** to come up with new products. Many firms do some form of R&D, but businesses that want to **innovate** depend on it.

> Innovating means thinking of a new idea or bringing out a product that's different to what's already on the market.

2) R&D has to turn raw ideas into **products** or **new processes**. This can take a long time.
3) R&D is **related** to market research, but they're not the same. Market research **discovers** what customers want and R&D comes up with new products to **meet** the customers' wants.
4) R&D can also be used to come up with new **production methods** — e.g. to improve productive efficiency.

Innovation can be Risky but is often the best way to make Big Profits

1) Research and Development is a very **costly** process.
2) It's also a **risky** process — it's estimated that in the **pharmaceutical** industry, only **1 in 12** new drugs **researched** are actually thought to have commercial potential and developed. Companies can end up developing something customers don't want, or they might not be able to produce the product on a large scale at a low enough cost.
3) However, market leaders normally invest in R&D. The most successful businesses have a **large portfolio** of products, **balanced** between **innovative new products** and proven older products.
4) The ability to successfully launch a new product in the market is of great value. A company can charge a high price for its innovative product (this is called market skimming), before competitors enter the market with **similar products** at **competitive prices**. The original Sony WALKMAN® was a great example of this.
5) Being innovative can be good for a firm's **reputation** — e.g. if they've been the first to launch exciting electrical products in the past, customers will naturally go to them if they want a cutting edge digital camera or whatever.
6) Some industries are particularly **fast moving**, and need to **constantly** develop new products — e.g. the pharmaceutical industry, the microchip industry and the mobile telecommunications industry.
7) Some organisations choose not to have a specific R&D department, but instead they **adapt** and **modify** new products brought out by their **rivals**. This may be because the business is risk averse, or because its shareholders prefer profits to be paid as dividends in the short term rather than invested for the long term.

Innovation affects what goes on in Other Departments

FINANCE

1) R&D for innovative products is **expensive**, so the finance department might need to raise extra **working capital** to pay for it. For more about ways of raising finance, see pages 106-107.
2) Innovation in **production methods** might mean that finance has to spend a lot on new **capital** (machinery). New machinery is expensive, but tends to make companies more **cost-effective** in the **long term**.

MARKETING

1) Companies might **increase** the amount of **market research** they do when researching an innovative idea — the risks and costs are high, so they need to be absolutely sure customers want or need the product.
2) An innovative product can lead to big changes in the **marketing mix**. For example, marketing will often use a different **pricing strategy** (usually skimming) for an innovative product. Promotional activities are affected too — there's often a lot of **PR** (public relations) activity when a radically new product is launched as everyone wants to feature it in their newspaper or on their TV show.

HUMAN RESOURCES

1) Innovation can mean there's a change in **staffing needs** — if a company suddenly decides to focus heavily on R&D they might need more **skilled staff**.
2) HR need to make sure that the business has the right **culture** for innovation to be successful. In a culture where staff are **scared** of the consequences of **failing** (e.g. that it might lead to dismissal), workers are unlikely to want to take risks. It's the job of HR to find ways of **encouraging** employees to take **risks**, e.g. by **rewarding** people who try **new things**, even if they don't work.

Operational Strategies: Innovation

New Product Development (NPD) has Six Stages from Idea to Launch

1) Idea

The business comes up with **new ideas**, explores and **develops existing ideas** or **modifies competitors' ideas**. New ideas can come from **brainstorming** in a group, from **employee suggestions** or from **R&D department meetings**. New ideas are also discovered through **market research** finding out what consumers want, or from customers submitting requests to a firm. Businesses can sometimes also use **already patented ideas**, for a fee.

2) Analysis and Screening

The business wants to see if the product can be produced and sold at a **profit**. All aspects of the idea are investigated — whether there's a **potential market** for it or not, based on market research, whether the **technology** and **resources** exist to develop it, whether a **competitor** has an existing patent on a similar idea. At this stage, a **prototype** may be made to see what the product will be like.

3) Development

The **R&D department** develop a **working prototype**. They test it **scientifically**, and tweak the design to make the **functional** design (how it works) and **aesthetic** design (how it looks, feels — or smells and tastes if it's a food) as good as possible. This is the real "meat " of research and development.

4) Value Analysis

The business tries to make the product good **value** for money. They look at the cost of **making**, **warehousing** and **distributing** the product to make sure the whole process is **good value** — for both **business** and **consumer**.

5) Test Marketing ← This is where the marketing department gets involved again.

The business sometimes sells the new product in a **limited geographical area**, and then analyses **consumer feedback** on the product, price and packaging. This allows **modifications** to be made before a wider launch.

6) Launch

A successful launch requires **enough stock** of the product to be distributed across the market. It also needs an effective **promotional campaign** in place to **inform** retailers and consumers about the product and **persuade** them to buy it.

The new product launch certainly went with a bang.

Practice Questions

Q1 What's meant by "research and development"?

Q2 Give two reasons why R&D is risky.

Q3 Give two ways that innovation can affect the marketing department.

Q4 What is value analysis?

Exam Question

Q1 Explain why some firms think it is important to invest in research and development. [10 marks]

R&D — not to be confused with R&B, which can also be fast-moving...

Hey, all those amazing new products have to come from somewhere. Just think, there are research and development eggheads beavering away as we speak, to come up with something utterly amazing that we'll all rush out to buy. Of course, it could turn out to be yet another shampoo for colour treated hair, or yet another web publishing tool. Yippee.

Operational Strategies: Location

Businesses have to find the optimal location — the best site their money can buy. I always like a location in town, so I can nip to the shops at lunch.

Quantitative Factors affect choice of Location

Businesses in the primary sector (e.g. mining and fishing) don't get much say in their location. They have to set up close to the natural resources that they're supplying.

1) Location is a big concern for most businesses. The wrong location could mean **high costs** or that potential **customers** won't notice you. Choosing the right location can be a huge **competitive advantage**.
2) When deciding where to locate or relocate, businesses analyse the potential impact on **costs** and **revenues**. **Investment appraisal** techniques such as **payback** and **average rate of return** (see p.110-111) can be used to calculate this.
3) Factors that can be measured in **financial** terms are called quantitative factors. The quantitative factors that affect the choice of location are:

Location decisions depend on distribution and supply costs

1) **Manufacturing** businesses which provide **bulky finished products** should be located near to their **customers** to cut down on distribution costs. Bulky products made from **lightweight** components are called "**bulk increasing**" goods.
2) Other products need **bulky raw materials** to make a **lightweight end product** — these are "**bulk decreasing**" goods. They need to be located near the source of **raw materials** to keep transport costs down.
3) A good **transport infrastructure** (see below) cuts distribution costs.
4) **Services** don't have large distribution costs. Decisions on where to locate services are based mainly on other criteria.

E.g. beer — made of water (available anywhere), plus hops and barley (low in bulk compared to the finished product). Breweries tend to be located near consumers and transport infrastructure, not near hop or barley fields.

E.g. the steel industry in South Wales. The three basic ingredients are iron ore (imported to local ports), coal and limestone (both from South Wales). The product is rolled steel, which is less bulky and can be transported by rail.

Location decisions depend on the availability and cost of resources

1) There must be a **good supply** of labour resources in the area where a business will be located.
2) The labour force must also be **suitable** — e.g. they might need special skills such as IT knowledge, technical knowledge of machinery, etc.
3) The area might need **local training facilities** for staff e.g. a college or university.
4) The area needs **facilities** such as affordable housing, suitable schooling, medical facilities, retail and leisure outlets to provide a good **standard of living** for staff.
5) Businesses can afford to pay workers less in areas where the **cost of living** is lower. To take full advantage of this, businesses need to locate **overseas** where labour costs are often lower than in the UK — see p.140.
6) Businesses also need the right land resources. They may need room for **future expansion**.
7) The **cost of land** and **property** for factories and business premises varies significantly from area to area — land in or near London is far more expensive than land in mid Wales, for example.

Location decisions depend on the market

1) Some businesses such as **retailers** need to locate **near to customers**, in order to catch the passing trade.
2) Business owners usually try to base their businesses in locations which will **maximise their revenue**.

A good location needs an efficient and appropriate infrastructure

1) Business organisations often benefit from access to **motorways**, fast **rail** links, **sea ports** and **airports**.
2) Transport infrastructure is needed for the **import** of **raw materials**, the **distribution** of **finished products**, and for **staff** to get to work.
3) Businesses also need **support services**. Most business organisations need some form of **commercial** support such as **banking**, **insurance** and **marketing** agencies.
4) They often need **technical** support such as engineering services and **IT** assistance.

Operational Strategies: Location

There are also **Qualitative Factors** involved in **Choosing** a **Location**

1) Entrepreneurs might choose to start a business near where they **live** — e.g. Dyson™ is based in Wiltshire, near the owner and inventor's home.
2) Some places have a **good image** which suits the image of the product. High fashion works better in New York, London and Paris than in Scunthorpe or Workington — New York, London and Paris already have a fashion image.

All these factors rarely, if ever, combine in one place to create an **ideal** location. It's more likely that the decision of where to locate a business is based on a **compromise** between different factors.

Businesses may have to **Relocate** — move facilities somewhere else

1) Established businesses sometimes have to up sticks and **move**. This may be because the firm has **grown too large** for its premises, or because **government incentives** have been withdrawn, or because taxes have risen.
2) Some firms have "**industrial inertia**" — it seems sensible for them to relocate, but other factors prevent them from doing so. For example, it might be make sense to relocate closer to suppliers or customers, but the **cost** of relocation might be too high to justify moving.
3) Deciding where to relocate is similar to deciding where to locate, with some **added problems**:
   - Production is likely to be reduced during the move — there may be **downtime**.
   - **Staff** may not **want** to move. They may need to be **paid** to relocate, especially if they have dependent family.
   - Notifying **suppliers** and **customers** costs money. Updating **headed notepaper** and **brochures** costs money.

Expansion is a common reason for businesses to relocate

1) **Expansion** is another word for **growth**. There's lots more about the different types of growth on pages 186-187.
2) When a company expands, they often have more **stock**, **staff**, **machinery** and even **customers** than they had before. This means they're likely to need **extra space**.
3) Some companies can **extend** their existing premises when they expand. However, if there's a lack of **available land** or the business fails to get **planning permission** the business might have to **relocate** instead.

Multi-site businesses operate from **Several** different **Locations**

1) A business can expand by opening new **factories**, **offices** or **stores** whilst also remaining in their **existing premises**. This is called a multi-site location. Shops and restaurant chains often expand this way.
2) Having a multi-site location can be a good way of increasing a company's **sales** and **capacity**. It can also make it easier for companies to respond to local **market conditions**.
3) The downside of multi-site locations is that they can make **communication** harder. The business might need to be **restructured** to remain efficient. Multi-site businesses often have a lot **more staff** than similarly-sized businesses operating from a single location (e.g. they might have a different manager overseeing each site) — this can lead to high **overheads**.

Multi-site locations need multi-sight managers.

Practice Questions

Q1 Identify and briefly explain three factors which affect location decisions.

Q2 Describe three problems that a company might face when relocating.

Q3 Give two disadvantages of multi-site locations.

Exam Question

Q1 One of the major decisions a business can face is where to locate a new factory.
What factors would be taken into consideration in the decision-making process? [10 marks]

Expansion — not just the result of too many chocolate biscuits...

At AS-Level, the focus was on how businesses choose a location when they're starting-up. Now you need to know what factors a business needs to consider if it's thinking of changing location or opening additional premises. Luckily, start-ups and relocations aren't really all that different. All the same, there's a lot of material on these pages, so learn them well.

Locating Abroad

Firms can locate some or all of the business abroad.

Offshoring means *Moving* parts of a business to *Cheaper Countries*

1) Increasingly, many businesses locate some of their **departments**, such as their call centres or payment processing departments, **overseas** — this is called **offshoring**.
2) The countries that firms move to most often are **China**, **India**, **Russia**, **Poland** and **Brazil**.
3) Offshoring can be a good way to **cut costs**, but it's not always good for a company's **image**. The media and trade unions often criticise companies for UK **job losses** caused by offshoring.

To everyone's surprise, staff loved the new offshore department.

Certain countries *Specialise* in particular *Goods* or *Services*

1) As a result of offshoring, some countries have become **specialised** in providing certain services. For example, **India** specialises in **communications** (e.g. call centres) and **IT services**.
2) If a country like India is providing a certain service to a large number of UK businesses, it **encourages** other companies to offshore that part of their business there as well. If India already has a large number of call centre providers, **prices** will probably be **competitive** and there is also likely to be a pool of suitably **trained workers**.
3) India has an **advantage** over other countries that provide communication services. Because it can provide communications relatively **cheaply** and **efficiently**, it's in a **strong position** to **sell** them to other countries.
4) Specialisation does have **risks**. Workers may lose **motivation** or the size of the industry may lead to **diseconomies of scale**. There's also a risk **another country** will find a way of providing a good or service even **more efficiently**.

Locating abroad can be a way of *Cutting Costs* or *Increasing Revenue*

Locating abroad can reduce costs

1) One of the main reasons why companies choose to move production overseas is that they can often pay **foreign workers** much **lower wages** than they would have to pay their UK employees. Some companies have been accused of not paying foreign workers enough to live on — this is **unethical**.
2) The cost of **land** and **office space** also tends to be **cheaper** overseas, especially in emerging markets. For example, it's estimated that it costs around **£114** per year to rent **1m²** of office space in the **UK**. In **Malaysia**, it only costs **£38** per **1m²** per year. Utilities like water and electricity might also be cheaper.

Locating abroad is a way of targeting new international markets

1) Targeting new, foreign markets is one way for companies to continue to grow when their existing market **stops growing** or becomes **saturated**.
2) Relocating overseas in order to sell your products to foreign markets also helps businesses to **survive** in times of **economic downturn** or **domestic recession**.
3) Locating a firm close to the overseas market it's trying to sell to makes it easier to spot local **market trends**. This makes it less likely a company will make expensive **marketing errors** and it might even spot new market **niches**.

Locating abroad helps companies avoid trade barriers

1) Some countries create **trade barriers** in order to **protect** domestic companies from **foreign competition**. These barriers might be things like **taxes** or **restrictions** on sales of goods from abroad.
2) Locating part of a business **within** a country with trade barriers helps companies **get round** these penalties.
3) Some people also think that trade barriers protect **domestic** industries from the realities of international competition, causing them to become **inefficient**. This could mean that a **foreign** company that locates in a country with trade barriers will have a **competitive advantage**, because it's likely to be more efficient.

Improved Transport and *Communication* links make it easier to locate *Abroad*

1) In recent years, the **cost** of **air travel** has **fallen** sharply and there are many **more flights** available than there used to be. This means it is relatively **easy** for people to **travel** between overseas business locations.
2) Trading overseas has also been made easier because countries with **emerging markets** are **investing** heavily in **infrastructure**. This means that they have much better road and rail networks and ports than they had in the past. For example, in 2008, China spent 12% of its GDP on improving its infrastructure.
3) Doing business overseas has also been made easier by **technological** developments. Businesses can communicate internationally by **email** and hold meetings using **videoconferencing** — so people don't have to leave the UK.

Locating Abroad

Locating Abroad has Public and Private Costs and Benefits

1) **Private costs** and **benefits** affect a firm directly — they're often **financial**. For example, the **private cost** of constructing a new shop unit might be £120 000. The **private benefit** of the new shop is the added **revenue** it will bring in.
2) **Public costs** and **benefits** are the **positive** and **negative effects** that a firm's activities have on the **outside world**. For example, **training** is a public benefit because it results in a more highly-trained workforce, and air **pollution** is a public cost. Public costs and benefits are also called **externalities**.
3) The **private benefits** for companies of locating abroad include **cheaper wage bills** and a **reduction in trade barriers**.
4) There can also be **private costs** to companies of locating abroad. Companies can get a **bad reputation** if consumers think that their behaviour in developing countries is **unethical**.
5) Locating abroad also has some **public benefits**. Companies that locate in developing countries create **new jobs**, which increases the local **income** and **standard of living**. Companies also **invest** in the host country by paying for factories, roads, etc to be built, and by paying **taxes** to the local government, which might be spent on things like schools and hospitals.
6) The **public costs** of locating abroad include the **loss of jobs** and **investment** in the original country. Also, some businesses may **exploit** foreign workers in developing countries — e.g. by using **child labour**, making employees work **long hours**, not providing a **safe** working environment, and **not paying** employees enough to live on.

Cost-benefit Analysis finds out which is Greater — Costs or Benefits

1) **Cost-benefit analysis** involves calculating the **private** and **public costs** of a project and **weighing** them up against its **private** and **public benefits**.
2) The basic formula for cost-benefit analysis is **social benefit – social cost**. The **social benefit** is **private benefits** and **public benefits** added together and the **social cost** is **private** and **public costs** combined.
3) The main **advantage** of this kind of analysis is that it ensures **all costs** are **taken into account**. It also allows a **value** to be put on **environmental effects**, e.g. the pollution and waste caused by building a factory abroad.

It can be Difficult to carry out an Accurate cost-benefit analysis

1) It's difficult to put a **financial value** on a lot of costs and benefits — e.g. it's almost impossible to know the real **monetary cost** of **pollution**. If costs and benefits are **wrongly calculated**, it might mean that a company makes the **wrong choice**.
2) Cost-benefit analysis might fail to **take account** of **all** the **groups** affected by a decision. For example, a new airport runway affects local homeowners, airport workers, airlines and many more individuals. Cost-benefit analysis might not consider the impact on **everyone** who might **benefit** or **suffer** as a result of the project.

Practice Questions

Q1 Give two advantages of offshoring your IT department to a country that specialises in IT services.

Q2 Describe three advantages of locating abroad.

Q3 Give two potential problems with cost-benefit analysis.

Exam Question

Q1 Flimby Toys Ltd wants to relocate to China. Explain why it would be a good idea to use cost-benefit analysis. [10 marks]

Offshoring communication — sending messages in bottles...

I don't think it's that difficult to understand why companies might like to locate abroad. After all, who wouldn't rather stare out of the window at a sunny beach rather than at a rainy, grey town centre. Make sure you learn the other advantages of international location too though, and also the stuff on cost-benefit analysis, which is a bit more complicated.

Lean Production

Lean production is all about "trimming the fat" from production methods. Shame — I like a bit of fat.

Lean Production means Eliminating Waste

1) **Lean production** is an **efficient** form of production that keeps **waste** (of time and resources) to a **minimum**.
2) **Inefficient** production methods increase **costs**, so **lean** production can **save** businesses a lot of money.
3) **Lean** production methods include **just-in-time**, **total quality management** (see p. 144) and **kaizen** (see p. 145).

It's Costly to hold lots of Stock

1) **Stock** is all the **raw materials** needed for making a product and the store of **finished goods** that a firm holds to supply to customers. These days firms don't tend to hold much stock — because of the **costs** involved.
2) **Storage costs** are the most **obvious cost** of holding stock. Storage costs include rent for the warehouse and also the non-obvious costs of heating, lighting, refrigeration, security etc. Don't forget those.
3) **Wastage costs** are the costs of **throwing away** useless stock. The longer a business holds stock, the more likely it is to create waste. Stock gets **physically damaged** as time goes on, and can also go **out of fashion**.
4) **Opportunity cost** is the cost of **investing** money in stock instead of **something else**. Capital tied up in stock is **unproductive** and could be used more productively elsewhere, such as financing a marketing campaign.

Stock Control aims to keep levels of stock Just Right

1) Most businesses try to reduce the level of stocks they're holding. The **maximum** level of stock a business wants to hold depends on the size of their warehouses, their production method (see p. 133) and also on **opportunity cost**.
2) Businesses that use **flow production** need a **large stock** of **raw materials**, whereas **batch production** leads to large **stocks** of **work-in-progress**. **Job production** often means there are **no stocks** of **finished goods** to be stored and **cell production** usually relies on **just-in-time** stock control (see below).
3) A business needs a **minimum** level of stock so that it **won't run out** of raw materials or finished goods. This minimum stock level is called **buffer stock**.
4) The **amount** of **buffer stock** needed depends on the warehouse **space** available, the kind of product (**perishable**, or something which keeps), the **rate** at which stocks are used up, and the **lead time**.
5) The **lead time** is the time it takes for goods to **arrive** after ordering them from the supplier. The **longer** the lead time, the **more buffer stocks** you need to hold — if customer demand suddenly went up, you wouldn't want to wait a long time for stocks to arrive from the supplier.
6) Stock control charts allow managers to **analyse** and **control** stock over a period of time — as shown below.

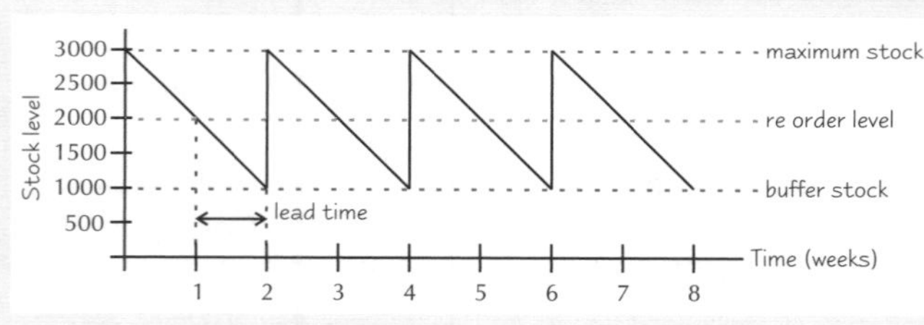

1) The **buffer stock level** is **1000 units**. The **lead time** is 1 week, and the business goes through **1000 units** a week. That means they have to **re-order** stock when they've got **2000** units left — just so they don't go below their buffer stock level. 2000 units is the **re-order level**.
2) The firm re-orders **2000 units** each time. This takes them back to their **maximum stock level** of 3000 units.

Just-In-Time (JIT) Production keeps stock levels Very Low

1) **Just-in-time** production aims to have as **little stock** as possible. Ideally, all raw materials come in one door, are made into products and go straight out another door — all **just in time** for delivery to customers.
2) JIT is based on very efficient stock control. **Kanban** is the JIT system of triggering **repeat orders**. When staff reach coloured kanban cards towards the end of a batch of components, they order more straight away. The **supply** of raw materials is **linked directly** to the **demand** for raw materials, and there's no need for lots of stock.
3) JIT has **advantages** — **storage costs** are reduced and **working capital control** is improved. There's **less waste** because there's less out-of-date stock lying around.
4) There are **disadvantages** — no stock means customers can't be supplied during **production strikes**. Businesses using JIT can't respond to **sudden rises** in **demand**. Suppliers have to be **reliable** because there isn't much stock of raw materials to keep production going.

Lean Production

Time-based Management means companies have to be Flexible

1) Time-based management means that as well as competing on price and quality, companies can also **compete** on **time** by trying to be the **fastest** to get their product on the market. It's often used to produce **technological** items and **high fashion** clothes — areas where consumer needs change fast.
2) Time-based management depends on **flexible production facilities**, e.g. machines that can do more than one thing. For example, a fashion retailer might need a machine that can sew buttons onto coats one week and attach zips the next.
3) For time-based management to work, **effective communication** between managers and production staff is essential, so the business needs to have a culture of **trust**. Staff also need to be **multi-skilled** — so **training** is important.

Tim knew he had to get his 'real-life effect' baby ice sculpture to consumers as quick as possible — otherwise it would melt.

ADVANTAGES OF TIME-BASED MANAGEMENT:

1) It **reduces lead times** — so the cost of holding stock falls (see p.142).
2) Reduced lead times also mean that **customer needs** can be satisfied **quicker**, giving the company a **competitive advantage**.
3) **Machinery** with more than one function makes it possible to offer a more **varied** product range.

4) However, some people have **criticised** time-based management for placing speed above **quality** — customers get a product sooner, but it might be faulty or not last as long.

Companies can also take a Time-based approach to R&D

1) The pressure of **intense international competition** and **rapidly changing technology** means that larger, multinational businesses need to come up with new, better products **all the time**. Businesses need to use **R&D** to develop new products so that they maintain or increase their global market share.
2) The **demands** of the market **change rapidly**, and manufacturers are under pressure to **react rapidly** to meet these changing demands. New product development, like production, is squeezed into as **short** a time as possible, to get the product out to consumers as quickly as possible.

The Advantages of Lean Production depend on Customers and Competitors

1) Lean producers tend to have **small volume** production runs and are more **flexible** than typical mass producers, who produce large quantities of identical products. This gives them an edge over mass producers when **product life cycles** are **short**, e.g. when fashions change quickly. They benefit when customers demand more new, fashionable, "now" products — which they certainly seem to be doing these days...
2) Of course, the advantage a business gets from lean production depends on what **other businesses** are up to. If they've all got the lean production bug as well, it won't give as much of a **competitive advantage**.

Practice Questions

Q1 What is lean production?

Q2 What is meant by 'stock'?

Q3 Name two advantages of just-in-time production.

Q4 Why might a company take a time-based approach to R&D?

Exam Question

Q1 Samuel Owen owns a women's fashion brand. A friend has recently suggested that he tries using time-based management techniques. Explain what advantages and disadvantages he might encounter if he does this. [10 marks]

Just-in-time production is a good idea — just-in-time revision isn't...

Hopefully you're reading this a good few weeks before the exam and you've got time to read and scribble until it's properly embedded in your memory. If you are tight for time though, don't panic. Do as much as you can, but don't stay up all night or you'll just be frazzled and not even remember your name when you get into the exam — get some zzzzzz.

Quality

Quality control, quality assurance or Quality Street® — I know which I prefer. You might remember a lot of this from AS level, but you'll need it again for A2.

Quality Control and *Quality Assurance* are *Different Things*

Staff had taken quality assurance to a new level — if they didn't turn up to work, things couldn't go wrong in the first place...

1) It's **important** that companies produce **quality** goods. Most **customers** realise that **lower priced** goods won't be as **high** quality as more **expensive** ones, but they do expect a product to be **fit for purpose** (to do the job it's intended for).
2) There are **two** ways for a company to check it's producing goods of a suitable quality — **quality control** and **quality assurance**.
3) **Quality control** means **checking goods** as you make them or when they arrive from suppliers to see if anything is wrong with them. It's often done by specially trained **quality inspectors**.
4) **Quality assurance** means introducing measures into the **production process** to try to ensure things don't go **wrong** in the first place. It assumes you can **prevent errors** from being made in the first place, rather than **eliminating faulty goods** once they've been made.

Quality Control	Quality Assurance (QA)
Assumes that errors are **unavoidable**.	Assumes that errors are **avoidable**.
Detects errors and **puts them right**.	**Prevents errors** and aims to get it **right first time**.
Quality control inspectors check other people's work, and are responsible for quality.	**Employees** check their own work. **Workers** are **responsible** for passing on good quality work to the next stage of the production process.

Quality Circles are *Groups* of *Employees* who work on quality issues

1) **Quality circles** meet a couple of times a month to discuss quality control issues.
2) They include employees from **various departments** and **all levels** of the organisation.
3) Quality circles aim to **identify** and **solve** specific quality problems that arise.

Strengths of Quality Circles	Weaknesses of Quality Circles
Quality circles can be very effective because they use the **knowledge** and **experience** of factory floor staff.	Factory floor staff might make **unrealistic** suggestions if they don't know what kind of measures the business can **afford** to introduce.
Quality circles are a good way of making staff feel involved and increasing **motivation**.	Quality circles are only useful if management actually **listen** to the suggestions and **make changes** accordingly.
Quality circles often lead to an increase in **productivity** as well as quality.	They only work if participation really is **voluntary** — staff who feel pressured into taking part are unlikely to make useful suggestions.

Total Quality Management assures *Commitment To Quality*

1) **Total Quality Management** (TQM) is a **lean production** method (see p. 142-143). It means the **whole workforce** has to be committed to quality improvements. The idea is to have **every department** focusing on quality in order to improve the **overall quality** of the products and services.
2) With TQM, every employee has to try to **satisfy customers** — both **external** customers that the business sells things to, and **internal** customers within the business.

Advantages of TQM	Disadvantages of TQM
Because all employees are involved with maintaining quality, TQM can help them to bond as a **team**.	It can take a **long time** to introduce TQM — so the company might not see immediate improvements in quality.
TQM boosts a company's **reputation** for providing quality services or products.	TQM can **demotivate staff** — it can seem like a lot of effort to think about quality in all parts of the business.
TQM usually leads to fewer **faulty** products being made — so the business creates less **waste**.	TQM is usually **expensive** to introduce — it often means investing in **training** for all employees.

Quality

Benchmarking Learns *from* **Other Businesses**

1) Benchmarking studies **other businesses** with excellent **quality standards**, and aims to **adopt** their **methods**. Companies can sometimes do this by joining benchmarking groups, where firms agree to share information about their way of doing things.
2) Businesses can **benchmark internally**, by studying similar activities in different departments.
3) It's also possible to benchmark across **different industries** — for example, an electronics manufacturer buys different raw materials than a food producer does, but the food producer might still find it useful to benchmark the **purchasing methods** and **negotiation techniques** used by the electronics company.
4) Benchmarking tends to **motivate** staff. It's more encouraging to introduce something that you've already seen being **used successfully** somewhere else than it is to introduce something completely **unknown**.
5) Another advantage is that it provides **early warnings** to businesses about **technology** or **methods** that might allow their competitors to **overtake** them.
6) One of the disadvantages of benchmarking is that the **firm** whom you're most **keen** to **benchmark** may **not** want to **share** their methods. **Competitors** are unlikely to **release** information if they're not part of a benchmarking group.
7) Another downside is that **working practices** can't always be transferred between different **corporate cultures**.

Kaizen *is Japanese for* **Continuous Improvement**

1) The **kaizen** approach is another **lean production method** that means that employees should be **improving** their work slightly **all the time**, instead of just making one-off improvements when management tell them to.
2) The **5 whys** are also important in kaizen. Whenever there's a problem, companies need to ask **'why?'** five times. For example, the firm's **reputation** seems to be getting worse. Managers investigate why and discover that an **unhappy customer** has talked about her poor experience. Further investigation shows that she didn't receive an order **on time**. The reason for this is that it took more than a week to **process** her order, which was due to a **lack** of **call centre staff**. Asking why there aren't enough call centre staff shows that business has **increased** 10%, but no extra staff have been **recruited**. So the real solution to the problem lies in **recruitment**, not in **PR** to improve the firm's image.
3) Workers are also responsible for keeping their equipment **clean**, their work area **tidy**, and making sure that everything is kept in the **right place**. For kaizen to work, they need to do this **every day**, not just occasionally.
4) For kaizen to work, employees at the bottom of the hierarchy have to be given some control over **decision-making** so that they can actually **implement** quality improvements.
5) Kaizen helps workers feel **involved** in quality assurance. It's also **cheap** to introduce.
6) The downside of kaizen is that, because it makes **small changes** over time, it's not great for businesses that **urgently** need to improve quality. It needs the firm to be willing to commit to the method in the **long term**.

Practice Questions

Q1 What's the difference between quality control and quality assurance?

Q2 Describe two advantages and two disadvantages of TQM.

Q3 What is 'kaizen'?

Exam Questions

Q1 Paul Newby wants to benchmark his business against similar firms. Explain the benefits of doing this, as well as some of the problems he might encounter. [10 marks]

Q2 Bella Stevens makes table lamps. Recently a large number of customers have been returning products, saying they're unhappy with the quality. Explain how kaizen might help Bella to better understand the problem. [8 marks]

Benchmarking — the defence method favoured by lazy footballers...

It's often expensive for companies to do a really good job of monitoring quality, but it's usually worth it — if customers know you can be counted on to provide a quality product it gives you a real competitive advantage. Make sure you learn the pros and cons of these methods inside out in case you get asked to recommend a method or assess an existing one.

Critical Path Analysis

Critical Path Analysis is used to find the most cost-effective way of doing a complex project.

Critical Path Analysis works out the Quickest Way to Finish a Set Of Tasks

Critical Path Analysis (CPA) identifies the most **efficient** and **cost-effective** way of completing a complex project — i.e. a project made up of a series of activities. Critical path analysis is sometimes just called 'network analysis'.

1) The various activities which make up the project are **identified**, and the **order** or **sequence** that these activities must be performed in is identified.
2) The **duration** (how long each activity will take) is **estimated**.
3) These factors are then arranged as a **network** or graph, showing the whole project from start to finish, and showing which tasks can be performed at the same time. For large, complicated projects made up of lots of steps, computer programs are used to construct the network.
4) The **shortest time** required to get from start to finish can then be identified. The sequence of tasks which have to be done one after another with **no gaps in between**, to get the project done as fast as possible, is called the **critical path**. Activities on the critical path are called **critical activities** — if they're delayed, the **whole project** is delayed.

Example

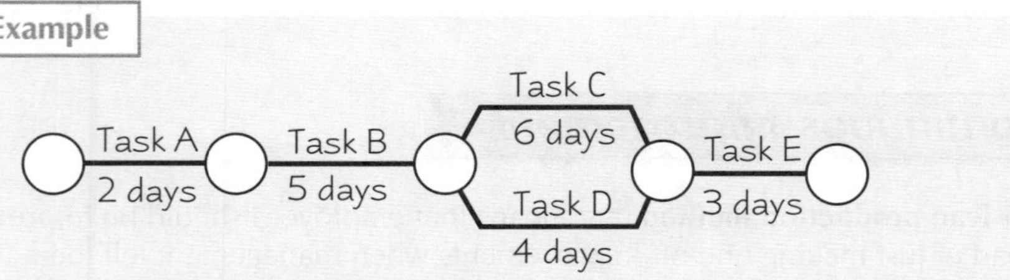

In this example, **task C** and **task D** can start at the **same time** once task B is completed.

The **critical path** here is task **A**, task **B**, task **C** and task **E** — task D **isn't** on the critical path because if task C and task D start at the same time, there will be a **gap** of two days between task D finishing and task E starting, while you wait for task C to finish.

Dearest, we really must get back to the path before we ruin our skirts. It's absolutely critical.

Nodes show when one task Must Finish and when the next task Can Start

1) The **circles** on the network are called **nodes** — they show where one activity **stops** and another activity **begins**.
2) Each node is split into three parts. The numbers inside each node are really useful, because they show the latest time that the previous task can finish, and the earliest time that the next task can start:

- The **left** part of the node shows you which **number** node it is.
- The number in the **top right** is the **earliest start time** (EST) of the activity **following** the node. That's the **earliest** time from the beginning of the project that the activity can **start**, assuming that all the activities before it are completed in as short a time as possible. See the next page for how to calculate the earliest start time of an activity.
- The number in the **bottom right** of the node is the **latest finishing time** (LFT) of the activity immediately **before** the node (or the LFT of the activity with the longest duration if there's more than one activity going into the node). That's the **latest** time that the activity can **finish** without having the knock-on effect of making the whole project **late**. See the next page for how to work out latest finishing times.

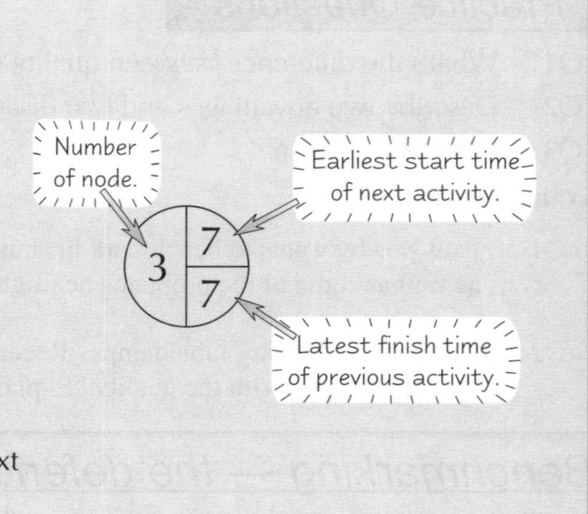

Critical Path Analysis

Critical Paths include Start Times, Finishing Times and Float Time

It's really important to know the **earliest** and **latest start** and **finishing times** for each activity so that you can make sure the whole project can be completed **on time** — if you **miss** the latest start time of an activity, there's **no way** you can finish the project on time (unless you can do individual activities **more quickly** than you predicted).

1) **EST** = **earliest start time**, in number of days since the start of the project. An activity can't start until the activity before it has been completed — e.g. you can't ice a cake before it's baked. EST is worked out by **adding** the **duration** of the **previous activity** to its **EST**. The EST of the first activity is always 0.

   E.g. a business needs a sign for the door. The sign needs to be **constructed (3 days)**, **painted (2 days)**, left to **dry (4 days)** and then **hung (1 day)**.
   So, the **EST** of **drying** is: **0 + 3 + 2 = 5**

2) **EFT** = **earliest finishing time**. It's the time that an activity will **finish** if it's **started** at the **earliest start time**. You can work out the EFT for an activity by **adding** its **duration** (in days here) to its **EST**.

   Using the same example, the **EFT** of **drying** is: **5 + 4 = 9**

3) **LFT** = **latest finishing time**. This is the **latest** time by which the activity can be completed without **holding up** the **completion** of the project. It's calculated by **subtracting** the **duration** of the **next activity** from its **LFT** — you have to work out the LFTs by **working backwards** from the **end** of the project.

   If the business needs the sign to be hung by the end of **day 14**, the **LFT** of **painting is: 14 – 1 – 4 = 9**

4) **LST** = **latest start time**. It's the **latest time** an activity can be **started** and still be **finished** by its **LFT**. To calculate LST, **subtract** the **duration** of the activity from its **LFT**.

   The **LST** of **painting** in the example above is: **9 – 2 = 7**

5) **Float time** is the **spare time** available for an activity. Only **non-critical** activities have **float time**.
   - **Free float** is the length of **time** you can **delay** an individual **activity** for without **affecting** the **EST** of the **next** activity. An activity only has free float if the next activity can't start until the completion of **another** activity, which is scheduled to take longer. You can work out the free float by:

     EST (next activity) – **duration** (this activity) – **EST** (of this activity) = **free float**

   - **Total float** is the length of **time** you can **delay** an activity without delaying the **completion** of the **project**. You can work it out by:

     LFT (this activity) – **duration** (this activity) – **EST** (this activity) = **total float**

Practice Questions

Q1 What is meant by the "critical path"?
Q2 What do the three numbers inside each node show?
Q3 What do the initials EST and LST mean?
Q4 How do you calculate the latest finishing time of an activity?
Q5 Explain the term "total float time".

Exam Question

Q1 Explain how a critical path network is produced. [8 marks]

What did the critical path say — "get your badly-dressed self off my gravel"...

To be honest, this is hard to learn from scratch. Once you've got a diagram to show the order of tasks in a project, and which ones can be done simultaneously, you can figure out where there's some spare time. Remember that you work out EST by working forwards from the start date, and you work out LFT by going backwards from the end date.

Critical Path Analysis

These are the last two pages on critical path analysis. And the last two pages of the section too.

Here's an **Example** of **Critical Path Analysis**

A project is made up of **nine separate tasks** — A to I:

- **Task A** takes **4 days** to complete and can be done at the same time as **task G** (5 days).
- **Task B** (7 days) and **task C** (9 days) can be done at the **same time** once **task A** is finished.
- **Task D** (6 days) can start once **task B** is completed.
- **Task E** (5 days) can start once **task B** and **task C** have **both** finished. **Task E** can be done at the **same time** as **task D**.
- **Task F** (3 days) can start once **task D** and **task E** have both finished.
- **Task H** (7 days) can start once **task G** has finished.
- **Task I** (4 days) can start once **task F** and **task H** have both finished.

The network looks like this:

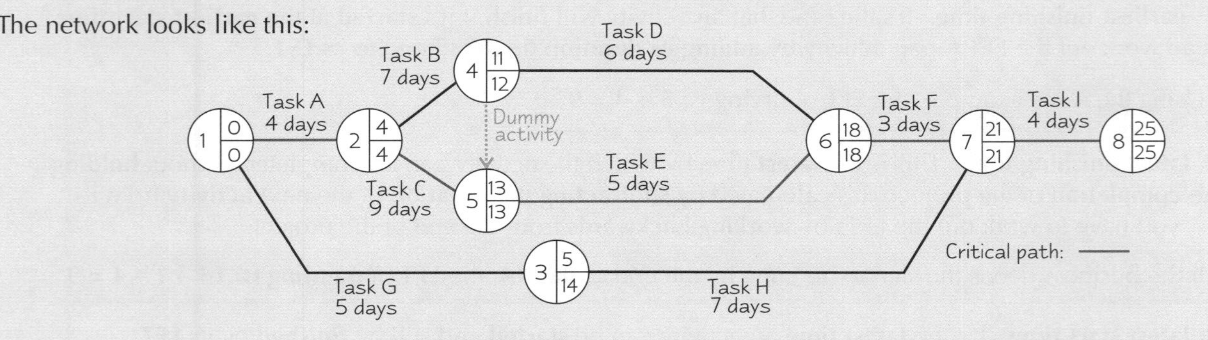

1) The **critical path** (in red) is task **A** (4 days) then task **C** (9 days), task **E** (5 days), task **F** (3 days) and finally task **I** (4 days). If you add up the time taken to do each task, it shows that the project can be completed in **25 days** in total. The LFT of task I in the final node is 25 days, and if there was another activity, its EST would be 25 days.
2) You can work out the **ESTs** of all the tasks by working **forwards** from the start of the project, and then work out the **LFTs** of the tasks by working backwards from the end of the project.
3) In each node on the **critical path**, the **EST** equals the **LFT**. For nodes that are off the critical path, the **EST** and **LFT** are **different**.
4) **Task B** and **task D** both have a total **float time** of 1 day, and **task G** and **task H** have a total float time of 9 days. These tasks are **non-critical activities** — if there is a **delay** in starting them, it's still possible to complete the project **on time**. E.g. if task G starts on day 5 instead of day 0, it will still be completed before its latest finishing time. If **critical tasks** start **late** or take **longer** than they're expected to, the project **can't** be completed on time.

There is a **dummy activity** between node 4 and node 5. A **dummy activity** is an **imaginary activity** — it just shows that one activity is **dependent** on another. In the example, the dummy activity shows that **task E can't start** until **task B** and **task C** have **both** finished. **Without** the dummy activity it would look as though **task E** was only dependent on **task C**, but having only **one node** between tasks B and C and tasks D and E would imply that **task D** was dependent on **both task B** and **task C**, instead of just **task B**.

Critical Path Analysis is used for **Scheduling** and **Allocating Resources**

1) Critical path analysis is used when **planning** a **complicated project**, such as the launch of a new product or building a new office block.
2) It allows companies to work out when they'll need **resources** to be **available**, e.g. that a certain **machine** will need to be **free** on Friday or that **raw materials** will need to be **ordered** so they arrive on day 25 of a project.
3) In many cases, it's possible to **shorten** the **critical path** by allocating **additional resources** to an activity. For example, sewing buttons onto a batch of jumpers might be expected to take 5 days, but if the company hired extra machinists, it might be possible to reduce that to 3 days.
4) Some **resources** can be **switched** between activities — e.g. multi-skilled staff can be moved from construction to painting. It's easier to switch resources between activities if the firm has **flexible production facilities** (see p.143).
5) Critical path analysis also helps managers with **decision-making**. Knowing the **latest finish time** of a project makes it easier to decide when to launch an **ad campaign** or when to schedule a **launch party**.

Critical Path Analysis

Critical Path Analysis has several *Advantages*

1) CPA identifies the **critical activities** (activities on the critical path), which need to be supervised closely, to make sure they meet their deadlines.
2) Labour resources can be transferred from activities with **float time** to **critical activities**, to make sure that deadlines are met.
3) CPA allows managers to operate **just-in-time** production. **Resources** such as raw materials, labour and equipment can be employed efficiently from the **earliest start time**, instead of hanging around waiting to be needed. This saves on the **storage costs** and opportunity costs of stock holding, and **improves liquidity**.
4) Critical path analysis helps firms forecast their **cash flow** — it gives definite earliest start times when cash will need to be spent on raw materials, which allows the firm to predict its liquidity.
5) Critical path analysis finds the shortest time possible for completing a complex project. This can give a competitive advantage. It's an important element of **time-based management**.
6) It's an excellent **visual aid** to communications, because it shows at a glance which steps take place at the **same time**, and which have any **float time**.
7) Critical path analysis forces managers to think about the **activities** involved in the project. Without the **systematic approach** of critical path analysis, something might be forgotten.
8) CPA can be used to review progress on **individual tasks**, e.g. if a task overruns its free float time or total float time you can see if it will delay the overall project or just the next activity. If there are changes and modifications to the progress of the project, the critical path can be **updated** as the project goes on.

Critical Path Analysis has *Disadvantages* as well

1) Critical path analysis relies on **estimates** of how long each task will take. If these aren't accurate, the whole analysis will be inaccurate.
2) Unless **critical activities** are identified and supervised closely, there'll be **delays** to the whole project. Critical path analysis can sometimes put **excessive pressure** on managers to **meet deadlines**.
3) Managers must make changes to the CPA once they know that delays are likely. Otherwise, it'll be inaccurate.
4) Constructing the CPA will require a significant amount of **planning** and **time**.
5) Critical path analysis sets **tight deadlines**, especially for critical activities. It's tempting for employees to **cut corners** in the rush to meet deadlines. **Quality** can suffer.
6) Critical path analysis can't tell you anything about **costs** — or anything about **how good** the project is.

Practice Questions

Q1 What is a dummy activity?

Q2 Give two examples of projects that managers might use critical path analysis for.

Q3 Give two advantages to managers of using critical path analysis.

Q4 Give two disadvantages of critical path analysis.

Exam Question

Q1 A project contains six separate activities. Activity A must be completed first, and it has an estimated duration of eight days. Activities B, C and D can take place at the same time — B takes four days, C six days and D four days. E can only be started once B, C and D are completed and will take seven days. Once E is completed, F and G can take place at the same time — F taking three days and G five days.

Answer on p.203

(a) Construct a critical path network to show this data. [5 marks]

(b) Mark in the critical path and state the minimum number of days the project will take to complete. [2 marks]

(c) What are the free float times at B and F? [2 marks]

You take the high road and I'll take the critical path...

Well that's it — the end of section four. These are a nice couple of pages to end it on too. Critical path analysis can seem a bit tricky, but don't be put off by the scary-looking network on page 148 — just break it down and it'll seem a whole lot simpler. Don't forget to learn the advantages and disadvantages of CPA too — they could easily come up in the exam.

HRM

These pages are all about managing "human resources" — otherwise known as people.

Human Resource Management is about Managing People

1) The role of Human Resource Management (HRM) is to ensure that a business achieves the **maximum benefit** from its employees at the **minimum cost**.
2) HRM objectives are influenced by the objectives of the business **as a whole**. For example, if the business is going to expand into a new market, the HR department might need to **recruit new staff** to suit the business needs.
3) They also work closely with **other departments**. These departments help HR to anticipate **workforce needs** and react to them — by **recruiting** new staff or **providing training**. HR also needs to work with the finance department to determine a **suitable budget** for the HR department.

Objectives help HR to Manage People Effectively

HRM objectives help them to manage staff successfully. Objectives for the HR department might include:

1 — Matching the Workforce to Business Needs

- HR needs to anticipate the **future size** of the workforce — if the organisation is **expanding** they'll need more workers, if it's **contracting** they won't need as many.
- They decide what **skill-level** the workforce **needs**, and whether staff should be employed **full-** or **part-time**. If the requirements of the business change, HR can decide whether to **train** current staff or **recruit** new workers from **outside** the business.
- They also work with other managers to decide **where** employees are needed if a business has several sites or branches, and **which departments** within a business require specific staff.

2 — Controlling Labour Costs

- HR has a **budget** like all other departments.
- They have to make sure that staff wages are **appropriate** to the job and employee. They have to get the **balance** between staying within the budget and **rewarding** more highly skilled and senior positions.
- Controlling costs means controlling the **number of staff**. **Too many staff** means that the business pays a **bigger wage bill** than it needs to, which reduces profits. **Not enough staff** with the right skill level results in a **fall** in **productivity**, leading to a fall in **profits**.
- Extra costs such as **training** and **recruitment** can be expensive but should have **long term benefits**, e.g. employing the **right** person for the right job means they're more likely to **stay** in the job.

3 — Helping Employees Reach their Full Potential

- HR invests in **training** so workers can improve their **productivity**. They also make sure that employees have the right equipment to do their job properly.
- HR make sure there are opportunities for **career progression**. Employees work better if they have **something to aim for**, like a **promotion** or taking on extra responsibility at work.
- They need to match **workforce skill-levels** to jobs. If a job is too **challenging** for an employee, this can lead to **demotivation** and **low self-esteem**. If the work is not demanding enough, employees become **bored**.
- Effective **management**, good staff **organisation** and a pleasant **working environment** help to improve **morale** — happy employees are more likely to work to their full potential.

4 — Supporting Employee/Employer Relations

- Employee/employer relations are based upon **good communication**. HR **listens** and **reacts** to employee concerns. They can **advise** managers how to deal with problems in their departments.
- Employees who are given **responsibility** and involved in decision-making feel **valued** and **trusted**.
- Improving the **relationship** between **employees** and **management** can reduce absenteeism and labour turnover. If employees feel **valued**, they're more likely to be **loyal** to the business.
- **Breakdown in relations** can lead to decreased productivity, low morale and even strike action.

HRM

HRM Strategies can be Hard or Soft

There are **two schools of thought** in human resource management — **hard HRM** and **soft HRM**.

Hard HRM

1) Employees are seen as a **resource** like any other.
2) Employees are hired on a **short-term basis.**
3) Managers believe that employees are mainly motivated by **money**.
4) Managers tend to be **Theory X** managers (they think that staff will do as **little** work as possible).
5) Appraisals are **judgemental.**
6) Training is only done to meet **production** needs.

Soft HRM

1) Employees are the **most important** resource.
2) Employees are managed on a **long-term basis.**
3) Managers motivate employees through **empowerment** and **development**.
4) Managers tend to be **Theory Y** managers (they think that working is **natural** for employees).
5) Appraisals are **developmental.**
6) Training is done to meet **development** needs.

1) **Hard HRM** can be **good** for businesses because managers keep **control** of the workforce, so people are less likely to make **mistakes**. Since employees are seen as just another resource, it's easy for the business to **replace** them if they leave.
2) One problem with hard HRM is that the business **doesn't** use its employees to their **full potential**, so it could be **missing out** on opportunities to increase its **profits**. Hard HRM can also be very **demotivational** for the workforce. Boring, repetitive jobs can make employees feel **undervalued**. They're unlikely to be loyal to their organisation, leading to **high staff turnover**.
3) **Soft HRM** is likely to increase **staff morale** because employees will feel **valued**. This will make it easier to **retain** staff, and the business will also benefit from the **skills** and **experience** of its staff. It encourages **commitment** and good performance from its **workers**, because they feel loyalty to the organisation.
4) Soft HRM **isn't** always **appropriate** though — employees might not be interested in **development** or **empowerment**, and soft HRM usually involves more **costs** for businesses because it encourages **investment** in employees. The extra training is also **time-consuming**. There's also a risk that employees who have completed all the training might want to **leave** for a better job.

Internal and External Factors influence HRM Objectives

Internal factors

1) The **culture** within the business influences **HRM objectives**. E.g. some businesses, like fast food restaurants, might not be worried about having a high labour turnover, so they wouldn't want HR to spend time and money trying to reduce it.
2) Other **departments** within the business influence HR. They give HR the information that they need to **predict** workforce needs.

External factors

1) The amount of **funding** available within the business and the general state of the **economy** (boom or recession) will also affect HR activities such as **recruitment** and **training**.
2) All UK businesses are subject to **UK** and **EU employment laws**. HR might have to change their objectives to fit in with **new legislation.** They inform other departments about changes in the law so they can **update working practices**.

Practice Questions

Q1 What are the problems of having too many staff?

Q2 How can HRM help employees reach their full potential?

Q3 What are the external factors that influence HRM objectives?

Q4 Why is it important for HR and other departments to work together?

Exam Question

Q1 Explain the difference between hard and soft HRM and evaluate the costs and benefits of each. [10 marks]

Soft HRM is always practised in pillow factories...

HRM sounds quite tricky — you've got to make sure you've got the right kinds of staff and the right number of staff, then try to stop too many of them from leaving, and try to get them to turn up for work and leave at the end of the day in one piece. Phew. It's a bit easier to learn about it all than to actually do it, which is lucky because that's what you've got to do.

Workforce Plans

Workforce plans are plans about, well, the workforce.

Workforce Planning starts with anticipating Future Staffing Needs

The **purpose** of workforce planning is to make sure that the business always has the **right number** of staff with the **right skills** to meet its needs. To do this, the HR department **predicts** the firm's future staffing needs by:

- working out **how many workers** will be needed.
- deciding what kind of workforce will be needed — **skilled** or **unskilled**, **full-time** or **part-time**.
- predicting what the **staff wastage** will be — how many workers will **leave** due to retirement, dismissal, etc.

HR departments try to predict Staff Demand and Supply

HR departments in a business assess **what workers** will be **needed** in several ways:

1) HR departments ask other **experienced managers** for their **opinions** and **advice**.
2) **Past statistics** are used to see if employee numbers have **risen**, **fallen** or **stayed the same**.
3) An increase or decrease in **demand** for a **product** means an increase or decrease in **need** for **workers**, so the HR department uses the company's sales forecasts to see whether demand for the firm's products will rise, fall or stay the same.
4) HR analyse the **current staff details** to see how many are likely to **leave** or **retire** in the near future.
5) The introduction of **new technology** and **techniques** will alter the number of workers needed.
6) HR do an **internal staff stocktake**. They look at the number of employees and their **qualities** and **skills**.

HR also need to assess the potential **supply** of **new workers**:

1) They check the **level of unemployment** in the area to find out how many people are looking for work.
2) **Local infrastructure** is important — good housing, transport and schools can **attract** people to the area.
3) HR departments see how many **school** and **college leavers** are seeking employment locally.
4) They see if **competitors** are recruiting a similar workforce — if so there'll be **competition** for workers.

Workforce Planning includes Recruiting, Training and Retaining staff

1) When they've decided what new staff the business needs, HR **recruit** staff. They draw up a **job description**, including the job title, the main **roles** and **responsibilities** of the job, salary, etc. They also write a **person specification**, detailing the **qualities** and **qualifications** required. HR also decide **where** to advertise the job.
2) HR take charge of the **selection** procedure for new staff — organising **interviews**, etc.
3) HR organises **induction** and **training** programmes for new staff to teach them the **specific skills** they need.
4) Recruiting and training staff is **expensive**, so HR try to **retain** staff. They can do this in various ways, including giving staff opportunities for promotion, providing social facilities, etc.

Workforce Plans are influenced by Internal and External Factors

Internal factors influencing workforce plans

1) Workforce plans have to **fit in** with the firm's other plans, and the overall **corporate plan**.
2) They must be coordinated with the **marketing plan** and the **production plan** — e.g. a plan to expand production and increase market share will require **more workers** and **new training**, and a plan to promote **innovation** might require a more **diverse** workforce (of different ages, genders, cultural backgrounds, etc).
3) Changes in **production style** may require **retraining**, **recruitment** or **moving** workers to another job in the firm.

External factors influencing workforce plans

1) **Employment legislation** (see p. 178-179) protects employees' rights and **restricts** companies' ability to dismiss or transfer workers as they might like.
2) **New technology** might change the **number** of staff and the **skills** needed in a business, and might mean that businesses have to **train** their staff differently.
3) **Labour market trends** like **migration** and the **ageing population** have an effect on workforce planning because they alter the **supply** of workers — e.g. in some areas the supply of workers has increased due to immigration from new EU countries like Poland and Hungary.

Workforce Plans

There can be **Problems Implementing Workforce Plans**

1) **Collecting** and **analysing** workforce data is **time-consuming** and **expensive**, so not all businesses can afford to do it. **Recruitment** and **training** programmes are also **costly**.
2) Businesses don't always have the **resources** needed to carry out the HRM department's suggestions. E.g. there might not be anyone in the company who's **qualified** to give the training that the HRM department suggests, and managers might be reluctant to spend time **training** staff if they think that it's not a **productive** use of their time.
3) The company might **ignore** HRM's recommendations if they don't fit in with the **image** the company wants to portray. E.g. managers might choose to go ahead with a **recruitment drive** even if HRM says they **don't need** any more staff, because it will give their competitors and the public the impression that they are doing really well. For the same reason, companies are often reluctant to make employees **redundant** — they don't want to **publicise** the fact that things aren't going well.
4) **Bad relationships** between employers and employees might make it **difficult** to implement workforce plans — e.g. HRM won't be able to stop employees from **leaving** the company if they **don't get on** with their managers.

Workforce Planning can be **Useful**... or **Not Very Useful**

1) **Workforce plans** can be **useful** for businesses because they allow them to **prepare** for **changes**. E.g. it's much easier for businesses if they know **in advance** that they're going to need an extra 50 employees to cope with extra **demand**, rather than realising **too late** that they're **understaffed** and having to take on **any** employees who are available, even though they might not be qualified, and then not having time to **train** them properly.
2) **Predictions** in workforce plans **aren't** always **correct** though, so workforce planning can end up being a huge **waste of money** for businesses. E.g. HRM might believe that **extra staff** are needed because demand is going to increase by 25%, but if demand **doesn't** actually increase, the business is stuck with extra staff they **don't need**. The business will also have spent a lot of money **unnecessarily** on **recruiting** and **training** the new staff, in addition to the time and money spent **making** the inaccurate **predictions** in the first place
3) Businesses need to **weigh up** the **costs** and **benefits** of workforce planning to decide whether they think it's **worthwhile** or not.

Workforce plans aren't much use at all if you've got them upside down.

Practice Questions

Q1 What factors do HR consider when trying to predict the firm's future staffing needs?

Q2 Once they've decided what staff are needed, what do HRM do next?

Q3 How can a company's image affect its workforce plans?

Q4 Why can workforce planning sometimes be a waste of time?

Exam Questions

Q1 Describe the main factors that influence a business' demand for workers, and the supply of workers available to them. [8 marks]

Q2 The HRM department of a large business is considering carrying out a major workforce planning exercise. Explain how they might carry out the workforce planning, and what internal and external factors they will need to take into account. [12 marks]

May the (work)force be with you...

Workforce planning is all about predicting what's going to happen in the future. Sometimes you get it right, and everything goes along swimmingly. Other times you get it wrong, and end up paying eighty people to sit and drink coffee all day. Make sure you're clear on how HRM carry out workforce planning, and the factors that can make it all go horribly wrong.

Competitive Organisational Structures

Hurray, two pages on organisational structures. It must be your lucky day.

Adapting Organisational Structures can improve Competitiveness

1) Changing the **organisational structure** of a business can make the business more **competitive**.
2) Many businesses change their structure **regularly** to keep up with the **changing demands** of the **market**.
3) Businesses might **decentralise** in **fast-changing** markets in order to **respond** to changes more quickly. E.g. in fashion chains, each **store manager** (rather than head office) might be allowed to choose the stock for their store, because they know what **trends** the customers in their particular store are likely to be interested in.
4) The most common reason for changing the structure of a business is to **keep costs low**. If competitors keep their **prices** low, businesses might **delayer** in order to **cut costs** so that they can keep their prices **competitive**.

Centralised Structures keep Authority for decisions at the Top

In **centralised** organisations, all decisions are made by **senior managers** at the **top** of the business.

Advantages of centralisation

1) Business leaders have lots of **experience** of making business decisions.
2) Managers get an **overview** of the whole business, so decisions are **consistent** throughout the business.
3) Senior managers **aren't biased** towards one department so they can make the best decisions for the business as a whole.
4) Senior managers can make big decisions **quickly** because they don't have to **consult** anybody else.

Disadvantages of centralisation

1) Not many people are **expert** enough to make decisions about all aspects of the business.
2) **Excluding employees** from decision-making can be **demotivating**.
3) The organisation **reacts slowly** to change, allowing its **competitors** to get ahead. This is because the senior managers who make the decisions don't spend time on the shop floor, so they're slow to notice **consumer trends**.

Decentralised Structures share out the Authority to make decisions

1) Decentralisation **shares out authority** to more **junior** employees.
2) Giving responsibility for decision-making to people below you is called **delegation**.
3) **National** and **multinational** firms **decentralise** decision-making, and delegate power to **regional** managers.
4) Managers have to make sure that the **work** of **all** a company's **employees** is **contributing** to the **goals** of the **business**. This can be **difficult** to achieve when a lot of **power** has been **delegated**.

Advantages of decentralisation

1) Involvement in decision-making **motivates employees**.
2) Employees can use **expert knowledge** of their sector.
3) Day-to-day decisions can be made **quickly** without having to ask senior managers.

Disadvantages of decentralisation

1) Junior employees may not have enough **experience** to make decisions.
2) **Inconsistencies** may develop between **divisions** in a business.
3) Junior employees may not be able to see the **overall situation** and needs of an organisation.

Delayering removes layers of Hierarchy

1) Delayering means **removing** parts of an organisation's hierarchy — usually a layer of managers from around the middle.
2) Delayering helps to **lower costs**. Cutting management jobs can save a lot of money in salaries. However, it can **cost businesses money** in the short term because the remaining staff might need to be **retrained** in their new roles.
3) After delayering, you get a **flatter** structure with **broader** spans of control. If you **overdo** it, managers can end up **stressed** and overworked with **huge** spans of control.
4) Delayering can give junior employees **enhanced roles** with more responsibility.
5) Delayering improves communication because there are fewer layers of hierarchy for messages to pass through.
6) Some businesses use delayering as an **excuse** to cut jobs rather than to create a flatter structure.

Competitive Organisational Structures

Flexible Working adapts working patterns to suit Employees

Flexible working is when **working hours** and **patterns** are adapted to suit the **employees**.
There are several types of flexible working, including:

1) **Part-time work** — employees work **less** than 35 hours a week.
2) **Flexi-time** — employees work **full-time hours**, but they can **decide** when to work, around fixed **core hours**. E.g. employees might have to work for 8 hours a day, but they have to be in the office between 10am to 3pm.
3) **Compressed hours** — employees work a set number of **hours** per week, but over **fewer days**.
4) **Annual hours** — employees work a certain number of **hours** over the **year**, but they choose when to work them. E.g. employees with children might not work as much in the school holidays.
5) **Job-sharing** — **two people** share **one job**, e.g. by working alternate weeks.
6) **Home working** — employees work from **home** instead of at the business premises.

Advantages of flexible working

1) Flexible working improves **motivation** so employee **productivity** should improve.
2) Flexible working helps employees with **children**.
3) Home working suits **families**, **disabled** workers and those who live in **remote** places.

Disadvantages of flexible working

1) It can be impractical for businesses that need to serve the **public** during normal working hours.
2) Home-workers may be easily **distracted** at home.
3) Job-sharing can lead to **confusion** over responsibilities and **unequal** workloads.

Businesses can Outsource some of their Activities

1) **Outsourcing** (or **subcontracting**) is when businesses **contract out** some activities to other businesses (called "outsourcers") rather than doing them **in-house**. This is most common with things like finance, recruitment, advertising and IT — things that the business doesn't specialise in but sometimes needs.
2) Outsourcing can be a good idea for businesses because they benefit from the **specialised knowledge** and **economies of scale** of the businesses they outsource to. Outsourcing also means that the business doesn't have to pay for permanent staff when they're only needed occasionally, so it **reduces costs**.
3) The main **disadvantage** of outsourcing is that the business doesn't have **control** over the quality of the outsourcer's work, and if the outsourcer's work is bad, it can have a **negative effect** on the business' reputation.

Employees can be Core Workers or Peripheral Workers

1) **Core workers** are employees who are **essential** to a business, like senior managers and skilled workers. Core workers are employed on **full-time**, **permanent** contracts.
2) **Peripheral workers** are employees who **aren't essential** to a business, but that the business employs when they need to increase their **staffing levels**. Businesses keep their **fixed costs down** by employing peripheral workers on **temporary**, **part-time** or **zero-hours** contracts (so the business only gives employees hours as and when they are needed). Employing peripheral workers gives the business a lot of **flexibility**.

Practice Questions

Q1 What's the difference between centralised and decentralised structures?

Q2 List four types of flexible working, and explain what they mean.

Q3 What is a peripheral worker?

Exam Question

Q1 Christine and Bryan run a small B&B. Christine usually does the cleaning and laundry herself, but Bryan has suggested outsourcing it to a specialist cleaning company.
Discuss the potential benefits and drawbacks of Bryan's idea. [4 marks]

Gymnasts are always keen on flexible working...

It's a shame you can't do a job-share for your A2 Business Studies, and just learn half the stuff. But then I guess you'd miss out on the joy of knowing the difference between centralised and decentralised structures, and ways that staff can be employed. Now all you need to do is make sure you know it all, then you can turn the page for even more knowledge.

Communication

Communication is really important in business. I bet you never would've guessed that...

Communication between **Managers** and **Employees** is **Essential**

1) The purpose of communication is to pass on **information** and **ideas**.
2) Communication **within** the business is necessary for making **plans**, giving **instructions** and **motivating** staff. Managers need to communicate goals and objectives to staff so that they know what they're meant to be doing.
3) Businesses also need to communicate with people **outside** the business, e.g. suppliers, shareholders, customers and potential customers.

Managers need to make sure that they **Communicate Effectively**

1) For communication to be effective, the message that's **received** should be the **same** as the message that was **sent**.
2) Good communication is **clear** and **unambiguous**. If a manager arranges a conference in Perth, Scotland, but half the people who are supposed to be there end up in Perth, Australia, communication has obviously failed.
3) Effective communication is a **two-way thing**. Managers have to tell employees what they want them to know, and they also need to listen to what their employees have to say to them.

I'll put the four candles in the post to you straight away.

There are several **Categories** of **Communication**

1) **Formal communications** are **officially endorsed** by the business. They include corporate notice boards, company newsletters, letters from managers or the HR department.
2) **Informal communications** are unofficial, e.g. gossip, emails between employees and leaked information.
3) **Vertical communication** travels **up** and **down** the hierarchy. **Authoritarian** corporate cultures often only have downward communication — but a mixture of upward and downward communication is best. **Downward** communication is used to give employees **instructions** and to **inform** them about goals and objectives. **Upward** communication is used by employees to give feedback, suggest ideas and ask for help.
4) **Horizontal** (**lateral**) communication occurs between staff on the **same level** within the hierarchy. Horizontal communication can be used to discuss issues and offer suggestions.
5) **Internal communication** remains within the organisation, e.g. office notice board, internal email.
6) **External communication** (e.g. websites) is aimed at **external stakeholders** like customers and suppliers.

Different **Methods** of **Communication** are suitable for different **Purposes**

Communication can be **verbal** (e.g. meetings), **written** (e.g. letters and emails) or **visual** (e.g. graphs and images).

1) Face-to-face **verbal communication** is the most **personal** form of communication.
2) The main **disadvantage** of verbal communication is that there's **no record** of what's been said, and different people might remember meetings or conversations differently.
3) Verbal communication is often used in **meetings** between managers and employees, especially to discuss issues that employees might have **questions** about or want to give their **opinion** on.

1) The main benefits of **written communication** are that there's a **permanent record** of it, and it can reach **lots of people** — companies can send out emails to all their employees or customers at once.
2) However, the sender doesn't know if the message has been **understood**, and they can't get instant **feedback**.
3) Written communication is also used when it's not **practical** to speak to someone in person, e.g. companies respond to customer complaints by letter or email rather than phoning or visiting them.

1) **Visual communication** can be used in **addition** to other forms of communication to make information easier to understand, e.g. companies might use graphs to show sales figures.
2) Company logos and visual adverts communicate a particular **image** of the business to the public.

Communication

Organisations face **Barriers** that **Threaten Communication**

There are seven main barriers that can prevent communication from being effective:

1) **Attitudes** — For example, the receiver may be **distracted**. The receiver may **dislike** the sender, or feel **threatened** by the communication.
2) **Intermediaries** — The **longer** the chain of communication, the more **mangled** the message can get between sender and receiver (a bit like Chinese whispers).
3) **Language barriers** — One word can mean **different things** in different cultures. Translation can **distort** meaning. **Jargon** can be confusing.
4) **No sense of purpose** — Staff who **don't understand why** they're being told something may start ignoring future messages.
5) **Communication overload** — If employees are **swamped** with communication, they won't be able to deal with it all. This can be a problem with emails in particular.
6) **Remoteness** — It's easy to **misinterpret** the tone of emails because of the **distance** between the sender and the receiver. In phone and face-to-face conversations, the speaker's **voice** gives you clues about how things are meant, but in emails the receiver has to guess the sender's "**tone of voice**", and it's easy to imagine that emails are meant to be rude or sarcastic when they're actually not.
7) **Group behaviour** — The way that employees behave in groups can also be **detrimental** to communication, e.g. some employees might be overbearing, making others too **afraid** to speak up in meetings, etc.

Betty soon began to regret telling her boss she was fluent in Japanese.

Organisations can **Overcome** the **Barriers** to **Communication**

If businesses recognise the barriers to communication, they can take steps to overcome them:

1) Businesses can **encourage** face-to-face and telephone conversations, and **limit** email use, to avoid misunderstandings.
2) Managers can have **individual** meetings with employees or allow staff to give feedback **anonymously**, so that all employees can have their opinions heard.
3) Businesses can employ professional **translators** for foreign communication, so that messages get across properly.

Example — Phones 4U

1) In 2003, bosses at Phones 4U estimated that **3 hours a day** were being spent on email.
2) The company **banned email** for internal communication. Head office communicated to managers and staff via the corporate **intranet**. Employees were encouraged to use the **phone** or have face-to-face **meetings**.
3) The company found that this made communication within the business much more **efficient** — there were **fewer misunderstandings**, and the volume of unnecessary information being passed around was **reduced**.

Practice Questions

Q1 What is the difference between horizontal communication and vertical communication?

Q2 Give two examples of external communication.

Q3 How can businesses avoid communication overload?

Exam Questions

Q1 Give examples of when verbal, written and visual communication are used in business, and explain the advantages and disadvantages of each method of communication. [10 marks]

Q2 Discuss the barriers to communication that businesses face. [8 marks]

Emails aren't usually meant to be rude or sarcastic...

Good communication is incredibly important in business. Managers and staff have to communicate with each other to get the job done properly. There's also communication between the business and its customers and suppliers to think about. You'll need to be able to put these facts and ideas into context if you get a question on communication in the exam.

Employer/Employee Relations

Obviously all businesses like their employees to participate in doing some work, but sometimes they let them get a bit more involved than that. Employee participation is when employees get involved in making decisions.

Employees can Participate in the Decision Making Process

1) All businesses need ways of **communicating** with their workforce. They also need a way to **consult** the workforce so that employees can **share ideas** with their managers.
2) In very small businesses, employees can talk **directly** to managers about business decisions. In larger companies, employees need a **representative** to give them a **voice** at a higher level.
3) Participation is **different** from employee representation. Participation **involves** workers in the decision making process. It helps managers and employees to **work together** to improve the day to day running of the business.
4) Employee participation also helps the **workforce** because employees are more likely to feel **valued** if their manager **listens** to them. It shows that their manager **trusts** them to take on **responsibility** and **make decisions**.
5) Employee representation focuses more specifically on **employee demands**, like pay and working conditions, which don't always **match** what the business offers. There's more on employee representation on p.159-161.

There are different Forms of Employee Participation

Ways businesses can **introduce participation** include:

Employee groups give workers more control

1) Managers may **delegate** responsibility and give a team (or employee group) more **freedom** to **plan** and carry out their own work. This improves motivation.
2) Employee groups may also be able to suggest **improvements** in **working practice**.
3) Employee groups elect a **leader**, and **appoint new staff**.
4) For this to work out, the **type** of work they're doing must be **suitable**, the group must **work well together** as a team, and they must have a good **blend** of skills.
5) Even then, it doesn't always work perfectly — some individuals may not want the **hassle** of deciding their own work plans.

Works councils (or employee associations) discuss work issues

1) Works councils are committees made up of employee representatives and employer representatives. Employee representatives are usually **elected**.
2) They **meet regularly** to discuss **general work issues** e.g. training, new technology and methods of work.
3) The sharing of ideas and information in a relatively **relaxed** atmosphere does a lot to improve **cooperation** between workers and management.
4) Where there's **no trade union presence**, works councils take care of **collective bargaining** (see p. 161).
5) **Quality circles** are like works councils, but they only discuss **quality** issues. They meet regularly to discuss ways of improving quality. Quality circles include employees from **all levels** of the business.
6) In 1994, the EU brought in the idea of **European Works Councils** for employees of businesses based in more than one European country.

Employee shareholders have more of a stake in the business

1) Employees can buy **shares** in the business. This gives them a higher **stake** in the business, and promises financial rewards in the form of **dividends** if the business performs well.
2) Shareholders can vote at the Annual General Meeting (AGM).
3) In practice, this is actually more of a **financial motivator** than an instance of industrial democracy. There aren't usually enough employee shareholders to have any real influence at the AGM.

Some groups, like **employee groups**, are mostly just meant for participation. Others, like works councils, involve representation as well as employee participation. Works councils can do the job of a trade union if there is no union present, but usually **employee representation** is carried out by **trade unions**.

Employer/Employee Relations

Trade unions represent the workforce and can influence the way the business is run.

Trade Unions Negotiate with Employers on behalf of Employees

1) Trade unions act on behalf of **groups of employees** in the workforce when negotiating rates of **pay** and **working conditions** etc. with the employer.
2) By joining with others and belonging to a union an employee **strengthens** his or her **bargaining power** in a way that wouldn't be possible if he/she tried to bargain as an **individual** (see p. 161).
3) Trade unions allow employers and workers to **communicate** with each other.
4) Trade unions give **advice** and **assistance** to **individual** employees who are having problems with their employer.

Trade unions take action in the workplace

1) Trade unions **negotiate** with employers on behalf of their members to secure fair rates of pay and/or productivity bonuses for their work.
2) Trade unions help negotiate reasonable hours of **work**, and **paid holiday** entitlement.
3) Trade unions help members get **safe** and civilized **working conditions.**
4) Trade unions help their members get greater **job security** with protection against **mistreatment**, **discrimination** and **unfair dismissal**.

Trade unions take action at a national level

1) Trade unions **put pressure on the government** to bring in legislation that serves trade union members' interests.
2) The **minimum wage** was introduced in **1998** by the government after discussions with trade unions.
3) Trade unions pushed the government to make **redundancy payments** compulsory.
4) Following demands from trade unions, the **Pension Protection Fund** was set up in April 2005 to protect the pensions of employees in private company pension schemes if their employer **goes bust**.

Trade unions take action in party politics

1) Many unions donate money to the **Labour Party** because they think its policies represent their interests.
2) In the 1970s and 80s, unions had a lot of **power** in the Labour Party. Since the **90s** they've had **less power**.

Trade Unions can influence decisions about changing Working Practices

1) When employers want to make **changes** to the **working practices** of the business (e.g. if the employer wants to reduce employees' contracted hours, or change the way it pays staff from an hourly wage to a piece rate, or vice versa), trade unions can help staff if they want to **resist** the change, e.g. by organising strikes.
2) Trade unions can also **facilitate change** by **liaising** between employers and union members, and communicating the **benefits** of the change in working practices to their members.
3) **Employees** are more likely to be **open** to change if union representatives are involved in decisions, because they **trust** trade unions to protect their interests, but may **not** trust their employers to do the same.

Trade Unions can influence decisions about changing Employment Levels

1) Trade unions stand up for employees' rights if employers want to make **redundancies**. They can negotiate with employers to persuade them to make **fewer** employees redundant, or negotiate better **redundancy payouts** for employees who are made redundant.
2) If employers are planning changes that might **adversely affect** the current workforce, trade unions try to **prevent** these changes from taking place. E.g. if employers want to take on **cheaper** staff (e.g. foreign workers), current employees' wages could be **driven down**, or **overtime** hours might be offered to the new, cheaper workers instead of the current staff. A trade union would try to **stop** the recruitment of cheaper workers from going ahead.
3) If staffing levels are **too low** and current staff are **overworked**, trade unions can try to convince employers to take on **more staff**.

Employer/Employee Relations

There are Different Types of Trade Unions

The trade union that employees belong to can depend on what type of **job** they do, or what **industry** they work in:

Craft unions	Members of craft unions share a **common skill** but often work for **different industries**. Most of them started out as a traditional guild of craftsmen. Examples: Equity (the actors' union), the Writers' Guild of Great Britain, the PFA (Professional Footballers' Association).
Industrial unions	Members all work in the **same industry** but do a **wide range of jobs**. Their bargaining power is strong because strike action could bring production to a stop. Examples: RMT (the transport workers' union), NUM (National Union of Mineworkers).
General unions	Members range across **many different industries** and **many different occupations**. General unions tend to have a very **large number** of members. Example: Unite — a merger between TGWU (Transport & General Workers Union) and Amicus.
White-collar unions	Members work in **administration** or **non-manual occupations**. The number of **members** of this type of union is **increasing**, because more and more people are working in **white-collar jobs**. Examples: NUT (National Union of Teachers) and NUJ (National Union of Journalists).

Trade unions are particularly strong in the **public sector** (e.g. teaching and nursing) and **transport and communication** (e.g. railways and ports). There's also strong union membership in **utilities** (e.g. gas and electricity).

Cooperation with Trade Unions helps businesses achieve their Objectives

1) **Cooperation** between employers and trade unions can be **beneficial** for businesses as well as their employees.
2) Employers and union reps can **share ideas** for the benefit of everyone in the firm. If the business is profitable, it's good news for both the employers and the employees, so it's in the **interests** of the trade union to help the business achieve its objectives.
3) Trade union representatives often have a lot of **knowledge** and **experience** about issues such as **employment law**, **health and safety**, **training**, etc. This knowledge can be helpful to employers, especially during periods of **change** such as a merger or if a firm is making redundancies.

Employee Representation has Advantages and Disadvantages

Employers and employees need to **cooperate** with each other to maintain a successful working relationship.

Advantages of employee representation

1) It's often more **effective** to approach an organisation as a group. Groups have a bigger **influence** and can be more **forceful**.
2) **Collective bargaining** can be a way of achieving **long-term aims** because employers may sign **contracts** which lock them into **agreements**.
3) It can be helpful for management to have a **small representative group** of workers to negotiate with rather than consulting every individual.
4) Senior management get a **direct insight** into the concerns of the workforce.

OK, so let's decide the birdseed budget now.
What about the vote on annual migration policy?

Disadvantages of employee representation

1) The biggest disadvantage of employee representation is that it can lead to **industrial action** (see p. 162-163). This can take the form of deliberately decreased **productivity** (work to rule) or **strike** action.
2) Strike action can **get out of hand** or turn **violent**.
3) Industrial action leads to a **drop in productivity** and **lost profits**.
4) The majority vote within a trade union may **overrule** the demands of the individual. The individual is then denied the **opportunity** to represent themselves as they might want to.
5) Industrial action can **undermine the trust** between employer and employee and this can take time to recover. A **breakdown** in communication damages employer/employee **relationships**.

Employer/Employee Relations

Collective Bargaining is used to agree *Pay* and *Working Conditions*

1) In some cases, **groups of employees** negotiate **working arrangements** or **pay** with their employer.
2) Negotiation is often done **collectively** by a **trade union** or **professional association**, representing a group of employees and negotiating pay and working conditions **on their behalf**. The union **bargains** for them all with their employer.
3) The result of collective bargaining for pay is a **common pay structure**, which is often called the **"going rate"** for the job. The employer can't pay anyone less than this going rate without causing trouble.
4) Employees and unions usually prefer **collective bargaining**, because it strengthens their position at the bargaining table and prevents **"divide and rule"** tactics by employers.

Collective bargaining for pay does create some **problems**, though...

1) Having a single wage rate makes it **difficult** to **reward** variations in work **effort** between staff doing jobs with a similar rate of pay. This may **reduce** the levels of **motivation** if good staff are not recognised and rewarded.
2) In some large companies, the collectively bargained rate of pay covers employees working in **different locations** across the country. This one-wage-for-all approach doesn't recognise differences between different parts of the country — e.g. cost of living, house prices, level of unemployment, or even the wages paid by other local employers. A **variation** in wage rates to take account of these factors might be more appropriate.

Collective bargaining isn't just used for discussing pay. Employees also negotiate collectively with employers in order to come to agreements about other **working conditions**, e.g. pension contributions from employers, holiday allowance, etc.

Each *Employee* also has an *Individual Relationship* with their *Employer*

1) All employees of a company are treated as **individuals** for some purposes, such as employee appraisals. When **individual employees** negotiate with their employer about their own **working conditions**, it's known as **individual bargaining**.
2) **Individual bargaining** for **pay** means that employers can decide to pay an employee what they think he or she is **worth** to the firm. It might be **more** or **less** than other employees in the same role. This provides a financial **incentive** to the employee to work productively.
3) **Individual bargaining** is also used for things like **flexible working arrangements** — they're often based on the employee's **personal circumstances**, e.g. if an employee cares for young children or an elderly parent, the employer might allow that employee to work from home or work flexi-time.

Practice Questions

Q1 What is an employee group?

Q2 What is a works council?

Q3 What do trade unions do for their members?

Q4 Give two examples of ways that trade unions have influenced government policy.

Q5 How can unions influence employment levels in a company?

Q6 What's the difference between a craft union and an industrial union?

Q7 What type of workers belong to white-collar unions?

Q8 What is collective bargaining?

Exam Question

Q1 Snapdragon Fashion Ltd. is a medium-sized clothes retailer employing 600 people in 10 stores spread across the country. Discuss the potential advantages and disadvantages to the employer of its staff being trade union members. [6 marks]

Detergent company employees belong to bright white-collar unions...

There's a fair old bit of detail on trade unions here. In the exam you could get asked about the different types of unions or the pros and cons of joining a union. There are also other ways that workers can influence the way their business is run like joining works councils or employee groups. There's a lot to learn on these four pages and it's all important stuff.

Industrial Disputes

Industrial disputes can get pretty ugly, so businesses try to resolve them as quickly as possible.

Industrial Disputes happen when Employers and Employees Can't Agree

1) Many industrial conflicts appear on the surface to be a dispute over **wages** and **working conditions**. However, there may be **other grievances** caused by various human factors:
   - **Frustration** and **alienation** caused by **lack of communication** from managers, or frequent **changes** in work practices.
   - **Stress** and **insecurity** caused by changing work patterns and **fears of redundancy**.
2) It can be **difficult** to **express** these kinds of feelings **clearly** in an argument — so it's often **easier** to turn the dispute into one about the more **usual workplace issues**.
3) Managers who **communicate effectively** and organise their staff's work responsibilities **consistently** will have a more **motivated workforce**, who'll be less likely to start a dispute.

Industrial Action — Work to Rule, Overtime Bans and Strikes

If the trade union fails to reach an agreement with the employer through negotiation, then they can apply more pressure by taking **industrial action** to reduce production. There are various tactics used, which gradually increase pressure.

1) **Work to rule** — employees stick 100% to the terms of their **contract**. They only do the tasks that their contract **specifically** requires them to do. This usually **slows production**.
2) **Go slow** — employees simply work more **slowly**.
3) A **ban on overtime** — exactly what it says. Employees don't work **overtime** when they're **asked** to. They don't come in early or work late or work at weekends.
4) **Strike** — employees withdraw their labour and **don't go to work**. This might be a **one-day strike** to **warn** the employer that they're serious about the issue, or a more **prolonged** strike.

Collective Employment Law Controls what Unions can do

1) Unions can represent their members in discussions with the employer and ultimately call them out on strike, but this has to be done **within the law**.
2) During the **1980s** and **1990s**, the government passed a series of **laws** to control the way that **industrial relations** (negotiations between union and employer) were conducted.
3) At the time the government thought trade unions had **too much bargaining strength** in industrial relations. This pushed up **wage rates**, which in turn pushed up production costs and **prices**. This **wage and price inflation** made British goods **less competitive** in the global market.
4) "**Voluntarism**" was also common at the time — this is where an employer and the trade union(s) representing the employees at a particular workplace came up with an agreement that only applied to that particular union and/or workplace (e.g. not to strike, or to inform the employer a few days before a strike). Voluntary agreements have now been **replaced** by the **collective labour laws** brought in by the government.
5) The changes in the law **reduced** the **bargaining power** of unions. They're summarised below.

Employment Act 1980	Firms could **refuse to recognise** a union. Picketing was restricted to workers' **own place of work**.
Employment Act 1982	Trade unions could be sued. **Union-only clauses** were **banned**.
Trade Union Act 1984	Unions had to have a **secret ballot** before striking.
Employment Act 1988	Unions **couldn't punish** members who didn't strike.
Employment Act 1990	Employers could **sack** workers who went on **unofficial strike. Closed shop agreements** were **ended** — no one could be refused a job because they weren't in the right union.
Trade Union Reform and Employment Rights Act 1993	Unions had to give employers **7 days' notice** of strike action. Secret ballots had to be done by **post**.

Industrial Disputes

Industrial disputes have to be **Resolved Eventually**

A **slow-down** or **stoppage** of production means less output, sales and profit for the employer. It also means **lower earnings** for the employee. Because **both parties** are suffering, they need to reach an agreement quickly.

As well as the employer and employee, **other stakeholders** suffer from lost production.

1) Local businesses suffer from the **reduced spending** of those employees.
2) **Customers** can't get the goods or services they want.
3) Other firms may rely on this firm for their raw materials or components.
4) The **firm's suppliers** suffer, especially if the firm is an important customer.

"Look, we'll have to sort it out eventually — so if you want to keep this tooth here, admit that I'm right..."

Employers and **Unions** often use **Other Organisations** to act as a **Mediator**

If the employer and union can't reach an agreement that **satisfies them both**, they might call on **another organisation** to act as **mediator** and / or **jury** to help resolve the dispute.

Industrial tribunal

This usually meets to deal with claims of **unfair dismissal** or **discrimination**. If it decides **against the employer** it may make them pay **compensation** to the employee. See p. 179 for more on industrial tribunals.

ACAS — the Advisory, Conciliation and Arbitration Service

The Advisory, Conciliation and Arbitration Service does exactly what the name says.

1) **Conciliation** — ACAS **meets both parties** in the dispute, usually separately, and tries to develop **common ground** that they can both eventually accept.
2) **Arbitration** — It can appoint an **independent arbitrator** who considers the claims and says what the outcome should be. If both sides agree, this outcome can be **legally binding**. There are two types of arbitration:
   - **Compromise arbitration** is a result which lies somewhere between what the employer wants and what the union wants. It sounds good, but the downside is that it may encourage the **union** and **employer** to adopt **extreme** first demands in order to **bias** the eventual compromise towards their position.
   - **Pendulum arbitration** makes a simple choice between the competing claims — there's no compromise, and **no middle ground**. This encourages parties to adopt a more **reasonable** position to try to get the arbitrator to pick their side.

Practice Questions

Q1 Explain why some industrial disputes about pay and conditions might have a different underlying cause.

Q2 List and describe the different kinds of industrial action a union might take in a dispute with an employer.

Q3 List five laws regarding trade unions that have been brought in since the 1980s, and explain how they've affected the power that trade unions have.

Q4 Explain the roles performed by ACAS in industrial disputes.

Exam Questions

Q1 "Trade union members will lose more than they gain when they enter into a dispute with an employer." Evaluate this claim. [8 marks]

Q2 Consider a recent industrial dispute and analyse it in terms of the following: its causes, the tactics used by the union and the final settlement. [8 marks]

I hear they've gone on strike again at the match factory...

Industrial disputes aren't much fun for anyone involved in them. It's not in the employees' best interests to be on strike for a long time — they lose pay, and damage their job prospects by damaging the industry. It's best to get things sorted ASAP. What you need to know is how disputes affect businesses and how they get resolved — through tribunals, ACAS, etc.

Mission, Aims and Objectives

Ooh, a whole section on objectives and strategies — you lucky thing.

The **Corporate Aims** and **Objectives** of businesses are mainly **Financial**

1) Setting **objectives** helps businesses achieve their **aims**. The **main aim** of most businesses is to make a **profit**.
2) Corporate objectives are **different** from functional objectives (see p.84). **Corporate objectives** are the **goals** of the business as a **whole**, e.g. increase sales, expand abroad. **Functional objectives** are the objectives of each department which outline what they can do to **contribute** to the business' aims.
3) **New businesses** that are currently making a loss might aim to become **profitable**. Established businesses that are already profitable might want to **increase** their profits (e.g. by 10% within three years).
4) Businesses might also want to increase their **market share**. E.g. a company that makes perfumes might aim to have a 20% share of the perfume market.
5) Businesses might aim to **expand geographically**. E.g. a business with four sandwich shops in Hull might aim to open other sandwich shops in cities around Yorkshire, and a successful UK clothes retailer might aim to expand into Europe or the USA.

Sally needed to work on her corporate aim.

6) Businesses might also aim to **expand** their **product range**. A business that makes toys might expand into organising children's parties, or a pizza restaurant might start offering pasta dishes too. Companies like Virgin have successfully expanded into areas completely **unrelated** to each other, like travel, music and cosmetics.

Corporate Strategies are **Plans** for the **Future**

1) A business' **corporate strategy** outlines **how** the firm plans to meet its corporate objectives.
2) A strategy can only be put into place once an organisation has **outlined** its aims and objectives. Businesses need to decide **what** they want to achieve before they can work out **how** to achieve it.
3) All businesses need to have a strategy. In **small firms**, these plans may not be **formally** written down. Strategies can simply be a **sequence** of business decisions made over time with the aim of reaching a particular **goal**, e.g. expanding into a new market segment.
4) In **larger firms**, the corporate strategy is usually more **clearly defined** because it will influence the plans of **individual departments**, e.g. a strategy outlining how a company wants to expand into a new market will affect the **Marketing strategy** (see p. 124-125), **HRM work plans** (see p. 152-153), etc.
5) Corporate strategy is a useful way of **planning** for the future and making sure employees are **aware** of the business' aims. The **actual performance** of the business will probably not match the corporate strategy exactly. In a **rapidly changing** global economy, **unforeseen** circumstances or **unexpected** events will probably force managers to **adapt** their corporate strategy.

Different Stakeholders have **Different Objectives**

1) Businesses have a lot of different **stakeholders** — groups that are **connected** with the business in some way. Stakeholders include employees, shareholders, customers, suppliers, etc. Stakeholders all have their own **objectives**, which are often **conflicting**:

- **Shareholders** usually want high **dividends** and a high **share price**.
- **Employees** want good **pay** and **working conditions**.
- **Suppliers** want to be paid a **fair price**, and be paid **on time**.
- **Customers** want the best possible **quality** at the lowest possible **price**.
- Local **residents** want the business to create **jobs**, and not to **pollute** or damage the local area.

2) Many businesses are mainly interested in keeping their **shareholders** happy. In order to achieve high share prices and dividends, the business would have to maximise its profits, and wouldn't be able to reinvest money into the business for expansion.
3) Businesses have to strike a **balance** to try and keep all their stakeholders as happy as possible. E.g. a business might cut costs in order to increase its profits if it's trying to keep its shareholders happy, but if this reduces the quality of the products, customers won't be happy and will stop buying products from the business — so the plan will **backfire**.

Mission, Aims and Objectives

Mission Statements give Clues to corporate culture

1) **Mission statements** are written **descriptions** of corporate objectives. They set out what the business does, and why they do it. Mission statements are intended to make all **stakeholders** aware of the corporate objectives, and to **encourage** all employees to **work towards** them.
2) Mission statements usually state the **purpose** of the business (e.g. "to make the best chocolate in the UK"), its **values** (e.g. "to pay a fair price to our suppliers"), its **standards** (e.g. "to treat customers with respect at all times") and its **strategy** (e.g. "to have a 20% share of the UK chocolate market within 10 years").
3) Mission statements give clues about the company's **culture** (see p. 192-193). For example, a mission statement that mentions **ethics** and **principles** gives a big hint that the corporate culture is focused on **ethical practice** as well as **profitability**.
4) Some mission statements **explicitly** state what the business believes its corporate culture is. After a short statement of corporate aim and vision for the future, there may be a **statement of shared beliefs**, e.g. "We believe in providing outstanding service to customers", "We believe that we gain strength through our diversity".
5) Businesses can have underlying cultures within **departments**, known as **subcultures**. For example, a design department might be relaxed, whereas the head of sales might run a very tight ship. One benefit of a mission statement is to try and **prevent** this by creating a **unifying**, visible culture for all employees to **identify** with.
6) **Changing** the mission statement can help change corporate culture.

There are Advantages and Disadvantages to having a Mission Statement

Advantages

1) Mission statements can give **staff** a sense of **shared purpose**, and encourage them to work towards **common goals** — having the cooperation of all the staff makes it more likely that a business will achieve its aims.
2) A mission statement gives **consumers** a clearer idea of the company's **values**. This allows consumers to choose companies whose values match theirs.

Disadvantages

1) Companies sometimes use mission statements to try and create good **public relations** for themselves rather than to state their **actual aims**. E.g. a company might say in its mission statement that it is committed to protecting the **environment** just to encourage more consumers to use its products. Companies **don't** have to **prove** that what they say about themselves in their mission statement is accurate, so they can say what they think consumers want to hear, without having to do anything about it.
2) Since mission statements are only a **few lines** long, and the aims and values of a business are usually quite **complex**, it's almost **impossible** for a mission statement to sum up what an organisation is all about. That's why some companies choose not to produce one.

Practice Questions

Q1 Give three examples of objectives that a business might have.

Q2 What is a corporate strategy?

Q3 List three stakeholder groups and the main objectives you would expect them to have.

Exam Question

Q1 Explain what a mission statement is, and discuss why some businesses see mission statements as valuable and others choose not to produce one. [8 marks]

Mission Statement Impossible — I think I saw that at the cinema...

Ok, so it might not be the most exciting part of Business Studies, but this is really important stuff. The stuff about mission statements is quite good anyway — you can just imagine the scene in the boardroom: "Your mission, if you choose to accept it, is to provide quality sofas and dining furniture." Anyway, your mission is to get these two pages learnt.

The Business Cycle

The business cycle is the way the economy grows and shrinks. At least it's not the carbon cycle.

GDP (Gross Domestic Product) indicates the **Size** of a **Nation's Economy**

GDP is the **total market value** of **goods** and **services** produced **within** a nation over a period of time (usually a year).

GDP = total **consumer spending** + business **investment** + **government spending** + the value of **exports** – the value of **imports**.

GDP is calculated in **real terms**, i.e. by ignoring **inflation**.

The **Business Cycle** is a regular pattern of **Growth** and **Recession**

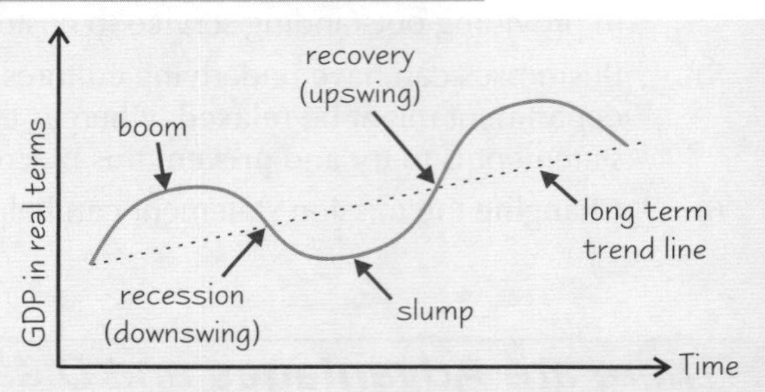

1) In a **recovery** or upswing period, **production increases**, and **employment** increases. People have more money to spend.
2) In a **boom**, GDP is high. As production reaches **maximum capacity**, there are **shortages**, and price increases. Shortages of skilled labour mean **wages rise**.
3) In a **recession**, incomes start to go down, and **demand** goes down. Business **confidence** is reduced.
4) In a **slump**, GDP is at a **low**. Businesses close factories and there are a lot of **redundancies**. **Unemployment** is **high**. A lot of businesses become **insolvent** or **bankrupt**.
5) How much a business is **affected** by the business cycle depends on the **income elasticity of demand** of its products. Businesses selling **income elastic** goods such as luxury holidays find that demand shoots **up** in a **recovery**, and dives **down** in a **recession**. Firms selling **income inelastic** goods such as staple foods **aren't affected** all that much by the business cycle.

Income elasticity of demand = extent to which demand depends on customer income.

Businesses deal with **Changes** in **Economic Activity Locally** and **Globally**

1) During **booms**, businesses can **raise prices**. This increases profitability, and it slows down demand a bit. Businesses may have to increase prices to cover their own costs if there are wage rises due to shortages of labour.
2) In a long lasting boom, businesses **invest** in **production** facilities to increase capacity. They may come out with **new products** to take advantage of increased consumer income.
3) During **recessions**, businesses may make workers **redundant** to **save wage costs** and **increase capacity utilisation**.
4) During a **local recession**, businesses can **market** their goods elsewhere in the country — a local shop could go mail-order. In a **national recession**, businesses can **market** their products **overseas**.
5) When the national recession or slump lasts a long time, some businesses choose to **relocate** abroad.
6) In general, **global upswings** provide growth opportunities for **everyone**, and **global recessions** are bad for **everyone**.

Supply and **Demand** can **Vary Seasonally**

1) As well as cyclical variations in demand caused by the business cycle, there are **yearly variations** in **demand** and **supply**. This is called **seasonality**.
2) **Weather** and **holidays** such as Christmas produce variations in **demand**. For example, **Christmas** creates high demand for **toys**. Hot weather creates demand for ice lollies, paddling pools and air conditioning units.
3) They can also cause variations in **supply** — there are more strawberries available in summer, for example.
4) It's impossible to avoid seasonality. Businesses must have **strategies** to deal with it. After Christmas, demand for retail goods drops, so shops **cut prices** (the **January sales**) to artificially boost demand, and get rid of stock.
5) Food producers can cope with seasonality in supply by **preserving food** — e.g. by canning or freeze-drying.

Economic Growth

Economic Growth is the Increase in Size of a nation's Economy

1) Economic growth is an **increase** in the nation's production of **goods** and **services**.
2) It's measured as the **rate of increase in GDP** (Gross Domestic Product).
3) Economic growth means the same thing as "an increase in **economic activity**" — growth means there's **more demand** in the economy and **more output** to meet that demand.

Economic Growth is determined by Resources and Productivity

1) The **growth potential** of an economy depends on the **amount** and **quality** of economic **resources** available — e.g. labour and fixed assets.

Quantity and quality of labour	**Quantity** of labour depends on **population size and age**, and on its **gender** composition (e.g. if lots of the female population are of childbearing age then they may not be available to work). The **quality** of labour is the level of **education and training** that workers have reached. **High quality** of labour enables an economy to **grow faster**.
Investment	**Investment** increases the amount of **productive assets** (machinery etc. used for production). For the **value** of **productive assets** to **grow**, the **level of investment** in productive assets has to be greater than the amount of **depreciation** (the amount by which machines wear out) during the year.

2) Economic growth also depends on **productivity** — how hard the nation is willing to work.
3) **Governments** can encourage **short-term** growth by cutting taxes and interest rates (see p.169). This encourages businesses to borrow money and invest it in production. It also encourages consumers to borrow money and spend it on goods, which increases demand in the economy.
4) Most modern economists think it's better to encourage **steady growth** by using "supply-side policies" (see p.172).

Economic Growth has Mainly Positive Effects for business and government

Positive effects of economic growth for individual businesses

1) On the whole, **growth** in GDP means **higher revenues** and higher **profitability** for **businesses**.
2) Economic growth gives the potential for **economies of scale**.
3) Sustained growth increases **confidence** and helps businesses **plan** for the future.
4) Economic growth affects the type of **strategic decisions** that a business makes. In periods of sustained growth senior managers might decide to **expand** the business, launch **new products** or try to break into **new markets**.
5) On the down side, fast growth may cause **shortages** of raw materials and skilled labour.

Positive effects of economic growth for governments

1) **Higher revenue** encourages investment in new projects, which creates jobs. This is good for the government — there's less need to pay welfare benefits.
2) Growth also enables the government to earn **increased revenues** through **taxes**.
3) Very high rates of growth are usually followed by **recession**. Governments try to avoid this boom-and-bust situation by keeping growth at a **sustainable level**.

It appears someone's gone a bit wild with the fertiliser.

Practice Questions

Q1 What happens to production during a boom period?

Q2 What is economic growth and how is it measured?

Q3 What are the effects of economic growth on governments?

Exam Question

Q1 Discuss the negative effects to a business of rapid economic growth. [6 marks]

Tip for the January sales — if it's beige (or yellow), don't buy it...

Trust me, they don't suit anybody. Growth in the national economy is a good thing for businesses. The problems start when growth is too fast — production can't keep up, and a pleasant period of growth swings round into an unpleasant recession. Learn the whys and wherefores of the business cycle, and learn a couple of things that firms do to cope with it.

Businesses and the Economic Environment

Here are three more delectable pages on how the economy affects businesses. Enjoy.

Inflation** is an **Increase** in the **Price** of **Goods** and **Services

1) The **Consumer Price Index** measures UK inflation — it tracks the prices of hundreds of goods and services that an average household would buy. There are **two types** of inflation:

Demand-pull inflation

High inflation can be caused by **too much demand** (more than the economy can supply) — it happens when there's an increase in disposable income so people buy more and companies can't supply goods quickly enough and **increase** their **prices**. This is **demand-pull** inflation. Excess demand when the economy is near its full capacity is called **overheating**. **Demand-pull inflation** can actually make **profit margins** go **up**. Businesses can put up prices in response to **high demand** without their **costs** going up by as much.

Cost-push inflation

Rises in inflation can be due to **rising costs** pushing up **prices** — this is **cost-push** inflation. **Wage rises** can make prices go up — especially if productivity isn't rising. **Cost-push inflation** can make **profit margins** go **down** if businesses decide not to put up their prices.

2) When inflation is **high**, spending goes **up** temporarily — people rush to buy more before prices go up even more. If **wages** don't go up in line with inflation, however, spending goes **down** as people can afford less.
3) **Expectations** of inflation can make inflation worse. A business which expects its **suppliers** to put their prices up will put its **own** prices up to cover increased costs. Employees' expectations of rising prices makes them demand **higher wages**, so prices go up. This is the **wage-price spiral** — it's a big cause of cost-push inflation.
4) When inflation in the UK is high, it makes UK **exports** expensive abroad. UK businesses become **less competitive**. When inflation in the UK is low, UK businesses have a competitive advantage.
5) Inflation that's **too high** is bad for the economy. The Bank of England aims to keep the inflation rate within a **target range** set by the government — they do this by changing **interest rates** (see next page).

High inflation isn't always a problem.

Inflation** affects **Business Strategy

1) Companies producing **premium goods** are the **most** likely to be **affected** by inflation because if customers have less to spend they start to look at **cheaper** alternative **products**. Manufacturers of premium products can react by **reducing prices** (although they have to be careful not to reduce them so far that the product loses its premium image) or by investing heavily in **advertising**.
2) Periods of high inflation can be a **good time** for firms to **expand** — if **interest rates** are **lower** than the rate of **inflation** it's **cheap** for them to **borrow money** to invest in **new premises** or **machinery**. The **interest** they'd earn on their savings would be **less** than the amount prices would have gone up by in the same time, so it makes sense to **spend** rather than save. However, the Bank of England often **raises** interest rates in times of high inflation to encourage saving, so businesses don't always benefit from high inflation.
3) It's harder for businesses to **plan** when inflation is **high**. They need **stable prices** in order to be able to make **accurate sales forecasts**.

Deflation** is a **Decrease** in the **Price** of **Goods** and **Services

1) **Deflation** is the **opposite** of inflation — it's when there's **not enough demand** so companies **reduce** their **prices**.
2) Deflation causes a **fall** in **productivity** because companies won't keep endlessly supplying the market with goods that nobody wants. **Lower productivity** usually means firms don't need as many workers — so deflation often leads to a **rise** in **unemployment**. This makes **demand drop** further and causes firms to **lower prices** even more.

Businesses and the Economic Environment

Interest is the Price Paid for Borrowing Money

1) Interest rates show the **cost of borrowing**. A **fall** in the interest rate **increases** businesses' levels of activity — it's **cheaper** for them to borrow money to invest. A **rise** in interest rates makes firms **decrease** their activity, because it's **more expensive** to borrow money to invest.
2) Interest rates affect **consumer spending**. High interest rates mean most consumers have less money to spend. People with existing **borrowing** like **mortgages** have to pay more money back in **interest**, so they have less **disposable income** (the money left over after essential payments like tax and mortgage repayments). Many people also **save more money** because they get a better rate of return on it, so market **demand** goes down.
3) The effect of interest rates on demand depends on the **product**. Products that require **borrowing** (e.g. cars, houses, new kitchens and high-end consumer electronics) are more **sensitive** to interest rate changes. When interest rates go up significantly, firms change strategy to diversify away from these goods and into cheaper ones.
4) Firms compare **UK** and **foreign** interest rates. When the UK interest rate is high or volatile, firms tend to expand into **other countries** with low, stable interest rates, as it's **cheaper** to borrow money there to invest in expansion.
5) When **interest rates** are **high**, **foreign investors** want to **save money** in **UK** banks. To do this, they **buy British pounds**, which boosts demand for the currency and makes the **exchange rate go up**, affecting **imports** and **exports**. When **interest rates** are **low**, investors prefer to invest abroad, so they **sell** their pounds and the **exchange rate falls**.

Exchange Rate is the Value of One Currency in terms of Another Currency

1) Exchange rates affect the amount of **foreign trade**.
   - When the exchange rate is **high** (e.g. more euros to the pound), UK **exports** are relatively **expensive** in Europe and **imports** into the UK are relatively **cheap** for Brits. A **strong pound** is **bad** for UK exporters because their goods aren't competitively priced abroad.
   - When the exchange rate is **low** (e.g. **fewer euros** to the **pound**), UK **exports** are relatively **cheap** for foreigners (which is **good** for UK **exporters**) and **imports** into the UK are relatively **expensive** for Brits.
2) A **strong pound** and **cheaper imports** mean **lower costs** for UK businesses importing raw materials from abroad, but they're bad news for UK manufacturers who export goods abroad.
3) When a rise in the value of the pound is predicted, a business might decide to move its **production** abroad. The business can also consider **importing** the **raw material** from abroad.
4) **Cheaper exports** should lead to increased **demand** and therefore higher **output**.

"Today's exchange rate is two sheep to the goat."

Exchange Rate Fluctuations create Uncertainty

1) For example, a UK manufacturer agrees a contract to sell to France, and agrees to be paid in **euros**. After the deal is made, the pound rises in value against the euro. The euro payment in the contract is now worth **fewer pounds** than before, so the UK manufacturer makes **less profit** from the contract than predicted.
2) Let's say that the UK manufacturer insists on being paid in **pounds**. When the pound rises in value, the goods are more expensive in euro terms for the French firm. They put the **selling price** up to compensate. The increase in price reduces **demand** for the goods, and there may be **less revenue** than predicted.

Some manufacturers based in the UK and **exporting to the EU** are considering **relocating** to **Euro zone** countries (i.e. countries where the currency is the Euro), so that their costs are in Euros — the same currency their customers pay in. They may also decide to pay UK suppliers in Euros, again to keep costs in the same currency that their customers pay them. See p.174 for more on the Euro.

Taxation Rates have an impact on Businesses

1) **All** individuals and businesses have to pay taxes. The tax rate set by the government can have a big impact on businesses.
2) **High** tax rates for **businesses** mean that their **net profits** (after-tax profits) are **reduced**.
3) **High** tax rates for **individuals** reduce consumers' disposable income, so people tend to **spend less** — this is bad news for businesses because it's likely to **reduce** their **turnover**. **Low** tax rates encourage people to spend, so businesses make **bigger profits**.
4) See p. 171 for more on taxation.

Businesses and the Economic Environment

Unemployment is measured by the number of People Seeking Work

1) Unemployment is measured by the number of jobless people who are a) **available** for work and b) **actively seeking jobs**.
2) There are five main **types** of unemployment.

   Structural unemployment is due to changes in the structure of the economy, e.g. a **decline** in a **major industry** such as coal mining. When structural unemployment is concentrated in a particular region of the country it's called **regional unemployment**.

   Frictional unemployment is temporary, caused by the delay between **losing** one job and **getting** another.

   Cyclical (**demand deficient**) unemployment is due to a **downturn** in the business cycle, e.g. a lack of **demand** for labour because production has decreased and businesses are trying to cut costs.

   Seasonal unemployment is due to the **season**, e.g. ice cream sellers in the winter.

3) High unemployment can affect **sales**. Producers of **luxury** goods are badly affected by **cyclical** unemployment. Businesses producing **essentials** aren't affected all that much unless people can easily switch to cheaper brands.
4) **Structural** and **regional** unemployment affects **local** businesses — unemployed people in the area have little money to spend.
5) When unemployment is **high**, businesses can hire staff easily. There's a good **supply** of labour, so businesses won't have to pay **high wages**. People in work will be extra **productive** to protect their job.
6) If unemployment is **structural** or **regional**, it's not all that easy to hire staff. Unemployed workers often aren't in the **right place** or the **right industry** for the jobs that are out there. They need **training**.
7) The government has various ways of trying to reduce unemployment. There's more about them on p. 171-172.

Low Unemployment is linked to Skills Shortages

Skills shortages are bad news for most businesses, but good news for recruitment consultants.

1) As well as a labour surplus or shortage, you can also have a **skills surplus** or **shortage**.
2) There are **shortages** of skilled labour in many industries.
3) Skills shortages are solved by **training**, but training is **expensive**. Governments can help by providing **training schemes** and encouraging colleges to offer **vocational** (job-related) courses and qualifications. Businesses who invest in training can find that competitors **poach** employees once they're trained.
4) Businesses can get round skills shortages by investing in labour-saving **machinery** — in other words, switching from labour-intensive production to **capital-intensive** production.
5) Businesses can also get round skills shortages by **relocating production** or service provision **abroad** where there are plenty of skilled workers.
6) It's possible to have **too many** skilled workers in a particular industry — this is a **skills surplus**. It can lead to a lot of skilled workers with the **same skills** being **unemployed** if they aren't willing to accept lower-paid unskilled jobs.
7) **Shortages** and **surpluses** of skills can be caused by having **too few** or **too many workers** in the country. To work out if the population of working age has grown or shrunk, you **subtract** the number of working-age **people** who've **left** the **UK** from the number who've **come** to live in the UK. If there are **lots of jobs** it's better if there's **more immigration** (people arriving) than emigration (people leaving). If jobs are scarce, the reverse is true.

Practice Questions

Q1 Explain what is meant by 'inflation' and 'deflation'.

Q2 Name the five types of unemployment and briefly explain what each one means.

Exam Question

Q1 Jemmy McDougal sells Scottish smoked salmon to catering companies in the US and Canada. She's noticed that the pound has been very strong in recent months. Explain the impact this is likely to have on her firm and why. [10 marks]

Structural unemployment — when buildings can't find work...

Personally, I think this stuff's quite interesting — it gives you a feel for how companies actually operate in the real world. They have to be on the lookout for changes in all kinds of factors and they need to know what they'll do if interest rates suddenly shoot up. Think of it like juggling — businesses have to keep all the balls in the air if they want to be successful.

Businesses and the Political Environment

Politics — you know you love it really. Even if you don't, you've still got to learn what's on these next three pages.

The Government plays Four Roles in the Economy

Not that kind of role play...

1) The government **provides** services like education, healthcare and defence.
2) The government **supports** businesses and individuals with things like tax credits and subsidies.
3) The government is a **legislator** — it makes laws and regulations (e.g. health and safety).
4) The government is a **consumer** — it buys products and services.

The government uses a combination of **fiscal policy** (see below), **monetary policy** (p. 172) and **supply-side policies** (p. 172) to try to keep the economy under control.

Taxation Rates affect Economic Activity

1) **Individuals** are taxed on their **income**. Businesses are taxed on their **profits** — sole traders and partnerships pay **income tax**, and limited companies pay **corporation tax**. These taxes are **direct taxes**.
2) Businesses also pay **business rate** tax based on the **value** of their **premises**. The rate is the same all over the country. However, because **property values** are generally **higher** in the **South** than in the North, **businesses** in the **South** generally end up **paying more**. This can **reduce** their **competitiveness**.
3) There are also **indirect taxes on spending**, e.g. VAT, taxes on pollution, tax on tobacco and tax on alcohol.
4) A business' **local competitiveness** can be affected by **local taxes** such as **congestion charges**. E.g. if a bakery is located within a congestion charge zone and customers can buy bread from another bakery that they don't have to pay to get to, they're more likely to go to the other bakery instead.
5) **High** tax rates **discourage** individuals from **spending**, and businesses from **expanding**. Increasing income tax **reduces spending power**, **cuts demand** and **lowers economic activity**.
6) **Reducing taxes** or giving businesses **subsidies** (financial assistance) encourages businesses to expand.
7) The effect of a tax cut or tax rise depends on the **income elasticity** of the good or service. Rises in income tax hit **luxury goods** (e.g. expensive kitchen appliances) harder than **staple goods** (e.g. petrol or bread).

Fiscal Policy changes Taxes and Spending

1) **Fiscal policy** does **two** things — it sets **tax rates** and the amount of **government spending**.
2) **Raising taxes** reduces spending in the economy, and cutting taxes increases it. **Low rates of tax** give businesses more profit, and **encourage business activity** like expansion and new start-ups.
   - It's fairly easy to predict the effects of a change in **direct taxation**. Raising **income tax** reduces consumer spending, and raising **business taxes** reduces economic output.
   - **Indirect taxation** is a bit harder to predict. In the **short term**, an **increase** in VAT tends to cause **inflation**, because the **higher tax** means that goods and services **cost more**. In the **longer term**, a rise in VAT **decreases** consumer spending, and **prices** have to **fall** to meet the **drop** in **demand**, so it causes **deflation**.
3) **Government spending** on social services, health, education etc. also pumps more money into the economy.
   - Changing government expenditure on **welfare benefits** has a **quick** impact on the economy, because poorer people who receive benefits will change their spending habits straight away.
   - Government spending on **infrastructure** such as roads has a **slower** effect on the economy.
4) **Fiscal policy** is really about the **balance** between tax and spending. The Chancellor of the Exchequer decides what the balance is going to be in the yearly Budget.

Fiscal Policy	When it's done	How it's done	Change in government borrowing	The effect it has
Expansionary fiscal policy	Economic slowdown / high unemployment	Cutting taxes and/or Raising spending	Government **borrowing increases** (or government **surplus decreases**)	**Demand** for goods and services **increases**
Contractionary fiscal policy	Production at 100% capacity / risk of high inflation	Raising taxes and/or Cutting spending	Government **borrowing decreases** (or government **surplus increases**)	**Demand** for goods and services **decreases**

5) Expansionary fiscal policy helps to **lower unemployment**. **Cutting taxes** gives people **more to spend** and increased **consumption** boosts **production** and creates **jobs**. It can cause **inflation** though, so it needs to be monitored.

Businesses and the Political Environment

Monetary Policy controls the Interest Rate

1) Monetary policy means **tweaking the interest rate** to control **inflation** and **exchange rates**.
2) Interest rates are set by the Bank of England, **not** by the government, but the Bank of England Monetary Policy Committee bears the **government's fiscal policy** in mind when it makes its decisions.
3) Monetary policy aims to:

    1) Control **inflation**.
    2) Control the overall rate of **economic growth**.
    3) Manage **unemployment** levels (e.g. if interest rates are low, people have more money to spend and increased demand leads to a rise in production so more workers are needed).
    4) Influence **foreign exchange rates**.

4) See p.169 for more on the **impact** of changes in the interest rate on **business activity**.

Supply-side Policies encourage Growth in the Market

Economic policies like increasing taxes aim to control the level of **demand** in the economy. Governments also use **supply-side policies** — policies that aim to help **markets work freely** by increasing **supply** in the economy (i.e. by encouraging business activity). Supply-side policies attempt to **reduce unemployment** and **increase output** and the **supply** of **labour**. They work by:

1) **Privatisation** (see below) and **deregulation** (opening up a market to new competitors, e.g. parcel delivery).
2) **Encouraging international trade** (e.g. by setting up trade agreements like the European Single Market). See p. 174-175 for more on this.
3) **Promoting entrepreneurship** by offering loans to new businesses.
4) **Lowering corporation tax** to attract investors from outside the country and encourage growth.
5) **Decreasing income tax** (people are more motivated to work when they keep a larger proportion of their wages).
6) **Cutting benefits** and **spending** more on **training** to encourage people to work.

Privatisation is when State-Owned Businesses are sold to Private Investors

1) In the 1980s many state-owned firms were sold into the private sector to **improve efficiency** and make a **profit**. Examples include **British Telecom**, **British Gas**, **British Steel**, the **water** companies and the **electricity** distributors.

Benefits of privatisation	Drawbacks of privatisation
Privatisation **promotes competition**, which **increases efficiency**, and offers **better quality** products at **lower prices**.	**Some** privatised companies have **raised prices** and **cut quality** to **exploit** consumers — especially if they're effectively a **monopoly**.
The **government** made a big **profit** from privatisation. This helped the government to **cut taxes** and **reduce its borrowing**, which in turn **encourages business activity**.	Privatised companies tend to have **lots of shareholders** — often **private citizens** holding just a few shares. Shareholders tend to look for **quick profit** at the expense of **long term strategy**.

This profit is one-off profit — the privatisation can't be repeated.

2) Some industries are **natural monopolies** — for example, you wouldn't have several sets of rail tracks from one city to another. When privatising a natural monopoly like the **railways**, the government needs to build in regulations to prevent the new owners from exploiting their position and raising prices or cutting quality.

Case study: Network Rail

Privatisation: In 1994 the UK government privatised the railways, and placed them under the control of a company called Railtrack. Railtrack went into administration in 2001, and since 2002 the railways have been owned by Network Rail. Network Rail is effectively a monopoly, with train operating companies as its customers.

Regulation: The Office of Rail Regulation (ORR) was set up by the government to regulate the rail industry and make sure that Network Rail doesn't allow its commercial interest to get in the way of public standards and safety.

Businesses and the Political Environment

Nationalisation is Government Ownership and Control of Businesses

1) **Nationalisation** means taking businesses into **government ownership**. It's a risky move because it usually creates a **legally protected monopoly**. This means there's a lack of competition, which can lead to inefficiency and poor quality. Nationalised industries often don't make much profit. See p. 183 for more on monopolies and competition.
2) Despite the problems with nationalisation, sometimes it **makes sense** for **certain industries** to be nationalised — usually when they supply **essential public services** or **goods**. That's why the **NHS** is state-run.

The State is a Consumer — it uses Goods and Services

1) The state **buys products** and **services** just like individuals do. For example, if the government is planning to build a new motorway it will need to pay a road construction company to do the work. For **some products**, e.g. pharmaceutical drugs, the **state** is the **biggest consumer**.
2) **Depending** on the **government** to buy your product can be **risky**. For example, if your company makes submarines and the government cuts defence spending, there might not be any **other market** for your product. This often leads to **regional unemployment**.

"And the Prime Minister will have the steak and chips..."

Intervention vs Laissez-Faire — whether governments Interfere in the economy

1) The idea of **laissez-faire** means that **governments don't interfere** in the economy. The idea of **interventionism** means they **do** get involved.
2) Governments **intervene** by charging **taxes**, passing **laws** which affect business, providing **public services** and taking part in the economy as a **consumer**. They also provide **subsidies** — payments to certain essential industries (e.g. farming) to encourage them to keep trading when it might not be financially viable to do so otherwise.
3) Governments that take a **laissez-faire** approach **dismantle** existing regulations that **constrain** business, abolish wage controls and **reduce taxation rates**.

Arguments for Laissez-faire	Arguments for Intervention
Intervention raises **costs** and makes businesses **less efficient** and **less profitable**.	Governments need to step in to make sure there's **fair competition** in the market.
Allowing businesses to **cut wages** makes them **more competitive**.	Totally **free**, profit-driven **markets** usually have **social** and **environmental costs**.
Encourages businesses to **behave responsibly**, rather than relying on the state to bail them out.	**Subsidies** help **pay** for the **costs** of production and ensure that businesses make a **reasonable income**.

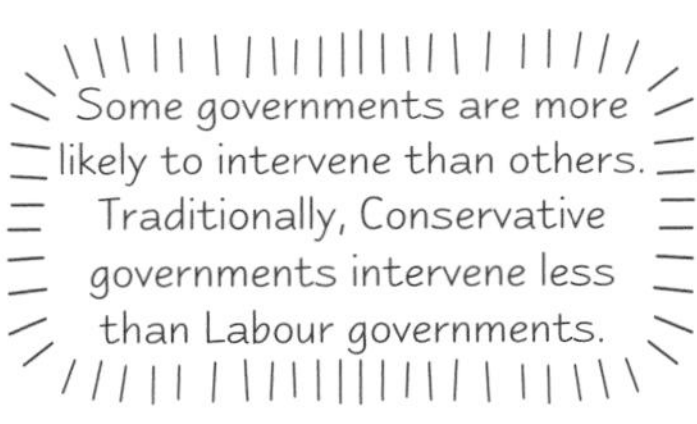

Some governments are more likely to intervene than others. Traditionally, Conservative governments intervene less than Labour governments.

Practice Questions

Q1 What are the four roles the government plays in the economy?

Q2 How do supply-side policies work?

Q3 Give two advantages and two disadvantages of privatisation.

Q4 What's the difference between intervention and a 'laissez-faire' approach to the economy?

Exam Question

Q1 The Chancellor of the Exchequer has just announced a contractionary fiscal policy.
Assess the impact that this will have on businesses, explaining what risks they might face. [10 marks]

Political change — what's left over from government spending...

There's a lot of material to cover on these pages, but stick with it — this stuff has the power to make or break businesses. The key point to learn is that not everyone agrees about how involved governments should be — some people find government intervention reassuring, other people just think they should keep their hands off. Which is better? You decide...

The European Union

The EU is a union of 27 independent countries, with a population of over 495 million — bigger than the US and Japan put together. So it's a pretty big deal.

The EU is a **Single Market** — **Trade** between member states is **Easy**

1) The European Single Market means there are very few **trade barriers** between EU member states. Firms don't pay **tax** when they **import** goods from other EU countries, so the EU provides easy export opportunities for UK firms.
2) The Single Market **smooths out price differences** between member states. **Producers** can look for the **highest selling price** within the EU, and consumers can look for the **lowest purchase price** within the EU. When the price in part of the EU is high, producers flood that area with their product, driving down prices. Low prices attract more buyers to the market, pushing prices up.
3) The EU **customs union** means the **same customs duties** apply to all goods entering the EU irrespective of which non-member country they come from, and which EU country they're going to.
4) There's freedom of movement within the EU for all **raw materials**, **finished goods** and **workers**. EU citizens can work in any country of the EU.
5) A **common EU competition law** controls anti-competitive activities — e.g. setting up a **monopoly**.
6) There are **common policies** on **product regulation** as well.

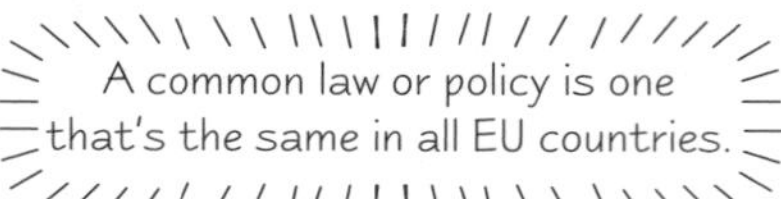

A common law or policy is one
that's the same in all EU countries.

The **Growth** of the **EU** has increased **Business Opportunities**

1) Whenever the EU expands, the **size of the market** available to an EU-based producer increases. Businesses can enjoy **increased sales** and take advantage of **economies of scale**.
2) The EU collectively has **more political whack** than its member states. For example, the EU can negotiate any trade dispute with the USA on equal terms. This increases competitiveness.
3) **Production costs** are **low** in the **new EU countries** that joined in 2004 (Poland, Hungary, etc) and 2007 (Romania and Bulgaria). Businesses can locate production facilities there to increase their competitiveness.

Increased Competition in the EU can be a **Threat**

1) The expansion of the EU brings **businesses** from **new member states** into the market.
2) There's **increased competition** in industries where new member states like Hungary and Poland have an advantage — e.g. **manufacturing** and **agriculture**. This threatens UK manufacturers and farmers.
3) **High tech** UK businesses keep their **competitive advantage**.
4) Increased competition may also hurt **inefficient** producers in the new member states, who were previously serving protected national markets.

Ian found that the best way to deal with the competition was just to trip them all up.

The **Euro** is the **Common Currency** of **Most** EU countries

The euro became the **common currency** of 11 EU member states in **1999**. They stopped using their old currencies completely in **2002**. These countries are commonly called the **eurozone**. More countries have joined the eurozone since the euro was first introduced, and there are now **16** eurozone countries. The **UK isn't** part of the eurozone — there are **benefits** and **drawbacks** to not being a member:

Benefits of keeping the pound

The UK still has power over its **interest rates**. For countries in the eurozone, the **European Central Bank** sets the interest rates, which causes problems if different countries have different **economic situations** (e.g. if inflation is high, higher interest rates are needed to control it).

Drawbacks of keeping the pound

1) **Changing money** on the foreign exchange market **costs money**. A common currency would **reduce transaction costs** between businesses in the UK and eurozone countries.
2) It's harder to **compare prices** when they're not in the same currency.
3) UK businesses exporting abroad face the **uncertainty** of fluctuating exchange rates. When the **pound rises** in value against the euro, UK exporters **lose** international competitiveness because their goods are more **expensive** for eurozone countries. Eurozone businesses don't have the uncertainty of constantly changing exchange rates.

The European Union

It's **Difficult** for businesses to come up with **Pan-European Strategy**

1) It's easy for businesses to think of the EU as a big single market, with the same rules and regulations throughout. In reality, it's tricky to come up with a **pan-European strategy** — one that works all over Europe.
2) There are still **cultural differences** between countries, and lots of **different languages**, so EU businesses need to market products in different ways to suit **different countries**.
3) Having to do lots of marketing campaigns for one product **reduces economies of scale**.
4) There are also still **legal** differences between EU countries.

EU Institutions pass **Laws** which affect **Business**

EU laws are divided into **four main categories**:

1) **Regulations** are **binding laws** that apply to **all** EU citizens as soon as they're passed.
2) **Directives** tell **member-state** governments to **pass a law** that meets a specific objective — e.g. reducing working time to 48 hours per week, or reducing pollution. It's up to member-state governments how to word the law. Some member governments make **strict** laws in response to EU directives, while others are more slack.
3) **Decisions** are **binding laws** that apply to a **specific country** or a **specific business**.
4) **Recommendations** aren't really laws at all, because they're **not legally binding**.

Most EU laws are directives.

The European Commission and the Council of Ministers decide on policies and laws

1) The **European Commission** puts forward new laws. The EU Commission is **appointed**, not elected.
2) The Council of Ministers **decides** whether or not to bring in **new laws** suggested by the Commission. It's made up of **government ministers** from **each member state**.

There's one commissioner from each member state.

The European Parliament is involved in making new laws

1) The European Parliament is **directly elected**, so it gives some democratic legitimacy to European law.
2) Most decisions on new EU laws are made **jointly** by the Council of Ministers and the European Parliament.

The European Central Bank (ECB) controls the euro

1) The **ECB** decides monetary policy (i.e. it sets interest rates) in the eurozone.
2) Only the eurozone countries have a say in the running of the bank.

The European Court of Justice interprets EU law

1) The European Court of Justice makes sure that **EU law** is applied in line with the **Treaty of Rome** — the treaty that says how the EU must be run.
2) It also sorts out disputes between member states.
3) The decisions of the court take precedence over the laws of each member state.

Practice Questions

Q1 Give an example of a benefit to business of the EU Single Market.

Q2 Give one benefit to business if the UK adopted the euro.

Q3 What is an EU directive?

Exam Questions

Q1 Analyse the ways in which a Welsh toy manufacturer would be affected if the UK decided to adopt the euro. [10 marks]

Q2 "The bureaucrats in Brussels can't change the way I run my business."
Do you agree with this statement? Justify your answer. [6 marks]

The Single Market's the place to go if you're looking for love...

The EU is a big deal for businesses — as the Single Market grows, there's more opportunity for easy importing and exporting. The EU is also another source of laws and regulations that businesses have to follow. Whether you're generally pro-Europe or anti-Europe doesn't change the fact that you need to revise both these pages to be prepared for the exam.

Businesses and the Legal Environment

There are a number of laws that affect the production and sale of goods, and so any business that's involved in either of these activities must be aware of their implications.

The Law protects Customers and Consumers

Libby's microwaveable lasagne looked quite different from the photo on the packet.

The Trade Descriptions Act (1968)

This law ensures that businesses don't **mislead** consumers with **false descriptions** on **packaging** or **advertising materials.**

The Sale of Goods Act (1979)

1) This Act sets out the main **rights** of customers when making a purchase.
2) It's been updated by the **Sale and Supply of Goods Act (1994)**, and the **Sale and Supply of Goods to Consumers Regulations (2002)**. Together, these laws mean that goods must be **fit for their purpose** and of **satisfactory quality**.

The Consumer Protection Act (1987)

1) This Act says that **new consumer goods** must be **safe**.
2) Along with this law, there are **regulations** governing things like **furniture fire safety** — all new products made after the regulations came into effect have to conform to the regulations. Manufacturers had to **change the materials** they used for sofa and chair cushions, which meant they incurred costs.

The Food Safety Act (1990)

1) Under this Act producers must ensure that foodstuffs are **not harmful**.
2) If any **part** of a batch of food is considered unfit for human consumption, then the whole lot is unfit, and it all has to be **destroyed**. This has serious implications for cost and revenue.
3) Foods must also not be **labelled** in a **misleading** way. The **Food Labelling Regulations** of 1996 say:
   - Food must be labelled with a **descriptive name** and a list of **ingredients**.
   - Labels can only claim "low in fat" or "high in vitamins" if the food meets **set standards**.
   - You can only claim that a food has **health benefits**, e.g. "lowers cholesterol", if it's been **scientifically proven** to do so.
   - Food labels must also have a **Best Before** or **Use By** date, and should say how to store the food.
4) The Act also requires that workers **handling food** should be trained in **basic food hygiene**.

The Law protects the Community and the Environment

1) Industries which release waste into the **water** or **land** are regulated by the **Environment Agency**. Businesses have to ensure their production processes don't cause unnecessary pollution, or risk heavy fines.
2) Light industrial processes which only release pollution into the **air** are regulated by **local authorities**. Businesses must get **authorisation** from the local council before carrying out processes which create **smoke** or make **noise**. **Environmental health** officers can force factories to **stop making noise** at night, if it's disturbing **local residents**.
3) Here are some examples of specific laws:
   - The EU directive on **Waste Electrical and Electronic Equipment (WEEE)** forces businesses to increase **recycling** of waste electrical and electronic equipment, much of which previously ended up in landfill sites. From August 2005, manufacturers have increased responsibility for ensuring that goods such as computers, TVs and VCRs are recycled once they've come to the end of their useful life.
   - **The Landfill Tax** was introduced in 1996 to **reduce the amount of waste** being dumped into **landfill** sites.
   - The **EU Packaging Waste Directive** forces businesses to increase the recycling of packaging. There are targets for the % of wood, paper, glass and plastic that must be recycled.

The Law protects Workers

1) **Employment law** covers things like ensuring people are **recruited** fairly and have a certain amount of **job security**.
2) **Health and safety** law makes sure people don't have to work in **dangerous** conditions. See p.179 for more on this.

Businesses and the Legal Environment

The **Law** says **Where** companies can and can't **Build** factories

1) There are laws which prevent businesses from **building** wherever they want to or from **extending** their existing premises without **permission**. These are called **planning laws**.
2) A business that's planning to build new premises has to submit **paperwork** to the **local authority** saying exactly what it wants to do. The local authority then has a **meeting** and decides whether or not to give the business **planning permission**.
3) If a business builds **without** planning permission, they'll be asked to apply for **permission** even if they've already **completed** the work. If they don't get permission, the council can force them to **take** the building **down**.

Vicarious Liability means it's all the **Employer's Responsibility**

1) Workers are also protected by **vicarious liability**. This means that an **employer** will normally be **liable** for any act committed by an employee in the normal course of their job.
2) The idea of vicarious liability has **serious implications** for businesses. Imagine a situation where a lorry driver has loaded his vehicle incorrectly, and while he's driving the load comes loose and causes an accident. The **employer** will be responsible for paying **compensation** to any people injured as a result of the accident.

Companies are **Punished** if they **Break** the **Law**

"What do you mean I broke health and safety law so I won't be getting any presents?"

1) If a company breaks the law then the **local council** can step in to **penalise** them. **Fines** are the most common penalty — for example, if a company is convicted in a magistrates' court of not having complied with the **Trade Descriptions Act** they can be fined up to **£5000** per offence.
2) **Inspectors** check that restaurants and cafés aren't breaking **food safety** laws. If a business is preparing food in a way that isn't hygienic, they'll be given a **deadline** by which they have to **improve standards**. If the standards of hygiene are **really bad**, they can **close** the business **down** for a certain number of **weeks** or **months**.
3) The penalties for breaking **health and safety** law were made tougher in 2008. The maximum **fines** have **gone up** and, in cases where somebody has **died** as a result of **serious neglect** or the law being broken **repeatedly**, it's possible for the person responsible to be sent to **prison**.

New Laws cost **Money**

1) The introduction of a new law might mean that manufacturers have to **change** their **production processes**.
2) Changing production processes costs money. There may be **reduced productivity** during changeover if a firm has to **stop production** while new **machinery** is **installed** and **workers** are **retrained**. It's also possible that the new processes won't be as **efficient** as the old ones or that new materials required by law may be **more expensive**.

Practice Questions

Q1 What does the Trade Descriptions Act prevent businesses from doing?

Q2 Give two examples of European Directives that affect manufacturers.

Q3 How do inspectors enforce food safety laws?

Exam Questions

Q1 Clare McFadden is planning to open a teashop. Explain the impact that the Food Safety Act is likely to have on her business. [8 marks]

Q2 Bob Stevens runs a construction firm. One of his employees erected some scaffolding incorrectly and it collapsed, injuring 3 people. Explain what is meant by vicarious liability and how it might affect Bob. [6 marks]

I fought the law and the law took my profits and stopped me from trading...

Most businesses comply with the law, so it's unlikely you'll ever see health inspectors shut down your favourite restaurant because of cockroaches. Sadly, there'll always be some firms who try to get away with endangering employees, cheating customers and selling dangerous tat. The law's there to make sure that all firms obey the rules, or face the consequences.

Employment Law

Ok, time for employment law. If you've ever fancied yourself as a bit of an Ally McBeal, you've come to the right page.

***Individual Labour Law** controls what rights **Employees** have*

1) An employee has a legal right to **fair treatment** while at work, and also while looking for employment.
2) These anti-discrimination laws **prevent** employers from **acting unfairly**, and ensure fair treatment for individuals:

Equal Pay Act (1970)	A man and woman doing the **same** or an **equivalent** job should receive the **same rate of pay**. Followed up by EU Equal Pay Directive in 1975.
Sex Discrimination Act (1975)	A person cannot be discriminated against on grounds of **gender** or **marital status** for recruitment, promotion, training or dismissal.
Race Relations Act (1976)	A person cannot be discriminated against on grounds of **colour**, **race**, **national origin**, or **ethnic origin**.
Disability Discrimination Act (1995)	The employer must make efforts to ensure that **disabled people** can be employed in that place of work (e.g installing wheelchair ramps).
The Equality Act (2006)	A person cannot be discriminated against on the grounds of their **religious** or **philosophical beliefs**, or **lack** of beliefs.

3) Anyone feeling **discriminated against** on the basis of sex, race, religion or disability can go to an **industrial tribunal** (see next page) to seek **compensation**. The tribunal listens to the arguments and makes a judgement.

The Data Protection Act** gives **Employees** rights to **Privacy

1) Businesses hold **data** about their employees and customers on **computer** and filed away on **paper** — this includes things like their date of birth, address, and bank account details. Employees wouldn't want this information getting into the wrong hands.
2) The **Data Protection Act (1998)** prevents the misuse of personal data. It says that:
   - businesses **can't** obtain data **unfairly** or **illegally**.
   - businesses can only use the information for the purposes it was collected for, and they **can't** use it for anything **illegal**.
   - businesses **can't keep hold** of data they **don't need**.
   - the data has to be **accurate** and **up-to-date**.
   - businesses have to **allow people** to **see** the data that they hold about them.
   - people have the right to **correct** data that's held about them if it's incorrect.
   - businesses have to take measures to make sure that the data **isn't used**, **changed** or **stolen** by **unauthorised** people, or **lost** or **destroyed**.

Angie and Steve had been given new identities under the Date Protection Act.

***Discrimination Laws** affect **All Aspects** of businesses*

Recruitment:

1) Employers aren't allowed to **state** in job adverts that candidates have to be a particular age, race, gender, etc. They can't use **discriminatory language**, e.g. advertising for a "waitress" excludes men.
2) Businesses are only allowed to advertise for someone of a specific age, gender, etc if it's a **genuine requirement** of the job — e.g. a female toilet attendant for ladies' toilets.
3) Businesses have to make **decisions** about who to employ without discriminating — they can't just bin all applications from women. Businesses have to be able to **justify** why they gave a job to a particular candidate, in case an unsuccessful candidate takes them to a tribunal.
4) The same rules apply when **promoting** staff — employers can't make decisions based on race, religion, etc.

Pay:

1) Businesses have to give male and female employees the **same pay** for work of **equal value**.
2) Women are entitled to the same **benefits** as men too (e.g. company car).
3) If a business pays a woman less than a man, they have to be able to prove that the work the woman does is **less valuable** for the business.

Redundancies:

If businesses need to make redundancies, they **can't** deliberately select staff who are disabled, who've taken maternity leave, etc.

Employment Law

Employers have to pay staff at least the Minimum Wage

1) A **national minimum wage** was introduced on 1st April 1999, to prevent employees from being paid unfairly low wages.
2) The minimum wage rises in October every year. From **1st October 2009**, it's **£5.80** for people aged over 22, £4.83 for people aged 18-21, and £3.57 for 16 and 17 year olds.
3) Employers who don't pay their staff enough can be **fined** up to **£5000**, and also have to **reimburse** their staff with the total amount that they've been underpaid.

An Employment Contract sets out the Conditions of Employment

1) Employees are entitled to receive a **written contract** of employment within **two months** of starting work.
2) A contract of employment is a **legally-binding** agreement between the employer and the employee about what the **duties** and **rights** of the employee and the employer are. It sets out the duties of the employee (e.g. what hours they're expected to work), and what the employee can expect from the employer (e.g. what the salary is).
3) There are some **responsibilities** that are **common** to all employers and employees:

Employers' responsibilities towards employees

- Employees have the right to a **safe** working environment. The **Health and Safety at Work Act (1974)** states that the employer must ensure the working environment is **safe** (e.g. electrical equipment, moving machinery, etc must be safe). Under the **Control of Substances Hazardous to Health Regulations 2002** (COSHH), businesses also have to protect employees from the risks of any **hazardous substances**.
- In April 2009, the **European Working Time Directive** gave full-time workers the right to **28 days** of **paid holidays** per year, including bank holidays. There's also a maximum working week of **48 hours** — although in the UK an employee can **opt out** of this and work longer hours if they want to.
- Employees have the right to be **paid** at least the **national minimum wage**.
- Employees have the right to **paid maternity** and **paternity** leave, although usually not on full pay. **Mums** get 39 weeks of paid leave, and can take 13 more weeks unpaid. **Dads** get up to 2 weeks of paid paternity leave.

Employees' responsibilities towards employers

- Employees have to **attend work** when they're supposed to, and be **on time**.
- They must be willing to carry out any **reasonable task** that's asked of them.

Employment Tribunals can settle Disputes

1) If employees feel that they've been treated **unfairly** by their employers (e.g. if they've suffered discrimination, been paid less than minimum wage, etc), they can make a claim to a tribunal.
2) At a tribunal, representatives of the employer and the employee put forward their cases, and an **experienced lawyer** (sometimes a panel) decides who's in the right.
3) If the employer loses the tribunal case, they're usually ordered to pay the employee **compensation**. If it's an unfair dismissal case, they might have to give the employee their job back too.

See p. 162 for more on industrial disputes.

Practice Questions

Q1 What's the purpose of the Data Protection Act?

Q2 How does the Health and Safety at Work Act protect employees?

Q3 How can employment tribunals settle disputes between employers and employees?

Exam Question

Q1 Discuss the role of anti-discrimination laws in the workplace. [15 marks]

Can tribunals settle disputes about whose turn it is to make the tea...

There's an awful lot of law to learn on these pages. Don't be too downhearted though, because it's possible to learn it all — just break it down into manageable bits and you'll be fine. This is all handy stuff to know anyway for when you get a job — if you know your rights then you can stand up to any unscrupulous employers who try to fiddle you. That'll teach 'em.

Businesses and the Social Environment

Social concerns affect business — not the 'what shall I wear to the party' type of social concerns though.

Businesses have to **Respond** to **Social Changes**

"Ooh yes, since we've been watching Jamie, we love a bit of lemongrass..."

1) The **structure** of the UK **population** changes over time in terms of **age**, **sex** and **race** — this is **demographic change**.
2) Demographic change is important to businesses because it has an **impact** on the **workforce**. The UK has an **ageing population**, which means that the number of people **available to work** (those aged 16-65) is **falling**. It's a bad thing if businesses **can't find** enough **workers** to fill all their vacancies, because it makes them **inefficient**.
3) However, the **ageing population** also creates **opportunities** for some firms, such as private healthcare providers. Retired people often travel a lot — so it's good news for holiday companies, too.
4) **Consumer tastes** are another thing that **change** over time. In recent years lots more people have started watching cookery programmes, so **supermarkets** stock far more **exotic ingredients** than they used to. Another example is the switch from CD to MP3 players, which means that companies now supply **music** for **download**.

Changes in **Employment Patterns** mean **Businesses** have to be more **Flexible**

In recent years, the concept of **work-life balance** has become more important and businesses have had to adapt to give workers more **choice** over **where**, **when** and **how** they work.

1) **Flexible working** (see p. 155) gives employees more **choice** about **when** they work and **how many hours** they do — it's popular with **mums** who have to fit their working hours round **childcare**. It's good for **reducing absenteeism** and increases a company's **choice** of **potential employees**, but can **increase administration** costs.
2) **Homeworking**, unsurprisingly, means **working from home**. New **technology** like **remote access** has made it far more common. Like flexible working, it **reduces labour turnover** and **absenteeism**, but it can be hard to **monitor** employees' **performance**. Also, not being in a social working environment can cause **worker morale** to **drop**.

Case study: BT

BT recognises that a lot of its workforce have responsibility for either a **child** or an **ageing parent**. It aims to help staff fit work around their caring duties. The firm used its broadband technology to help introduce flexible working. In 2008, **71%** of BT's employees were on some kind of flexible scheme. The company says flexible working has **increased productivity** by **20%**.

Business Ethics help businesses make **Socially Responsible Decisions**

1) In recent years, changes in **consumer concerns** have led many firms to consider whether their **behaviour** is **ethical**. Not everyone **agrees** on what's ethical and what's not. For example, most people **agree** that **child labour** is **unethical**, but **opinions differ** on whether it's **unethical** to **sell cigarettes** even though they cause cancer.
2) In the UK, one of the ethical issues that manufacturing businesses have to consider is the **balance** between **capital** and **labour**. It might be most efficient for them to replace some of their workforce with machines, but some people think that this is **unethical** if it leads to high numbers of **redundancies**.

Morals are personal beliefs about what is right and wrong. Ethics are rules which say what is acceptable behaviour for members of a group. Business ethics are about doing the "right thing".

3) Ethical behaviour can affect **profit**, e.g. if it means paying **suppliers** a **higher price**. However, it has **positive effects** too — behaving ethically **attracts customers** who **approve** of this approach. It can be a **unique selling point**, particularly in retail (e.g. The Body Shop® products, Co-op's fair trade chocolate etc). Ethics can be **good PR**.
4) **Growth objectives** can also be affected by ethical behaviour. So a company producing **fairtrade clothes** (giving their suppliers in developing countries fair pay and fair conditions) is likely to have longer **lead times** (see p. 142-143) than a non-fairtrade company, so the **delay** in stocking new trends might stop it expanding rapidly.
5) Businesses might also try to accommodate their employees' **spiritual needs**. This might mean providing separate **kitchen facilities** for employees with **religious dietary needs** or providing a quiet **place** to **pray**.
6) Sweatshops are a big ethical issue currently. A sweatshop is a **factory** (usually overseas) where workers are forced to work **long hours** in **poor** and **unsafe conditions** for **low pay**. Some firms, e.g. **Marks and Spencer**, have **voluntarily promised** not to buy from suppliers who use sweatshops, but many **other companies** either still **use** them or have only **stopped** following **pressure** (e.g. boycotting) from **customers**. Another problem is that some companies aren't very good at **checking up** on the behaviour of their **suppliers**.

Businesses and the Social Environment

Social Responsibility means being responsible towards the *Whole of Society*

1) Corporate social responsibility (CSR) is the **voluntary** role of business in looking after **society** and the environment.
2) Businesses have special responsibility to their **stakeholders** — everyone who's affected by the business, e.g. **employees**, **suppliers**, **creditors**, **customers**, **shareholders** and local **communities**.

Employees

1) Every firm has **legal responsibilities** to its staff.
2) Firms have a responsibility to **train** employees.
3) Firms can **choose** to give their employees a better deal than the bare legal minimum. Firms that operate internationally can **choose** to give workers abroad similar rights to workers in the UK.

Examples — providing a safe work environment, not discriminating based on race or gender, giving lunch breaks and paid holiday. See p.178-179.

Suppliers

1) It's not in a firm's best interest to treat their **suppliers** badly. For good results, be **honest** and **pay** on time.
2) Firms can build **long-term relationships** with suppliers — e.g. by offering **long-term exclusive supply contracts** and placing **regular orders**. A good relationship makes it more likely that the supplier will pull all the stops out to deliver **fast service** when it's really needed.
3) There's also a responsibility to the rest of **society** to choose suppliers who don't **exploit** their workers or **pollute** excessively. Firms may not see this as worthwhile, **unless** customers care enough to **boycott** the product.

Customers

1) Firms who treat their **customers** well can build up **customer goodwill**. Good customer service, good quality products and reasonable prices all encourage **customer loyalty** and **repeat business**.
2) Customers are more and more willing to **complain** when firms don't treat them well. Customers can even **campaign against** firms who disappoint, and **persuade** other people **not to buy** their goods and services.

Local Community

1) Firms can be responsible to the local community by keeping **jobs secure**, and using **local suppliers**.
2) They can also avoid **noise pollution**, **air pollution** and excess **traffic** on local roads.
3) Businesses can **earn goodwill** by making **charity** donations or **sponsoring** schools, leisure centres, parks etc.

Some people claim that it's **unethical** to produce certain types of product, e.g. tobacco and weapons, and that even if the companies who make these things behave in a **socially responsible** way in terms of how they treat their staff, etc, it's only to distract consumers and get **positive PR**. These people tend to think that **government regulations** and **laws** are the only real way of getting businesses to behave responsibly.

Here are *Two* corporate social responsibility *Case Studies*

Case study: The Coca-Cola® Company

The Coca-Cola® Company's corporate social responsibility policy covers **four areas** — **employees**, the **environment**, the **community** and **customers**. The company's social goals include **reducing** the amount of **water** it takes to produce each litre of Coke®, helping consumers make healthy choices by having a **product portfolio** which is **36% low sugar** or **sugar free**, and using **flexible working** to help **women** reach senior positions.

Case study: Cadbury

Cadbury have set themselves **CSR targets** to meet by **2010**. These include **sustainably sourcing** half of their **raw materials**, ensuring all packaging is recyclable or biodegradable and donating **1%** of their **pre-tax profit** to **community** projects. Cadbury Dairy Milk has also been **Fairtrade certified** since summer 2009, and Cadbury is committed to making more of its products Fairtrade in the future.

Businesses and the Social Environment

*Being **Socially Responsible** has an impact on the **Decision-making process***

1) Traditionally, the **decision-making process** put the **needs** of **shareholders first** — which meant that the business was concerned with its **profits** above all else.
2) Corporate social responsibility means that the **needs of other stakeholders** also have to be **considered** during the decision-making process. E.g. a company that makes chocolate bars for children might put some information on their website about the importance of healthy eating and being active.
3) In reality though, it can be **hard** to take into account the needs of all shareholders. If a company has promised to **invest** in a **local school** for the next **5 years** but its **profits fall** sharply, it has to decide which is more important — keeping **shareholders happy** or the need to **behave ethically**.

*__Business Activity__ can be **Harmful** to the **Environment***

1) Businesses pollute the environment through **production** processes, through **traffic pollution** caused by **transporting** raw materials and finished goods, through **dumping waste** in waterways and seas, and through **burying** or **burning waste**. **Packaging** creates a large amount of **landfill** waste.
2) Businesses also damage the environment through **unsustainable resource management** — e.g. cutting down rainforest for mining developments, building on greenfield sites.
3) The **Environment Act (1995)** set up the **Environment Agency**, which coordinates pollution control. Businesses can't release dangerous substances into waterways or the air without a **permit** from the Environment Agency. There are also a lot of **EU directives** relating to pollution.
4) Most environmental costs are **external costs**, i.e. they affect society, not the business itself. External costs include health issues caused by air pollution, the greenhouse effect and acid rain.
5) The government **fines** businesses that pollute more than a certain level. Pollution is also controlled through **taxes**.
6) Many businesses now try to **minimise** the **impact** they have on the environment. One way they can do this is to ensure that their activities are **sustainable**, e.g. **replacing resources** as they use them. This might mean **cleaning waste water** before it's pumped back into rivers and lakes, **planting new trees** to replace trees that are cut down for timber or making sure that **overfishing** doesn't endanger certain species or cause them to die out altogether.

*__Environmental Auditing__ shows how a firm is affecting the **Environment***

1) An environmental audit is a review of the **environmental effects** of the firm's activities. It assesses whether the firm is meeting legal environmental protection requirements, and whether it's meeting its own **targets**. Environmental audits show businesses where they need to **change** their **waste management** practices.
2) For example, one of the environmental costs of business activity is the emission of **greenhouse gases**. A business which has decided to **reduce** the amount of **greenhouse gases** emitted into the atmosphere would set a clear **objective** for reducing emissions and **check their progress** towards this objective through an **environmental audit**.
3) Environmental audits only work if a company has something to **compare** its **waste output** to (e.g. **legal requirements** or **company policy**) and if it knows what **action** will be taken to reduce the amount of waste if it's too high. Firms aiming to reduce their waste output over time need to keep **accurate records** of waste levels.

Practice Questions

Q1 What is demographic change? What are its positive and negative effects on businesses?

Q2 How does ethical behaviour affect profit?

Q3 What does corporate social responsibility mean?

Q4 What is an environmental audit?

Exam Question

Q1 Evaluate the following statement: "Profit should be a higher priority than social responsibility for businesses." [9 marks]

CSR — just a new TV crime series....

Corporate social responsibility has become far more important over the last 20 years — lots of consumers worry about the way the products they buy were made. Some firms take these concerns very seriously and try to make sure their behaviour is ethical, others don't care much at all. Learn to spot examples of firms behaving in a socially responsible way...

Businesses and the Competitive Environment

Here's a nice page on the competitive environment. Not a competitive environment in an "I'm greener than you are" kind of way, but the competition businesses face when they're trying to get consumers to buy their products.

Market Structure affects Strategy and Competitive Behaviour

1) **Perfect competition** is where all firms compete on an **equal** basis — their **products** are near-enough **identical** and it's **easy** for businesses to **come** and **go** from the market. In this environment, the consumer has lots of sellers to choose between and can easily find out who's offering the best price, so they get **high quality** products for **low prices**. Perfect competition often leads to **low profit margins**, so firms try to keep **costs low** and focus on **efficiency**.
2) A **monopoly** is where one business has **complete control** over its market. There's **no** competition. Since there are no alternatives, if the consumer **needs** the product, the monopoly can charge whatever **price** it wants. But although monopolies are **very powerful**, they can be **inefficient** and **don't** often **innovate**. In the UK, the Competition Commission treats any firm with over 25% market share as a monopoly and can stop monopolies from occurring (e.g. by preventing a takeover or merger if the resulting company will have a market share over 25%). See p. 187 for more on takeovers and mergers. If a state-owned business is **privatised** (see p. 172), the business could go from being a monopoly to having to **compete** with other businesses.
3) **Monopolistic competition** is when there are a lot of businesses in the same market but their products are sufficiently **different** for competition to **not** be based just on price — consumers choose based on how closely the product matches their needs, so a company's focus should be on making their **product** stand out.
4) In an **oligopoly**, a **small** number of **large** firms dominate a market, and charge **similar prices**. If the consumer **needs** the product, they must pay this price. Firms in an oligopoly focus more on **marketing** and **brand image**.
5) Businesses have to **rethink** their **strategies** if a **new competitor** enters the market. For example, if a high street music retailer launches a music download website, existing online music retailers might either have to **lower** their **prices**, invest in a fresh **marketing campaign** or **diversify** into new areas (e.g. film downloads).
6) A **dominant business** is the **strongest business** in a particular market. If a new dominant business emerges in the market then the **strategies** of its **competitors** will **change** based on the **decisions** made by the **dominant business**. E.g. if the dominant business decides to charge £300 for its product, rival firms will generally charge slightly less. Equally, if the dominant firm starts researching new technology, its competitors usually end up doing the same.

Companies are affected by how Powerful their Customers are

1) The **amount** that **people spend** in shops is mostly determined by their **disposable income** (see p. 169), so changes in customers' disposable income have an impact on the competitive environment.
2) If people have **less disposable income** (e.g. in an economic downturn) then they will **spend less**. This means that retailers' **power** to set prices is **reduced** — customers can demand **reduced prices**, and if businesses don't lower their prices they're likely to **lose custom**.
3) When customers have **more disposable income**, they tend to **spend more** — that means that businesses are in a more **powerful** position and can charge higher prices. The **more disposable income** customers have, the **less** businesses have to **compete** on **price**.

Companies are also affected by how Powerful their Suppliers are

1) If a **supplier gains power** in a market, then they can sell their products to businesses for **higher prices**. E.g. PC manufacturers nearly all buy software from **Microsoft®** because most customers are already using Microsoft® products — using a different supplier's software would probably put some customers off buying the finished PC. This means that businesses are sometimes **forced** to use **powerful suppliers** and pay **high prices**. Using **powerful suppliers** pushes businesses' **costs up**.
2) Suppliers that **don't** have a lot of power (e.g. new suppliers) **can't** charge high prices to businesses — if they tried, businesses would just use a different supplier. Using cheaper suppliers allows businesses to keep their **costs down**.

Derek was the proud winner of the 2009 'Most Powerful Supplier' championships.

Businesses and the Technological Environment

It's all about technology these days. Technology is the reason why things are quicker and more exciting and why nobody reads books any more. Oh, wait, this is a book...

Production Methods have Changed as a result of new Technology

1) Production technology is changing all the time. New technology tends to make production **faster**, more **efficient** and more **accurate**. It also makes **innovation** easier.
2) **Computer-aided design** (CAD) involves using computers to help design new products, or make alterations to existing products. CAD produces 3D mock-ups on screen, so it can show managers exactly what a product will look like before it's actually made. This can also be useful for **marketing** things like new kitchens.
3) **Computer-aided manufacture** (CAM) uses computers to produce a product, usually involving **robots** or 'computer-numerically controlled' (**CNC**) machines — machine tools which form a material into a finished product from a computer design. CAM is often combined with the CAD process — products are designed on computer, and the design data fed straight into the production machine. This is called **CAD/CAM**.
4) Computers make **stock control** easier. Holding stock information in a database makes it much easier to monitor when you need to order new stock. In retailing this is often combined with **Electronic Point of Sale (EPOS)** systems that rely on barcodes to record which products are being purchased by customers. This means stocks can be re-ordered automatically. Having a good stock control system makes it easier for companies such as supermarkets and big retailers to move to a **just-in-time** supply system (see p.142).
5) New technology can also improve **quality control**. For example, in 2008, **Cadbury** introduced a new system which allows them to test **more** product samples for **harmful bacteria** in a **shorter** amount of **time**.

Robots do the Boring, Repetitive bits of production

1) **Robots** are mostly used to replace human staff for **tasks** which are **dangerous**, **repetitive** or **boring**.
2) **Factories** and **production plants** often use **automated pickers** to take goods from the production line and pack them into boxes. It's usually **cheaper** and **faster** for robots to do this job instead of humans.

Susie wasn't actually a big, orange robot.
A bad spray tan had just made her look like one.

Case study: Ocado

Traditional Method:	Most supermarkets that offer internet shopping use shopfloor workers to pick goods from stores, load them into vans and deliver them to customers. Accuracy rates are usually roughly 90%.
New Method:	Ocado uses remote-controlled machines to guide human workers to the right product, so they pick goods more accurately. Accuracy levels have been shown to be much higher, at around 99%.

Marketing has Changed as a result of new Technology

1) Many companies now use **technology** to gather **information** about the **lifestyles** of their **customers** and the **products** that they **buy** or are likely to buy. This helps them to make sure that **promotions** are **targeting** the right people and stand the best chance of causing **sales** to **increase**.
2) Lots of supermarkets offer **loyalty cards** which give customers money back according to how much they spend. One **benefit** for the supermarket is that it allows them to form a **database** of customer names and addresses which they can then use to create **mailing lists** for **direct marketing** campaigns.
3) **Loyalty cards** also tell the supermarkets what **products** a particular customer is **buying**. This means they can send out **offers** which **relate** to the kind of products that the person buys **most often**.
4) **Social networking websites** are another way that businesses can use technology to find out more about customer likes and dislikes. People who use these sites often list information about themselves, including the type of **music** they like, where they go on **holiday**, what **car** they drive etc. Companies who advertise on these sites can make their adverts visible only to the people who are **likely** to **buy** their product — this is **cheaper** and more **effective** than targeting everyone who uses the website. **Search engines** like Google™ often use **targeted advertising** — they show adverts that are **relevant** to the topic the user searched for.
5) New technology has also made it easier to extend a product's life cycle using an **extension strategy**. For example, **Apple®** have harnessed new technology which allows them to extend the life of the **iPod classic™** by increasing its **memory** and simplifying its **controls** and **software** .

Businesses and the Technological Environment

New **Technology** can cause the **Culture** of a **Business** to **Change**

1) Developments in **communication technology** have had a big impact on business culture. For example, a small business with a close-knit team used to face-to-face contact might find that employees become **demotivated** if they're encouraged to communicate more by **email**. On the other hand, email has been a good thing for businesses because it allows messages to be sent with **speed** and **ease**.
2) **Flexi-working** has also been made much easier by technology — **remote access** means employees can now access their work computer from their home PC.
3) Many businesses have **software** which allows companies to **monitor** exactly what employees are doing on their computers. This might increase **productivity**, but there's a big risk that **trust** between employee and employer could break down if the employee feels they're being **watched** the whole time.
4) A firm that switches to **automated** production processes might find that employees lose the desire to be **creative** and help with **problem-solving**. Making them responsible for **quality assurance** can help with this.
5) Developments in technology can encourage firms to be more **innovative**. If a firm is going to pursue a **diversification** strategy (see p.124), the culture of the business will need to encourage **risk-taking**.

New Technology isn't **Always** a **Good Thing**

1) A new piece of **CAM** equipment or a new computer system doesn't automatically make the **design** process **faster** or **cheaper**. Equally, just because a product is designed using an **advanced computer system** does not guarantee it will be a **success** in the market place — the customer still needs to **want** the product.
2) It can be difficult to **integrate** new technology with existing machines. The business might be less **efficient** during the time that it takes to **coordinate** multiple systems.
3) The **initial cost** of installing new technology is usually very high. The business needs to look carefully at the impact that buying new technology will have on its **cash flow**. The good news is that up-to-date machinery usually makes a business more **cost-effective** in the **long-term**.
4) New technology often requires workers to be **retrained**. Training can be **expensive** and it also has **opportunity costs**, e.g. the workers could be producing goods in the time it takes to train them.
5) New technology can mean that the business doesn't need as many workers. This might mean that workers need to be **retrained** and moved to **other departments** or it might lead to **redundancies**. Redundancies often have a **demotivating** effect on remaining staff. Trade unions in the car industry have been very resistant to automation because it reduces labour requirements.
6) New technology can affect the level of **customer service** a firm is able to provide. **Automated telephone switchboards** and **answering machines** are **cheaper** than telephone operators but many customers don't like listening to a machine and would rather deal directly with a **person**.

Practice Questions

Q1 What's the difference between a monopoly and monopolistic competition?

Q2 What are CAD and CAM technologies?

Q3 Describe three ways that technology can affect the culture of a business.

Q4 Give two potential disadvantages to a business of introducing new technology.

Exam Questions

Q1 Explain how businesses are affected by the power of customers and suppliers. [8 marks]

Q2 "Adopting new technology is always beneficial to the long-term success of a business." Discuss. [14 marks]

Computer says no...

Technology is a great thing for businesses, it really is. It's just that sometimes it has an annoying habit of crashing at really crucial moments. That's just one of its many disadvantages — make sure you learn the others on this page too. If your brain just doesn't seem to want to store the information, why not turn it off, wait ten seconds, then turn it back on again.

Internal Causes of Change

Change isn't always caused by external factors like competitors — it can come from within the business too.

Growth, Leaders and Business Performance can cause Change

1) **Growth** causes big changes to businesses — e.g. if businesses grow, they might have to relocate to bigger premises. See below for more on how growth affects businesses.
2) **New leaders** or **owners** can introduce changes into businesses (see p.193). These could be **small** changes like introducing flexible working hours, or **bigger** changes like making staff redundant.
3) If a business has been **performing badly**, managers are likely to make changes to try to **improve** the business' performance — e.g. if sales have fallen due to customer services staff being rude and unhelpful to customers, managers might **change** the customer services policy and **retrain** staff.

Organic Growth is when a business Grows Naturally

1) To see if a business is growing, you need to know what **size** it was in the first place. Business size is usually **measured** either by **revenue** or **number of employees**.
2) If a business is **successful**, it will **grow naturally** as demand for the company's products grows.
3) When an **existing** business expands as a result of its success, it's known as **organic growth** (or internal growth).
4) Businesses that grow organically are often able to **finance** their growth (more machinery, bigger premises, more staff, etc.) by **reinvesting profits** into the business. If they need **external finance**, it's **easier** to get hold of if they can demonstrate that they've been successful in the past.
5) Organic growth is **slower** and **more gradual** than external growth (i.e. mergers and takeovers — see next page), which means that it's easier for the company to **adapt** to growth.

Growing in Size brings its Own Problems

1) When a company changes from a **private limited company (Ltd)** to a **public limited company (PLC)**, the original owners won't find it so easy to maintain **control**, as they'll be responsible to a wider range of **shareholders**.
2) Once a company becomes a **PLC** then it's more open to being **taken over**. Anyone with enough money could buy enough of its shares to take a **controlling interest**.
3) Becoming a **PLC** can make managers more **short-termist**. Shareholders often want a **quick return** on investment through **dividend** payments, so they're sometimes **unlikely** to favour investment in **long-term projects**.
4) The process of **floating** the business on the **stock market** is **expensive** and **complicated**.
5) When companies **expand overseas** they need to be familiar with the **commercial law** of the host country (see p.127). Companies operating abroad may also have to deal with **different languages** and **cultures**.
6) Large companies can suffer from **diseconomies of scale** (see p.134). Diseconomies of scale are when the business grows so much that the **cost** of producing each unit **rises**.
7) Businesses have to avoid growing so much that they **dominate** their market and become a **monopoly** (see p.183) — companies can be penalised by the **Competition Commission** if they **damage competition** in a market.
8) Business owners may choose to **restrict** growth for the following reasons:
    1) They may want to **maintain the culture** of a small business.
    2) If the business "**overmarkets**" their products they could let customers down — the productive, administrative or distributive capacity may not be enough to handle the **increased demand**.
    3) The business will become more **complicated** to manage as it gets bigger.
    4) Growth requires the business to **secure additional financial resources**, which can be complicated.
    5) They may not want to put too much **strain** on their **cash flow** position.

Businesses may become Smaller — this is called Retrenchment

1) Businesses can choose to become smaller if they are suffering from **diseconomies of scale**.
2) They can **downsize** by choosing to **focus** all their energy on one area of the business. Doing too many different activities makes it hard to stay competitive.
3) Businesses can be forced to become smaller if they're **forced out of a market** by a larger competitor. They can also be forced to stop making some types of product by changes in **consumer taste**.
4) Also, changes in the **economy** such as **recession** or high interest rates may force a business to **downsize**.

Internal Causes of Change

Changes of Ownership can be Takeovers or Mergers

Watch out with these terms, because they're often used incorrectly.

1) The definition of a **takeover** is when one business buys enough shares in another, so that they have more than 50% of the total shares. This is called a **controlling interest**, and it means the buyer will always win in a vote of all shareholders.
2) A **merger** happens when two companies **join together** to form **one company**. They might keep the name of one of the original companies, or come up with a new name. The **shares** of the merged company are **transferred** to the shareholders of the old companies.

Takeovers can be Agreed or Hostile

1) **Hostile takeovers** happen when one **public limited company (PLC)** buys a **majority** of the shares in **another** PLC against the will of the directors of that company. It can do this because the shares of PLCs are **traded** on the stock exchange and **anyone** can buy them. The company will encourage existing shareholders to sell them the shares by offering a **premium** — an extra payment on top of the actual value of the shares.
2) **Agreed takeovers** happen when shareholders or other types of owners such as sole traders **agree** that they'll sell the business to someone else. This is usually because the owners believe it would benefit the **survival** of the business.

There are Many Reasons why companies Take Over or Merge With others

1) Some businesses decide to **diversify** and buy **existing** businesses operating in the market they want to **enter**. They **gain** from the **experience** of those employed by the businesses they buy, so they can make **profits** faster.
2) They may want to buy out companies that **operate in the same market** so that they can **reduce** the amount of **competition** that they face.
3) Businesses might buy out their **suppliers** or the **retailers** that sell their products in order to have more **control** over how their products are produced or sold.
4) Other companies will want to **extend** their market in the **same industry** but in **other countries**. E.g. T-Mobile (a German mobile phone operator) bought One-2-One (a British mobile phone operator).
5) Some businesses make profits from "**asset stripping**". They buy poorly performing businesses **cheaply** and then sell off the assets at a profit. The land on which the original business had its factory may be more valuable as building land, and could be **sold off** by the buyer at a nice profit.
6) Two large companies in the same industry may merge so that both could benefit from increased **economies of scale**. This is called **corporate integration**. In the car industry, companies such as Ford, Peugeot, BMW, and General Motors have bought out car manufacturers overseas. They can **switch production** from country to country where **labour costs** may be lower but the **expertise** already exists.

Practice Questions

Q1 What is organic growth?

Q2 Give three reasons why a business might choose not to grow.

Q3 What's the difference between a takeover and a merger?

Q4 When would you consider a takeover to be "hostile"?

Exam Question

Q1 A high street fashion retailer is concerned that the overall group profits are falling, despite turnover going up. The Board of Directors receive a report from their management consultants which indicates that the problem is one of rising costs. There have been delays in receiving deliveries from suppliers due to delays at the suppliers' factories. After some discussion the Board decides that they should buy two of their suppliers, both of which are small PLCs. Explain why you believe the Board took this decision. [4 marks]

Could a fertiliser business ever choose not to promote growth...

Growth might seem like a straightforward topic, but there's a fair amount to learn here. Make sure you learn the reasons why a business might want to grow or stay small. It's not just a case of "to grow or not to grow" either — two companies can merge together or one business can take over another business. Just don't have nightmares about hostile takeovers.

Planning for Change

Businesses decide on their corporate objectives and strategy, and then write it all up in a nice corporate plan.

Businesses make **Corporate Plans** which set out their overall **Strategy**

1) Corporate plans set out the **corporate objectives** for the business as a whole, and set out the **overall strategy** the business will use to reach its objectives.
2) For example, a corporate plan lays out **how** the business intends to **survive**, whether the business intends to **grow**, and **how** it might go about growing.
3) The corporate planning process involves several stages:
    1) Senior managers decide on the long-term **corporate objectives** of the business.
    2) They research the **market** to identify **opportunities** and **threats** to the business.
    3) They look at **each department** to identify the **strengths** and **weaknesses** of the business.
    4) They develop **strategies** to achieve the corporate objectives, focusing on the external **opportunities** and the internal **strengths** of the business.
    5) They **review** each strategy and make any **adjustments** that are necessary.
4) The corporate plan will also include an outline of **functional objectives** for each department. The details of the functional objectives are decided by the managers of each department.
5) The **purpose** of having a corporate plan is to make sure that all the parts of the business are **working together** towards the **same goal**. Businesses are much more likely to achieve their objectives this way.

Corporate plans are sometimes called 'strategic plans'.

External Factors can affect a business' **Corporate Plan**

The **external factors** that can affect a corporate plan are:

1) **Political and legal factors**
New laws can affect businesses. E.g. the ban on smoking in public places could be a **threat** to restaurants, because it might discourage smokers from eating out. On the other hand, it created an **opportunity** for restaurants to grow by targeting **families**, who might be more willing to eat in restaurants because of the smoking ban.
2) **Economic factors**
Customers' **spending habits** are affected by **economic factors**. High interest rates, low GDP, high unemployment and high inflation all mean that consumers have **less money** to spend, which is a threat to businesses. When interest rates, inflation and unemployment are low, and GDP is high, consumers will have **more disposable income**.
3) **Social factors**
Businesses need to consider migration patterns, an ageing population, etc.
4) **Technological factors**
Trends like the popularity of internet shopping and the availability of new machinery affect businesses.
5) **Environmental factors**
Customers are starting to consider the **environment** more, so businesses have to take things like **pollution** and the use of carrier bags into account when they make plans.

Internal Factors can also affect the **Corporate Plan**

1) **Skilled** and **motivated staff** help businesses to **achieve** their **objectives**. If staff are **unskilled** and **unmotivated**, this **limits** the plans that businesses can make.
2) Businesses also need to take into account how **good** their **products** are — it's hard to increase **sales** if there's no **demand** for your products.
3) The business' **finances** affect their **corporate plan** — e.g. poor cash flow restricts the plans that the business can make.
4) **Production capacity** can also limit the plans a business can make — e.g. if a business can't increase output, there's no point in trying to increase demand.

With a product like liver and kidney milkshake, achieving sales objectives is tricky.

Planning for Change

Contingency Plans prepare for Out Of The Ordinary Events

1) Corporate plans include **contingency plans** — planning what to do if something **unexpected** happens.
2) Contingency planning can help a business **respond** to lots of different types of **crisis**, such as:
   - **Faulty** or **dangerous products**.
   - A **hostile takeover bid**.
   - A **fire** that destroys a factory.
   - **Bad news** or **PR** in local papers.
   - A sudden **change in demand** for products caused by competitor activity or an economic crisis.
   - An **overseas** factory having to be shut down because it doesn't comply with **foreign law**.
   - **Lost** or **corrupt data** caused by computer network problems.
3) For example, most businesses have a **contingency plan** in case of **IT** disasters. They might take **backups** of their data at the end of each day. Some of these backups must be **stored off-site** — otherwise if there was a fire at the site, all the data would be **lost**, even the backups. That would be very expensive.
4) Businesses **can't** plan for **every unforeseen event**. Some adverse events are hard to plan for. Contingency planning is very **expensive**, so it's not worthwhile to plan for every single thing that could possibly go wrong. Managers have to decide **how likely** a particular adverse event is to happen, and how **badly** it would damage the business if it did happen.

Crisis management is when an unexpected situation **occurs**, and a business has to respond.

- It's **less effective** if managers haven't carried out **contingency planning** — they're **not prepared** so they have to make **snap decisions** about what to do. If they've done contingency planning then they've already decided what to do in that situation, which makes crisis management **much more straightforward**.
- Managers need to **act quickly** and **decisively** to **limit** the amount of **damage** caused. This is best achieved through **strong leadership**, e.g. an autocratic leader (see p. 190).

Corporate Plans can Help and Hinder businesses

1) Corporate plans can be **helpful** because they give the business a **clear direction**, and everyone working for the business knows what they're trying to achieve.
2) Corporate planning is also helpful because it makes managers think about the **strengths** and **weaknesses** of the business, and its **external threats** and **opportunities**. This helps managers to spot ways to **improve** the business that they might not have noticed otherwise.
3) The **drawback** of having a corporate plan is that it can **restrict** the business' **flexibility** — employees might think that they have to follow the corporate plan even if the situation has **changed** since it was made, or if they can think of a **better way** of doing things.

Practice Questions

Q1 What is included in a corporate plan?

Q2 List two external factors and two internal factors that affect corporate plans.

Q3 Give three examples of situations that a business might have a contingency plan for.

Q4 What's the difference between contingency planning and crisis management?

Exam Question

Q1 Discuss the extent to which corporate plans are helpful for businesses. [6 marks]

What's your contingency plan for falling down a well on the way to the exam...

Any of this stuff about corporate plans could come up in your exam, so make sure you're clear on what it's all about. You need to know what corporate plans are, the internal and external factors that affect them, and their pros and cons for businesses. Don't leave out the best bit — contingency plans and crisis management. I love a good crisis.

Leadership

There are different styles of leadership — different ways of getting things done and different ways of dealing with people.

Leaders Influence employees, **Managers Control** employees

1) **Leaders motivate** people. They **inspire** people to do things which they wouldn't do otherwise.
2) **Leaders'** power comes from their **personalities** — people do what their leaders tell them to do because they **want to**.
3) Managers are not always good leaders. **Managers set objectives** for their department and for the people in it. They **organise resources** to get the job done and **achieve** their objectives. Their power comes from their **position** — employees do what their managers tell them to do because they **have to**.
4) It's always helpful if managers have **leadership** qualities. **Managers** who are good **leaders** can **persuade** people that the decisions they make and the objectives they set are the **best** ones.

There are various different **Leadership Styles**

1) **Authoritarian** or **autocratic** style — the **leader makes decisions** on his or her own. The leader identifies the objectives of the business and says how they're going to be achieved. It's useful when you're dealing with lots of **unskilled** workers and in **crisis management**. This method requires lots of **supervision** and monitoring — workers can't make their own decisions. An authoritarian style can **demotivate** able and intelligent workers.
2) **Paternalistic** (fatherly) style is a softer form of the autocratic style. The leader **consults** the workers before making decisions, then **explains** the decisions to them to **persuade** them that the decisions are in their interest. Paternalistic leaders think that getting **involved** and caring about human relations is a **positive motivator**.
3) **Democratic** style — the leader encourages the workforce to **participate** in the decision-making process. Leaders **discuss** issues with workers, **delegate responsibility** and **listen** to advice. Democratic leaders have to be good communicators, and their organisations have to be good at dealing with a lot of **to and fro communication**. This leadership style shows leaders have a lot of confidence in the workforce — which leads to increased employee **motivation**. It also takes some of the **weight** of decision making off the leader.
4) **Laissez-faire** style is a **weak** form of leadership. **Managers** might offer employees coaching and support, but they **rarely interfere** in the running of the business. The workforce is left to get on with trying to achieve the objectives of the business with minimal input and control from the top. This **hands off** style of leadership would only be appropriate for a small, highly motivated team of **able** workers.

Internal and **External Factors** influence **Leadership Styles**

A leader's **behaviour** is influenced by factors inside and outside the business. The **best leaders** are the ones who can **adapt** their style to suit the situation.

Internal Factors

1) **Urgent** tasks need different leadership from **routine** tasks. Urgent tasks, like an **unexpected** large order coming in, may need an **authoritarian** leader to **tell** employees what to do and how to do it.
2) A **large**, **unskilled** workforce suits **authoritarian** leadership, whereas a **small**, **educated** workforce suits a **democratic** approach much better. E.g. when a business is **growing** and takes on lots of new employees, the owner might take an authoritarian approach — once the new employees are more familiar with the business, the owner can give them more responsibility and use a more democratic approach.
3) The way the organisation's been run in the **past** affects the **expectations** of the workforce, which affects how they might **respond** to leadership.

External Factors

1) In a **recession**, a business needs strong leadership to guide it through difficult economic times. **Authoritarian** or **paternalistic** leaders can be efficient in times of crisis — they can issue **clear, quick commands** because they don't have to consult others. This can **reassure** workers during a recession.
2) When the economy is **growing**, managers don't always need such a strong leadership approach. **Democratic** leaders can take the time to **communicate** with employees.
3) **Increased competition** requires **democratic** leaders who can **motivate** their employees to **adapt** to change or expansion. **Laissez-faire** leaders are more **complacent** and don't always provide enough **leadership** to guide their workforce during times of change.

Leadership

Leadership is important in **Managing Change**

1) Businesses often need to make **changes** in order to stay **competitive**. They might change teams around, bring in new technology, move to a new location or alter their product range.
2) When businesses make changes, the employees affected by the changes are likely to be **uncomfortable** with the idea of changing, and to be **afraid** of the unknown. E.g. they might worry that they'll lose their job, that they won't see the same colleagues any more, or that their role will change and it will be too difficult for them.
3) Employees might react to the idea of change by being **demotivated** and **uncooperative**, and they might even actively **resist** the change, e.g. by going on strike.
4) Effective leadership can **avoid** the problems that can be caused by change. Leaders can use several methods to persuade employees to accept change:
   - leaders need to **communicate** with employees and help them **understand** why the change is necessary.
   - leaders can **retrain** employees if their job is changing, so that they feel **comfortable** in their new role.
   - leaders can **involve** employees in making decisions about how and when changes are made — this will make employees feel more **in control** and **less fearful** of the changes.
5) In times of change, **authoritarian** leadership might make employees more **fearful** of change, and they might be more likely to go on strike or resist the change in another way. **Laissez-faire** leadership can mean that employees don't have **confidence** that changes will work out well, so they won't be **supportive**. The most **suitable** forms of leadership for helping employees cope with change are the **paternalistic** and **democratic** styles.
   See p. 196-197 for more on managing change.

Good Leadership can **Transform** the **Workforce** and the **Business**

Leaders have a big **impact** on the people they work with. **Effective leaders** can meet the needs of the workforce and the demands of the business. **Good leadership** is really important for a successful business.

1) Good leadership is often based on **listening** to the workforce. Employees whose contributions are valued are **happier** and more **productive**. Increased production leads to increased **profits**.
2) When employees **trust** their leader, they're more likely to feel **secure** in their jobs. They're more likely to stay **loyal** to their company and want to contribute to its success by **working hard** and **adapting to change**. **Low staff turnover** is also good for morale.
3) Good leaders can look to the **future** and see the **potential for expansion**. They consider the options and take **sensible risks** for the good of the organisation. They are **not complacent** — they take every **opportunity** to help their business grow. Sensible expansion can lead to **increased profits**.
4) Effective leaders can think **"outside the box"**. This means they can find **creative** solutions to problems and **inventive** new ways to expand the business which allow the company to stay **ahead** of its competitors. Thinking **"outside the box"** can be seen as a bit of **cliché** and there's a danger that managers get **carried away** trying to find **unconventional** solutions to problems.

Practice Questions

Q1 What's the difference between a manager and a leader?

Q2 Give three internal factors which affect leadership style.

Q3 Why is leadership important when changes are happening in a business?

Exam Question

Q1 Manufacturer DCP Furniture must increase productivity by 25% by next March. Manager Sam Raynes has an easy-going, friendly attitude to his staff and likes to involve them in decision making. Explain how Sam might need to adapt his leadership style in order to meet the productivity targets. [12 marks]

Take me to your leader...

The key to all this is being able to say what is appropriate for a particular situation — in the exam, you might get a case study of two managers with different leadership styles, and be asked to assess whose ideas are best for the situation the business is in. A lot depends on whether the issue is related to business practices or the needs of the workforce.

Organisational Culture

Organisational culture isn't about going to the opera or reading Dostoevsky novels — it's to do with a company's values.

Organisational Culture is the Way a business Does Things

1) **Organisational culture** is the way that a business does things, and the way that people in the business expect things to be done. It shapes the **expectations** and **attitudes** of staff and managers.
2) Because organisational culture **affects staff behaviour** and how they make decisions, it has an effect on planning, objective setting and strategy.
3) Organisational culture is **created** and **reinforced** by company **rules**, **managerial attitudes** and behaviour, **recruitment** policies that recruit people who "fit in", **reward** systems (e.g. how bonuses are calculated and allocated), etc.
4) A company's culture can be **identified** by looking at its **heroes** (people who exemplify the company's values), the **stories** that are told repeatedly within the company, **symbols** (like staff mottos and sayings) that represent the company's values, and the **ceremonies** (such as office parties) that the business holds.

Organisational Culture can be Strong or Weak

Strong culture

Organisational culture is strong when employees **believe** in the corporate values of the company. Having a strong corporate culture has several advantages:

- Employees need **less supervision**, because their behaviour will naturally tend to fit in with the company's values.
- Staff are more **loyal** to the business, so **staff turnover** is lower.
- It increases employees' **motivation**, so they work more productively.

Weak culture

Weak culture is where the employees of a company **don't** share the company's values, and have to be **forced** to comply with them (e.g. through **company policies**).

There are Four Main Types of Organisational Culture

Charles Handy identified the following **four types** of organisational culture in 1993:

1) **Power culture** — organisations where decision-making authority is limited to a **small number** of people — perhaps just **one person**.
2) In these businesses, objectives reflect the wishes of the person at the **top**.

1) **Role culture** — **bureaucratic** firms where authority is defined by job title.
2) These organisations tend to **avoid risk** for fear of failure, so they develop **cautious** aims and objectives.
3) The danger here is that overcautious companies can lose out in the long run, especially in **new** or **expanding** markets where strategies need to be developed and implemented quickly. Organisations with role culture often fail to **exploit opportunities** before their competitors do.

1) **Person culture** — loose organisations of individual workers, usually **professional partnerships** such as solicitors.
2) The objectives of these firms will be defined by the **personal ambitions** of the individuals involved. The firms have to ensure that the individuals actually have **common goals**.

1) **Task culture** places an emphasis on getting specific **tasks** done.
2) Task culture gets **small teams** together to work on a project, then disbands them. There may be **conflict** between teams for resources and budgets. It can be confusing if a firm has too many products or **projects**.
3) This culture supports objectives which are based around **products** (e.g. make Product X the market leader).
4) Task cultures respond well to **management by objectives**. Management by objectives translates corporate objectives into **specific targets** for each **department** and for each **individual employee**.

In addition to Handy's models, **Stephen McGuire** identified another model of organisational culture in 2003 — **entrepreneurial culture**. In entrepreneurial cultures, employees are encouraged to look for **new ways** of bringing **revenue** into the company. **Innovation** and **creativity** are valued.

Organisational Culture

Managers might want to Change the Organisational Culture

There are **two** main reasons why the managers of a business might want to **change** the organisational culture :

1) The organisational culture of a business depends on the **preferences** of its **leaders**. When a new manager joins a business, they might change it to make it more **similar** to businesses they have worked in **before**. E.g. if a manager who is used to working in a business with a **role culture** starts working in a business with a **task culture**, they might **force** the business to adopt a role culture because that is what they are used to.
2) A business might change its culture in order to be more **competitive**. E.g. businesses with a **power culture** can be **slow** to spot ways to **save money**, or more **efficient** ways of working, so adopting an **entrepreneurial culture** where all the staff are constantly looking for ways to **improve** the business could make the business more **competitive**.

Changing the Organisational Culture can be Difficult

1) Employees usually **resist** any kind of change, including changes in **organisational culture**. Employees who have worked for the business for a long time are **especially likely** to resist changes to the organisational culture, because they have been used to one way of working for a long time.
2) Changing organisational culture means changing the **attitudes** and **behaviour** of staff, so it's much more **complicated** than changing things like pricing structure. E.g. the managers of a clothes retailer might want to introduce a more **customer-focused** culture, but bringing in loyalty cards and generous refund policies **won't** achieve that if staff are **rude** to the customers.
3) Changing the organisational culture can also be very **expensive**. It might involve buying new **equipment**, changing **office layout**, or changing the company **logo** or **motto** on stationery, advertising, etc. This means that businesses can't always afford to change their culture, as much as they would like to.

Corporate Culture is Important for the Stakeholders of the business

The **organisational culture** of a business affects its **staff**, **customers** and **shareholders**:

Staff
Culture affects the **motivation** of the employees. E.g. a **power culture** or **role culture** can **demotivate** creative staff who can see ways to **improve** things but don't have the **power** to put changes into practice.

Customers
Organisational culture affects **customers' loyalty** to a business. Businesses with a **customer-focused** culture are more likely to have loyal customers.

Shareholders
The level of **risk** that businesses take depends on their organisational culture. Shareholders might get **low returns** on their investment if they invest in a company with a **low-risk culture**, whereas investing in a company with a **high-risk culture** gives shareholders the possibility of **high returns**, but there's also the risk that they'll **lose money**.

Practice Questions

Q1 What is organisational culture?

Q2 Describe the power culture, and its approach to setting objectives.

Q3 Why is changing organisational culture difficult?

Exam Question

Q1 Explain the importance of organisational culture for the stakeholders of a business. [6 marks]

Organisational Culture Club — an 80s tribute band formed by executives...

This stuff on organisational culture's pretty interesting I reckon. Remember that the organisational culture of a business affects all sorts of things — from whether or not they take financial risks, to whether they have office parties. When you get a case study, look for clues about the culture of the business — it can tell you a lot about what's happening and why.

Making Strategic Decisions

Ah, decisions, decisions...tricky business.

Decision-Making is essential for Planning

There are **three types** of decisions that businesses have to make — **strategic**, **tactical** and **operational**.

Strategic decisions

1) These are **long-term** decisions affecting the **general direction** of the business. They are made to help the business achieve its **long term aims**.
2) Strategic decisions are usually **expensive**, so they are **high-risk** decisions. It's not always obvious whether the business made the right decision until a long time **after** they make it. E.g. in 2001 Marks & Spencer opened its first **'Simply Food'** stores in the UK. Launching the stores was **expensive**, and M&S would have lost a lot of money if they had failed. However, the 'Simply Food' stores have proved **successful** and there are now **more than 300** branches in the UK, so the strategic decision seems to have been a good one.
3) Strategic decisions are usually taken by the **owners** or **directors** of a business.

Tactical decisions

1) These are **medium-term** decisions that are made **after** the **strategic decisions** have been agreed. E.g. Marks & Spencer's decisions about the **exact location** of 'Simply Food' shops was a **tactical decision.**
2) It's usually much **easier** to predict the **impact** of tactical decisions than strategic decisions.
3) Tactical decisions are usually taken by the **senior managers** of a business.

Operational decisions

1) These are **routine decisions** that are taken on a **daily** basis, e.g. store managers at Tesco decide how many check-outs to open at different times of the day.
2) Operational decisions are usually taken by **middle** or **junior managers.**

Information Management involves Collecting and Processing Data

Managers rely on having the right information when they need it so they can make the most sensible decisions.

1) Raw data is **gathered** by the relevant department, e.g. the Marketing department conduct market research to work out what the consumer market thinks about their product, or to find out more about the shopping habits of the market segment. This data can be quantitative or qualitative (see p. 118-119).
2) The information is then **processed** by that department and **organized** e.g. into graphs, charts, tables.
3) Data needs to be **maintained** and **updated** to make sure the most up to date information is accessible.
4) The most useful data is:

- directly **relevant**
- **up to date**
- **correct** and **verified**
- in the right amount of **detail**

Management Information Systems and ICT help managers make Decisions

1) **Management information systems** (MIS) are the **computerised systems** in a business that **gather** and **analyse information** for managers to use when making their decisions.
2) The types of data stored and analysed by management information systems are:
   - **Marketing and sales** data (e.g. sales levels for each product, number of sales made by each salesperson)
   - **Production** data (e.g. output levels, quality standards)
   - **HRM** data (e.g. employee turnover)
3) If managers receive **too much data** from their management information system, they can become **overwhelmed** when trying to make decisions. This is **information overload**. Businesses need to focus on the **quality** rather than the **quantity** of data that a management information system produces.
4) Using **ICT** can also help improve decision-making, or help with tasks such as **planning** their cash flow. ICT also helps make **forecasts** more **accurate** — e.g. managers can use computer programs to assess past sales for a product and then extrapolate the information to predict future sales (see p. 121).

Making Strategic Decisions

Several **Factors** influence **Decision-Making**

1) **Pressure groups** sometimes try to influence company decisions, e.g. by using the threat of **bad publicity** to persuade decision-makers to act in the interest of the pressure group. They can use the media, leaflets and petitions to **raise awareness** of their cause. **Consumer response** to pressure groups can affect business practices, e.g. if a pressure group publishes **evidence** that a clothing brand has been using child labour or sweatshops, consumers may switch to a competitor brand, depending on how strongly they feel.
2) **Corporate culture** (see p.192-193) also influences decision-making. A business with a **risk-taking culture** will encourage people to take **risky decisions** if the potential **rewards** are **high**. A firm with a more **conservative** culture will **discourage risk taking**, e.g. by not promoting people whose decisions have led to costly mistakes in the past.
3) The business' **stakeholders** also try to influence decisions — e.g. **shareholders** might not want businesses to make risky decisions, because they won't want to **lose money** on their investment. Stakeholders **don't always agree** so managers have to think about which stakeholder group is most **important** to them.
4) The firm's **ethics** have an effect too — e.g. they might decide not to switch to a cheaper supplier if that supplier is less environmentally aware than their current one. A company's **actual ethics** do not always agree with their **perceived ethics**. A business can decide to **market itself** as an ethical company to influence the public's perception. Managers need to decide whether an ethical policy is part of the organisation's strategy.
5) **Resource availability** is also a factor — the business might not plan to grow if there's a **shortage** of local **labour**.

Decisions can be made **Scientifically** — or based on **Gut Feeling**

Tony's gut feeling told him it was nearly time for dinner.

1) Scientific decision-making means **collecting** data, **analysing** it to arrive at a **conclusion** (or decision) and then **testing** that decision to see if it works (see p.120-123). It allows businesses to **predict** the outcomes of complex decisions. The **alternative** to the scientific approach is **inspired guesswork** based on **experience** or **gut reaction**.
2) There are three common scientific decision-making **techniques**:
   - **Break-even analysis** shows how much businesses need to **sell** to cover their **costs**.
   - **Investment appraisal techniques** help managers predict which **capital investment project** will give them the most favourable **financial return**.
   - **Decision trees** allow managers to **measure** the likely **financial impact** of alternative decisions. They do this by considering the **probability** of different events occurring.
3) Scientific decision-making is **costly** and **time-consuming** because it involves **collecting** and **analysing** a lot of data. However, it **reduces** the risk of making **expensive mistakes** if the company has to make a big decision.
4) Some managers have **good intuition** — they can **sense** when a decision is the right one based on **past experience**. When their intuition is right, it can lead to great business decisions and keep the company ahead of its competition. It's risky to rely on intuition all the time though, because people can make mistakes.
5) The **type** of problem influences how managers make decisions. **Routine problems** can be handled with an experience-based approach. **Unfamiliar** problems and **big decisions** need research and analysis.

Practice Questions

Q1 What does MIS stand for?

Q2 Describe five things that can influence strategic decision-making.

Q3 What is the main advantage of using scientific decision-making rather than 'gut feeling'?

Exam Question

Q1 Explain the difference between strategic, tactical and operational decisions. [6 marks]

My gut feeling is it's nearly the end of the book...

Not much more to go now — just two more pages in this section and then a few maths and exam-type bits and bobs, and you'll be done. Anyway, using ICT can help managers to analyse lots of different information, but it can also make them want to throw the computer out of the window if the information is wrong or there's too much information to take in.

Managing Change

You're probably ready for a change from all this learning about change. Well don't worry, because you're almost at the end of Section 8 now — phew.

Managers need **Strategies** to **Overcome Resistance** to change

1) The most **successful changes** happen when all employees have opportunities to be **fully consulted**.
2) Staff don't like being kept **in the dark**. They cope better when they have **information** about what's going on. **Lack of information** can lead to rumour and **distrust** of management's **intentions**, which affects **motivation** and **morale**.
3) Employees also don't like to feel **powerless**. They cope better when they're given the opportunity to **have their say**, and **influence decisions** in some way.

There are **two strategies** commonly used by managers to overcome resistance:

1) Everyone who may be affected by the change is expected to **become involved** at the **planning stage**. This helps them to understand **why change** is necessary. When a decision needs to be taken, all employees affected have an opportunity to **comment** on the proposal, **suggest** changes and eventually reach an **agreement**. This is easier to achieve when change is incremental but more difficult at times of crisis. This strategy is used by **democratic** managers.
2) All staff affected by change are kept **informed** at each stage of the process, but don't get the chance to become involved in planning the change. Managers try to **persuade** employees that the changes are a good idea. This is the strategy that **paternalistic** managers use.

Project Champions and **Project Groups** can help change **Succeed**

1) A **project champion** is a manager within the company whose role is to **encourage** employees to **support** changes. They do this by being **enthusiastic** about the changes, and trying to spread their enthusiasm among the staff. They explain to people why they think the changes are a **good idea**, and what the **benefits** will be. This makes employees feel more **positive** about the changes.
2) **Project groups** are groups of **employees** who are involved in the change process. They might be involved in making **decisions** about the changes, or they might just sit in on **meetings** so that they're kept **informed** about what's going on. Other employees are likely to be **less suspicious** of changes when a project group is involved, because they know that they're getting the full picture of what's going on, rather than just hearing what managers want them to know.

Being the project champion was ok, but what Jon really wanted was a pay rise.

Teamwork and **Motivation** can help to **Achieve Change**

1) Employees are usually **resistant** to changes at work. But if change is **managed well**, businesses can get the staff on their side, which will make the whole process a lot **easier**.
2) Staff who want to **avoid** change can cause a lot of **trouble** for businesses — times of change are already difficult for businesses because there's a lot to organise and adjust to, but if staff are uncooperative then implementing changes becomes almost **impossible**. E.g. if a business wants to bring in a new, more efficient, system for taking orders but staff refuse to use it or deliberately make mistakes, the business will be in a **worse position** than it was to start with. If staff go on **strike** then no work will get done at all.
3) On the other hand, if managers can **motivate** employees using the techniques described above, changes will happen much more smoothly, because staff will be **committed** to making the changes successful, so they'll be willing to do whatever they need to do to make it work.
4) When all the employees in a business work **together** as a team, there's a much greater chance that the changes will work than if some of the employees are **resisting** the changes or trying to make things go wrong.

Managing Change

The way businesses **Manage Change** depends on their **Corporate Culture**

Organisational culture (see p.192-193) has a big impact on how companies handle change, and whether staff are **open** to change or **resistant** to it:

Task culture

Staff working in a company with a task culture are likely to be **comfortable** with change because they are used to **changing teams** often and working with a variety of people. This means that they are likely to be **less resistant** to change in general.

Power culture

All the **decisions** are made by **one** person or **a few** people at the **top** of the business. This means that employees are likely to be **more resistant** to change, because they don't have the opportunity to give their **opinions** on what changes should and shouldn't be made. They might also be resistant to changes because they don't have enough **faith** in senior managers who they feel are **out of touch** with the day-to-day activities of the business.

Role culture

In companies with a role culture, **decisions** come from **senior managers**, so employees don't have the opportunity to be involved in the decision-making process. Change is also quite **rare** in companies with a role culture because they **avoid** taking risks and trying new things — this means employees are likely to resist any changes that are brought in because they're **not used** to doing things differently.

Entrepreneurial culture

Change is a big part of entrepreneurial culture, and **all employees** are responsible for coming up with ideas to **improve** how the business is run. If employees are encouraged to be **creative** and **innovative**, they are likely to be much more **open** to change, especially when changes are made based on their suggestions.

Person culture

Change in businesses with a person culture can only happen when the **goals** of each person in the business change. **Decisions** are made **jointly**, so employees are likely to be **comfortable** with changes that are made because they have agreed to them.

Involving Employees in change **Reduces** their **Resistance**

Employees are likely to be more open to change if they are **involved** in planning changes, kept **informed** about how changes are progressing, and provided with the **training** and **resources** they need to adapt to the new way of working. The **two main ways** of involving employees in the change process are through **total quality management** and **kaizen**.

1) **Total quality management** (TQM) is a process where **every worker** is **responsible** for the quality of the product. Workers who are encouraged to take responsibility for tasks and get involved in improving working practices every day are often **less resistant** to change when it comes. It may have been one of the **workers** on the factory floor who spotted a change that could be made to improve quality. See p.144 for more on TQM.
2) **Kaizen groups** promote **continuous improvement** and so when workers meet to discuss **improvements** that can be made, they are **expecting** change to happen, and are **open** to it. See p.145 for more on kaizen.

Practice Questions

Q1 What are the two main strategies that managers can use to overcome resistance to change?

Q2 What is a project champion?

Q3 How does total quality management reduce employees' resistance to change?

Exam Question

Q1 Explain how corporate culture affects how changes are made, and whether they are successful. [8 marks]

We are the (project) champions...

Yep, you've done it. That's the last page of the last section in the book (except for the handy maths and exams tips that are up next). Before you get too excited and start jumping up and down on the furniture and singing with joy at the top of your voice, make sure you know everything really well — project champions, corporate culture, and all the rest. The end.

Maths Bits

You need to understand a bit about maths if you want to do well in Business Studies.

Businesses work out **Percentage Changes** in figures

1) Businesses work out **percentage increases** or **decreases** in sales, revenue, profit, etc. so that they can see how the business' performance is **progressing** over time. Percentage changes can show **trends** in performance.
2) The **formula** for calculating percentage change is →

$$\text{Percentage change} = \frac{\text{new figure} - \text{previous figure}}{\text{previous figure}} \times 100$$

3) E.g. if a company's profits have gone up from £20 000 to £23 000, this is a percentage increase of (23 000 – 20 000) ÷ 20 000 × 100 = 15%.
4) It's important not to **underestimate** the importance of large changes in figures even if they only produce a **small percentage change**. E.g. a fall in revenue of £1 million shouldn't be overlooked even if it's only a 2% decrease.

Index Numbers show **Changes** in data over time

1) **Index numbers** are a way of showing **changes** in revenue, profits, etc. over a period of time.
2) The **earliest figure** is the **base figure** — this base figure is given an index value of **100**. The index values for the later figures are worked out by **dividing** each figure by the **base figure** and then **multiplying** by **100**.
3) The main **advantage** of index numbers is that they make it easy to see **trends** within the business.

Year	Total revenue	Revenue index (2005 = 100)
2005	£35 200	100
2006	£38 700	110
2007	£43 200	123
2008	£56 600	161

base figure

Graphs can display **Data Clearly**

1) It can sometimes be difficult to get a clear picture of what's happening in a business just by looking at the figures.
2) Displaying data in **graphs** and **charts** makes it easy to **understand** without wading through pages of figures.
3) **Bar charts** and **line graphs** make **trends** in data more obvious. They can also be used to **compare** sets of data (e.g. a company's sales figures can be plotted against its competitors', or against its own sales figures from previous years).
4) **Pie charts** are useful for showing **market share**, or for showing what proportion of a company's sales come from each of its products.

Graphs can sometimes be **Misleading**

1) Graphs are a **useful** way of displaying data, but they can sometimes give a **false impression** of what's going on.
2) If you're given a graph in an exam, keep an eye out for axes that don't start at **zero** — they can make differences look much bigger than they really are. If you're comparing graphs, check that they both use the same **scale**.

The two graphs below both show profits made by Lulu's, a chain of hair salons, over a four-year period.

This graph seems to show that profits have **more than doubled**. But look at the axis — it starts at **100**, not 0.

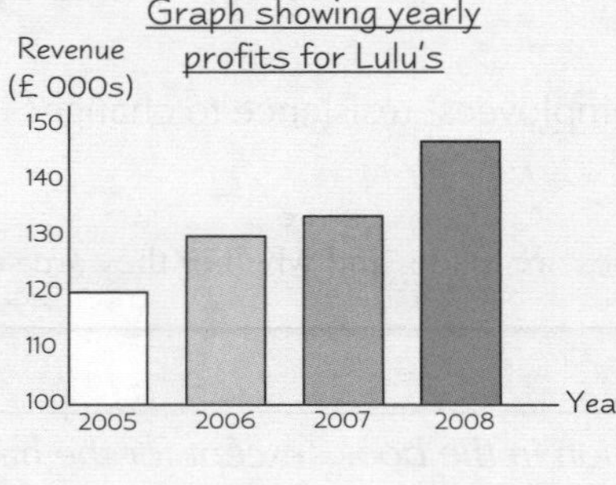

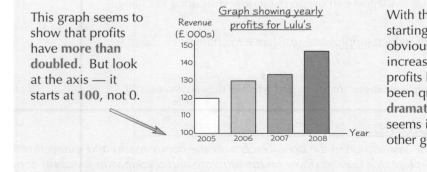

With the axis starting at **0**, it's obvious that the increase in profits hasn't been quite as **dramatic** as it seems in the other graph.

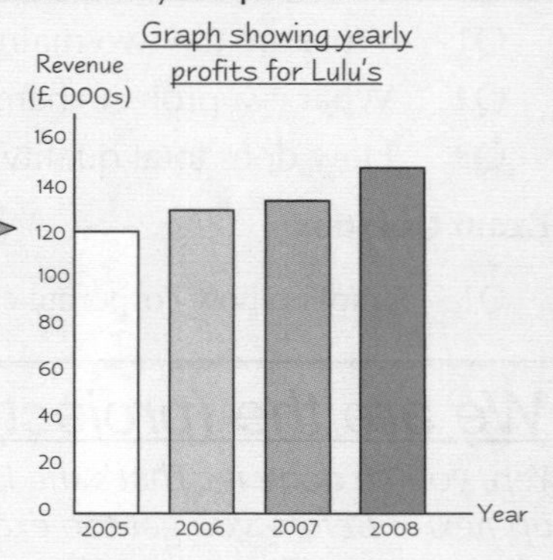

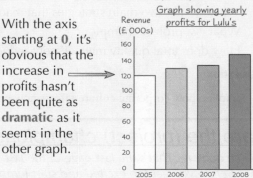

Maths Bits

The Mean is the Average Value in a set of data

1) The **mean** is the **sum** of all the **values** in a data set divided by the **number of values** in the set.
2) It's calculated using this formula:

$$\text{Mean} = \frac{\text{total amount}}{\text{number of values}}$$

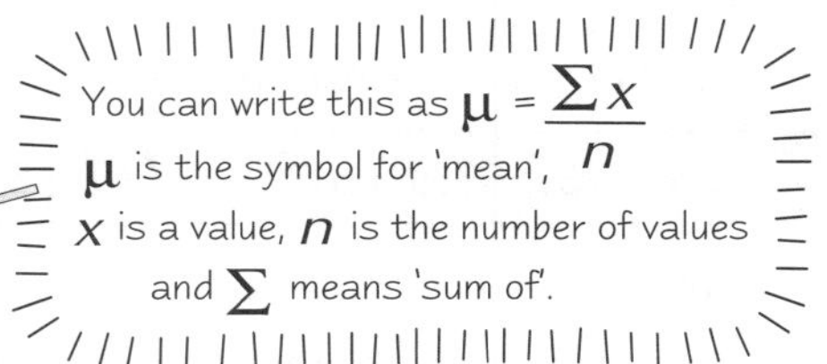

You can write this as $\mu = \frac{\Sigma x}{n}$
μ is the symbol for 'mean',
x is a value, n is the number of values
and Σ means 'sum of'.

Anna is thinking of opening a restaurant. She wants to know if there's enough **demand** for a new restaurant in her town, so she asks five people **how often** they eat out on average per month. The results are: 3, 2, 12, 8 and 10.

The **mean** is: $\frac{3 + 2 + 12 + 8 + 10}{5} = 7$

3) The **median** is the **middle value** in a set of data when all the numbers are listed in **order** from lowest to highest.
4) The **mode** is the **most common** value in a data set.

In the following set of data: 4, 5, 7, 10, 11, 12, 12, 13, 16
- the **median** is **11**, the 5th value out of 9. If there's an **even** number of values, you take the **mean** of the two middle numbers to get the median.
- the **mode** is **12**, because it's the only number that appears more than once.

Standard Deviation shows how Spread Out values are around the Mean

1) **Standard deviation** is used to measure the **distribution** of values around the **mean**. A **low** standard deviation means that all the data is **clustered** around the mean, and a **high** standard deviation means that the data is **spread out** a lot.
2) The **formula** for standard deviation looks pretty scary, but it's actually quite straightforward when you know what all the **symbols** stand for:

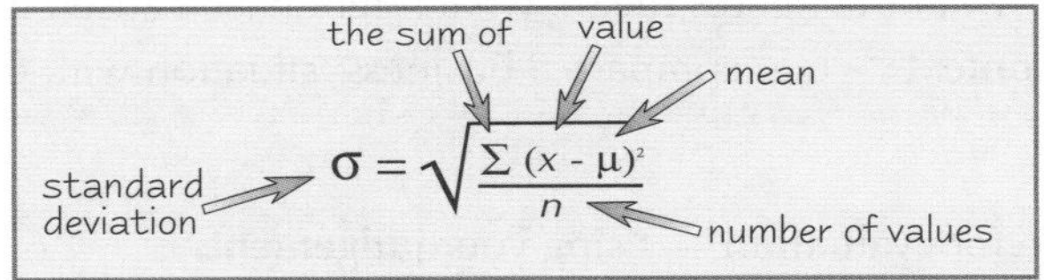

Anna can work out the **standard deviation** of her data about how often people eat out. She already knows that the **mean** is 7 (see above), so she **subtracts 7** from each value, **squares** the results and **adds** them all together, **divides** the total by **5** (the number of values) and takes the **square root** of the result. This is shown in the table:

x	3	2	12	8	10		
$x-\mu$	-4	-5	5	1	3	**sum**	**SD**
$(x-\mu)^2$	16	25	25	1	9	76	3.9

Anna could do similar market research in **other towns** and work out the standard deviation of those data sets to see if people's eating-out habits are **more varied** (a standard deviation of more than 3.9), or **more similar** to each other (a standard deviation of less than 3.9) than in her town.

Practice Questions

Q1 How are percentage changes worked out?

Q2 What do index numbers show?

Q3 What's the formula for standard deviation?

Exam Question

Q1 Explain how graphs can sometimes be misleading. [3 marks]

It's a bit "mean" to make you learn all this maths, isn't it...

You might have thought that you left maths behind after GCSE, but here it is, popping up again like a long lost friend/ bad penny. Even if you hate maths, you still need to know these few bits because you're more than likely going to have to analyse a graph or some figures in the exam. So learn it all and then you've just got 'Do Well in Your Exam' left. Hurray.

Do Well in Your Exam

These pages tell you what the actual exams will be like — so it won't be too much of a surprise on the day. You don't need to learn this stuff as such, but it's worth making sure you understand it.

*You get marks for **AO1 (showing knowledge)** and **AO2 (applying knowledge)***

AO1

1) **AO1** marks are for **content** and **knowledge**.
2) You'll only get about **a few marks** for this, whether the question is worth 10 marks, 18 marks or even over 30 marks. At A2 level, they assume you know what most **basic business terms** mean.

AO2

1) **AO2** marks are for **applying** your **knowledge** to a **situation** — e.g. thinking about the type of ownership of the business in the question, the product or service it's selling, the type of market it's in.
2) There's usually only a **small number** of marks available for this too.

*You get marks for **AO3 (analysis)** and **AO4 (evaluation)***

Most of the marks for any **long-answer** question are for **AO3** and **AO4**.

AO3

1) **AO3** marks are for **analysis** — thinking about benefits, drawbacks, causes, effects and limitations.
2) Use your knowledge to **explain** your answer and **give reasons**.
3) With data, say what the figures **mean**, what might have **caused** them and what the **consequences** might be.
4) Write about **context** — e.g. compare a business' situation with the industry as a whole, or with a competitor.

AO4

1) **AO4** marks are for **evaluation** — using your **judgement**.
2) Give **two sides** of an argument, and say which you think is **strongest**. Consider **advantages** and **disadvantages** and weigh them up.
3) You don't need a definite answer. You can point out that it depends on various factors — as long as you say what the factors are, and say why the right choice depends on those factors. Use your **judgement** to say what the **most important factors** are.
4) Relate your answer to the **business** described in the **question** and to the **situation** in the **question**. Give reasons **why** the business would make a particular decision, and how and why the particular circumstances might **affect** their **decision**.

"I might...maybe...we'll see" — there are some situations in life where it is important to give a definite answer.

Most** questions cover **All** the **Assessment Objectives

You might get a couple of questions that are **just** marked on AO1, AO2 and AO3. These are likely to be the **shorter** questions that ask you to **"analyse"** or **"examine"** something. But because this is A2, **most** of the questions you get will have marks for **all** of AO1, AO2, AO3 and AO4.

For example, an **evaluation** question has some AO1 marks for **content**, some AO2 marks for **application**, some AO3 marks for **analysis** and some AO4 marks for **evaluation**.

- You can **lose marks** for poor content, application and analysis.
- If the question's based on a **case study**, you'll **lose marks** if you don't **relate** the answer **specifically** to the situation in the **case study** (e.g. if it's a question about the pros and cons of relocating abroad, write about the pros and cons for the company in the question, not just businesses in general).

There are still **more** marks for analysis and evaluation than for **basic facts**, though.

Do Well in Your Exam

A2 Material is Based on AS Material — your AS Work is Relevant

Even though you're taking the A2 exams, you'll still be expected to **use information** from the AS course:

1) As **background knowledge** to help you **apply knowledge**, and **analyse** and **evaluate** business decisions.
2) "**Synoptic**" questions test knowledge from the AS part of the course as well as the A2 part. The **Unit 3** exam paper contains synoptic questions based on a **case study**. For your **Unit 4** exam, the paper will have **some questions** specifically about **A2 topics** and **some synoptic questions**. There's more about synoptic questions below.

Synoptic questions test Everything you've Learnt in the last Two Years

Both the papers you did at AS-Level were based on **specific topics**, which meant you could pretty much tell what the examiners were going to ask you about. As part of the A2, you'll sit two **synoptic papers** which test your knowledge of **everything** you've learnt since the **beginning** of **AS**. It sounds **hard**, but it doesn't have to be, as long as you remember these things:

Synoptic papers for goldfish test everything they've learnt in the last three seconds.

1) Synoptic papers are a great chance for you to show the examiner just **how much** you **know**. You **choose** what material to include in your answer, so it's a good opportunity to **focus** on the bits of the course you were **good at** or **enjoyed**.
2) However, you can only focus on issues that are **relevant** to the question. Don't go on and on about motivation if it's not at all **related** to what you're being asked. The best way to get **high marks** is to always clearly **link** what you're talking about back to the **original question**.
3) **Practise** linking ideas together. You don't need to write whole essays when you're revising. Just try to get a big supply of **practice questions** and give yourself **15 minutes** to scribble down all the things you can think of that are linked to the question. It's a good idea to get used to spotting all the **different factors** that are involved when a business makes a **decision**. There's an **example** of a synoptic question essay plan below:

"The balance sheet is the only thing stakeholders need to look at to get a good picture of a company's activities." Discuss this view.

Balance sheet might be more important to certain groups of stakeholders than others, e.g. shareholders.

Government is a stakeholder — they'll want to know that laws (e.g. minimum wage) aren't being broken to achieve high levels of profit. This information isn't on the balance sheet.

The business plan and the company's corporate objectives are important because they show future plans as well as current position.

Corporate Social Responsibility Policy — CSR could have an impact on long-term profitability. Many companies have a written CSR document which stakeholders could look at alongside balance sheet.

Don't forget to include a conclusion at the end of your essay.

You get marks for Quality of Written Communication

Jotting down a quick essay plan will help.

1) You have to write a **well-structured essay**, not a list of bullet points.
2) You need to use **specialist vocabulary** when it's appropriate, so it's worth **learning** some of the **fancy terms** used in this book (check out the glossary for the ones you really need to know).
3) Write **neatly** enough for the examiner to be able to read it and use good **spelling**, **grammar** and **punctuation**. You don't get many marks for this — but remember that if the examiner can't **read** or **understand** your writing, you won't get the **other marks** either.

Make sure you thoroughly revise Words and Concepts you often get Mixed Up

Everybody has certain topics they find it **difficult** to get their head around. The important thing is to spend **extra time** revising the bits you find really **tricky**, rather than concentrating on the things you find easy and hoping the tough stuff doesn't come up. It might also be helpful to **check** you're absolutely clear on the **difference** between these **frequently confused terms**.

Price and **cost**
Productivity and **productive efficiency**
Liquidation and **bankruptcy**
Interest rate and **exchange** rate
Differentiation and **diversification**
Quota and **stratified** sampling

Do Well in Your Exam

There are two **Exam Units** at A2

1) There are **two examinations** at A2 — one covers **unit 3** and one covers **unit 4**. They're each worth **25%** of the total A level marks. Each exam lasts **1 hour 45 minutes** and has a total of **80 marks**.
2) **Unit 3** is called **Strategies for Success**. It's a **synoptic** paper based on an **unseen case study**. It has about four **extended answer** questions worth between **10** and **34** marks. It focuses on **functional objectives and strategy**; **financial strategies and accounts**; **marketing strategies**; **operating strategies**; and **human resource** strategies. You'll be expected to show knowledge of the material you covered at **AS Level** too.
3) **Unit 4** is called **The Business Environment and Managing Change**. It has **two** parts and is also **synoptic**, although the focus of the paper is on **corporate aims and objectives**, **assessing change in the business environment**, and **managing change**. **Section A** is based on **pre-released research tasks** that you'll have covered in the run-up to the exam — these tasks should give you a pretty good idea of the kind of questions that might come up. **Section B** contains a choice of three long essay questions. You must answer **one question** which is worth **40 marks**.

Here's an **Example Answer** to give you some tips:

Malvern Holdings manufactures electronic components for domestic appliances. The company has recently received some large orders after a successful marketing campaign. To meet these orders it must increase its capacity and replace existing machines with new technology. Analyse the benefits to Malvern Holdings of using critical path analysis to meet these large orders. (10 marks)

Critical path analysis is a tool used by firms to work out the quickest way of doing things. Before Malvern Holdings can get the products to their customers it needs to increase the size of its factory and replace existing machinery, CPA will help them do this in the quickest way by identifying the critical path. This will not only allow them to satisfy customers orders but give them an advantage over their competitors.

> 1 mark (A01) — understands the term 'critical path analysis'.

> 1 mark (A02) — applies knowledge to Malvern Holdings.

By using a CPA managers at Malvern Holdings can establish which activities can take place at the same time. For instance, Malvern Holdings may be able to order raw materials whilst improvements to the factory are taking place. There is a risk though that managers may have wrongly estimated the time needed to do each activity and orders could be late to customers.

> 1 mark (A03) — analyses disadvantages of CPA.

> 2 marks (A02) — refers to Malvern Holdings.

CPA can also help firms forecast their cash flow, it gives earliest start times when cash will be needed and may also indicate when they are likely to receive inflows of cash. This will help the firm avoid cash flow problems .

> 1 mark (A01) — shows knowledge of CPA and cash flow.

> Relating this knowledge to the question would score more marks.

Given the number of orders that Malvern Holdings has received for its products it may have to adopt a just-in-time production system. Resources used to produce the components such as raw materials and labour can be employed at the earliest start time, instead of hanging around and waiting to be needed. This will reduce both storage and opportunity costs. This may be especially important for the firm as the successful marketing campaign is likely to have cost them a large sum of money.

> 2 marks (A02 and A03) — analyses benefits of just-in-time production for Malvern Holdings.

There are of course lots of problems with CPA. The earliest start and latest finish times are estimates made by managers. There is a risk these could be inaccurate and therefore the whole CPA will be incorrect. Once a CPA has been constructed it is important that the process is then supervised. If it is not, delays may occur and customers won't be satisfied.

> The conclusion is weak — it doesn't fit in well with the answer and doesn't show analysis.

This is a good answer and would get about **8** out of **10 marks**. It examines a range of points **relevant** to Malvern Holdings, but the answer is **let down** by a **weak conclusion**. **More analysis** would improve the answer.

Answers to the Numerical Questions

Section Two — Financial Strategies and Accounts

Page 103 — Exam Questions

Q1 (a) Net profit margin = net profit ÷ turnover × 100 ***[1 mark]***
Net profit margin = (£750 000 – £250 000) ÷ £2 000 000 × 100
= 25% ***[1 mark for working, 1 mark for answer.]***

Page 105 — Exam Questions

Q1 (a) Dividend cover = net profit after tax ÷ total dividends ***[1 mark]***
= £300 000 ÷ (6p × 100 000) = £300 000 ÷ £6000 = 50
[1 mark for working, 1 mark for answer.]

(b) Dividend Yield = dividend per share ÷ price per share × 100
= 6p ÷ 300p × 100 = 2%
[1 mark for working, 1 mark for answer.]

Page 111 — Exam Questions

Q1 ARR = (average annual profit ÷ investment) × 100 ***[1 mark]***
Overall net cash flow = £320 000 – £40 000 = £280 000 ***[1 mark]***
Average annual profit = (£280 000 – £200 000) ÷ 8 ***[1 mark]***
= £10 000
ARR = £10 000 ÷ £200 000 × 100 = 5%
[1 mark for working, 1 mark for answer.]

Q2 Payback period = amount invested ÷ annual profit from investment ***[1 mark]***
Payback period = £5000 ÷ £1500 = 3.33 years (or 3 years and 4 months) ***[1 mark for working, 1 mark for answer.]***

Section Three — Marketing Strategies

Page 121 — Exam Question

Q1

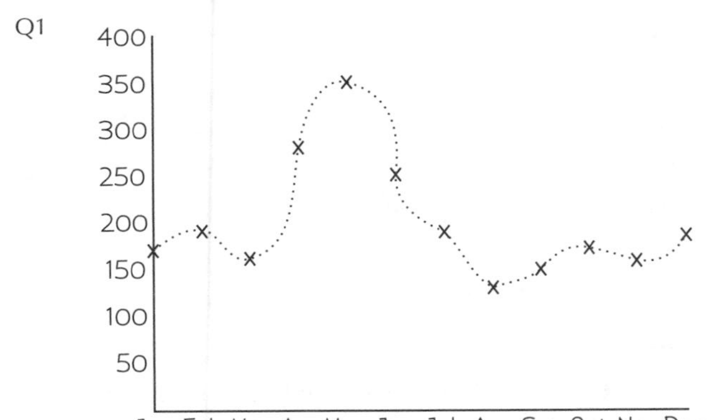

[6 marks]

Page 123 — Exam Question

Q1(a)

Year	Quarter	Sales revenue (thousand £s)	4 quarter moving total	8 quarter moving total	Quarterly moving average
2006	1	630			
	2	567	~~2427~~		
	3	552	~~2418~~	4845	605.63
	4	678	~~2429~~	4847	605.88
2007	1	621	~~2420~~	4849	606.13
	2	578	~~2342~~	4762	595.25
	3	543	~~2323~~	4665	583.13
	4	600	~~2295~~	4618	577.25
2008	1	602	~~2254~~	4549	568.63
	2	550	~~2214~~	4468	558.50
	3	502	~~2201~~	4415	551.88
	4	560			
2009	1	589			

[14 marks]

(b)

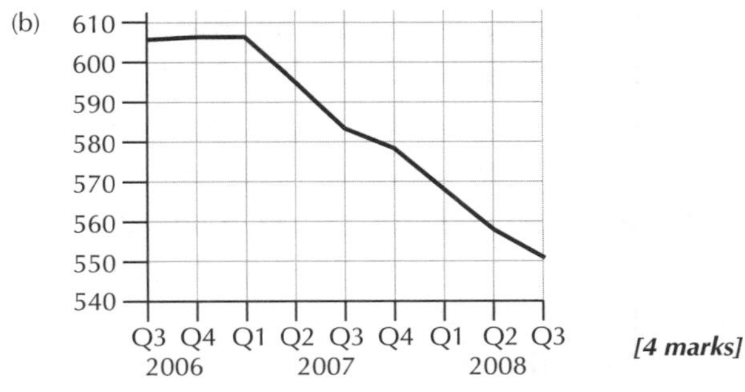

[4 marks]

Section Four — Operational Strategies

Page 149 — Exam Question

Q1 (a)

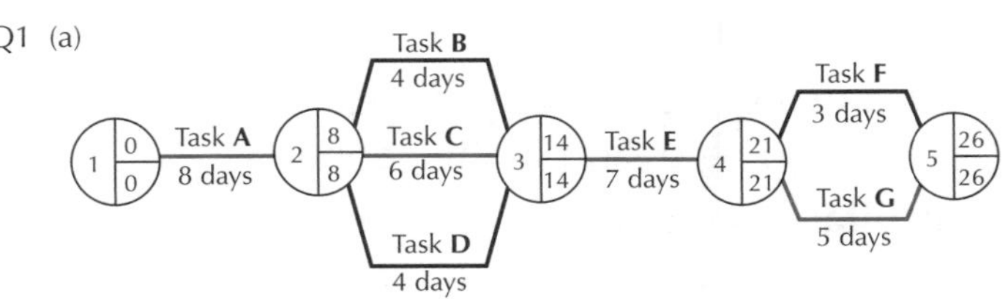

[3 marks for putting (A), (B, C and D), (E), and (F and G) in the right order. 2 marks for one error. 1 mark for 2 errors], [1 mark for B, C and D as simultaneous], [1 mark for F and G as simultaneous].

(b) ***[1 mark for the critical path — it's a thick pink line on the diagram] [1 mark for the total time — 26 days]***

(c) *Float times for B and F are both 2 days.* ***[1 mark for each]***

Glossary

ACAS The Advisory, Conciliation and Arbitration Service, which acts as a mediator in industrial disputes and aims to improve employment relations.

Ansoff's Matrix Shows the strategies that a firm can use to expand, according to how risky they are.

asset Anything that a business owns.

balance sheet A snapshot of a firm's finances at a fixed time.

budget Forecasts future earnings and future spending.

business cycle The regular pattern of growth and recession in the economy.

capital A company's finances or resources (land, premises and machinery).

cash flow Money that comes into and goes out of a firm.

competition policy Government policy to prevent anti-competitive behaviour by businesses, such as the formation of monopolies.

contingency plan A plan for when something goes wrong.

corporate culture The way a business does things — it affects the attitudes and expectations of employees.

corporate objectives The goals of the whole business.

corporate plan Sets out the business' corporate objectives and the strategy the business will use to achieve them.

corporate social responsibility (CSR) When a business' objectives consider the needs of all its stakeholders, not just shareholders.

cost centre Part of a business that directly incurs costs.

cost-benefit analysis Assessing the financial and social costs of an activity and its financial and social benefits.

critical path analysis Works out the most efficient and cost-effective way to finish a set of tasks.

deflation Decrease in the price of goods and services.

depreciation Losing value over time — fixed assets often depreciate.

developing market A country with rapid economic growth.

diversification Expanding to produce new products or enter new markets.

economic growth Increase in the amount of goods and services that a country produces. Measured in rate of increase of gross domestic product (GDP).

environmental audit Independent check on the environmental impact of a firm's activities. Also called a green audit.

ethical Morally and professionally acceptable.

exchange rate The value of one currency in terms of another.

final accounts A company's balance sheet, profit and loss account and cash flow statement at the end of the financial year.

fiscal policy Government policy that sets tax rates and government spending.

fixed assets Things businesses keep long-term or use repeatedly — e.g. property, equipment, land, computers.

fixed costs Costs that stay the same — no matter how much or how little a firm produces.

forecasting Trying to predict what will happen in the future.

functional objectives The objectives of individual departments.

gearing The proportion of a business financed through debt rather than equity or reserves.

GDP (gross domestic product) The total value of goods and services produced in a country, over a year.

globalisation The breakdown of traditional national boundaries with the growth of communications, transport and global organisations and businesses.

Human Resource Management (HRM) Looks after all the people-related aspects of a business — like recruitment and training.

income statement Statement showing how much money's gone into and out of a company over a period of time.

Glossary

industrial democracy Allowing the workforce to have some input into an organisation's decision-making process.

inflation The increase in the price of goods and services.

interest rate Shows the cost of borrowing.

just-in-time (JIT) production Manufacturing process which operates with very small amounts of stock.

kaizen Japanese for "continuous improvement", an approach used to improve quality control and efficiency.

lean production Techniques that aim to reduce waste to an absolute minimum (e.g. JIT production).

liabilities Debts a business owes.

liquidity How easily assets can be turned into cash.

market analysis Finding out about the market a company is operating in, e.g. its size, growth, classification and the market share of the company and its competitors.

market classification Identifying a market's characteristics (by geography, seasonality, etc.).

market growth When demand for a product or service increases.

market research Finding out about customers, markets and competitors.

market segmentation Identifying the different types of customer in a market, e.g. by gender or spending power.

market share The percentage of sales in a particular market that belong to a particular company or brand.

marketing mix The four Ps firms use to market their goods / services — price, product, promotion and place (distribution).

merger Where two companies agree they should join together into one business.

mission statement A written description of a company's corporate objectives.

monetary policy Policy that controls the interest rate.

monopoly Where one firm controls most or all of the market share.

motivation Anything that makes you work hard and achieve things.

moving average A way of finding trends in a set of data over time by smoothing out cyclical and seasonal variations.

multinational A business with its headquarters in one country and bases in other countries.

nationalisation When the government takes over the running of a private company or an industry.

objective A medium- to long-term target.

offshoring When a firm has one or several of its activities carried out abroad.

operations management Planning and monitoring business operations to ensure they're as efficient as possible.

opportunity cost The idea that money or time spent doing one thing is likely to mean missing out on doing something else.

organic growth When a business grows naturally.

outsourcing When a firm has one or several of its activities carried out by another, specialist company.

privatisation Selling publicly-owned companies to private individuals and firms.

profit centre Part of a firm that directly generates revenue.

protectionism When a country tries to protect its own companies by making it harder for foreign companies to trade in that country.

qualitative analysis Non-scientific method of analysing why people buy a product, e.g. using focus groups.

quantitative analysis Analysing sales using mathematical calculations (e.g. calculating market share).

Glossary

return on capital employed (ROCE) Shows you how much money is made by the business compared to how much money's been put into the business.

SMART objectives Objectives which are Specific, Measurable, Agreed, Realistic and doable within a certain Time period.

social benefits Internal benefits + external benefits

social costs Internal costs + external costs

specialisation Breaking a job into smaller tasks so that workers become expert at their given task.

stakeholders Everyone affected by a business including workers, shareholders, customers and the public.

strategy A plan for achieving objectives.

subsidy Money paid by the government to certain industries to keep the costs of production down.

supply-side policies Government policies that aim to allow markets to work as freely as possible.

sustainability Whether a production process can continue indefinitely, bearing in mind its impact on resources like oil.

SWOT analysis A method of assessing a business' current situation — looks at the Strengths, Weaknesses, Opportunities and Threats facing the firm.

takeover Where one firm buys over 50% of the shares of another firm, giving them the controlling interest.

tariff Tax paid on an imported product.

time series analysis (TSA) Recording data over time to help identify trends.

trade barrier Measures such as tariffs or quotas that make it more difficult for foreign goods to enter a country.

trade unions Groups that act on behalf of groups of employees in negotiations with employers.

trading bloc A group of countries that trade freely with each other.

variable costs Costs that vary, depending on how much business the firm does.

vicarious liability Where an employer is responsible for any act committed by an employee during the normal course of their job.

waste management Keeping levels of waste as low as possible and within legal limits.

working capital Money available for day-to-day spending.

Index

Index

Index

Index

Index

Index